**CITE THIS VOLUME
AS FOLLOWS:**
ALM Spec L c — § —

ANNOTATED LAWS OF MASSACHUSETTS

with pocket upkeep service

Containing all the Laws of Massachusetts of

a general and permanent nature

completely annotated

SELECTED SPECIAL LAWS OF MASSACHUSETTS
Chapters S67 through S137

By the Editorial Staff of the Publishers

1992

Lawyers Cooperative Publishing
Aqueduct Building, Rochester, New York 14694

Library of Congress Catalog Card Number 33–1118

FOREWORD

This volume contains special laws which, although not part of the General Laws of Massachusetts, have been selected by the editors for inclusion herein for the convenience of the practitioner because of statewide application, general interest or current importance.

The selected special laws have been unofficially codified by the editors to facilitate the legal research of the practitioner. Similar to the style found in the General Laws, the selected special laws are arranged in broad, logical divisions called titles. Each title is divided into chapters. Each chapter, divided into sections, is a separate selected special law. Titles are assigned consecutive odd numbers. Chapters are also assigned odd numbers, preceded by 'S' to distinguish Selected Special Law Chapters from the General Law Chapters. Numerical gaps appear at the end of each title to accommodate new selected special laws inserted in the future supplementation of this volume. Except where the section number is enclosed in brackets, sections carry the numbers assigned by the General Court when the selected special laws were originally enacted or subsequently amended.

In addition to the text of the selected special laws, other helpful features are provided for the practitioner. As in the General Laws, up-to-date, accurate legislative histories follow the text of each section. These histories reflect additions and amendments made by the General Court up to and including the 1991 legislative session. Where pertinent, editorial notes are appended to the statutory provisions, providing the text of sections of helpful related special laws. Cross references are made to related provisions of the General Laws. Case notes have been prepared by the editors to reflect accurately and completely opinions construing and applying the statutes.

An index has been prepared for the volume with a convenient form of citation similar to the form of citation used in the index to the General Laws. The citation is composed of two numbers, the chapter number, on the left of the colon, and the section number, on the right.

THE PUBLISHER

THIS VOLUME CONTAINS

Statutes:

This volume covers the full text of selected laws enacted or amended by the General Court through the 1991 Session. Consult the pocket supplement and the Advance Legislative Service for the Annotated Laws of Massachusetts for later enactments.

Case notes and collateral matters:

The sources of the case notes and collateral matters construing and applying the statutes referred to in this volume have been brought down through the following volumes:

    410 Mass
     30 Mass App Ct
  1991 Mass App Div 127
    580 NE2d 398
    941 Fed 2d
    768 F Supp
    501 US
    116 L Ed 2d (Supreme Court decisions)
    111 S. Ct
     89 ALR4th
    104 ALR Fed
    106 L Ed 2d (annotations)
    105 Harvard Law Rev #2
     76 Mass Law Rev (Quarterly) #3
    101 Yale Law J #2

Attorney General Opinions through
recently published reports

Auto-Cite®: Cases and annotations referred to herein can be further researched through the Auto-Cite® computer-assisted research service. Use Auto-Cite to check citations for form, parallel references, prior and later history, and annotation references.

TABLE OF TITLES AND CHAPTERS
SELECTED SPECIAL LAWS OF MASSACHUSETTS

TITLE I
BUSINESS AND FINANCE

TITLE III
CIVIL DEFENSE, MILITARY AFFAIRS AND VETERANS

TITLE V
PUBLIC HEALTH, EDUCATION AND WELFARE

Auto-Cite®: Cases and annotations referred to herein can be further researched through the Auto-Cite® computer-assisted research service. Use Auto-Cite to check citations for form, parallel references, prior and later history, and annotation references.

ANNOTATED LAWS
OF
MASSACHUSETTS

TITLE V (Cont'd)
PUBLIC HEALTH, EDUCATION AND WELFARE
IN PREVIOUS VOLUME

IN THIS VOLUME

CHAPTER S67
Massachusetts Water Resources Authority
(Acts 1984, Ch. 372)

1

> **Auto-Cite®:** Cases and annotations referred to herein can be fur-
> ther researched through the Auto-Cite® computer-assisted
> research service. Use Auto-Cite to check citations for form,
> parallel references, prior and later history, and annotation
> references.

§ 1.   Massachusetts Water Resources Authority Established.

It is hereby determined that:

(a) Providing water supply services and sewage collection, treatment and disposal services to areas of the commonwealth made up
of the cities and towns now served by the metropolitan district
commission is an essential public purpose. The preservation and
improvement of the health, welfare and living conditions of the cit-
izenry, the promotion and enlargement of industry and employment
and all other aspects of commerce, the protection, conservation,
management and development of water supplies and the environment depend upon the sound maintenance, operation and improvement of an adequate water supply distribution system and an adequate sewage collection, treatment and disposal system. The
financing requirements for such water supply and sewage collection,
treatment and disposal systems are substantial and require independent financial resources, including the ability to rely on user charges
to recover costs of providing such services and the ability to fund
capital programs without undue reliance on the general obligation
credit of the commonwealth.

(b) It is in the best interests of the commonwealth and its citizens
to create an authority to achieve the following goals, purposes and
objectives:

(i) efficient and economical operation of water delivery and
sewage collection, disposal and treatment systems including programs for leak detection and reduction of infiltration and inflow
for the service areas of the Authority;

(ii) repair, replacement, rehabilitation, modernization and extension of the delivery of water and sewage collection, disposal and
treatment systems for the service areas of the Authority, including the financing on a self-sustaining basis of capital and operating expenses relating thereto;

(iii) establishment and administration of equitable charges, consistent with the objectives of this act to conserve water and
improve the quality of the environment, for water delivery and
sewage collection, disposal and treatment services;

(iv) professional and productive management of and system-wide planning for the delivery of water and sewage collection, disposal and treatment services; all of which are declared to be for the public benefit, to necessitate the creation of the authority, and to make it necessary and expedient to vest in the authority the powers granted by this act.

(c) The commonwealth faces important needs for fostering efficient use of water, for efficient planning and improvement of the delivery of water and sewage collection, disposal and treatment services to which and an authority should be established and vested with extensive operating, financing and regulatory powers to provide appropriate means for addressing these needs.

Therefore, it is declared to be in the best interest of the commonwealth and its inhabitants, to promote the general health and welfare, to improve commerce and living conditions, to conserve water, and to develop and protect in the public interest the natural resources of the commonwealth, that there be established the Massachusetts Water Resources Authority empowered to operate, regulate, finance, and improve the delivery of water and sewage collection, disposal and treatment systems and services, and to encourage conservation, as provided in this act.

This act may be cited as the Massachusetts Water Resources Authority Act.

History—

1984, 372, § 1; 1987, 770, § 1.

Editorial Note—

Section 63–71 of the 1984 inserting act provide as follows:

SECTION 63. Grants made under clause (iii) of the first sentence of the second paragraph of section thirty-three of chapter twenty-one of the General Laws shall be made in accordance with a priority system to be established by regulation of the director of the division of water pollution control, which priority system may include criteria applied in administering the FWPCA as defined in said chapter twenty-one of the General Laws and shall also include supplemental preferential criteria for the following factors: (a) that the project is necessary in order to abate violation of law found in a judicial proceeding or ordered to be abated under section thirty-three D of chapter twenty-one of the General Laws or other administrative proceeding of proper jurisdiction; provided, however, that the division may deny priority to a project where unreasonable and wilful dilatory conduct of a public entity has contributed to the entry of such judicial or administrative order; and (b) that the project will offer water quality improvements benefitting shellfish cultivation and saltwater recreation. Nothing in this section shall require the director in establishing such priority system and making such grants to take any action which would disqualify the commonwealth from the receipt of maximum available federal assistance under federal programs for wastewater treatment construction grants.

SECTION 64. It is the intention of the general court with respect to grants authorized by section thirty-three of chapter twenty-one of the General Laws provided from the proceeds of any bond issues previously authorized and lawfully available therefore and, as necessary, from future authorizations of bonds or other future appropriations, that: (a) total state expenditures in any fiscal year for the sum of all grants made under clauses (i), (ii) and (iii) of the first sentence of the second paragraph of said section thirty-three, computed on the basis that such grants under clause expenditure in said fiscal year for the aggregate of grants under clauses (i) and (ii) of said sentence of said paragraph of said section thirty-three, computed on the basis that such grants under clauses (i) and (ii) are made or deemed to be made in accordance with federal grant participation levels in effect on the effective date of this act, and (b) total aggregate expenditures in all years for grants under said clause (iii) of the first sentence of said second paragraph of said section thirty-three shall not exceed three hundred million dollars. It is also the intention of the general court that from the effective date of this act, that the share of eligible costs to be borne by a public entity sponsoring any water pollution abatement facility funded by a grant from the federal government under the Federal Water Pollution Control Act shall not exceed ten per cent.

SECTION 65. Chapter seven hundred and thirty-seven of the acts of nineteen hundred and seventy-two shall continue in full force and effect.

SECTION 66. Notwithstanding any other provision of this act, employees of the metropolitan district commission whose duties as of the effective date of this act are directly or primarily related to forestry, biology, wildlife, police, management, maintenance or operation in any watershed system property shall be transferred on January first, nineteen hundred and eighty-five to the division of watershed management.

SECTION 67. Any community, any part of which is within ten miles of the state house, may continue to use any source of water presently used by it, or may develop any source not presently used by it for domestic or industrial purposes. If the commissioner of the department of environmental protection shall declare a source of water to be unfit for consumption, said town or community or part thereof, may abandon said unfit source and derive its entire water supply or portion thereof from the Authority. No water company owning a water pipe system in the towns of Hingham, Hull, Dedham, or Westwood shall charge more for water than a reasonable sum measured by the price ordinarily charged for a similar service in towns in the water works system of the Authority. The selectman of either of said towns or any persons deeming themselves aggrieved by the price charged for water by any such company in either of said towns may, in nineteen hundred and twenty-three and every fifth year thereafter, apply by petition to the supreme judicial court, asking to have the rate fixed at a reasonable sum measured by the standard above specified; and two or more judges of said court, after hearing the parties, shall establish such maximum rates as they shall deem proper; and said maximum rates shall be binding upon said water company until the same shall be revised or altered by said court pursuant to this section.

SECTION 68. The executive director of the Authority shall conduct a feasability study for construction of a septage waste processing facility for towns which have used in the past or now use the MDC sewer lines to discharge waste from septic systems. Said feasibility study shall require that the entire cost of building and maintaining such processing facility shall be born by the towns using it.

SECTION 69. The Authority shall not take any structural action in any donor basin, including any capital inprovements or expenditure of capital funds, which could reasonably be expected to (i) create a new interbasin transfer of water or (ii) increase the rate of any existing interbasin transfer of water without the express approval of the general court; provided, however, that this provision shall not be construed to require general court approval for actions undertaken to reduce leakage in an existing interbasin transfer. Any determinations made under the provisions of this section shall be made by the division.

SECTION 70. The Authority shall take all reasonable steps expeditiously to continue planning on design and to commence construction of wastewater treatment and delivery projects for which planning or design contracts have been approved by the metropolitan district commission prior to the effective date of this act and which are listed on the Construction Grants Project Priority List established by the department of environmental quality engineering and the division of water pollution control in effect on the effective date of this act.

SECTION 71. Notwithstanding any provision of this act to the contrary, the supply of water by the Authority to any political subdivision to which the metropolitan district commission was not providing water at the time of the effective date of this act shall be made only upon the determination by the Authority and the department of environmental protection that the water supply source used by said political subdivision at the time of the passage of this act is unfit for drinking and cannot be economically restored for drinking purposes. (Amended by 1990, 177, §§ 384, 385, approved, with emergency preamble, Aug 7, 1990).

The 1987 amendment after "water" in clause (ii) of paragraph (b), inserted "and".

Code of Massachusetts Regulations—

Massachusetts Water Resources Authority, general provisions, 360 CMR 10.001-10.012.

§ 2.   Definitions.

As used in this act, unless the context clearly indicates otherwise, the following words and phrases shall have the following meanings:

(a) "Advisory Board", the advisory board established by section twenty-three;

(b) "Authority", the Massachusetts Water Resources Authority created by section three;

(c) "Bonds", bonds, notes or other evidences of indebtedness of the Authority;

(d) "Cost", as applied to any project of the Authority, any or all costs, whenever incurred, of carrying out and placing such projects in operation, including, without limiting the generality of the foregoing, amounts for the following: acquisition, construction, expansion, improvement and rehabilitation of facilities; acquisition of real or personal property; demolitions and relocations; labor, materials, machinery and equipment; services of architects, engineers and environmental and financial experts and other consultants; feasibility studies, plans, specifications and surveys; interest prior to and during the carrying out of any project and for a reasonable period thereafter; reserves for debt service or other capital or current expenses; costs of issuance; and working capital, administrative expenses; legal expenses and other expenses necessary or incidental to the aforesaid, to the financing thereof and to the issuance therefor of bonds under the provisions of this act;

(e) "Costs of issuance", any amounts payable or reimbursable directly or indirectly by the Authority and related to the sale and issuance of bonds and the investment of the proceeds thereof and of revenues securing the same including, without limiting the generality of the foregoing, printing costs, filing and recording fees, fees and charges of trustees, depositories, authenticating agents and paying agents, legal and auditing fees and charges, financial consultant fees, costs of credit ratings, premiums for insurance of the payment of bonds and fees payable for letters or lines of credit or other credit facilities securing bonds, underwriting or placement costs, fees and charges for execution, transportation and safekeeping of bonds, costs and expenses of refunding and other costs, fees and charges in connection with the foregoing;

(f) "Current expenses", the authority's current expenses, whether or not annually recurring, of maintaining, repairing and operating the systems and engaging in other activities authorized by this act including, without limiting the generality of the foregoing, amounts for administrative expenses of the division including costs of salaries and benefits, as provided in this act, cost of insurance, payments for engineering, financial, accounting, legal and other services rendered to the authority, taxes upon the authority or its income, operations or property and payments in lieu of such taxes, costs incurred or payable by the authority with respect to the system real property, costs of issuance not financed in the cost of a project, and other current expenses required or permitted by law to be paid by the authority, including the funding of reasonable reserves for upgrading, maintenance, repair, replacements, insurance, emergency contingencies or operations;

(g) "Division", the division of watershed management established by section forty-two.

(h) "Local body", a city, town, district, commission, or other political subdivision or instrumentality of the commonwealth responsible for providing by itself or through an officer, board, department or division thereof local water supply or local sewer services; except as otherwise expressly provided herein, in any case where local water supply or local sewer services within the territorial boundaries of a local body are provided in whole or in part by a political subdivision or public instrumentality of the commonwealth separate from such local body, the term "local body" as used in this act shall mean, within the service area thereof, that political subdivision or public instrumentality.

(i) "MDC sewer system", the sewers and other works of the metropolitan district commission which comprise the system of sewage disposal of the metropolitan sewage district on the effective date of this act, including all interests in real and personal property, equipment, appurtenances, structures and facilities held by the commonwealth or the metropolitan district commission in connection with the ownership, maintenance and operation thereof;

(j) "MDC water system", the water works of the metropolitan district commission which comprise the system of metropolitan water works of the metropolitan water district on the effective date of this act, including all interests in real and personal property, equipment, appurtenances, structures and facilities held by the commonwealth or the metropolitan district commission in connection with the ownership, maintenance and operation thereof;

(k) "Person", any natural or corporate person, including bodies politic and corporate, public departments, offices, agencies, authorities and political subdivisions of the commonwealth, corporations, societies, associations and partnerships, and subordinate instrumentalities of any one or more political subdivisions of the commonwealth;

(l) "Project", any undertaking or other activity by or on behalf of the Authority to maintain or improve the systems, including, without limiting the generality of the foregoing, any extension, expansion or addition thereto, any acquisition, construction, reconstruction or alteration of any part thereof and any other investment therein;

(m) "Revenues", all charges and other receipts derived by the Authority from operation of the waterworks and sewer systems and from all other activities or properties of the Authority including, without limiting the generality of the foregoing, proceeds of grants, gifts or appropriations to the Authority, investment earnings and proceeds of insurance or condemnation, and the sale or other disposition of real or personal property;

(n) "Safe yield", that amount of water that can be safely withdrawn from a water supply source without impairing the ability of such source to supply said amount of water on an average annual basis, as determined by the division of watershed management and commented on by the division of environmental protection within the department of the attorney general.

(o) "Sewer system", the sewer system of the Authority, consisting of (i) the system personal property formerly a part of the MDC sewer system transferred to the Authority in accordance with section four, (ii) the interest of the Authority created by this act in the system real property which was a part of the MDC sewer system immediately prior to the effective date of this act, (iii) all extensions, enlargements, improvements and additions to the former MDC sewer system acquired, constructed or operated by or on behalf of the Authority, and (iv) each other system for collection, treatment or disposal of sewage acquired or constructed by or on behalf of the Authority in accordance with the provisions of this act or as otherwise authorized by law. The sewer system shall include, without limiting the generality of the foregoing, sewers, pipes, conduits, pump stations, force mains, interceptors, treatment works and other structures, devices, appurtenances and facilities utilized for sewage collection, disposal and treatment and franchises, privileges, plant, equipment and real and personal property and rights and interests of every kind relating thereto;

(p) "System", the sewer system and the waterworks system of the Authority and the watershed system of the division.

(q) "System personal property", all personal property held by or on behalf of the commonwealth in the MDC sewer system and the MDC water system, including, without limitation, all equipment, machinery, vehicles and appliances.

(r) "System real property", all real property held by or on behalf of the commonwealth immediately prior to the effective date of this act in and for the MDC sewer system and the MDC water system, including all land, easements, and other interests in real property, including, without limitation, real property interests in buildings, structures and improvements and in sources of water supply.

(s) "Transfer date", for those employees being transferred to the Authority, July first, nineteen hundred and eighty-five; for those employees being transferred to the division, January first, nineteen hundred and eighty-five.

(t) "Users", local bodies, utilizing water or sewer services of the Authority;

(u) "Watershed system", (i) all real and personal property interests held by or on behalf of the commonwealth immediately prior to the effective date of this act in and for the MDC water system which were part of or appurtenant to the Quabbin watershed, Quabbin Reservoir, Ware River watershed, Wachusett watershed, Wachusett Reservoir, North and South Sudbury watersheds, Sudbury Reservoir, Framingham reservoirs 1, 2 and 3, Blue Hills Reservoir, Bear Hill Reservoir, Spot Pond Reservoir, Fells Reservoir, Weston Reservoir, Norumbega Reservoir, Chestnut Hill Reservoir, including land, easements, buildings, structures, all equipment, machinery, vehicles, and appliances, improvements, water rights and rights in sources of water supply and, (ii) all enlargements and additions to the former MDC water system acquired or constructed by the division for the purposes of the watershed system, including land, easements, building structures, equipment, machinery, vehicles, and appliances, improvements, reservoirs, dams, water rights and rights in sources of water supply; but excluding in each case the waterworks system as defined herein;

(v) "Waterworks system", (i) all real and personal property interests in the system of waterworks held by or on behalf of the commonwealth immediately prior to the effective date of this act in and for the MDC water system, including all plants, works, connections, aqueducts, mains, pipe lines, pumping plants and facilities, waterworks buildings and structures, standpipes, tanks and appurtenances, all equipment, machinery, vehicles, and appliances, and all lands and easements directly appurtenant or incident to the maintenance or operation thereof, and (ii) all extensions, enlargements, improvements and additions to the former MDC water system acquired, constructed or operated by the authority including all plants, works, connections, aqueducts, mains, pipe lines, pumping plants and facilities, waterworks building and structures, standpipes, tanks and appurtenances, all equipment, machinery, vehicles, and appliances, and all lands and easements directly appurtenant or incident to the maintenance or operation thereof;[.]

History—
1984, 372, § 2; 1987, 770, §§ 2–4.

Editorial Note—
The **1987 amendment,** after "whenever incurred," in paragraph (d), replaced "or" with "of", after "real" in paragraph (j), inserted "and" and, in paragraph (v), after "pumping", replaced "plans" with "plants."

Code of Massachusetts Regulations—
Massachusetts Water Resources Authority, general provisions, 360 CMR 10.001-10.012.

§ 3. Massachusetts Water Resources Authority Placed in Office of Environmental Affairs; Members; Term of Office; Oath; Removal; Vice-Chairman; Quorum; Expenses.

(a) There is hereby created and placed in the executive office of environmental affairs a body politic and corporate and a public instrumentality to be known as the Massachusetts Water Resources Authority, which shall be an independent public authority not subject to the supervision or control of the executive office of environmental affairs or of any other executive office, department, commission, board, bureau, agency or political subdivision of the commonwealth except to the extent and in the manner provided in this act. The exercise by the Authority of the powers conferred by this act shall be deemed to be the performance of an essential public function.

(b) The powers of the Authority shall be exercised by or under the supervision of a board of directors consisting of eleven members. One member of the board of directors shall be the secretary of the executive office of environmental affairs, serving *ex officio,* one member of the board of directors who is a resident of a Connecticut river basin community who represents water resources protection interests shall be appointed by the governor and shall serve coterminous with the governor, one member of the board of directors who is a resident of a Merrimack river basin community who represents water resources protection interests shall be appointed by the governor and shall serve coterminous with the governor, one member of the board of directors shall be appointed by the governor upon the recommendation of the mayor of Quincy in accordance with the procedure set forth in paragraph (c) and shall serve a term of four years, one member of the board of directors shall be appointed by the governor upon the recommendation of the board of selectmen of the town of Winthrop by majority vote, in accordance with the procedure set forth in paragraph (c) shall serve a term of four years; provided however, that one of the previous named five members shall be a minority person; three members of the board of directors shall be appointed by the mayor of the city of Boston and shall serve conterminous with the mayor, and three members of the board of directors shall be appointed by the advisory board as provided in section twenty-three of this act. Members appointed by the advisory board shall serve for terms of six years, provided, however, that, of the members first appointed by the advisory board, one shall serve for a term expiring on June thirtieth, nineteen hundred and eighty-six, one shall serve for a term expiring on June thirtieth, nineteen hundred and eighty-eight, and one shall serve for a term expiring on June thirtieth, nineteen hundred and ninety, with the term of each to be designated by the advisory board at the time of appointment. Persons appointed to terms succeeding the terms of members initially appointed by the advisory board, shall be appointed to terms of six years. For the purposes of this paragraph a Connecticut river basin community shall include any city or town in the commonwealth lying in whole or in part in the drainage area of the Connecticut river or its tributaries, a Merrimack river basin community shall include any city or town in the commonwealth lying in whole or in part in the drainage area of the Merrimack river or its tributaries, and a minority person shall be as set forth in the definition of "minority" contained in section forty C of chapter seven of the General Laws.

(c) The members of the board of directors to be appointed by the governor upon the recommendation of the mayor of the city of Quincy and the board of selectmen of the town of Winthrop shall be chosen by the governor from a list of three qualified persons submitted to the governor by said mayor and a list of three qualified persons submitted by said board.

The governor shall make such appointment within fourteen calendar days after receiving said list. If there should exist a vacancy in a position on the board of directors which is to be appointed in this manner, said vacancy shall be filled through the procedure set forth herein.

(d) Each member of the board of directors shall serve until his successor is appointed and qualified and each appointed member of the board of directors shall be eligible for reappointment. Each member of the board of directors appointed to fill a vacancy on the board shall be appointed for the unexpired term of the vacant position. Each member of the board of directors before entering upon his duties shall take an oath before the governor to administer the duties of office faithfully and impartially and a record of such oaths shall be filed in the office of the secretary of the commonwealth. Any member of the board of directors may be removed by the appointing authority for misfeasance, malfeasance or wilful neglect of duty upon the filing by the appointing authority with the secretary of the commonwealth of a statement of facts and circumstances which form the basis for such removal. The secretary of the executive office of environmental affairs shall be the chairman of the Authority. The board of directors annually shall elect one of its members as vice-chairman. Six members of the board of directors shall constitute a quorum and the affirmative vote of six members shall be necessary and shall suffice for any action taken by the board of directors. Any action of the board may take effect immediately and need not be published or posted unless otherwise provided by law. No vacancy in the membership of the board of directors shall impair the right of a quorum to exercise the powers of the board of directors. The members of the board of directors shall serve without compensation but each member shall be reimbursed for all reasonable expenses incurred in the performance of his duties. The board of directors shall be deemed to be a governmental body for purposes of and shall be subject to section eleven A and one-half of chapter thirty A of the General Laws. The Authority shall be deemed to be an agency for all other purposes under said chapter thirty A. The

Authority shall also be subject as an authority of the commonwealth to section forty-two of chapter thirty and section ten of chapter sixty-six of the General Laws. The Authority shall be deemed to be a public body and all monies of the Authority shall be deemed to be public funds for purposes of chapter twelve A of the General Laws.

(e) Notwithstanding any other provision of general or special law to the contrary, any member of the board of directors who is also an officer or employee of the commonwealth or of a city or town or other public body shall not thereby be precluded from voting for or acting on behalf of the Authority, the commonwealth or such city or town or other public body on any matter involving the Authority, the commonwealth or that city or town or other public body and any member, officer, employee or agent of the Authority shall not be precluded from acting for the Authority on any particular matter solely because of any interest therein which is shared generally with a substantial segment of the public. The Authority shall be deemed to be a state agency for purposes of chapter two hundred and sixty-eight A of the General Laws and a governmental body for purposes of chapter two hundred and sixty-eight B of the General Laws.

History—
1984, 372, § 3.

§ 4. Transfer of Property and Records to Authority; Powers and Duties as to Sewer and Waterworks Systems.

(a) On July first, nineteen hundred and eighty-five, ownership, possession and control of the system personal property as it relates to the sewer and waterworks system shall pass to and be vested in the Authority without consideration or further evidence of transfer and shall thereafter be in the ownership, possession and control of the Authority. All records in custody of the metropolitan district commission under chapter one hundred and seventy-two of the acts of nineteen hundred and thirty-nine shall remain in the metropolitan district commission. All books, maps, papers, plans, records and documents of whatever description pertaining to the design, construction, operation, and affairs of the MDC sewer system and the MDC water system, exclusive of those pertaining to the MDC watershed system, which are in the possession of the metropolitan district commission on January first, nineteen hundred and eighty-five, or which thereafter come into the possession of the metropolitan district commission also shall be transferred and delivered to the Authority to its use, ownership, possession and control. All such system personal property as it relates to the watershed system shall remain in the metropolitan district commission and be assigned to the watershed management division.

13

(b) As of July first, nineteen hundred and eighty-five, the commonwealth grants to the Authority, subject to limitations under other law in force on the effective date of this act and limitations contained in this act, the exclusive right for so long as the Authority shall not have been terminated in accordance with section twenty-one to utilize for water supply purposes all such quantities of water as may be safely yielded from the watershed system or as otherwise may have been provided by the general court for the watershed system. The Authority's right to utilize the watershed system shall include the delivery, distribution and sale of water thereof by the Authority and the receipt by the Authority as its revenues of the Authority's charges therefor.

(c) The ownership of the system real property, as it relates to the sewer and waterworks systems shall not be transferred to the Authority under this act, but the Authority, as of July first, nineteen hundred and eighty-five, shall have the rights to enter, use, improve, operate, maintain and manage that portion of the system real property in accordance with this act, such right to be subject to revocation by the commonwealth through legislation enacted by the general court. The commonwealth hereby covenants that in the event such rights are revoked by the general court, such rights shall be transferred to such other public body as the general court shall designate, and the commonwealth further covenants that whatever public body assumes such rights shall discharge and provide for the satisfaction of all the obligations of the Authority, including, but not limited to, its obligations to provide for payment of the bonds of the Authority. The ownership of the system real property as it relates to the watershed system shall remain in the commonwealth and the watershed management division of the metropolitan district commission shall manage all such properties provided for by this act.

Under this act (i) no lands or easements taken or acquired for the purposes authorized by article ninety-seven of the Amendments to the Constitution of the Commonwealth shall be used for other purposes or disposed of, and (ii) no lands devoted to a public use shall be diverted to another inconsistent public use, except in all instances in accordance with the laws and the Constitution of the Commonwealth.

(d) On July first, nineteen hundred and eighty-five, all proceeds, exclusive of such amounts for the purposes of equipment, capital project needs, or land acquisition and improvements of that portion of the MDC water system comprising the watershed system, if any, of bonds referred to in section eleven and grants and other aid which are held by the commonwealth at the effective date of this act shall then and thereafter be deemed to be held in trust for, and shall upon demand of the Authority be transferred to the Authority to be applied by the Authority to projects for which such bonds, grants or other aid was authorized. On July first, nineteen hundred and eighty-five, all proceeds, if any, of bonds referred to in said section eleven and grants and other aid which are for the equipment, capital project needs, or land acquisition and improvements of that portion of the MDC water system comprising the watershed system, shall then and thereafter be expended by the division on projects for which such bonds, grants or other aid was authorized. All proceeds if any, of bonds, grants or other aid referred to herein, which shall be so held in trust and transferred upon demand, shall be in the amount as certified by the commissioner of the metropolitan district commission to the state treasurer.

(e) The requirements respecting budgets of the Authority in paragraph (b) of section eight shall first be effective commencing with current expenses and costs paid or incurred on and after July first, nineteen hundred and eighty-five. The charges of the Authority provided for in section ten shall first become effective on July first, nineteen hundred and eighty-five. During the fiscal year of the commonwealth commencing July first, nineteen hundred and eighty-four, the commonwealth may make, enforce and receive assessments and charges relating to the MDC sewer and water systems, comprising the sewer system, watershed system, and waterworks system as defined in this act, with provisions of chapter ninety-two of the General Laws in effect immediately prior to the effective date of this act only as follows: (i) with respect to all expenses and costs other than debt service which shall have been expended for operation of the MDC sewer system in the fiscal year of the commonwealth commencing July first, nineteen hundred and eighty-three; (ii) with respect to debt service relating to the MDC sewer system which shall be incurred in the fiscal year of the commonwealth commencing July first nineteen hundred and eighty-four; (iii) with respect to all costs and expenses including debt service which shall be incurred for operation of the water supply system for the fiscal year of the commonwealth commencing July first nineteen hundred and eighty-four. No repeal or amendment of laws pursuant to sections thirty through seventy-two of this act shall revoke the obligation of any person to make payments to the commonwealth, including, without limitation, charges or assessments under chapter ninety-two of the General Laws and section twenty of chapter fifty-nine of the General Laws, made prior to July first, nineteen hundred and eighty-four, pursuant to the authorization contained in the preceding sentence and during the fiscal year of the commonwealth commencing July first, nineteen hundred and eighty-four, and all amounts received by the commonwealth on account of charges or assessments to be made under the authority of the preceding sentence and any other amounts derived from or related to the operation of said systems during the fiscal year of the commonwealth commencing July first nineteen hundred and eighty-four shall be received and held as funds of the commonwealth and shall not be transferred to the Authority. Notwithstanding any other provision of this act or other law, commencing on July first, nineteen hundred and eighty-five, all amounts of any kind received by the commonwealth, exclusive of amounts derived from or related to the activities authorized in section forty-two, which are derived from or related to the operation of the systems including the former MDC sewer system or MDC water system, exclusive of that portion of the MDC water system comprising the watershed system as defined in this act, shall be deemed to be held in trust for and shall be transferred and paid over to the Authority when received without further appropriation to be applied to the purposes of the Authority. For purposes of this section, all references to funds received by the commonwealth shall be deemed to include receipt of funds by the metropolitan district commission.

(f) All rules, regulations, licenses and permits duly promulgated by or on behalf of the metropolitan district commission respecting the MDC sewer system and the MDC water system, exclusive of that portion of the MDC water system comprising the watershed system as defined in this act, shall remain in full force and effect to the extent consistent with this act until revised or rescinded by the Authority. All such rules, regulations, licenses and permits respecting that portion of the MDC water system comprising the watershed system shall remain in full force and effect to the extent consistent with this act, including regulations promulgated pursuant to chapter seven hundred and thirty-seven of the acts of nineteen hundred and seventy-two. All contractual rights and liabilities of the metropolitan district commission pertaining to either the MDC sewer system, and the waterworks functions of the MDC water system, or the watershed functions of the MDC water system, shall continue in full force and effect and all benefits, obligations and duties thereunder shall be assumed by and imposed upon the Authority and the division, respectively, so far as consistent with the powers granted to the Authority and said division under this act. No liability in tort, or for water pollution under a statutory or other basis, arising prior to July first, nineteen hundred and eighty-five, however, shall be imposed upon the Authority and this sentence shall apply to all actions or proceedings, including those commenced prior to the effective date of this act. Except as expressly excepted by the previous sentence, actions and proceedings against or on behalf of the metropolitan district commission, pertaining to either the MDC sewer system and the waterworks functions of the MDC water system, or the watershed system functions of the MDC water system, shall continue unabated and may be completed against or by the Authority or by the division, respectively.

(g) On July first, nineteen hundred and eighty-five, each employee of the metropolitan district commission paid as of the effective date of this act from funds derived from the accounts of the metropolitan sewerage district or the metropolitan water district shall become an employee of the Authority without impairment of civil service status and seniority and without reduction in compensation, notwithstanding any change in job titles or duties and without loss of accrued rights to holidays, sick leave, vacation and benefits, and shall thereafter perform his or her duties under the direction, control and supervision of the Authority, provided, however, that any employee subject to transfer under the foregoing provision of this sentence whose existing duties and responsibilities are determined by the commissioner of the metropolitan district commission to relate directly and primarily to functions of the metropolitan district commission not passing to the Authority under this act and for whom a position at the metropolitan district commission is funded in whole or in part by items 2410-1000 or 2460-1000 of section two of chapter two hundred and thirty-four of the acts of nineteen hundred and eighty-four and any employee, so determined, to be transferred to the division of watershed management shall remain an employee of the commission, without change in civil service status, if any, without any reduction in seniority, compensation, salary, and without any loss of accrued rights to holidays, sick leave, vacation and other benefits of employment, and shall continue to perform duties under the direction, control and supervision of the metropolitan district commission, under funding arrangements not thereafter derived from the accounts of the metropolitan sewerage district or the metropolitan water district. It is the intention of the general court in the implementation of this provision that each employee of the metropolitan district commission whose compensation is funded from funds derived from the accounts of the metropolitan sewerage district or the metropolitan water district shall, upon the implementation of the foregoing provisions, then hold employment at the Authority or the metropolitan district commission, as the case may be, subject, so far as concerns the Authority, to the terms and conditions of employment established by this act, and so far as concerns the metropolitan district commission, to such rights as may now and hereafter be lawfully protected and provided. Terms or office of employees of the metropolitan district commission transferred to the Authority shall not be deemed to be interrupted by such transfer provided that all employees shall be governed by the provisions in section seven for retirement, pension and group insurance benefits and for protection and preservation of retirement and pension rights based on their prior service. Rights and obligations under collective bargaining agreements with respect to employees transferred from the metropolitan district commission, except to the extent expressly inconsistent with this act, shall be assumed by and imposed upon the Authority pursuant to section

17

seven (c). Every employee transferred to the Authority under this paragraph who immediately prior to such transfer holds a permanent appointment classified under chapter thirty-one or has tenure by reason of section nine A of chapter thirty of the General Laws shall be entitled to the rights and benefits of and shall be subject to the provisions relating to tenured employees under chapter thirty-one or section nine A of chapter thirty, respectively, with respect to that position.

(h) The deputy commissioner of capital planning and operations shall assist and cooperate with the Authority in making suitable office arrangements, exclusive of the office premises in the building located at twenty Somerset street in Suffolk county, in the city of Boston, for the administrative offices of the Authority including, without limitation of the foregoing, temporary arrangements in office premises of the commonwealth which may include such reduced rents prior to the transfer date as the deputy commissioner shall deem appropriate.

History—

1984, 372, § 4; 1987, 770, § 5.

Editorial Note—

The 1987 amendment, after "duties" in the third sentence of paragraph (f), inserted "thereunder shall be".

Acts 1987, ch. 307, §§ 1, 7, 8, 9, entitled "An act providing for the improvement of the Clinton wastewater treatment plant", provide as follows:

SECTION 1. Notwithstanding the provisions of any general or special law to the contrary, the ownership, possession and control of the town of Clinton wastewater treatment plant is hereby conveyed to and vested in the Massachusetts Water Resources Authority. With respect to the operation, improvement and enlargement of said plant, said Authority shall be subject to the provisions of chapter three hundred and seventy-two of the acts of nineteen hundred and eighty-four. Any political subdivisions served by said plant shall be subject to the provisions of clause (c) of section eight of said chapter three hundred and seventy-two.

SECTION 7. The ownership, possession and control of personal property at and associated with the town of Clinton wastewater treatment plant shall be transferred to the Massachusetts Water Resources Authority, and shall thereafter be in the ownership, possession and control of said Authority. All books, maps, papers, plans, records and documents of whatever description pertaining to the design, construction, operation and affairs of the plant which are in the possession of the metropolitan district commission shall be transferred and delivered to said Authority for its use, ownership, possession and control. The real property associated with said plant shall be deemed to be "system real property" as defined in section two of chapter three hundred and seventy-two of the acts of nineteen hundred and eighty-four. Said Authority shall not be liable for any claims, damages, penalties or liabilities arising out of or based upon matters occurring prior to the transfer to it of the legal responsibility for the operations of said plant.

SECTION 8. In order to compensate the town of Clinton for use of certain land in said town for watershed purposes, the division of watershed management within the metropolitan district commission shall make an annual payment to said town, subject to appropriation, in an amount equal to the user fees levied against said town by the Massachusetts Water Resources Authority for services provided by the town of Clinton wastewater treatment plant not to exceed five hundred thousand dollars; provided, however, that said Authority shall annually compensate said town for such purposes in an amount equal to the user fees levied against said town by said Authority which exceeds five hundred thousand dollars during each year.

SECTION 9. A duplicate copy of each sewage bill submitted to the town of Clinton shall be forwarded to the division of watershed management within the metropolitan district commission at the time said billing is made by the Massachusetts Water Resources Authority. Said division within thirty days of receipt of said billing shall forward an amount, subject to the provisions of section eight, to said town. Within ten days of receipt of such sum, said town shall forward such amount to said Authority. No amount of such payments by said division shall be included in the amount of the annual determination of fiscal year charges to said authority assessed to said authority under section one hundred and thirteen of chapter ninety-two of the General Laws.

Code of Massachusetts Regulations—

Massachusetts Water Resources Authority, adjudicatory proceedings. 360 CMR 1.00.

CASE NOTES

Affirming order of United States District Court awarding of fees under Clean Water Act (USCS §§ 1251-1376), judge's decision to focus on specific tasks and time fairly needed to accomplish them made eminently good sense. United States v Metropolitan Dist. Com. (1988, CA1 Mass) 847 F2d 12, 27 Envt Rep Cas 2087, 18 ELR 21233, 11 FR Serv 3d 387.

§ 5.   Appointment of Executive Director and Staff; Implementation of Rules and Regulations; Financing; Appropriations; Indebtedness.

(a) Notwithstanding any other provision of this act, on January first, nineteen hundred and eighty-five or as soon thereafter as a quorum of the board of directors may be appointed, the Authority shall undertake the following: (i) appoint an executive director and such additional staff as shall be necessary for the purposes of this section; (ii) develop its rules and regulations, including charges for implementation on July first, nineteen hundred and eighty-five; (iii) provide for the implementation of permanent financing and; (iv) any such other powers necessary for the provision of water delivery and sewer services on July first, nineteen hundred and eighty-five. Until the appointment and qualification of members of the board of directors of the Authority constituting a quorum of the board all such rights and powers authorized by the provisions of this section may be exercised by personnel of the metropolitan district commission with the approval of the secretary of the executive office of environmental affairs.

(b) An amount equal to all requirements incurred in the MDC Sewer Fund and the MDC Water Fund to the extent and in amounts expended for the purposes of the sewer and waterworks systems for the fiscal year of the commonwealth commencing July first, nineteen hundred and eighty-four and all amounts appropriated by the commonwealth for such period shall be repaid to the commonwealth by the Authority and credited on the books of the commonwealth as of no later than June thirtieth, nineteen hundred and eighty-six. The Authority shall also reimburse the commonwealth to be credited on the books of the commonwealth as of no later than June thirtieth, nineteen hundred and eighty-six for all then outstanding and unreimbursed cash advances of funds of the commonwealth made on or prior to that date for the funding of projects for MDC sewer system or the MDC water system and, from January first, nineteen hundred and eighty-five through June thirtieth, nineteen hundred and eighty-five, for costs of projects of the Authority for the waterworks system and the sewer system, to the extent of and in amounts expended for the purposes of the sewer and waterworks systems. All amounts transferred between the commonwealth and the Authority under sections four and five shall be subject to adjustment upon final audit to be completed within two years of the effective date of this act.

(c) In order to provide funds in addition to amounts appropriated by the commonwealth for current expenses of the sewer and waterworks systems during the period from the effective date of this act until December thirty-first, nineteen hundred and eighty-five the state treasurer, on behalf of the commonwealth, is hereby authorized and directed to loan to the Authority through investment in a note or other appropriate instrument of the Authority, and the Authority is authorized to borrow from the state treasurer, at any time and from time to time on or prior to December thirty-first, nineteen hundred and eighty-five, on such terms and conditions as the state treasurer and the Authority shall agree, an amount not in excess of sixty-five million dollars. Any amount so borrowed by the Authority, with interest thereon at such reasonable rate as the state treasurer and the Authority shall agree, shall be repaid to the commonwealth to be credited on the books of the commonwealth as of no later than June thirtieth, nineteen hundred and eighty-six. Of the amount so loaned, the Authority may transfer to the state treasury such amounts as it deems appropriate to be administered in trust for the purpose of the water and sewer divisions of the metropolitan district commission; provided, however, that such amounts may be expended only after transfer to and subject to the wording of the appropriate line-item appropriations of said divisions, all outside sections pertaining to said items, and all other laws regulating the expenditures of state funds. For purposes of the first sentence of paragraph (b), amounts expended from such transfers to the state treasury shall not be deemed requirements incurred in the metropolitan district commission sewer fund or the metropolitan district commission water fund. Said transfers shall be approved by the secretary of environmental affairs.

(d) The Authority is also authorized to issue at one time or from time to time prior to June thirtieth, nineteen hundred and ninety, notes of the Authority in the aggregate principal amount of six hundred million dollars outstanding at any one time, excluding notes refunded by other notes issued under this paragraph, for the purpose of providing funds for: (i) meeting the obligations of the Authority to repay or reimburse the commonwealth for all amounts described in paragraph (b) of this section; (ii) repaying the commonwealth for any amounts borrowed by the Authority from the commonwealth including interest thereon pursuant to paragraph (c); (iii) meeting the obligations of the Authority as required by section forty-two of this act; (iv) paying all or part of the cost of the Authority's projects undertaken at any time prior to December thirty-first, nineteen hundred and eighty-nine; (v) paying all or any part of the current expenses of the Authority in anticipation of receipt of revenues of the Authority, but in no event shall the aggregate amount of notes outstanding for this purpose exceed one-half of the budgeted current expenses of the Authority for the fiscal year in which such notes are outstanding; and, (vi) paying all or any part of the interest payable on any notes of the Authority issued under this paragraph. Notes issued by the Authority in accordance with this paragraph shall be issued for such term or terms as the Authority shall determine and may be renewed from time to time; provided, however, all such notes and any renewals thereof shall mature and be payable no later than June thirtieth, nineteen hundred and ninety except that notes issued in anticipation of revenues shall be payable and shall mature no later than one year from their date. Notes issued by the Authority in accordance with this paragraph, except notes issued in anticipation of revenues, shall be issued in anticipation of bonds to be issued by the Authority pursuant to section twelve. All notes issued pursuant to this paragraph shall be authorized, issued and sold in the same manner as, and shall otherwise be subject to, section twelve and the other provisions of this act relating to bonds; provided, however, that notes issued under this paragraph shall be issued at a fixed rather than a variable rate or rates of interest.

(e) The commonwealth, acting by and through the secretary of administration and finance with the approval of the governor, upon application of the Authority, shall guarantee the principal of and interest on notes of the Authority issued in accordance with paragraph (d). The secretary of administration and finance with the approval of the governor and without further authority may approve the form, terms and conditions of, and may execute and deliver on behalf of the commonwealth such guaranty and any related agreements with or for the benefit of the holders of such notes containing such terms, conditions and convenants of the commonwealth as the secretary of administration and finance may deem reasonable including provision for the payment of notes not paid or refunded by the Authority by application of the proceeds of the loan authorized in paragraph (f). Without limiting the generality of the foregoing, such guaranty may take the form of an agreement to reimburse the issuer of a letter of credit or other credit facility which relates to such notes. The full faith and credit of the commonwealth shall be pledged for the guaranty provided for in this paragraph. The total principal amount of notes to be guaranteed under this paragraph shall not exceed six hundred million dollars in the aggregate; provided, however, that any note being refunded by the issuance of a guaranteed note shall not, and the refunding note shall, be included within such total amount.

(f) If the Authority shall fail or otherwise be unable to refund or pay when due any guaranteed note or notes, or the interest thereon, issued by the Authority in accordance with paragraph (d), such notes, and the interest thereon, upon presentation to the state treasurer, shall be paid by the commonwealth. For the purpose of providing funds to pay any such guaranteed notes and interest or to reimburse the treasury for any such payments the state treasurer shall, upon the request of the governor, issue and sell bonds of the commonwealth in an amount specified by the governor from time to time, but not exceeding in the aggregate the sum of six hundred million dollars for principal and ninety million dollars for interest. Bonds issued by the commonwealth under this paragraph shall be designated on their face, Massachusetts Water Resources Authority Loan, Act of 1984. Such bonds shall be issued for such maximum term or terms not exceeding twenty years as the governor may recommend to the general court in accordance with section three of Article LXII of the Amendments to the Constitution of the Commonwealth. The Authority shall reimburse the commonwealth in accordance with a schedule to be determined by the secretary of administration and finance at the time such bonds are issued, from any moneys of the Authority which are available for such purposes, including funds provided from charges of the Authority in accordance with paragraph (a) of section ten. Bonds and interest thereon issued by the commonwealth under the authority of this section shall, notwithstanding any other provisions of this act, be general obligations of the commonwealth. In anticipation of the receipt of proceeds of such bonds, the treasurer may issue and sell temporary notes and renewals thereof in an amount outstanding at one time not in excess of the amount of bonds specified by the governor pursuant to this paragraph, for a term not to exceed three years, including any renewals thereof. The principal of and interest on such notes may be paid from the proceeds of said renewal notes or bonds and to the extent not so paid shall be paid from any other funds or receipts; provided, however, that if and to the extent that the principal amount of such notes is paid from other than the proceeds of said renewal notes or bonds, the principal amount of said bonds which may be issued under this section shall be reduced by a like amount. Such notes and any renewals thereof shall be general obligations of the commonwealth.

(g) The state treasurer may borrow, from time to time, on the credit of the commonwealth such amounts as may be necessary to make any loans required of the commonwealth under paragraph (c) and to pay any interest or other charges incurred in borrowing such money, and may issue notes of the commonwealth therefor, bearing interest payable at such times and at such rates as shall be fixed by him. No note issued under this paragraph shall mature more than one and one-half years from its date but notes may be refunded one or more times. Such notes shall be issued for such maximum term of years, not exceeding one and one-half years, as the governor may recommend to the general court in accordance with section three of Article LXII of the Amendments to the Constitution of the Commonwealth.

(h) The obligations of the Authority to make repayments and reimbursements to the commonwealth as described in paragraphs (b) and (c) and section forty-two shall be reduced by the sum of all amounts received by the commonwealth on account of operations of the system conducted in the fiscal year of the commonwealth commencing July first, nineteen hundred and eighty-four including, without limitation, all amounts so received on account of charges and assessments for purposes described in clauses (ii) and (iii) of the third sentence of paragraph (e) of section four. Attribution of charges and assessments received by the commonwealth during such year shall be made on a consistent basis with the certifications made to the state treasurer by the metropolitan district commission which are the basis of such charges. Except as otherwise expressly provided in this act, no amount to be repaid or reimbursed to the commonwealth by the Authority under this section five shall bear interest prior to such repayment or reimbursement. All amounts received by the commonwealth on account of operations of the system conducted in the fiscal year of the commonwealth commencing July first, nineteen hundred and eighty-four and all amounts repaid or reimbursed to the commonwealth by the Authority under this section and section forty-two shall be accounted for as appropriate on the books of the commonwealth in

23

the Metropolitan Sewerage District Fund and the Metropolitan Water District Fund and such funds shall be closed on the books of the commonwealth as of the close of the fiscal year ending June thirtieth, nineteen hundred and eighty-six.

History—
1984, 372, § 5; 1987, 770, §§ 6–8.

Editorial Note—
The 1987 amendment, in the first sentence of paragraph (f), replaced "paragraph (e)" with "paragraph (d)", in the first sentence of paragraph (h), replaced "of account of operations of the system conducting" with "on account of operations of the system conducted", and replaced "paragraph (f)" with "paragraph (e)".

§ 6.   General Powers and Duties of Authority.

The Authority shall have all powers necessary or convenient to carry out and effectuate the purposes and provisions of this act, including without limiting the generality of the foregoing, the powers:

(a) to adopt and amend by-laws for the regulation of its affairs and the conduct of its business;

(b) to adopt an official seal and alter the same at pleasure;

(c) to maintain an office at such place or places as it may determine;

(d) to adopt a fiscal year to conform with the fiscal year of the commonwealth;

(e) to adopt and enforce procedures and regulations in connection with the performance of its functions and duties and without limitation on other reasonable means of enforcement, to establish reasonable penalties for violation of its regulations commensurate with the seriousness of the violation; provided, however, that no penalty may exceed ten thousand dollars for each such violation but the Authority may in the case of a continuing violation, make each day's violation a separate violation;

(f) to sue and be sued, to prosecute and defend actions relating to its properties and affairs, and to be liable in tort in the same manner as a private person except that the Authority and its members, employees and agents shall be immune from tort liability for acts and omissions constituting (i) the exercise of a legislative or judicial function, (ii) the exercise of an administrative function involving the determination of fundamental governmental policy or (iii) the exercise of a discretionary function or duty; provided, however, that property of the Authority, other than, in actions to enforce payment of bonds, the revenues and funds pledged to the payment of bonds, shall not be subject to attachment nor levied upon by execution, and, provided, further, that the Authority is not authorized to become a debtor under the United States Bankruptcy Code;

(g) to employ personnel as hereinafter provided and to engage architectural, engineering, accounting, management, legal, financial and environmental consulting and other professional services;

(h) to receive and apply its revenues to the purposes of this act without appropriation or allotment by the commonwealth or any political subdivision thereof;

(i) to maintain, repair, operate, extend, enlarge, and improve the sewer and waterworks systems, to investigate, design, construct and acquire improvements and additions to said systems; to engage in activities, programs and projects on its own behalf or jointly with other public bodies; to provide technical assistance to local bodies and the division in furtherance of the management or improvement of water supply and sewage collection, disposal and treatment services; and to provide for the cost of activities, programs and projects from grants, the proceeds of bonds, or from other revenues available to the Authority for such purposes;

(j) pursuant to the provisions of section nine, to acquire and take and hold title in its own name, by purchase, lease, lease-purchase, sale and leaseback, mortgage, exchange, gift or otherwise, or to obtain options for the acquisition of, and to dispose of, any property, real or personal, improved or unimproved, tangible or intangible, or any interest therein, and to exercise the power of eminent domain;

(k) to establish, adjust, collect and abate charges for services, facilities and commodities furnished or supplied by it;

(l) to borrow money and issue bonds and to pledge or assign or create security interests in funds or revenues of the Authority to pay or secure such bonds;

(m) to obtain insurance and to enter into agreements of indemnification necessary or convenient to the exercise of its powers under this act;

(n) to apply for, receive, administer and comply with the conditions and requirements respecting any grant, gift or appropriation of property, services or moneys;

(o) to enter into contracts, arrangements and agreements with other persons in all matters necessary or convenient to the operation of this act including, without limiting the generality of the foregoing, matters of technical cooperation, planning, management, administration and operations and to execute and deliver instruments necessary or convenient to the exercise of its powers under this act;

(p) to apply for and to hold permits, licenses, certificates or approvals as may be necessary or desirable to construct, maintain and operate the sewer and waterworks systems;

(q) to appear in its own behalf before other public bodies, including, without limiting the generality of the foregoing, the Congress of the United States and the general court of the commonwealth, in all matters relating to its powers and purposes;

(r) to do all things necessary, convenient or desirable for carrying out the purposes of this act or the powers expressly granted or necessarily implied by this act.

Specification elsewhere in this act of powers of the Authority with respect to the Authority's regulations, charges and operations shall not limit the generality of the powers granted in this section and in section ten or powers the Authority may exercise under any other special or general law insofar as it relates to the purposes of this act.

History—
1984, 372, § 6; 1986, 557, § 208; 1987, 770, § 9.

Editorial Note—
   The 1986 amendment made a corrective change in clause (o), after the second occurrence of "matters", substituting "of" for "or".
   The 1987 amendment, in clause (o), replaced "or" with "of."
   Acts 1987, ch. 307, §§ 2, 3, entitled "An act providing for the improvement of the Clinton wastewater treatment plant", provide as follows:
   SECTION 2. Commencing on the effective date of this act, the Massachusetts Water Resources Authority may enter into contracts relating to, and shall be eligible for grants and other assistance for, improvements and enlargement to be made to said plant and any necessary appurtenances thereto. Projects for improvement and enlargement of said plant shall take into account the sewage treatment needs of the town of Clinton and the Lancaster sewer district and the septage needs of the towns of Sterling, Bolton, Lancaster, Clinton and Berlin. Said Authority is hereby authorized to take, pursuant to section nine of chapter three hundred and seventy-two of the acts of nineteen hundred and eighty-four, real property or any interests or rights therein in said towns deemed by it essential to achieve the purposes of this act and said chapter three hundred and seventy-two.
   SECTION 3. The share of the costs of projects improving and enlarging said plant to be borne by the Massachusetts Water Resources Authority shall not exceed the local share.

Code of Massachusetts Regulations—
   Massachusetts Water Resources Authority, adjudicatory proceedings, 360 CMR 1.00.

Continuation of contract water supply, 360 CMR 11.00 et seq.

CASE NOTES

Affirming order of United States District Court awarding of fees under Clean Water Act (USCS §§ 1251-1376), judge's decision to focus on specific tasks and time fairly needed to accomplish them made eminently good sense. United States v Metropolitan Dist. Com. (1988, CA1 Mass) 847 F2d 12, 27 Envt Rep Cas 2087, 18 ELR 21233, 11 FR Serv 3d 387.

§ 7. Appointment of Executive Director, Secretary and Treasurer; General Powers and Duties of Appointees; Indemnification of Officers and Employees; Representation in Labor Matters; Retirement System; Group Insurance; Deferred Compensation Program; IRA Accounts; Affirmative Action Program; Internal Special Audit Unit.

(a) An executive director, who shall be a person professionally skilled and experienced in law, finance, public works or public utility programs, or public administration with significant experience in wastewater pollution abatement, shall be appointed by the board of directors for a term not to exceed five years as chief executive officer of the Authority, and shall so serve until his successor is appointed and qualified and each such executive director shall be eligible for reappointment for like five year terms. An executive director may be removed at any time by the board for misfeasance, malfeasance or wilful neglect of duty upon the filing by the board with the secretary of the commonwealth of a statement of facts and circumstances which form the basis for such removal. The executive director shall administer the affairs of the Authority, including, without limiting the generality of the foregoing, matters relating to contracting, procurement, personnel and administration, under the supervision of the board of directors in accordance with such authorizations as the board of directors may from time to time reasonably adopt and continue in force. The Authority shall also appoint persons to hold the offices of secretary and treasurer to the Authority. The secretary shall be the custodian of the seal and of the books and records of the Authority and shall keep a record of the proceedings of the board of directors. The secretary may cause copies to be made of all minutes and other records and documents of the Authority and may give certificates under its official seal to the effect that such copies are true copies and all persons dealing with the Authority may rely upon such certificates. The treasurer shall have charge of the books of account and accounting records of the Authority and shall be responsible under the supervision of the executive director for financial control for the Authority. Upon the recommendation of the executive director, the board of directors shall also appoint and establish reasonable compensation, benefits and other terms of employment for other officers and other employees of the Authority as it deems necessary, including assistant secretaries and assistant treasurers in whom may be vested any of the powers of the secretary and the treasurer, respectively, and including architects, engineers, accountants, lawyers, planners and other management and professional personnel. Except as otherwise hereinafter provided for the appointment of said executive director, other officers and employees of the Authority shall serve at the pleasure of the board of directors or under collective bargaining agreements or contracts of employment; provided, however, that no contract of employment, except for that of the executive director, shall exceed a term of three years, which may be renewed upon the expiration thereof.

(b) The Authority may indemnify any present or past director, officer, employee or agent of the Authority and any member, officer, employee or agent of the retirement board established pursuant to paragraph (d) against liabilities, claims, costs and expenses, including legal expenses, in connection with any actual or threatened proceeding, including any settlement thereof approved by the Authority, arising by reason of any act or omission within the scope of his duties for the Authority; provided, however, that no indemnification shall be provided to a person concerning a matter as to which such person is finally adjudicated to have acted either without the belief held in good faith that his or her conduct was in the best interests of the Authority or with reason to understand that his or her conduct was unlawful. Costs and expenses may be paid prior to a final disposition upon receipt of an undertaking, which the Authority may accept without regard to the financial resources of the person indemnified, that the person receiving the benefit of payments shall repay such payments if he shall be finally adjudicated not to be entitled to indemnification hereunder. The Authority may purchase insurance on behalf of itself and any of its directors, officers, employees or agents and any member, officer, employee or agent of the retirement board established pursuant to paragraph (d) against any liability arising out of such person's status as such, whether or not the Authority would have the power to indemnify such person against such liability.

(c) The Authority and its employees shall be subject to the provisions of chapter one hundred and fifty E of the General Laws, and for purposes of said chapter, the Authority shall be deemed to be an employer or public employer and a legislative body. The Authority may designate a representative to act in its interest in labor relations matters with its employees. Rights and obligations under collective bargaining agreements with respect to employees transferred from the metropolitan district commission, except to the extent expressly inconsistent with this act, shall be assumed by and imposed upon the

Authority, and employees transferred to the Authority who are subject to such agreements shall continue to be represented by the employee organizations that are parties to such agreements until such time as they elect to be otherwise represented in accordance with the provisions of chapter one hundred and fifty E. Existing bargaining units as determined by the state labor relations commission for metropolitan district commission employees shall remain in full force and effect for those employees transferred to the Authority until the expiration date of collective bargaining agreements covering such employees. No collective bargaining agreement entered into by the Authority, however, shall limit inherent management rights which shall include, without limiting the generality of the foregoing, the following: (i) employment, assignment, and promotion of employees and the determination of standards therefor, (ii) termination and discharge of employees, provided that any collective bargaining agreement may protect employees against such actions on arbitrary, capricious or unreasonable grounds, (iii) determination of the Authority's levels of service, levels of staffing, and the methods, means and personnel for performing operations, (iv) supervision, control, and evaluation and establishment of productivity standards for employees, and (v) use of part-time regular employees and of independent contractors or vendors. Notwithstanding the foregoing, each collective bargaining agreement in force on the effective date of this act covering former employees of the metropolitan district commission transferred to the employment of the Authority under section four, shall continue to be a valid collective bargaining agreement in effect with respect to such employees until the date which is two years subsequent to the stated date of expiration of such agreement; provided, however, that the Authority shall negotiate in good faith pursuant to the provisions of chapter one hundred and fifty E of the General Laws with respect to wages, hours, and other terms and conditions of employment to become effective as of the stated date of expiration of such agreement for the balance of the term of such agreement as herein extended.

(d) All employees of the Authority not employed by the metropolitan district commission prior to July first, nineteen hundred and eighty-five shall become members of a contributory retirement system to be referred to as the Massachusetts Water Resources Authority Retirement System, hereinafter referred to as the "Authority Retirement System", which shall be a separate system from the state employees' retirement system and which shall be established and maintained in accordance with sections one to twenty-eight L, inclusive, and section one hundred and two of chapter thirty-two of the General Laws and for all purposes thereunder shall be deemed to be a contributory retirement system of a governmental unit governed by the provisions thereof for the state employees' retirement system except as otherwise expressly provided herein. The Authority Retirement system shall become effective without further acceptance by the Authority on July first, nineteen hundred and eighty-five. The Authority Retirement System shall be administered by a separate retirement board established by the Authority which shall consist of three persons and which shall have custody of the funds of the Authority Retirement System and shall have the general powers and duties set forth in subdivision five of section twenty of chapter thirty-two of the General Laws. One member of the retirement board shall be the secretary of the Authority, serving *ex officio*. The second member of the retirement board shall be initially appointed by the Authority for a term expiring June thirtieth, nineteen hundred and eighty-six and thereafter the second member shall be a person elected by members in service and members retired from service in the Authority Retirement System from among their number to serve for a term expiring June thirtieth, nineteen hundred and eighty-nine and for successive triennial terms thereafter. The third member of the retirement board shall be appointed by the Authority for successive triennial terms; provided, however, that the term of the member first appointed shall expire on June thirtieth, nineteen hundred and eighty-eight. Members of the retirement board shall serve until their successors are duly qualified and shall be eligible for re-election or reappointment. Members of the retirement board shall serve without compensation but each member may be reimbursed for all reasonable expenses incurred in the performance of his duties. Without limitation of other provisions of general law applicable by terms thereof to the retirement board, the retirement board shall be deemed to be a governmental body for purposes of and shall be subject to section eleven A and one-half of chapter thirty A of the General Laws and the members thereof shall be deemed to be state employees subject to chapter two hundred and sixty-eight A of the General Laws. Whenever a person, other than an employee of the metropolitan district commission transferred to the Authority under the provisions of this act, who is a member of a retirement system under chapter thirty-two of the General Laws shall become a member of the Authority Retirement System by virtue of employment by the Authority, that person shall be entitled to all creditable service and all rights and benefits to which he was entitled as a member of such prior retirement system. Within ninety days of such employment, the amounts of the accumulated total deductions, including accumulated interest on such deductions, credited to such employee's accounts in the annuity savings fund and pension reserve fund of the prior retirement system shall be transferred and credited to the employee's accounts in the annuity savings fund and pension reserve fund of the Authority Retirement System. The amounts required to finance pension benefits earned by employees of the Authority in a given year shall be determined by the retirement board and shall be paid over by the Authority. Funds paid into the Authority Retirement System pursuant to this section shall cease to be funds of the Authority and shall be used solely for the purposes of the Authority Retirement System. This provision shall be deemed to constitute a contractual right and benefit on behalf of members of the Authority Retirement System who are or may be retired pursuant to said chapter thirty-two, and no amendment or alteration shall be made which would result in a diversion of the funds of the Authority Retirement System from the purposes thereof. Nothing in this act shall be deemed in any way to decrease or abridge the annuities, pensions, retirement allowances, refunds or accumulated total deductions or any right or benefit to which an employee transferred to the Authority Retirement System pursuant to this act has become entitled by virtue of membership in any of the systems in the state retirement system prior to transfer to the Authority's employment, and the liability therefor shall become the liability of the Authority Retirement System upon the transfer of funds provided for in this paragraph. All persons transferred to the Authority on July first, nineteen hundred and eighty-five who are members of the state employees' retirement system on account of employment by the metropolitan district commission prior to said date shall continue to be members of the state employees' retirement system and subject to the laws applicable thereto, and neither the Authority nor the Authority Retirement System shall have any liability for retirement allowances to or on account of such persons.

The Authority shall not be liable for retirement allowances to or on account of metropolitan district commission employees who are not transferred to the Authority pursuant to the provisions of this act, except for the costs of retirement contributions of employees of the watershed management division properly chargeable to the Authority.

(e) Subject to the last sentence of this paragraph, every employee who upon employment by the Authority is covered by the group insurance provided by chapter thirty-two A of the General Laws shall continue in uninterrupted coverage and all other employees of the Authority are hereby made eligible for said group insurance to the same extent as if they were employees of the commonwealth. The share of the commonwealth of the cost of such insurance, with respect to the employees of the Authority, shall be borne by the Authority, but with respect to persons retired from service with the metropolitan district commission who have not been employees of the Authority, shall continue to be borne by the commonwealth. The Authority shall forward its contribution, together with all amounts withheld from the salaries or wages of its employees as provided in paragraph (a) of section eight of said chapter thirty-two A and all amounts paid by an employee as provided in paragraph (b) of said section eight, to the state employees group insurance commission at such time and in such manner as said commission may reasonably prescribe. The Authority is authorized to enter into reasonable alternative and substitute group insurance arrangements providing benefits to its employees substantially equivalent to or superior to benefits under said chapter thirty-two A, and thereupon may cease its arrangements for such benefits under said chapter thirty-two A.

(f) The Authority may contract, to the extent permitted by and in accordance with applicable requirements of the United States Internal Revenue Code, with any of its employees (i) to defer a portion of the employee's compensation and to invest such amounts under a deferred compensation program and (ii) to make contributions from amounts otherwise payable as an employee's current compensation to an individual retirement account; hereinafter referred to as IRA.

Investments of deferred compensation may be made in a life insurance or annuity contract, mutual fund or bank investment trust and investments of IRA amounts may be made in the foregoing or in other investments authorized by the Internal Revenue Code. The treasurer of the Authority, before making any such investment of deferred compensation or making any deductions from compensation for purposes of an IRA, shall solicit sealed bids to be opened at a time and place designated by the treasurer from insurance companies authorized to conduct business within the commonwealth pursuant to chapter one hundred and seventy-five of the General Laws, mutual fund managers and banks. As applicable to investment of deferred compensation and IRA amounts, as the case may be, bids shall clearly indicate the interest rate which shall be paid, any commissions for salesmen, any load imposed for purposes of administration, mortality projections, expected payments, tax implications for employees and such other information as the treasurer may require. For IRAs, upon the treasurer's determining which provider offers the product or products most beneficial to the employee in each category for which bids were solicited, the treasurer may offer such employee the opportunity to establish an IRA with one or more such providers. The employee who wishes to invest his IRA funds with any such provider, or combination of providers, may authorize the treasurer to deduct from amounts otherwise payable to the employee, at one time or on a periodic basis, amounts to be paid into the employee's IRA. If the employee so elects, the treasurer shall pay to the providers the amount designated by the employee, in the name of the employee, to the employee's IRA. Amounts so paid to the providers for the employee's IRA account shall belong exclusively to the employee. Except as otherwise provided herein, the treasurer may restrict an employee's right to contract to have contributions made to an IRA through deductions and payments by the treasurer to those providers selected as the result of the competitive bidding process outlined herein, but the authority conferred upon the treasurer shall not be construed to restrict or limit the right of any employee to establish one or more IRAs with such banks, insurance companies, or similar authorized institutions as the employee may choose in any manner other than through an authorized deduction by the treasurer of a portion of the employee's compensation as outlined herein. Notwithstanding any provisions to the contrary, the treasurer shall not be required to solicit bids from providers of investment products for deferred compensation investments or IRA contributions, provided: (i) the treasurer elects to invest such deferred compensation in, or is authorized by the employee to pay IRA contributions into, the same investment products as provided through a deferred compensation or IRA plan for employees of the commonwealth administered by the state treasurer, or a deferred compensation plan for employees of the Authority administered by the treasurer, provided such plan resulted from the solicitation of bids in accordance with bidding requirements comparable to those required under this section; or (ii) the treasurer elects to invest such deferred compensation in, or is authorized by the employee to pay IRA contributions into investment products offered pursuant to a deferred compensation plan or an IRA investment option program, developed through a competitive selection process resulting from the solicitation of bids by a group of any combination of three or more city, town, county or public authority treasurers acting as a Common Group for purposes of soliciting such proposals in accordance with bidding requirements comparable to those required under this section. Any contract entered into between an employee and the Authority pursuant to this section shall include all information in terms the employee can reasonably be expected to understand. Such deferred compensation and IRA programs shall be in addition to and not a part of the retirement program or pension system as provided under the Authority Retirement System, under said chapter thirty-two or under any other benefit program provided by law for such employee. Any compensation deferred under such a plan and any compensation contributed by an employee to an IRA under such plan shall continue to be included as regular compensation, as defined in section one of said chapter thirty-two, for the purpose of computing the retirement and pension benefits earned by any such employee, but any compensation so deferred shall not be included in the computation of any taxes withheld on behalf of any such employee. For purposes of this paragraph, the word "employee" shall have the same meaning as "employee" in section one of chapter thirty-two of the General Laws and shall also include consultants and independent contractors who are natural persons paid by the Authority and whose duties require that their time be devoted to the service of the Authority during regular business hours.

(g) The Authority shall not be subject to the jurisdiction of the division of personnel administration established by section four A of chapter seven of the General Laws and shall not be governed by sections forty-five, forty-six, forty-six C to forty-six G, inclusive, of chapter thirty, and sections twenty-six, twenty-seven and twenty-seven A to twenty-seven E, inclusive, of chapter one hundred and forty-nine of the General Laws. No employee of the Authority shall be covered by section nine A of chapter thirty of the General Laws or by chapter thirty-one of the General Laws except for certain former employees of the metropolitan district commission transferred to the Authority from the metropolitan district commission under section four, to the extent of the rights provided for those employees in said section four; provided, however, that a veteran transferred to the Authority under said section four shall be entitled to include his service at the metropolitan district commission toward the three years of service provided for in section nine A of chapter thirty, and if he completes such term of service at the Authority, he shall be entitled to rights under and shall be subject to the provisions of chapter thirty. All provisional employees who are transferred to the Authority and who are labor service employees as defined in section one of chapter thirty-one and who are not eligible for an examination as provided for in section twenty-six of chapter seven hundred and sixty-seven of the acts of nineteen hundred and eighty-one and who have worked in such positions for a period of one year prior to January first, nineteen hundred and eighty-five shall be made permanent employees.

The Authority shall engage consultants to perform only those services for the Authority which regular employees of the Authority are unable to perform owing to lack of special expertise or other inability to perform such services on the schedule or in the manner required by the Authority. The Authority shall be subject to section four of chapter one hundred and fifty-one B of the General Laws, shall be deemed to be an agency of the commonwealth for purposes of section two of said chapter, and shall be subject to the enforcement jurisdiction of the commission against discrimination under said chapter. The Authority shall develop policies and programs for affirmative action in employment, procurement and contracting in accordance with law and consistent with general policies and programs of the commonwealth.

The Authority shall also appoint a special assistant for affirmative action and compliance and provide appropriate support staff. The special assistant shall report directly to the chairman of the Authority and shall develop, supervise, monitor and provide for the enforcement of affirmative action plans for employment, procurement and contracting activities of the Authority. The chairman shall take such steps and impose such sanctions as may be appropriate to ensure enforcement. A quarterly report shall be filed at the close of each quarter with the state office of affirmative action and each member of the general court requesting a copy of such report on actions taken during the preceding quarter to implement the Authority's affirmative action plan and programs.

(h) The Authority shall establish an internal special audit unit which, under the direct supervision of the executive director, shall monitor the quality, efficiency and integrity of the Authority's operating and capital programs and make periodic recommendations and reports to the executive director and the board of directors. Employees of the Authority serving in the internal special audit unit shall devote their full-time efforts to the unit and shall not be assigned direct operating responsibilities.

History—
1984, 372, § 7; 1986, 557, § 209.

Editorial Note—
The **1986 amendment** made a corrective change in the last sentence in paragraph (c), after "terms" and preceding "conditions of employment", substituting "and" for "in".

§ 8.   Operation, Improvement and Enlargement of Sewer and Waterworks Systems; Budget; Designation of Service Areas for Sewer Division and Waterworks Division; Promotion of Water Conservation.

Without limiting the generality of the powers granted to the Authority under other provisions of this act, the following provisions are made for the operation, improvement and enlargement of the sewer and waterworks systems by the Authority and for the attainment of the Authority's other purposes:

(a) The operations of the Authority specifically related to the separate functions of sewage collection, treatment and disposal and delivery of water shall be organized respectively into a sewer division and a waterworks division. The Authority shall maintain, except to the extent otherwise permitted in this act, segregated accounts for each of its divisions with respect to the revenues, expenses, assets and funds pertaining to the operation thereof. The board of directors may act to provide specified administrative or technical support services on a combined basis when, in the board's opinion, it would be more efficient to do so, in which event the board shall provide for a fair and equitable allocation of the costs to the accounts of the divisions in accordance with generally accepted accounting principles.

(b) The Authority shall adopt an annual budget for its current expenses which budget the Authority shall have submitted for comment and recommendation to the advisory board not less than sixty days prior to the adoption thereof. Except in case of an emergency, no current expenses may be incurred in excess of those shown in the annual current expense budget. The Authority may from time to time adopt amendments to current expense budgets which the Authority shall have submitted for comment and recommendation to the advisory board not less than thirty days prior to the adoption thereof. The Authority periodically shall also adopt and revise capital facility programs for the sewer system and waterworks system and capital expenditure budgets based thereon. The current expense budgets, capital expenditure budgets and the capital facility programs of the Authority shall be deemed not to be regulations or adjudications for purposes of chapter thirty A of the General Laws. The Authority shall consult in the preparation of its capital facility programs for the sewer and waterworks systems with the advisory board and the executive office of environmental affairs, and may consult with other agencies of federal, state and local government concerned with the programs of the Authority. Proposed capital facility programs and capital expenditure budgets for said systems shall be submitted to the advisory board for such consultation no less than sixty days prior to adoption or revision by the Authority. The Authority shall prepare a written response to reports respecting its finances submitted to it by the advisory board which response shall state the basis for any substantial divergence between the actions of the Authority and the recommendations contained in such reports of the advisory board. The Authority shall file copies of its capital facility programs with the deputy commissioner of capital planning and operations in accordance with section thirty-nine C of chapter seven of the General Laws, shall prepare and file long-range capital facility development plans in accordance with section seven A of chapter twenty-nine of the General Laws, and shall be deemed to be a public agency subject to the recordkeeping and reporting requirements of paragraph (4) of section forty A of chapter seven of the General Laws.

(c) The sewer division of the Authority shall provide main sewer services for the area consisting of the following political subdivisions: Arlington, Ashland, Bedford, Belmont, Boston, Braintree, Brookline, Burlington, Cambridge, Canton, Chelsea, Dedham, Everett, Framingham, the north sewer district of Hingham, Holbrook, Lexington, Malden, Medford, Melrose, Milton, Natick, Needham,

Newton, Norwood, Quincy, Randolph, Reading, Revere, Somerville, Stoneham, Stoughton, Wakefield, Walpole, Waltham, Watertown, Wellesley, Westwood, Weymouth, Wilmington, Winchester, Winthrop and Woburn. The Authority may also enter into (i) arrangements for a limited term with any person within or outside the foregoing political subdivisions to provide sewage treatment, collection or disposal services not involving extension of the sewer system; provided, however, that no such arrangement shall continue for a period in excess of six months, including any renewals thereof, unless it shall have been approved by the advisory board created by section twenty-three, and (ii) arrangements with any local body pursuant to which a sewage collection, treatment or disposal system or any part thereof shall become a part of the sewer system, provided that no extension of the sewer system shall be made to local bodies not listed in the previous sentence unless the Authority shall obtain the approval of the advisory board and the department of environmental protection, after due consideration of feasible alternatives to such extension, and the Authority shall find (1) the safe capacity of the sewer system as extended will be sufficient to meet ordinary wet weather demand, (2) all feasible actions have been taken and shall continue to be taken by any local body to which the system is extended to minimize infiltration and inflow, and (3) an industrial pretreatment program is in effect within any such local body in accordance with applicable laws and regulations. Any local body within the limits of which any main sewer under the control of the Authority is situated shall connect its local sewers with such main sewers subject to the direction, control and regulation of the Authority and the Authority may also connect private sewers with such main sewers under such terms and conditions as the Authority may prescribe. Notwithstanding the foregoing, no new local body will be added to the sewer service area without prior approval of the governor and the general court.

(d) The waterworks division of the Authority shall provide water for local water systems of the following political subdivisions: Arlington, Bedford, Belmont, Boston, Brookline, Cambridge, Canton, Chelsea, Chicopee, Clinton, Dedham, Everett, Framingham, Leominster, Lexington, Lynn, Lynnfield Water District, Malden, Marblehead, Marlborough, Medford, Melrose, Milton, Nahant, Needham, Newton, Northborough, Norwood, Peabody, Quincy, Revere, Saugus, Somerville, Southborough, South Hadley Water District No. 1, Stoneham, Swampscott, Wakefield, Waltham, Watertown, Wellesley, Weston, Wilbraham, Winchester, Winthrop, Woburn and Worcester. The provisions of special acts and contracts in effect on January first, nineteen hundred and eighty-four under which water is supplied by the MDC water system shall continue in full force and effect under the respective terms thereof, subject to all rights of the Authority as successor to the metropolitan district commission. Continuation of delivery of water to local water systems supplied on a contractual basis on the effective date of this act upon the expiration of such contractual obligations, service to be supplied under willingness-to-service contracts on the effective date of this act and new communities entering the system, shall be made to the foregoing political subdivision on such reasonable terms and charges as the Authority may determine, provided that in each such instance the Authority shall find: (1) the safe yield to the watershed system, only on advice of the division, is sufficient to meet projected demand; provided, however, that a local body receiving water on a contractual basis as of the effective date of this act which meets the requirements of having no local water supply capable of being developed under the provisions of clause (5), in this subsection, shall not be denied such continuation; (2) no existing or potential water supply source for the local body has been abandoned unless the department of environmental protection has declared that the source is unfit for drinking and cannot be economically restored for drinking purposes; (3) a water management plan has been adopted after approval by the water resources commission established by section eight A of chapter twenty-one A of the General Laws; (4) effective demand management measures have been established, including but not limited to the establishment of a leak detection and other appropriate water system rehabilitation programs; (5) a local water supply source feasible for development has not been identified by the local body or the department of environmental protection; and (6) a water use survey has been completed which identifies all users in the area of the local body that consume in excess of twenty million gallons per year. Any provision for supply of water under special act in effect on the effective date of this act, and any contract for the supply of water by the metropolitan district commission in effect on the effective date of this act which does not provide for a specific term may be terminated by the Authority on or after, but not before, the fifth anniversary of the effective date of this act, in which case continuation of service shall thereafter be governed by the provisions of the preceding sentence. Subject to the approval of the advisory board established by section twenty-three and regulatory bodies within the executive office of environmental affairs with jurisdiction in the matter as a result of other general or special laws applicable to the Authority, the Authority may extend the waterworks system to additional local bodies on such reasonable terms as the Authority may determine; provided, however, that in each instance the Authority shall find: (1) the safe yield of the watershed system, only on the advice of the division, is sufficient to meet such new projected demand; (2) no existing or potential water supply source for the local body has been abandoned unless the department of environmental protection has declared that the source is unfit for drinking and cannot be economically restored for drinking purposes; (3) a water management plan has been adopted after approval by the water resources commission established by section eight A of chapter twenty-one A of the General Laws; (4) effective demand management measures have been established including, but not limited to, the establishment of a leak detection and other appropriate water system rehabilitation programs; (5) a local water supply source feasible for development has not been identified by the local body or the department of environmental protection; and (6) a water use survey has been completed which identifies all users in the area of the local body that consume in excess of twenty million gallons per year; and provided further that no new local body will be added to the water service area without prior approval of the governor and the general court. Connections to the water system shall be under the direction and control of the Authority, provided, however, that water shall be delivered by the Authority under sufficient pressure for use without local pumping, unless delivered in some other manner by agreement. The Authority may also enter into arrangements not involving the extension of the waterworks system to provide the delivery of water to any local body, any institution, agency or facility of the commonwealth or any institution, agency or facility of the United States provided (i) that as a condition to the entry into such arrangement the Authority shall find and declare that the demand on the waterworks system from the Authority's performance of the arrangement is not reasonably expected to jeopardize the delivery of water provided by the Authority to the inhabitants of the political subdivisions listed in the first sentence of this paragraph, after taking account of other water supply resources reasonably available to such political subdivisions, and (ii) no such arrangement shall extend for a period in excess of six months, including any renewals thereof, unless it shall have been approved by said advisory board. Subject to the provisions of section forty of chapter forty of the General Laws, in case of any emergency as determined by the department of environmental protection, any local body deriving its water supply in whole or in part from the waterworks system may provide a connection and a supply of water to any adjoining local body having an inadequate water supply of water subject to reasonable provision for payment to the Authority and for approval by the Authority of the means of connection. No local body or private water company shall abandon any local water supply source and substitute for it water from the waterworks system unless the department of environmental protection has declared that the water supply source abandoned or to be abandoned is unfit for drinking and cannot be economically restored for drinking purposes. Any local body which derives all or part of its water supply on the effective date of this act under a contract with the metropolitan district commission which contains a minimum purchase requirement may elect, upon such reasonable prior notice as the Authority may require, to terminate such minimum purchase requirement.

The Authority shall reimburse any community serviced by the waterworks division of the Authority for the cost incurred in carrying out measures ordered by the department of environmental protection to remedy total coliform level violations in their water distribution systems, for up to ten thousand dollars per community per calendar year, if it is determined by the director of the waterworks division and approved by the executive director, that there is a strong likelihood that activities conducted by the Authority in its system contributed to the cause of the total coliform level violation in the water distribution system. Such determination shall not be considered an assumption of any liabilities by the Authority.

(e) In order to attain its statutory purposes to promote water conservation, protect the adequacy of a pure water supply, reduce wastewater flow and improve environmental quality, the Authority is authorized and directed: (i) to promote water conservation and environmental quality through its schedule of charges, to which end, without limiting the generality of the foregoing and the generality of the regulatory powers conferred on the Authority under section six and the powers to establish charges under section ten, the Authority shall prepare and publish no later than the second anniversary of the effective date of this act a comprehensive study of environmental, social and economic impacts of its charges to serve as a basis for the implementation of charges fully consistent with the objectives of this act, and shall consult with the division for the determination of such environmental impact; (ii) to conduct public programs of education and technical assistance in support of water conservation and environmental quality objectives; (iii) to terminate as promptly as feasible, and thereafter not to institute or reinstitute, any charge or charges for the waterworks system by which the unit price declines as volume of use increases; (iv) to identify and consider demand management and water conservation solutions to new and existing water consumption requirements and, wherever reasonably practicable, to implement such solutions in preference to solutions which would increase water withdrawals from any natural or artificial source of ground or surface waters; and (v) to prepare and submit an annual report to the governor, the general court and the water resources commission stating the means by which future water requirements of the Authority's service areas will be met within the safe yield of the watershed system of the division, pursuant to any such determination made by the division.

Nothing contained in paragraphs (c) and (d) shall require a city or town not presently served by the Authority to accept an extension of the Authority's sewer and water works without a majority vote by the city council if a city or a majority vote of the town meeting if a town.

(f) Officers or agents of the Authority may enter at reasonable times any public or private property, connected directly or indirectly to the sewer system, for purposes of (i) inspecting, sampling and gauging any sewage, drainage, substances or wastes conveyed through such a connection, (ii) inspecting any monitoring equipment or procedures maintained with respect to discharges thereof, (iii) examining any records or matters pertaining to such discharges or to the operation of pretreatment works, and (iv) determining any matter of compliance with requirements under this act. Officers or agents of the Authority may also enter any public or private property supplied directly or indirectly by the waterworks system for purposes of (i) inspecting water works or fixtures, (ii) determining water usage, (iii) preventing improper use or waste of water, (iv) determining any matter for compliance with requirements under this act. Entry upon private property for purposes of this section shall be made (i) under warrant, including, without limitation, warrants for administrative inspection upon a probable cause showing of a reasonable and valid public interest in the effective enforcement of matters governed by this act in accordance with a general plan justifying administrative inspection of premises specified in the application for such warrant, or (ii) under procedures for warrantless entry of non-residential premises during business hours conducted by administrative inspectors in accordance with regulations which the Authority shall adopt to further the urgent governmental interest in environmental protection committed to the Authority. This section shall not limit entries and administrative inspections, including seizures of property, without a warrant (1) with the consent of the owner or person in charge of the premises, (2) in situations presenting imminent danger to health or safety, (3) in any other exceptional or emergency circumstances where time or opportunity to apply for a warrant is lacking, or (4) in all other situations in which a warrant is not required by the laws and constitutions of the commonwealth or the United States.

(g) The Authority shall be deemed to be a public agency for purposes of, and shall be subject to, sections forty-four A to forty-four H, inclusive, of chapter one hundred and forty-nine of the General Laws, section thirty-nine M of chapter thirty of the General Laws and sections thirty B to thirty M, inclusive, of chapter seven of the General Laws, and shall comply with requirements applicable to an independent public authority for publication of contract information in the central register established under section twenty A of chapter nine of the General Laws. The Authority shall not be subject to supervision under section twenty-two of chapter seven of the General Laws, but may enter into agreements under section twenty-two A and twenty-two B of chapter seven of the General Laws and in all respects not governed by general or special laws expressly made applicable to the Authority shall adhere to good business practices to be determined by the Authority in its procurement of equipment, materials, property, supplies and services.

(h) In operating its systems and performing its projects in relation thereto, the Authority may construct and maintain buildings, machinery, roads, conduits, pipes, sewers and aqueducts, may alter grades or directions of watercourses and may conduct aqueducts over or under any watercourse, railroad, pipeline, cable, or way, restoring the same to as good order and condition as practicable. Persons who sustain injury in their property by the entry upon or use thereof by the Authority under this section may recover their damages under chapter seventy-nine of the General Laws, unless a lawful alternative provision for such damages is otherwise made by the Authority.

(i) The Authority and division shall be subject to the provisions of, and to regulation by the department of environmental protection and any division thereof as may be duly exercised over an independent public authority of the commonwealth, including without limitation, sections fourteen, twenty-seven, thirty A to thirty-four C, inclusive, thirty-seven, forty and forty-two to forty-six A, inclusive, of chapter twenty-one of the General Laws, chapter twenty-one C of the General Laws, chapter twenty-one E of the General Laws, chapter ninety-one of the General Laws and sections two B, two C, five E, five G, seventeen, thirty-one D, one hundred and forty-two A to one hundred and forty-two E, inclusive, one hundred and fifty A, one hundred and fifty B, one hundred and sixty, one hundred and sixty A, one hundred and sixty B, one hundred and sixty-two and one hundred and sixty-five of chapter one hundred and eleven of the General Laws.

The Authority shall be deemed to be a public entity under section twenty-six A of chapter twenty-one of the General Laws and shall be eligible for grants and other assistance under the Massachusetts Clean Water Act and any other program of federal or state assistance for waterworks, wastewater treatment or related purposes to the most liberal extent of the eligibility of an agency of the commonwealth, a political subdivision of the commonwealth, or any other public body of the commonwealth. The Authority shall be subject to section four A and sections eight A to eight F, inclusive, of chapter twenty-one A of the General Laws, sections three, four, seven, ten and fourteen of chapter twenty-one D of the General Laws and sections one hundred and forty-two A to one hundred and forty-two E, inclusive, of chapter one hundred and eleven of the General Laws. The Authority shall be deemed to be an agency of the commonwealth for purposes of, and shall be subject to, section one hundred and fifty A and section one hundred and fifty B of chapter one hundred and eleven of the General Laws. Without limitation on other public health or environmental regulation over the Authority exercisable pursuant to other law without conflict with the Authority's purpose of serving critical public needs on a broad geographic basis as a public instrumentality of the commonwealth, the Authority also shall be subject to sections forty and forty A of chapter one hundred and thirty-one of the General Laws, to sections sixty-one to sixty-two H, inclusive, of chapter thirty of the General Laws and to sections twenty-six C and twenty-seven C of chapter nine of the General Laws. The Authority and the division shall be subject to sections thirteen to sixteen, inclusive, and section eighteen of chapter one hundred and thirty-two A of the General Laws. In accordance with section eleven D of chapter twelve of the General Laws, the Authority shall give written notice to the attorney general of all adjudicatory proceedings or public hearings conducted by it or to which it is a party in which damage to the environment is or may be at issue.

(j) All powers to be exercised under this act, including powers to be exercised by the division of watershed management and the Authority, shall be subject to provisions regulating interbasin transfers as set forth in sections eight B to eight D, inclusive, of chapter twenty-one of the General Laws, including without limitation all approvals therein required to be obtained from the water resources commission and to provisions for the protection of scenic and recreational rivers and streams as set forth in section seventeen B of chapter twenty-one of the General Laws and in section two of chapter nine hundred and eighty-four of the acts of nineteen hundred and seventy-three, including without limitation all approvals respecting water diversions therein required to be obtained from the general court.

(k) Notwithstanding any rule or regulation or any provision of any general or special law to the contrary, the commissioner of public safety or his designee in the division of inspection of the department of public safety shall have exclusive jurisdiction and responsibility with respect to projects or operations of the Authority for inspection, approvals, enforcement, permitting, and licensure authorized or required by (i) chapter one hundred and forty-three of the General Laws or (ii) any regulation adopted pursuant to chapter eight hundred and two of the acts of nineteen hundred and seventy-two.

(l) Notwithstanding the provisions of chapters one hundred and thirty-four and one hundred and forty-seven of the General Laws, if money, goods or other property which has been abandoned, mislaid or lost comes into the possession of the Authority and remains unclaimed in its possession for a period of one hundred and twenty days, the Authority may sell the same, excepting money so unclaimed, at public auction after notice of such sale has been published in a newspaper published in the city or town where such sale is to take place. The net proceeds of such sale, after deducting the cost of storage and the expenses of such sale, and all money so unclaimed, shall become revenues of the Authority. If in the opinion of the Authority any such property in the possession of the Authority and unclaimed in its possession for a period of one hundred and twenty days is of the value of one hundred and fifty dollars or less, the Authority may donate the same to a charitable organization.

(m) The powers of the Authority shall include the powers to be exercised by procedures, regulations, incentive and other charges, and licenses and permits to require persons who are users of the sewer system or of any tributary system to the sewer system to comply with applicable provisions of federal and state law respecting (i) toxic waste and pretreatment standards, (ii) construction, operation and maintenance of pretreatment facilities, (iii) monitoring, recordkeeping and reporting of discharges to the sewer system, (iv) notification of proposed new discharges or substantial changes in discharges to the sewer system, and (v) user charges in accordance with law, and to regulate the nature and quantity of discharge of sewage, drainage, substances or wastes by any person into the sewer system or any sewer tributary thereto. The procedures, regulations, charges and licensing, permitting and other programs of the Authority shall also reasonably provide for abatement, reduction and prevention of infiltration and inflow of ground waters, surface waters or storm waters into the sewer system; and the Authority is directed to continue, and is authorized in its discretion reasonably to require the extension and improvement of separation of sewers for the collection, treatment, and disposal of human and industrial sewage from drainage for surface or storm water. The procedures, regulations, charges, licensing, permitting and other programs of the Authority shall also reasonably provide for leak detection and repair, for programs for water conservation, including, without limiting the generality thereof, water use limitations in time of drought or other emergency, and may also reasonably provide for installation and maintenance of meters by any person and the metering of use made by any user or group of users of the sewer system or any system tributary thereto or by any user of water derived from the waterworks system. The Authority may regulate and require the taking of a permit from the Authority with respect to any building, construction, excavation or crossing within an easement or other property interest held by the Authority or in the immediate vicinity of a water or sewer main or other facility which is operated by the Authority. The provisions of this paragraph shall not limit the generality of the regulatory powers conferred on the Authority under section six and the powers to establish charges under section ten.

(n) The Authority is authorized to take all necessary action, consistent with applicable special or general law, administrative regulation or practice, to secure any federal assistance which is or may become available to the Authority, the commonwealth or any local body for any of the sewer or waterworks purposes of this act. If any federal law, administrative regulation or practice requires any action relating to such federal assistance to be taken by any department or instrumentality of the commonwealth other than the Authority, such other department or instrumentality is authorized to take all such action, including without limitation filing applications for assistance, supervising the expenditure of federal grants or loans and making any determinations and certifications necessary or appropriate to the foregoing, and the Authority is authorized to take all action necessary to permit such department or instrumentality to comply with all federal requirements; provided, however, that no such action or federal requirement shall be taken which is inconsistent with the provisions of any special or general law or the provisions of this act relating to waterworks, sewer works, wastewater treatment or water supply.

(o) Any person who without lawful authority injures, destroys or interferes with any property held or used by the Authority for the purpose of constructing, operating or maintaining the waterworks system or the sewer system, shall be subject to a criminal fine of not more than fifty thousand dollars, or imprisonment for not more than one year; provided, however, that in cases of continuing violation, such maximum fine may be ten thousand dollars per day for each day such violation occurs or continues. Notwithstanding any limitation on criminal penalties set forth in the preceding sentence, any person convicted of the wanton or malicious destruction of or injury to any property of the Authority used in the construction, operation or maintenance of the waterworks system or the sewer system shall also be liable in tort to the Authority for triple the amount of damages thereby caused. The provisions of this paragraph are in addition to and not in limitation of the Authority's power to adopt, issue and enforce regulations, permits and licenses and establish penalties for violation thereof and to set charges and provide for the collection and enforcement thereof.

(p) Authorized agents and employees of the Authority may enter upon any lands, waters and premises in communities listed in both paragraphs (c) and (d) for the purpose of making surveys, soundings, test pits, drillings, borings and examinations as the Authority may deem necessary or convenient for the purposes of this act, and such entry shall not be deemed a trespass, nor shall an entry for such purposes be deemed an entry under any condemnation proceedings which may be then pending. The Authority shall give at least fifteen days notice of its intent to enter such lands, waters or premises to the record owner(s) of the property and to the municipality wherein the property lies, and shall state in that notice the amount it proposes to pay as just compensation for such entry. Following such entry, the Authority shall pay the amount of compensation previously proposed and shall reimburse the owner for any actual damage resulting to such lands, waters and premises as a result of such activities. If the owner of said lands believes that the amount paid is insufficient to provide just compensation, the owner may petition to the superior court to have the amount increased. The provisions of this section shall in no way expand the powers of the Authority to take any of the properties investigated by eminent domain.

History—

1984, 372, § 8; 1987, 770, §§ 10–15; 1990, 145, § 1, approved July 28, 1990, effective 90 days thereafter; 1990, 177, §§ 380–382, approved, with emergency preamble, Aug 7, 1990; 1991, 261, approved Oct 11, 1991, effective 90 days thereafter.

Editorial Note—

The 1987 amendment, in both clauses (4) of paragraph (d), replaced "program" with "programs" after "areas" in clause (v) of paragraph (e), inserted "will be met" in the second paragraph of paragraph (e), replaced "town meeting of" with "the town meeting if" in the first paragraph of paragraph (i), replaced "pursuant to" with ", including without limitation," replaced "chapter twenty-one A" with "chapter twenty-one", replaced "sections four, six, seven and nine of chapter twenty-one C" with "chapter twenty-one C", and replaced "sections three, six, seven, nine and ten of chapter twenty-one E" with "chapter twenty-one E" in paragraph (n) after "all federal requirements", deleted ", such action" and added paragraph (p).

The first 1990 amendment, in paragraph (d), after the opening paragraph, following "Arlington", inserted ", Bedford". Section 2 of the amending act provides as follows:

SECTION 2. Notwithstanding the provisions of section one, the inclusion of the town of Bedford into the Massachusetts Water Resources Authority shall commence only after said Authority makes findings as set forth in paragraph (d) of section eight of chapter three hundred and seventy-two of the acts of nineteen hundred and eighty-four.

The second 1990 amendment in the second sentence of paragraph (c), substituted "environmental protection" for "environmental quality engineering", in paragraph (d), in clauses (2) and (5) of each of the third and fifth sentences and, in the seventh and eighth sentences, substituted "environmental protection" for "environmental quality engineering", in each instance, and, in the first paragraph of paragraph (i), substituted "environmental protection" for "environmental quality engineering".

The 1991 amendment, in paragraph (d), added a paragraph relative to requiring the Massachusetts Water Resources Authority to reimburse certain cities and towns for certain water purification work.

Code of Massachusetts Regulations—
Continuation of contract water supply, 360 CMR 11.00 et seq.

§ 9.   Acquisition or Disposal of Property or Interests.

(a) Except for the acquisition of any water supply source or right to a water source, which right is vested exclusively in the division of watershed management, the Authority may acquire from any person real property, or any interest or rights therein, deemed by it essential for operation, improvement or enlargement of its sewer and waterworks systems by eminent domain in accordance with the provisions of chapter seventy-nine or chapter eighty A of the General Laws subject to the prior approval of the governor and the general court; provided, however, that for takings related to main, trunk, intercepting and connecting sewers and pumping stations incidental thereto, and combined overflow treatment works and pumping stations incidental thereto, said prior approval shall not be required, and provided, that no property or rights, including water rights, comprising the watershed system shall be taken; and, provided further, that no property or rights already appropriated to public use shall be so taken without the prior approval of the governor and general court. Prior approval of the legislature and governor, to the extent otherwise required by the preceding sentence, shall not be required for takings within the communities listed in the first sentence of paragraph (d) of section eight, for purposes of maintenance or improvement of the waterworks system within such communities. Notwithstanding the provisions of this act, no taking by eminent domain of water or water rights shall be made by the Authority. No taking shall be made for a project of the Authority which requires regulatory approvals with respect to matters to which the Authority is subject under paragraph (i) of section eight until the Authority has certified that the Authority reasonably believes all such approvals will be obtained by the Authority in ordinary course. Before a taking is made by the Authority for which damages may be recovered under chapter seventy-nine, the Authority shall file with the secretary of the commonwealth security to the satisfaction of said secretary for the payment of all damages and costs which may be awarded for the property taken, and if, upon petition of the owner and notice to the Authority, any security taken appears to have become insufficient, the secretary shall require the Authority to give further security to the satisfaction of the secretary.

(b) The Authority may order the removal or relocation of any conduits, pipes, wires, poles or other property located in public ways or places, or in or upon private lands, which it deems to interfere with the laying out, construction, maintenance or operation of the sewer and waterworks systems, subject to the ability of the proper authorities lawfully to grant or otherwise make provisions for new locations for any such structure so removed or relocated. Such orders, to the extent specified therein, shall be deemed a revocation of the right or license to maintain such conduits, pipes, wires, poles or other property in such public ways or places, and the private owner of any such structures in public ways or places shall comply with such orders. If any such owner shall fail to comply with any such order of the Authority relating to any such structure in public ways and places within a reasonable time, to be fixed in the order, the Authority may discontinue and remove such conduits, pipes, wires, poles or other property, and may relocate the same, and the cost of such discontinuance, removal or relocation shall be repaid to the Authority by the owner. No such discontinuance, removal or relocation shall entitle the owner of the property thus affected to any damages on account thereof. Any such structure in or upon private lands may be removed and relocated by the owner thereof, the reasonable expense thereof shall be repaid to him by the Authority.

(c) Subject to the prior approval of the governor and general court, and to applicable provisions of the laws and constitution of the commonwealth, including without limiting the generality of the foregoing, article ninety-seven of the Amendments to the Constitution of the Commonwealth, doctrines of laws concerned with diversion of lands devoted to public use to other inconsistent public use the Authority may, at public or private sale, sell, lease or dispose of any interest in real property of the sewer and waterworks systems acquired by the Authority pursuant to paragraphs (b) and (c) of section four, upon compliance with the following conditions: (i) such property or interest in property is no longer needed for the construction, maintenance or operation of the sewer and waterworks systems; (ii) such disposition shall not impair the maintenance and operation of said systems; and (iii) the Authority shall so notify the deputy commissioner of capital planning and operations, and said deputy commissioner shall proceed in accordance with section forty F of chapter seven of the General Laws.

(d) Real and personal property, or interests or rights therein, may be acquired by the Authority after July first, nineteen hundred and eighty-five if deemed essential for operation, improvement or enlargement of its sewer and waterworks systems. The Authority may, at public or private sale, dispose of said real property, or interest or rights therein no longer needed for the construction, maintenance or operation of the sewer and waterworks systems, subject to prior approval of the governor and the general court, provided, however, that such disposition shall not impair the maintenance and operation of said systems.

Any interest in real property so disposed of may be conveyed, subject to such easements, reservations and restrictions as the Authority deems necessary to secure the maintenance and operation of said systems, by deed duly executed by the Authority, with or without warranty. In any case where the Authority may dispose of such property, it may convey it and receive in complete or partial consideration therefor other property or interests therein, for the purpose of the sewer and waterworks systems, the title of the same to be taken in the name of the Authority. The Authority shall give sixty days notice of the proposed lease or disposition of any such property or any such interest in real property to the chief executive officer, as defined in section twenty-three, of any city or town in which the real property is located and to the deputy commissioner of capital planning and operations. The Authority shall be deemed to be a public agency for purposes of and shall comply with sections forty J and forty K of chapter seven of the General Laws. The Authority also from time to time at public or private sale conducted in a commercially reasonable manner may sell or otherwise dispose of personal property of the Authority whether acquired pursuant to the provisions of paragraph (a) of section four or after the effective date of this act, which is no longer needed for the construction, maintenance or operation of said systems.

History—
1984, 372, § 9; 1987, 770, § 16.

Editorial Note—
The **1987 amendment,** in paragraph (a), inserted the second sentence, relat-

ing to prior approval of the legislature and governor for takings within the communities listed in the first sentence of paragraph (d) of section eight.

§ 10.   Charges, Fees, Rates, Assessments, etc.

(a) Said Authority shall establish and adjust charges which may be denominated as charges, fees, rates, assessments or otherwise as the Authority may reasonably determine, for services, facilities and commodities furnished or supplied by the Authority. The charges of the Authority shall be separately established in respect to the Authority's waterworks and sewer divisions and shall be fixed and adjusted so as to provide funds, in the aggregate and separately, with respect to costs and operations allocable to each division, sufficient in each fiscal year with other revenues of Authority, if any, available therefor (i) to pay all current expenses, (ii) to pay all debt service on bonds of the Authority as the same becomes due and payable, (iii) to create and maintain all reserves reasonably required by any bond resolution, trust agreement or other agreement securing bonds of the Authority or as otherwise determined by the Authority to be necessary or desirable, (iv) to pay all costs of maintenance and replacement of the sewer and waterworks systems, and costs of improving, extending and enlarging said systems as determined by the Authority to be necessary or desirable, to be funded as current expenses in order to carry out the purposes of the Authority, (v) to provide for payments to the commonwealth for debt service as herein provided, and (vi) to pay or provide for all amounts which the Authority may be obligated to pay or provide for by any law or contract including any bond resolution, trust agreement or other agreement securing bonds of the Authority and including any amount to be repaid to the commonwealth to reimburse the commonwealth for debt service paid by the commonwealth on a bond issued under paragraph (f) of section five. The charges of the Authority for delivery of water and for sewage collection, disposal and treatment services shall be established as charges of general application to be borne by the local body utilizing such services and shall be established at a level sufficient to meet the revenue requirements of the Authority as provided in this paragraph, notwithstanding the provisions of any other general or special law to the contrary.

Said Authority's charges of general application shall be adopted, and on not less than an annual basis reviewed and if necessary revised, in accordance with procedures for notice and a hearing as provided by chapter thirty A of the General Laws, and notice of such hearing shall also be delivered at least twenty-one days in advance of the hearing date, to the advisory board and published in newspapers of general circulation in cities and towns receiving services. No later than the date of such publication, the Authority shall transmit to the advisory board and reasonably provide for other public review for the period preceding the hearing including (i) its most recent financial statements, (ii) its current expense budgets and capital expenditure budgets for the current fiscal year and, if then adopted or proposed, for the next fiscal year, and (iii) the proposed charges on which the Authority seeks public comment. Prior to any public hearing as provided herein, the Authority shall comply with requests of the ombudsman acting under paragraph (g) of section twenty-three for the inspection of the books, records, financial statements and documents of the Authority relating to the proposed charges. In establishing its charges the Authority shall continue provisions for subsidization of water charges to which any local body is entitled in accordance with contract or other lawful obligations assumed by the Authority as successor to the metropolitan district commission, to the same extent as the metropolitan district commission would be bound to provide such subsidization if such charges had continued to be established by the metropolitan district commission. The Authority may also provide for charges of special application to any person for compensation for special or temporary services entered into in accordance with paragraphs (c) and (d) of section eight. Charges of special application shall not be regulations for purposes of chapter thirty A of the General Laws and may be computed in the Authority's discretion with respect to the services or commodities provided on the basis of the Authority's costs, or the value of the benefits conferred on the payer, or market value. The charges of the Authority, whether of general or special application, shall not be subject to supervision or regulation by any office, department, division, commission, board, bureau or agency of the commonwealth or any of its political subdivisions. The charges of the Authority, whether of general or special application, shall give account to (i) actual costs to the Authority of providing services, (ii) reasonable provisions in the nature of incentives and disincentives to promote conservation of resources and protection of the environment and to induce the protection, maintenance and improvement of the sewer and waterworks systems and of sewer and water systems of local bodies, (iii) reasonable provisions reflecting the contribution made by local bodies through expenditures including, but not limited to, leak detection, system rehabilitation and other water management programs, sewerage inflow/infiltration reduction projects, separation of combined sewers and other projects which improve the overall efficiency of the Authority's and local bodies' service delivery, (iv) reasonable provisions to reflect respective local bodies' disproportionate historic investment in the sewer and waterworks systems and in the former metropolitan district commission sewer system and metropolitan district commission water system used in the services delivered by the Authority, (v) reasonable interest charges and penalties for delinquency in payment.

(b) Said Authority, in such form as it determines, may certify to each local body to which services, facilities or commodities of the Authority are delivered or furnished the amounts of the Authority's charges to such local body. The Authority may adopt and enforce procedures and regulations for the purposes of making, collecting and enforcing its charges which, without limiting the generality of the foregoing or the general powers with respect to its regulations and charges provided herein or by any other general or special law, may impose requirements on any person including, but not limited to, local bodies and officers and boards thereof or subordinate thereto, respecting (i) the furnishing to the Authority of information reasonably deemed pertinent by the Authority concerning the volume and character of services, facilities and commodities furnished or supplied by the Authority, and the nature and quantity of services, facilities and commodities furnished to or to be furnished to or used by or to be used by users, and (ii) reasonable schedules for remittance to the Authority of its charges. In all actions pursuant to this paragraph, the Authority shall give due regard to local bodies' systems of billing and collection of water and sewer charges in order to avoid unnecessary expense and to achieve management and fiscal efficiency consistent with the attainment of the Authority's statutory objectives. Local bodies, and officers and boards thereof or subordinate thereto, shall cooperate with the Authority to effect the prompt, accurate and efficient billing and collection of the Authority's charges. In the event any local body, which has received a certification of the Authority's charges, shall fail to pay the same to the Authority when due after demand by the Authority, the Authority may without any requirement of election of remedy provided that there is no duplication of recovery, (i) certify to the state treasurer the amount owing to the Authority by said local body, whereupon the state treasurer shall promptly pay over to the Authority any amount otherwise certified to the state treasurer for payment to the local body as receipts, distributions, reimbursements and assistance under sections eighteen A, eighteen B, eighteen C and eighteen D of chapter fifty-eight of the General Laws and any other amount for local reimbursement, grant or assistance programs entitled to be received by such local body until such time as any deficiency in the local body's payment of charges to the Authority shall be set off by such payments from the state treasurer, and (ii) recover from the local body in an action in superior court the amount of such unpaid amount together with such lost interest and other actual damages the Authority shall have sustained from the failure or refusal of the local body to pay over said amount. Any amount paid to the Authority by the state treasurer as a set off under the provisions of the next preceding sentence which is later determined, upon audit, to be in excess of the actual amount of charges, interest and damages due to the

Authority, shall, upon demand of the local body, be repaid by the Authority to the local body.

History—
1984, 372, § 10; 1987, 770, §§ 17, 18.

Editorial Note—
The 1987 amendment, after "provided" in the second sentence of paragraph (b), inserted "herein" and, in clause (i) of paragraph (b), replaced ", to the Authority" with "to the Authority of."

Code of Massachusetts Regulations—
Massachusetts Water Resources Authority, user charges, 360 CMR 10.011.
Massachusetts Water Resources Authority, service charges or fees, 360 CMR 10.012.

§ 11.   [Repealed, 1991, 138, § 223, approved July 10, 1991, by § 393, effective July 1, 1991].

§ 12.   **Issuance of Bonds by Authority.**

(a) Said Authority may provide, by resolution of the board of directors, for the issuance from time to time of bonds of the Authority for any of its corporate purposes and for reimbursement, pursuant to section forty-two, to the commonwealth for costs associated with the division, or for the borrowing of money in anticipation of the issuance of such bonds. Bonds issued by the Authority may be issued as general obligations of the Authority or as special obligations payable solely for particular revenues or funds as may be provided for in any bond resolution, trust agreement or other agreement securing bonds. The Authority may also provide by resolution of the board of directors for the issuance from time to time of temporary notes in anticipation of the revenues to be collected or received by the Authority, or in anticipation of the receipt of other grants or aid. The issue of such notes shall be governed by the provisions of this act relating to the issue of bonds of the Authority other than such temporary notes as the same may be applicable; provided, however, that notes issued in anticipation of revenues shall mature no later than one year from their respective dates and notes issued in anticipation of grants, or other aid and renewals thereof, shall mature no later than six months after the expected date of receipt of such grant or aid. The aggregate principal amount of all bonds issued under the authority of this act shall not exceed the sum of two billion three hundred million dollars outstanding at any one time provided however, that bonds for the payment of redemption of which, either at or prior to maturity, refunding bonds shall have been issued, shall be excluded in the computation of outstanding bonds.

(b) Bonds of each issue shall be dated, may bear interest at such rate or rates, including rates variable from time to time as determined by an index, banker's loan rate or other method determined by the Authority, and shall mature or otherwise be payable at such time or times, as may be determined by the Authority, and may be made redeemable before maturity at the option of the Authority or the holder thereof at such price or prices and under such terms and conditions as may be fixed by the Authority. Prior to the initial issuance of each series of bonds the Authority shall advise the advisory board created by section twenty-three and the executive office for administration and finance of the timing and terms thereof and the Authority shall also communicate such information to the finance advisory board. The Authority shall determine the form of bonds, including interest coupons, if any, to be attached thereto, and the manner of execution of such bonds, and shall fix the denomination or denominations of such bonds and the place or places of payment of principal, redemption premium, if any, and interest, which may be at any bank or trust company within or without the commonwealth. In case any officer whose signature or a facsimile of whose signature shall appear on any bonds or coupons shall cease to be such officer before the delivery thereof, such signature or facsimile shall nevertheless be valid and sufficient for all purposes as if such officer had remained in office until delivery. The Authority may provide for authentication of bonds by a trustee, fiscal agent, registrar or transfer agent. Bonds may be issued in bearer or in registered form, or both, and, if notes, may be made payable to bearer or to order, as the Authority may determine, and provision may be made for the registration of any coupon bonds as to principal alone and also as to both principal and interest, for the reconversion into coupon bonds of bonds registered as to both principal and interest and for the interchange of bonds registered as to both principal and interest and for the interchange of registered and coupon bonds. The Authority may also establish and maintain a system of registration for any bonds whereby the name of the registered owner, the rights evidenced by the bonds, the transfer of the bonds and such rights and other similar matters are recorded in books or other records maintained by or on behalf of the Authority, and no instrument evidencing such bond or rights need be delivered to the registered owner by the Authority. A copy of the books or other records of the Authority pertaining to any bond registered under such registration system certified by an authorized officer of the Authority or by the agent of the Authority maintaining such system shall be admissible in any proceeding without further authentication. The Authority may adopt regulations with respect to the operation of such system. The board of directors may by resolution delegate to any director or directors or officer or officers of the Authority or any combination thereof the power to determine any of the matters set forth in this section. In the discretion of the Authority, bonds of the Authority may be issued with such terms as will cause the interest thereon to be subject to federal income taxation. The Authority may sell its bonds in the manner, either at public or private sale, for the price, at the rate or rates of interest, or at discount in lieu of interest, as it may determine will best effect the purposes of this act.

(c) Said Authority may issue interim receipts or temporary bonds, with or without coupons, exchangeable for definitive bonds when the bonds shall have been executed and are available for delivery. The Authority may also provide for replacement of any bonds which shall have become mutilated or shall have been destroyed or lost. The Authority, by itself or through such agent as it may select, may purchase and invite offers to tender for purchase any bonds of the Authority at any time outstanding, provided, however, that no such purchase by the Authority shall be made at a price, exclusive of accrued interest, if any, exceeding the principal amount thereof or, if greater, the redemption price of such bonds when next redeemable at the option of the Authority, and may resell any bonds so purchased in such manner and for such price as it may determine will best effect the purposes of this act.

(d) In the discretion of the board of directors, any bonds issued hereunder may be secured by a bond resolution or trust agreement or other agreement in such form and executed in such manner as may be determined by the board of directors between the Authority and the purchasers or holders of such bonds or between the Authority and a corporate trustee which may be any trust company or bank having the powers of a trust company within or without the commonwealth. Such bond resolution, trust agreement or other agreement may pledge or assign, in whole or in part, the revenues and funds held or to be received by the Authority, and any contract or other rights to receive the same, whether then existing or thereafter coming into existence and whether then held or thereafter acquired by the Authority, and the proceeds thereof. Such bond resolution, trust agreement or other agreement may contain such provisions for protecting and enforcing the rights, security and remedies of the bondholders as may be reasonable and proper, including, without limiting the generality of the foregoing, provisions defining defaults and providing for remedies in the event thereof which may include the acceleration of maturities, restrictions on the individual right of action by bondholders and covenants setting forth the duties of and limitations on the Authority in relation to the acquisition, construction, improvement, enlargement, alteration, equipping, furnishing, maintenance, use, operation, repair, insurance and disposition of the sewer and waterworks systems, the custody, safeguarding, investment and application of moneys, the issue of additional or refunding bonds, the fixing, revision, charging and collection of charges, the use of any surplus bond proceeds, the establishment of reserves and the making and amending of contracts; provided, however, that the Authority shall not mortgage its real property or fixed assets to secure its bonds.

(e) In the discretion of the board of directors any bonds issued under authority of this act may be issued by the Authority in the form of lines of credit or other banking arrangements under terms and conditions, not inconsistent with this act, and under such agreements with the purchasers or makers thereof or any agent or other representative of such purchasers or makers as the board of directors may determine to be in the best interests of the Authority. In addition to other security provided herein or otherwise by law, bonds issued by the Authority under any provision of this act may be secured, in whole or in part, by financial guarantees, by insurance or by letters of credit issued to the Authority or a trustee or any other person, by any bank, trust company, insurance or surety company or other financial institution, within or without the commonwealth, and the Authority may pledge or assign, in whole or in part, the revenues and funds held or to be received by the Authority, and any contract or other rights to receive the same, whether then existing or thereafter coming into existence and whether then held or thereafter acquired by the Authority, and the proceeds thereof, as security for such guarantees or insurance or for the reimbursement by the Authority to any issuer of such letter of credit of any payments made under such letter or credit.

(f) It shall be lawful for any bank or trust company to act as a depository or trustee of the proceeds of bonds, revenues or other moneys under a bond resolution, trust agreement or other agreement of the Authority and to furnish indemnification and to provide security as may be required by the Authority. Any pledge of revenues and other funds made by the Authority under the provisions of this act shall be valid and binding and shall be deemed continuously perfected for the purposes of the uniform commercial code and other laws when such pledge is made. The revenues and funds, rights therein and thereto and proceeds so pledged and then held or thereafter acquired or received by the Authority shall immediately be subject to the lien of such pledge without any physical delivery or segregation thereof or further act, and the lien of any such pledge shall be valid and binding against all parties having claims of any kind in tort, contract or otherwise against the Authority, whether or not such parties have notice thereof. The bond resolution, trust agreement or any other agreement by which a pledge is created need not be filed or recorded to perfect such pledge except in the records of the Authority and no filing need be made under the uniform commercial code. It is hereby declared that any pledge or assignment made under the Authority of this act is an exercise of the political and governmental powers of the Authority, and revenues or funds, contract or other rights to receive the same and the proceeds thereof which are subject to the lien of a pledge or assignment created under this act shall not be applied to any purposes not permitted by such pledge or assignment.

(g) Any holder of a bond issued by the Authority under the provisions of the act or of any of the coupons appertaining thereto and any trustee or other representative under a bond resolution, trust agreement or other agreement securing the same, except to the extent the rights herein given may be restricted by the resolution, trust agreement or other agreement, may bring suit upon the bonds or coupons and may, either at law or in equity, by suit, action, mandamus, or other proceeding for legal or equitable relief, including proceedings for the appointment of a receiver to take possession and control of the business and properties of the Authority, to operate and maintain the same, to make any necessary repairs, renewals and replacements in respect thereof and to fix, revise and collect charges, protect and enforce any and all rights under the laws of the commonwealth or granted hereunder or under such bond resolution, trust agreement or other agreement, and may enforce and compel performance of all duties required by this act or by such bond resolution, trust agreement or other agreement, to be performed by the Authority or by any officer thereof.

(h) Before the issuance of any bonds of the Authority each member of the board of directors and each officer of the Authority charged with responsibility for the issuance thereof shall execute a surety bond conditioned on the faithful performance of the duties of the office of each such director and officer, in the sum of one hundred thousand dollars payable to the Authority, or, in lieu thereof, the Authority shall obtain a blanket bond in the same amount covering all such persons, and such bond or bonds shall be filed in the office of the secretary of the commonwealth.

History—

1984, 372, § 11; 1986, 557, § 210; 1987, 770, § 19; 1989, 275, § 13, approved, with emergency preamble, July 25, 1989; 1990, 150, § 176, approved Aug 1, 1990, by § 383, effective July 1, 1990; 1991, 499, § 10, approved Dec 31, 1991, by § 46, effective upon passage.

Editorial Note—

The **1986 amendment** made a corrective change in paragraph (h), replacing "such bonds or bonds" with "such bond or bonds".

The **1987 amendment**, in the last sentence of paragraph (a), after "bonds for the payment", replaced "of" with "or".

The **1989 amendment**, in the fifth sentence of paragraph (a), substituted "one billion two hundred million" for "six hundred million".

The **1990 amendment**, in the fifth sentence of paragraph (a), between "shall not", deleted a comma, and substituted "two billion" for "one billion two hundred million".

The **1991 amendment**, in the fifth sentence of paragraph (a), substituted "two billion three hundred million dollars" for "two billion dollars".

§ 13.   Issuance of Refunding Bonds.

Said Authority may issue refunding bonds for the purpose of paying any of its bonds issued pursuant to this act at or prior to maturity or upon acceleration or redemption or purchase and retirement. Refunding bonds may be issued at such times at or prior to the maturity, redemption or purchase and retirement of the refunded bonds as the board of directors deems to be in the interest of said Authority. Refunding bonds may be issued in sufficient amounts to pay or provide for payment of the principal of the bonds being refunded, together with any redemption premium thereon, any interest or discount accrued or to accrue to the date of payment of such bonds, the costs of issuance of the refunding bonds, the expenses of paying, redeeming or purchasing the bonds being refunded, the costs of holding and investing proceeds of refunding bonds pending such payment, redemption or purchase and such reserves for debt service or other capital or current expenses from the proceeds of such refunding bonds as may be required by a bond resolution, trust agreement or other agreement securing bonds. The issue and sale of refunding bonds, the maturities and other details thereof, the security therefor, the rights of the holders thereof, and the rights, duties and obligations of the Authority in respect of the same shall be governed by the provisions of this act relating to the issue of bonds other than refunding bonds insofar as the same may be applicable.

History—
1984, 372, § 13.

§ 14.   Bonds of Authority as Securities for Purpose of Investment.

Bonds issued by said Authority are hereby made securities in which all public officers and agencies of the commonwealth and its political subdivisions, all insurance companies, trust companies in their commercial departments, savings banks, cooperative banks, banking associations, investment companies, executors, administrators, trustees and other fiduciaries may properly invest funds, including capital in their control or belonging to them. Such bonds are hereby made securities which may properly be deposited with and received by any state or municipal officer of any agency or political subdivision of the commonwealth for any purpose for which the deposit of bonds or obligations of the commonwealth or any political subdivision is now or may hereafter be authorized by law.

History—
1984, 372, § 14.

§ 15. Issuance of Bonds Without Consent of Commonwealth or Political Subdivision.

Bonds may be issued under this act without obtaining the consent of any executive office, department, division, commission, board, bureau or agency of the commonwealth or any political subdivision thereof, and without any other proceedings or the happening of any condition or acts other than those proceedings, conditions or acts which are specifically required therefor, and the validity of and security for any bonds issued by the Authority pursuant to this act shall not be affected by the existence or nonexistence of any such consent or other proceedings, conditions or acts. Provisions of this act relating to the preparation, adoption or approval of programs and budgets shall not affect the issue of bonds and bonds may be issued either before or after such preparation, adoption or approval.

History—
1984, 372, § 15.

§ 16. Bonds of Authority Deemed Not to be Debt or Pledge of Faith and Credit of Commonwealth or Political Subdivision.

Bonds issued under the provisions of this act, excepting any notes or bonds guaranteed or issued by the commonwealth under paragraphs (e) or (f), respectively, of section five, shall not be deemed to be a debt or a pledge of the faith and credit of the commonwealth or of any of its political subdivisions, but shall be payable solely from the funds of the Authority from which they are made payable pursuant to this act. Bonds issued under the provisions of this act, excepting any notes or bonds guaranteed or issued by the commonwealth under paragraphs (e) or (f) of section five, shall recite that neither the commonwealth nor any political subdivisions thereof shall be obligated to pay the same and that neither the faith and credit nor the taxing power of the commonwealth or of any political subdivision thereof is pledged to the payment of the principal of or interest on such bonds. Further, every bond shall recite whether it is a general obligation of the Authority or a special obligation thereof payable solely from particular revenues or funds pledged to its payment. The aggregate principal amount of all bonds issued under the authority of this act shall not exceed the sum of two billion three hundred million dollars outstanding at any one time; provided however, that bonds for the payment of redemption of which, either at or prior to maturity, refunding bonds shall have been issued, shall be excluded in the computation of outstanding bonds.

History—

1984, 372, § 16; 1989, 275, § 14, approved, with emergency preamble, July 25, 1989; 1990, 150, § 177, approved Aug 1, 1990, by § 383, effective July 1, 1990; 1991, 499, § 11, approved Dec 31, 1991; by § 46, effective upon passage.

Editorial Note—

The 1989 amendment, in the fourth sentence, substituted "one billion two hundred million" for "six hundred million".

The 1990 amendment, in the fourth sentence, substituted "two billion" for "one billion two hundred million", and following "dollars outstanding", substituted "at any one time;" for a comma.

The 1991 amendment, in the fourth sentence, substituted "two billion three hundred million dollars" for "two billion dollars".

§ 17.   Bonds of Authority as Investment Securities under Uniform Commercial Code.

Notwithstanding any of the provisions of this act or any recitals in any bonds issued hereunder, all such bonds shall be deemed to be investment securities under the uniform commercial code.

History—

1984, 372, § 17.

§ 18.   Moneys Received from Bonds or Revenues Deemed Trust Funds.

All moneys received pursuant to the provisions of this act, whether as proceeds from the issue of bonds or as revenues or otherwise, shall be deemed to be trust funds to be held and applied solely as provided in this act.

History—

1984, 372, § 18; 1987, 770, § 20.

§ 19.   Exemptions from Taxation.

(a) Bonds issued by the Authority, their transfer and the income therefrom, including any profit made on the sale thereof, shall, at all times, be exempt from taxation by and within the commonwealth.

(b) The Authority shall not be required to pay any taxes, betterments, assessments or excises upon its income, existence, operation or property; provided, however, that so long as there is no revocation of the Authority's title to sewer and waterworks systems as provided for in section four, the Authority is authorized and directed to make payments in accordance with sections five D to five F, inclusive, of chapter fifty-nine of the General Laws.

History—
1984, 372, § 19.

§ 20.   Water and Sewage Collection, Treatment and Disposal Services within Service Area on Exclusive Basis.

It is expressly contemplated by this act that the Authority, to the extent deemed by it to be necessary and convenient to achieve its purposes under this act and under such supervision from agencies of the commonwealth as is expressly authorized in this act, shall provide water and sewage collection, treatment and disposal services within its service area on an exclusive basis. It is intended that this section shall not (i) diminish the powers or responsibilities of local bodies, (ii) override other provisions of this act regulating the procedures for abandonment of local water supplies, (iii) limit the lawful exercise of any local body, subject to applicable approvals by the department of environmental protection and the water resources commission, to continue to use any source of water used by it or to develop or reactivate any source of water to be used by it, or (iv) impose responsibility on the Authority for operation of the sewer and waterworks systems except as the Authority is charged with responsibility or may elect to exercise responsibility under other provisions of this act. In addition to and without limiting the generality of the foregoing, said Authority shall be a "local government" insofar as concerns immunity under sections (4), (4A) or (4C) of the Clayton Act; 15 U.S.C.A. §§ 15, 15A, and 15C from damages, interest on damages, costs or attorneys fees for a local government, for any official or employee thereof acting in an official capacity or for a person against whom a claim is based on any official action directed by a local government, or official or employee thereof acting in an official capacity.

History—
1984, 372, § 20; 1990, 177, § 383, approved, with emergency preamble Aug 7, 1990.

Editorial Note–
The 1990 amendment, in clause (iii), substituted environmental "protection" for environmental "quality engineering".

§ 21. Termination of Authority.

The Authority and its corporate existence shall continue until terminated by law; provided, however, that no such law shall take effect so long as said Authority shall have bonds outstanding unless adequate provision has been made for the payment or satisfaction thereof. Upon termination of the Authority, the title to all funds and other properties owned by it which remain after provision for the payment or satisfaction of all bonds of the Authority shall vest in the commonwealth. The obligations, debts and liabilities of the Authority shall be assumed by and imposed upon the commonwealth, and the funds of the authority retirement system shall be transferred to the treasurer and receiver general or to such other successor as the general court may designate, to be held for the exclusive use and benefit of the members of the authority retirement system.

History—
1984, 372, § 21.

§ 22. Accounts; Reports; Costs of Reports.

(a) The Authority, shall, at all times, keep full and accurate accounts of its receipts, expenditures, disbursements, assets and liabilities which shall be open to inspection by any officer or duly appointed agent of the commonwealth or the advisory board. Said Authority shall submit an annual report, in writing, to the governor, the president of the senate, the speaker of the house of representatives, the chairman of the senate committee on ways and means, the chairman of the house committee on ways and means and the advisory board. Said report shall include financial statements relating to the operations, properties, and capital facility expenditures, including costs of land acquisitions, of the Authority maintained in accordance with generally accepted accounting principles so far as applicable, beginning with the fiscal year of the Authority commencing July first, nineteen hundred and eighty-five, and audited by an independent certified public accountant firm.

(b) Not later than December thirty-first, nineteen hundred and eighty-nine and every five years thereafter, the Authority shall submit to the governor, the president of the senate, the speaker of the house of representatives, the chairman of the senate committee on ways and means, the chairman of the house committee on ways and means and the advisory board a progress report on the Authority's attainment of its statutory purposes. Each such five-year progress report shall be prepared by the Authority with the assistance of an independent citizen panel which shall include persons selected by the Authority and approved by the advisory board who are experienced in environmental protection, civil engineering and public management and finance. Said reports shall include recommendations concerning the future activities of the Authority including, but not limited to, changes in the provisions of this act or the Authority's administrative procedures necessary or desirable for improving the delivery of services. The costs of preparing the reports of said Authority shall be provided for in the current expense budgets of said Authority.

History—
1984, 372, § 22.

§ 23. **Advisory Board to Authority; Members; Powers and Duties.**

(a) There shall be an advisory board to the Authority consisting of (i) a voting representative of each of the following cities and towns: Arlington, Ashland, Bedford, Belmont, Boston, Braintree, Brookline, Burlington, Cambridge, Canton, Chelsea, Chicopee, Clinton, Dedham, Everett, Framingham, Hingham, Holbrook, Leominster, Lexington, Lynn, Lynnfield, Malden, Marblehead, Marlborough, Medford, Melrose, Milton, Nahant, Natick, Needham, Newton, Northborough, Norwood, Peabody, Quincy, Randolph, Reading, Revere, Saugus, Somerville, South Hadley, Southborough, Stoneham, Stoughton, Swampscott, Wakefield, Walpole, Waltham, Watertown, Wellesley, Weston, Westwood, Weymouth, Wilbraham, Wilmington, Winchester, Winthrop, Woburn and Worcester and (ii) a voting representative of the metropolitan area planning council to be designated by the board of the council and six persons to be appointed by the governor who shall be voting representatives from the following categories: (1) one person who represents the interests of persons and communities in the Connecticut river basin area, (2) one person who represents the interests of persons and communities in the Quabbin and Ware watershed area, (3) one person who represents the interests of persons and communities in the Wachusett watershed area, provided, however, that no such person appointed for categories (1), (2) or (3) shall live in a community which has a representation on the advisory board by virtue of clause (i) of this sentence, (4) one person with skill and expertise in matters relating to environmental protection, and (5) two persons qualified by membership or affiliation in organizations directly concerned with the recreational or commercial uses of Boston harbor and who are further qualified by professional experience in an environmental or scientific discipline. The member of the advisory board representing a city or town shall consist of the chief executive officer thereof; provided, however, that any chief executive officer, by writing filed with the Authority may appoint a permanent designee to serve in his stead as a member of said advisory board until the expiration of each term of office of the designating chief executive officer or the earlier vacancy of the office of the designating chief executive officer. For purposes of this section, the term "chief executive officer" shall mean the person designated as the chief executive officer under the provisions of a local charter of laws having the force of a charter, and otherwise the mayor in every city and the chairman of the board or selectmen or president of the town council, as the case may be, in every town. The members of said advisory board appointed by the governor shall serve coterminous with the governor.

(b) The total voting strength of the advisory board shall be one hundred votes, of which ninety-five votes shall be divided on a fractional basis in the manner hereafter provided among the cities and towns listed in clause (i) of the first sentence of paragraph (a) of this section and five votes shall be divided on an equal fractional basis among the representatives provided for in clause (ii) of said sentence. The fractional vote of the representative of each city or town shall be determined on an annual basis by the Authority on a weighted basis by dividing a reasonable estimate of the charges for the Authority's services to users in that city or town by a reasonable estimate of the charges for the Authority's services to all users in all such cities and towns. For each year the determination of votes shall be certified to the advisory board by the Authority, provided, however, that within five days of the effective date of this act the executive office of environmental affairs shall prepare an interim voting value based on the most recent available annual records of the costs of water and sewer services of the metropolitan district commission, which interim voting value shall be conclusive upon the advisory board until July first, nineteen hundred and eighty-six. Said advisory board may act at a regular periodic meeting called in accordance with its by-laws or at a special meeting called by the Authority or by representatives of fifteen or more members of the advisory board. Except as specially provided in paragraph (a), a quorum of the advisory board shall consist of representatives who hold a total voting strength of fifty or more of the votes of the advisory board, and the advisory board may act, except as otherwise provided in paragraph (e), by the affirmative casting of a majority of the votes represented in the quorum. The advisory board shall be deemed to be a governmental body for purposes of, and shall be subject to, section eleven A and one-half of chapter thirty A of the General Laws and shall also be subject to section ten of chapter sixty-six of the General Laws.

(c) For the conduct of its business said advisory board shall adopt and may revise and amend by-laws. Said advisory board shall annually elect a chairperson, a vice chairperson and a secretary and such other officers as said advisory board may determine. Each officer shall serve until a successor is chosen and qualified. Each officer may be removed by vote of the advisory board with or without cause. In the event of a vacancy, said board shall fill the vacancy for the unexpired term. Each member of said advisory board shall serve without compensation but may be reimbursed, as an expense of said advisory board, for all reasonable expenses incurred in the performance of its duties as approved by the advisory board.

(d) The purposes of the advisory board shall be as follows:

(i) to appoint three members of the board of directors of the Authority, in the manner hereafter provided and in section three;

(ii) to consider matters committed to the approval of the advisory board under paragraphs (c) and (d) of section eight;

(iii) to make recommendations to the Authority on annual current expense expenditure budgets submitted to the advisory board in accordance with paragraph (b) of section eight;

(iv) to make recommendations to the Authority on its charges;

(v) to hold hearings, which may be held jointly with the Authority at the discretion of the advisory board and said Authority, on matters relating to said Authority;

(vi) to review the annual report of the Authority and to prepare comments thereon to the Authority and the governor, and to make such examinations of the reports on the Authority's records and affairs as the advisory board deems appropriate; and

(vii) to make recommendations to the governor and the general court respecting the Authority and its programs. The advisory board shall have all powers necessary or convenient to carry out and effectuate the foregoing purposes.

(e) Three members of the board of directors of the Authority shall be appointed by the advisory board. Members of the board of directors so appointed may also be members of said advisory board. Said advisory board shall appoint successor members, which successor members shall replace those members of the board of directors appointed by the advisory board whose terms have expired or otherwise terminated. With respect to appointment of any member of the board of directors the advisory board shall act only if there is a special quorum consisting of a majority of those persons who are voting members of the advisory board and only by an affirmative vote of the majority of the members present, each voting member voting one unweighted vote, and in this instance the total voting strength of the advisory board shall equal the total number of persons entitled to vote.

(f) Within thirty days of receiving any proposed current expense budget of the Authority or within fifteen days of receiving any proposed amended expense budget of the Authority, the advisory board shall hold a public hearing on matters relating to such budget for the purpose of ascertaining, for subsequent report to the Authority if necessary, the views of the public thereon.

(g) The advisory board shall provide for the appointment of an ombudsman who, with assistance from such staff and consultants as the advisory board may authorize and appoint, shall act for and in the name of the advisory board in the following respects:

(i) preparation of analysis for the advisory board of the Authority's current expense budgets, capital expenditure budgets and capital programs and their effect on the charges of said Authority;

(ii) representation of the advisory board to said Authority in all matters relating to said Authority's programs, operations, finances and charges;

(iii) reporting regularly to the advisory board on the activities of the ombudsman and other staff of the advisory board, on the affairs of the Authority, and on the effect of the Authority's program and operations on the costs to consumers of water and sewer services; and

(iv) exercising such other duties and responsibilities consistent with the powers of the advisory board as the advisory board may assign from time to time.

Reports of the ombudsman, after acceptance by the advisory board, shall be made available to the public.

(h) The advisory board may incur expenses, not to exceed thirty-five thousand dollars in the fiscal year commencing July first, nineteen hundred and eighty-four and not to exceed one hundred thousand dollars annually thereafter for expenses authorized under paragraph (c) and for personnel and office expenses. Such expenses shall be paid by the Authority in the fiscal year commencing July first, nineteen hundred and eighty-four from amounts appropriated to the Authority by the commonwealth, and thereafter shall be provided for in current expense budgets of the Authority. After the fifth anniversary of the transfer date, the maximum level of advisory board expenses may be increased from time to time upon the review and approval by the Authority of the justification for such increases submitted by the advisory board.

History—

1984, 372, § 23; 1987, 770, § 21.

Editorial Note—

The **1987 amendment,** after "the chairman of the board" in the next to last sentence of paragraph (a), replaced "of" with "or."

§ 24. Jurisdiction of Superior Court Department of Trial Court to Enforce Rights and Duties of Provisions Pertaining to Authority; Jurisdiction of Supreme Judicial Court as to State Actions; Appearance by Attorney General on Matters Involving Water Pollution.

The superior court department of the trial court shall have jurisdiction to enforce rights and duties created by the provisions of this act, and on complaint of the Authority may restrain violations of the Authority's regulations and otherwise enforce by any appropriate remedy, including without limiting the generality of the foregoing, injunctive relief, the regulations, licenses, permits, orders, penalties and charges of the Authority. Penalties and charges established by or under authorization of this act shall be collected for the account of the Authority and paid over to the Authority. Except for rights of action expressly conferred upon the Authority, no provision of this act shall create private rights of action in enforcement proceedings.

Notwithstanding any provision of the Massachusetts Water Resources Authority Act or of any special or general law to the contrary, the supreme judicial court shall have original and exclusive jurisdiction of all state actions in which the Authority is a defendant and water pollution is an issue. The attorney general shall appear on behalf of the Authority in any action involving water pollution in which the Authority is a plaintiff or defendant, and he shall do so to the same extent as is required by section three of chapter twelve when appearing on behalf of a state agency.

History—
1984, 372, § 24.

Code of Massachusetts Regulations—
Massachusetts Water Resources Authority, adjudicatory proceedings, 360 CMR 1.00.
Massachusetts Water Resources Authority, judicial remedies, 360 CMR 10.106.

§ 25.   Construction and Application of Provisions for Accomplishing Purposes of Authority.

The provisions of this act shall be deemed to provide an additional, alternative and complete method for accomplishing the purposes of this act, and shall be deemed and construed to be supplemental and additional to, and not in derogation of, powers conferred upon the Authority and others by laws; provided, however, that insofar as the provisions of this act are inconsistent with the provisions of any general or special law, administrative order or regulation, the provisions of this act shall be controlling.

History—
1984, 372, § 25.

§ 26.   Powers and Duties of Local Bodies and Public Agencies; Compensation for Water Diverted from Watershed System.

(a) All local bodies and all public agencies, instrumentalities, commissions and authorities of the commonwealth are hereby authorized and empowered to undertake activities, programs and projects in conjunction with the Authority in furtherance of the purposes of this act, including without limiting the generality of the foregoing, to join in investigations and studies, and to grant applications and applications for project approvals.

(b) Except with respect to real property acquired or held for purposes described in Article XCVII of the Amendments to the Constitution, all local bodies and all public agencies, instrumentalities, commissions and authorities of the commonwealth, are hereby authorized and empowered to lease, lend, grant or convey to the Authority upon such terms and conditions as the proper authorities of such public bodies, public agencies, instrumentalities, commissions and authorities of the commonwealth may deem appropriate and without the necessity of any action or formality other than the regular and formal action of said public bodies, agencies, instrumentalities, commissions and authorities of the commonwealth any interest in any real or personal property which may be necessary or convenient to effect the purposes of the sewer and waterworks of the Authority.

(c) All general and special laws relating to water and sewer services of local bodies shall be interpreted and construed liberally so as to effectuate the purposes and provisions of this act and the objectives of the Authority.

(d) For any local body in the service areas of the Authority, local officials lawfully so charged shall for their local body have the charge and control of the respective water, waterworks and sewer works owned and used by said local body and not in the ownership, possession and control of the Authority. Said local officials so charged shall have for their local body the charge and control of the water sources owned and used by said local body. Subject to the exercise of powers of the Authority provided for in this act or otherwise, and to other applicable law, said local officials shall manage and improve municipal water works and sewer works, extend the pipes and other works as they may deem expedient, keep the pipes, fixtures and other works under their charge in good condition and repair, and prescribe for local water and sewer systems, rules and regulations under other law, provided, however, that without limiting the generality of the foregoing, written notice of rules and regulations relating to local sewer and delivery of water services proposed for adoption by any local body shall, except in an emergency, be given to the Authority not less than sixty days prior to adoption.

(e) Notwithstanding any provision of general or special law to the contrary, a local body may (i) for furnishing water supply, establish rates, fees or other charges on a flat rate per volume of water consumed or on an ascending unit rate based on quantity of water consumed, and (ii) for furnishing water supply and sewer services, provide in its charges or through abatement proceedings conducted in accordance with its regulations for assurance of service to persons who by reason of age, infirmity or poverty are unable to pay the charges of the local body otherwise applicable, provided that the aggregate liability of the local body for the total amounts owed to the Authority under section ten shall be in no way diminished thereby. Without limiting the generality of regulatory powers and powers with respect to charges established elsewhere in this act, the Authority may require that each local body adopt and administer user charges for local water services and sewage services which shall be in compliance with (i) all applicable requirements of state and federal law, and (ii) policies of the Authority directed to conservation of water, elimination of infiltration and inflow of surface water and ground water into the sewage collection, treatment and disposal system, and removal or pretreatment of industrial wastes. No action shall be taken by the

Authority, however, in violation of clause 1 of section 10 of Article I of the United States Constitution which shall substantially impair a contractual expectation entered into prior to the effective date of this act by a local body pursuant to a power granted it by law to issue revenue bonds.

(f) If, except in circumstances of temporary emergency, any volume of water from the watershed system of the division shall be directed under any provision of law for delivery of water purposes which are not subject to the charges of the Authority provided for in section ten, the Authority shall receive compensation from the user or users thereof in lieu of revenues which otherwise would have been received by the Authority in respect of the use of such water.

History—
1984, 372, § 26; 1986, 557, § 211; 1987, 770, §§ 22, 23.

Editorial Note—
The **1986 amendment** made a corrective change in the last sentence of paragraph (d), replacing "deep" with "deem".

The **1987 amendment,** in the third sentence of paragraph (d), replaced "deep" with "deem" and, in paragraph (e), replaced "; and may (ii) provide for furnishing water supply and sewer services" with ", and (ii) for furnishing water supply and sewer services, provide."

Code of Massachusetts Regulations—
Continuation of contract water supply, 360 CMR 11.00 et seq.

§ 27. Power of Authority to Enter Into Consent Decree.

Notwithstanding the provisions of any general or special law or provision of this act to the contrary; no officer of the Authority shall enter into any consent decree in any court of any jurisdiction without prior approval of the governor and the general court.

History—
1984, 372, § 27.

§ 28. Application of Provisions of Chapter 12A of General Laws.

The provisions of chapter twelve A of the General Laws shall apply to the Authority.

History—
1984, 372, § 28.

§ 29. Severability of Provisions.

The provisions of this act are severable, and if any provision hereof shall be held invalid in any circumstances, such invalidity shall not affect any other provisions or circumstances. This act shall be construed in all respects so as to meet any constitutional requirements. In carrying out the purposes and provisions of this act, all steps shall be taken which are necessary to meet constitutional requirements.

History—
1984, 372, § 29.

TITLE VII
HIGHWAYS, WATERWAYS AND TRANSPORTATION

CHAPTER S71

Massachusetts Parking Authority

(Acts 1958, Ch. 606)

73

20. Act Liberally Construed.
21. Constitutional Construction.
22. Labor Relations Policy.
23. Repeal of Statutes, Other Laws Inapplicable.
24. [Amended ALM GL c 63 § 12]
25. Effective Date.

Auto-Cite®: Cases and annotations referred to herein can be further researched through the Auto-Cite® computer-assisted research service. Use Auto-Cite to check citations for form, parallel references, prior and later history, and annotation references.

---

§ 1.   Declaration of Necessity.

It is hereby declared that the free circulation of traffic of all kinds through the streets of the city of Boston is necessary for the rapid and effective fighting of fires and disposition of police forces in said city and for the health, safety and general welfare of the public, whether residing in said city or traveling to, through or from said city in the course of lawful pursuits; that in recent years the parking of motor vehicles in the streets of said city has so substantially impeded such free circulation of traffic as to constitute at the present time a public nuisance endangering the health, safety and welfare of the general public, as well as endangering the economic life of said city; that this parking nuisance is not capable of being adequately abated except by the construction and operation of a garage under Boston Common in said city; that notwithstanding chapter two hundred and ninety-four of the acts of nineteen hundred and forty-six, and subsequent acts amendatory thereof, and chapter seven hundred and one of the acts of nineteen hundred and fifty-seven, such a garage has not been constructed; and a public exigency exists which makes the provisions of this act a public necessity.

History—
1958, 606, § 1.

§ 2.   Definitions.

As used in this act, the following words and terms shall have the following meanings, unless the context shall indicate another or different meaning or intent:—

(a) "Authority" shall mean the Massachusetts Parking Authority, created by section three of this act, or, if said Authority shall be abolished, the board, body, authority or commission succeeding to the principal functions thereof or to whom the powers given by this act to the Authority shall be given by law.

(b) "City" shall mean the city of Boston.

(c) "Cost of the project" shall embrace the cost of preparing plans and specifications for, and constructing the garage, tunnel, and underground passageway, as hereinafter defined, including all necessary and convenient approaches thereto and all extensions and improvements thereof, the cost of restoring gardens, lawns, trees and shrubs in the area included in the project to substantially the same condition as prior to construction, except at the point of ingress and egress, the cost of acquiring all land, rights-of-way, property, rights, easements and interests acquired by the Authority for such construction, the cost of demolishing or removing any buildings or structures on land so acquired, including the cost of acquiring any lands to which such buildings or structures may be moved, the cost of all machinery and equipment, financing charges, interest prior to and during construction, and, if deemed advisable by the Authority, for one year after completion of construction, cost of removal or relocation of any public utilities' facilities, cost of traffic estimates and of engineering and legal services, surveys, estimates of cost and of revenues, other expenses necessary or incident to determining the feasibility or practicability of constructing the garage, tunnel and underground passageway, administrative expenses, and such other expenses as may be necessary or incident to the construction of the garage, tunnel and underground passageway, and the cost of issuing revenue bonds or interim receipts under the provisions of this act. Any obligation or expense hereafter incurred at the request of the Authority by the state department of public works or by the city for traffic surveys, borings, preparation of plans and specifications, and other engineering services in connection with the construction of the garage, tunnel and underground passageway, shall be regarded as a part of the cost of the project and shall be assumed and paid by the Authority or reimbursed to the commonwealth or to the city out of the proceeds of the Common garage revenue bonds hereinafter authorized.

(d) "Current expenses" shall mean the reasonable and necessary current expenses of the Authority in maintaining, repairing, operating or leasing the garage, tunnel and underground passageway including, without limiting the generality of the foregoing, ordinary and usual expenses of maintenance and repair, including expenses not annually recurring, engineering expenses relating to operation and maintenance, insurance premiums after completion of construction, all administrative and legal expenses after such completion, charges of paying agents and fees and expenses of the trustee after such completion, and any other expenses accruing after such completion which are required to be paid by the Authority under the provisions of the trust agreement or resolution hereinafter mentioned or by law.

(e) "Garage" shall mean a garage for motor vehicles under Boston Common in the city within the following boundaries: Bounded westerly by the easterly line of Charles street; northerly by the southerly line of Beacon street; easterly by the Soldiers and Sailors Monument and the westerly perimeter of the Parkman bandstand; southerly by the Central Burying Ground, together with all necessary and convenient approaches above and below ground; provided, that on the Charles and Beacon street frontages combined there shall be an average setback of not less than ninety feet except at the points of ingress and egress and except that the Authority, its employees and constractors may cross and recross said setback during the period of construction; and provided, further, that the Authority shall require that the work of construction be so carried on that the gardens, lawns, trees and shrubs in the area will, after construction, remain in, or be restored to, substantially the same condition as prior to construction except at the points of ingress and egress, and that the filling or relocation of the Public Garden pond, or any part thereof, will not be required. "Garage" shall include such service station and other facilities for administration and storage which the Authority may deem necessary for the operation of the garage, and also all property, rights, easements and interests which may be acquired by the Authority for the construction of the garage.

(f) "Common garage project" or "project" shall mean the "garage" as defined in (e), the "tunnel" as defined in (h), and the "underground passageway" as defined in (j) and all approaches thereto and extensions and improvements thereof.

(g) "Fiscal year" shall mean the calendar year.

(h) "Tunnel" shall mean a two-lane traffic tunnel to be constructed under the provisions of this act under the Public Garden, Charles street and Boston Common from Commonwealth avenue at or near Arlington street to the garage within boundaries substantially as follows:—Beginning at a point on Commonwealth avenue at about midway between Arlington street and Berkeley street and running in an easterly direction on and under Commonwealth avenue, and under Arlington street, the Public Garden and Charles street at a location on Charles street approximately midway between Beacon and Boylston streets to the garage, so located as not to disturb permanently the Washington Monument or the bridge over the

Public Garden pond. "Tunnel" shall include all property, rights, easements and interests which may be acquired by the Authority for the construction or the operation of the tunnel.

(i) "Trustee" shall mean the bank or trust company acting as trustee under the resolution whereby the revenue bonds herein provided for are issued by the Authority or under a trust agreement made and entered into by and between the Authority and a bank or trust company.

(j) "Underground passageway" shall mean the underground passageway for the convenience of persons using or employed in the garage to be constructed under the provisions of this act from the garage to a point at or near the corner of West and Tremont streets, together with machinery and equipment for conveying passengers, and all property, rights, easements and interests which may be acquired by the Authority for the construction or the operations of the underground passageway.

History—
1958, 606, § 2.

§ 3. Massachusetts Parking Authority.

There is hereby created and placed in the state department of public works a body politic and corporate to be known as the "Massachusetts Parking Authority," which shall not be subject to the supervision and regulation of the department of public works or of any other department, commission, board, authority, bureau or agency of the commonwealth except to the extent and in the manner provided in this act. The Authority is hereby constituted a public instrumentality and the exercise by the Authority of the powers conferred by this act in the construction, operation and maintenance of the garage shall be deemed and held to be the performance of an essential governmental function.

The Authority shall consist of three members, two of whom, hereinafter referred to as the governor's appointees, shall be appointed by the governor and the third member shall be such person as the mayor of the city shall from time to time designate. The chairman of the Authority designated by the governor, as hereinafter provided, shall receive a salary of ten thousand dollars and each of the members shall receive seven thousand five hundred dollars annually. Said sums referred to heretofore shall be payable solely from revenues received by the Authority.

The members of the Authority first appointed by the governor shall serve for terms expiring on July first, nineteen hundred and sixty-five, and July first, nineteen hundred and sixty-six, the terms of such members to be designated by the governor, and until their respective successors shall be duly appointed and qualified. The governor shall designate one of the governor's appointees as chairman who shall serve as such during his term of office. Upon the expiration of the term of office of such chairman, the governor shall appoint one of the governor's appointees as his successor as chairman. The successor of each of the governor's appointees shall be appointed for a term of eight years, except that any person appointed to fill a vacancy shall serve only for the unexpired term. Any member of the Authority shall be eligible for reappointment. Each member of the Authority before entering upon his duties shall take an oath before the governor to administer the duties of his office faithfully and impartially, and a record of such oaths shall be filed in the office of the secretary of the commonwealth.

The Authority shall elect one of the members as vice chairman thereof and shall also elect a secretary-treasurer who need not be a member of the Authority. Two members of the Authority shall constitute a quorum and the affirmative vote of two members shall be necessary for any action taken by the Authority. No vacancy in the membership of the Authority shall impair the right of a quorum to exercise all the rights and perform all the duties of the Authority.

Before the issuance of any Common garage revenue bonds under the provisions of this act, each member of the Authority shall execute a surety bond in the penal sum of twenty-five thousand dollars, and the secretary-treasurer shall execute a surety bond in the penal sum of fifty thousand dollars, each such surety bond to be conditioned upon the faithful performance of the duties of his office, to be executed by a surety company authorized to transact business in the commonwealth as surety and to be approved by the attorney general and filed in the office of the secretary of the commonwealth. Each member shall be reimbursed for his actual expenses necessarily incurred in the performance of his duties. All expenses incurred in carrying out the provisions of this act shall be paid solely from funds provided under the authority of this act and no liability or obligation shall be incurred by the Authority hereunder beyond the extent to which moneys shall have been provided under the authority of this act.

History—
1958, 606, § 3; 1971, 1037; 1979, 254.

Editorial Note—
The 1979 amendment in the second paragraph, added a sentence providing for compensation of members of the Massachusetts Parking Authority.

Cross References—
Authority's structures defined as public buildings, see ALM GL c 22 § 13A.

§ 4.   Credit of Commonwealth or any Political Subdivision not Pledged.

Common garage revenue bonds, interim receipts, temporary bonds and Common garage revenue refunding bonds issued under the provisions of this act shall not be deemed to constitute a debt of the commonwealth or of any political subdivision thereof, or a pledge of the faith and credit of the commonwealth or of any such political subdivision; but all such bonds and interim receipts shall be payable solely from the funds herein provided therefor from revenues. All such bonds and interim receipts shall contain on the face thereof a statement to the effect that neither the Authority nor the commonwealth nor any political subdivision thereof shall be obliged to pay the same or the interest thereon except from revenues of the Common garage project, and that neither the faith and credit nor the taxing power of the commonwealth or of any political subdivision thereof is pledged to the payment of the principal of or the interest on such bonds and interim receipts.

All expenses incurred in carrying out the provisions of this act shall be payable solely from funds provided under the authority of this act, and no liability or obligations shall be incurred by the Authority hereunder beyond the extent to which monies shall have been provided under the provisions of this act.

History—
1958, 606, § 4.

§ 5.   General Grant of Powers.

The Authority is hereby authorized and empowered—

(a) To adopt by-laws for the regulation of its affairs and the conduct of its business;

(b) To adopt an official seal and alter the same at pleasure;

(c) To maintain an office or offices at such place or places within the commonwealth as it may determine;

(d) To sue and be sued in its own name, plead and be impleaded;

(e) To prepare plans and specifications for, construct, reconstruct, extend, improve, insure, repair, maintain, operate or lease a garage under Boston Common for the parking and the servicing and repairing of motor vehicles, together with all necessary and convenient approaches to such garage above and below ground, including the underground passageway and the tunnel;

(f) To issue Common garage revenue bonds of the Authority, interim receipts, and temporary bonds, payable solely from revenues as hereinafter provided, and to refund its bonds, all as provided in this act;

(g) To fix and revise from time to time and charge and collect fees for the parking of motor vehicles in the garage and for the servicing and repair of motor vehicles;

(h) To establish and revise from time to time rules and regulations for the use of the common garage project, and to provide penalties for the violation of said rules and regulations not exceeding fifty dollars for each such offence, which upon payment into courts shall be accounted for and paid to the Authority;

(i) To acquire by conveyance under section seven of this act, and hold such interest in and under the lands constituting Boston Common and in Commonwealth avenue, Arlington street, the Public Garden, Charles street and any other public street as it may deem necessary for carrying out the provisions of this act;

(j) To acquire, hold and dispose of real and personal property in the exercise of its powers and the performance of its duties under this act, provided that any sale of real property shall be sold, after advertisement for bids, to the highest responsible bidder. The authority shall have the right to reject all bids and to readvertise for bids. No real estate shall be sold unless notice of the sale shall have been advertised in two daily newspapers published in the city of Boston, and, if such real property is located in any other city or town, in a newspaper published in such other city or town, once a week for three successive weeks. Such advertisements shall state the time and place where all pertinent information relative to the real property to be sold or conveyed may be obtained, and the time and place of opening the bids in answer to said advertisements, and that the authority reserves the right to reject any or all such bids. All bids in response to advertisements shall be sealed and be publicly opened by the authority. The authority may require, as evidence of good faith, that a deposit of a reasonable sum, to be fixed by the authority, accompany the proposals.

(k) To acquire in the name of the Authority by purchase or otherwise, on such terms and conditions and in such manner as it may deem proper, or by the exercise of the power of eminent domain in accordance with the provisions of chapter seventy-nine of the General Laws or any alternative method now or hereafter provided by law insofar as such provisions may be applicable, such public lands, parks, playgrounds, reservations, highways or parkways, or parts thereof or rights therein, and any fee simple absolute or any lesser interest in such private property as it may deem necessary for carrying out the provisions of this act, which taking or purchase may be fixed by planes of division, or otherwise, below or above or at the surface of the soil, with no taking of upper or lower portions, provided, that no compensation shall be paid for public lands taken; provided, further, that whenever a parcel of private property so taken is used in whole or in part for residential purposes, the owner or owners of said parcel may, within thirty days of the date of the Authority's notice to vacate such parcel, appeal to the Authority for a postponement of the date set for vacating, whereupon the Authority shall grant to the owner or owners of the property a postponement of three months from the date of such appeal; provided, however, that the appeal for such postponement shall be in the form of a written request to the Authority sent by registered mail return receipt requested; and provided, further, that the Authority shall give security to the state treasurer for the payment of such damages as may be awarded in accordance with law for such taking, and that the provisions of section forty of said chapter seventy-nine, insofar as the same may be applicable, shall govern the rights of the Authority and of any person whose property shall be so taken;

(l) To make and enter into all contracts, leases and agreements necessary or incidental to the performance of its duties and the execution of its powers under this act, including leases with any person, partnership, association, or corporation for the operation of the project, provided that sections twenty-six to twenty-nine, inclusive, and sections forty-four A to forty-four L, inclusive, of chapter one hundred and forty-nine of the General Laws and sections thirty-nine F to thirty-nine M, inclusive, of chapter thirty of the General Laws shall apply to contracts of the authority to the same extent and in the same manner as they are applicable to the commonwealth. All general or special laws, or parts thereof, inconsistent herewith, are hereby declared to be inapplicable to the provisions of this act.

(m) To employ consulting engineers, accountants, attorneys, construction and financial experts, superintendents, managers and such other employees and agents as may be necessary in its judgment, and to fix their compensation;

(n) To receive and accept from the federal government or any federal agency grants for or in aid of the construction of the Common garage project, and to receive and accept aid or contributions, from any source, of money, property, labor or other things of value, to be held, used and applied only for the purposes for which such grants and contributions are made.

(o) Without license under section thirteen of chapter one hundred and forty-eight of the General Laws, but subject to any applicable rules and regulations of the board of fire prevention regulations under said chapter, to buy, store, sell and deal in gasoline and other motor vehicle fuels and oils, accessories, goods, wares, and merchandise in any way connected with motor vehicles and to service motor vehicles including the right to make minor repairs, and to lease the rights to exercise such powers; and

(p) To do all acts and things necessary or convenient to carry out the powers expressly granted in this act.

History—
1958, 606, § 5; 1971, 693, §§ 1, 2.

§ 6. Incidental Powers.

The Authority shall have power to change and adjust the lines and grades of public highways so as to accommodate the same to the design of the Common garage project and any damage incurred in changing and adjusting the lines and grades of such highways shall be ascertained and paid by the Authority as a part of the cost of the project.

The Authority may, with the approval of the traffic commissioner of the city, establish satisfactory detours over existing public ways during the construction of the project.

If the Authority shall find it necessary to change the location of any portion of any public way, it shall reconstruct the same at such location as the Authority shall deem most favorable with the approval of the public improvement commission of the city, and of substantially the same type and in as good condition as the original highway. Land or rights in land may be acquired for this purpose by eminent domain under chapter seventy-nine by the Authority in behalf of the city or in behalf of the Authority, at the option of the Authority. Control of the land or rights in the land acquired under this paragraph on behalf of the city shall not vest in the city until such time as the work for which the land or rights in land have been acquired has been completed by the Authority. Any person whose property has been taken by the Authority under this paragraph may recover from the Authority under chapter seventy-nine. The cost of such construction and the damages incurred under this paragraph shall be paid by the Authority as part of the cost of the project.

Any public highway affected by the construction of the Common garage project may be abandoned or relocated by the Authority, and any damages awarded on account thereof shall be paid by the Authority as a part of the cost of the project.

The Authority and its authorized agents and employees may enter upon any lands, waters, and premises in the city of Boston for the purpose of making surveys, soundings, drillings and examinations as they may deem necessary or convenient for the purposes of this act, and such entry shall not be deemed a trespass, nor shall an entry for such purpose be deemed an entry under any eminent domain proceedings which may be then pending. The Authority shall make reimbursement for any actual damages resulting to such lands, waters and premises as a result of such activities.

The Authority may order the removal or relocation of any conduits, pipes, wires, poles or other property located in public ways or places, or in or upon private lands, which it deems to interfere with the laying out and construction of the Common garage project, and the appropriate authorities shall grant new locations for any such structure so removed or relocated, and the owner thereof shall be reimbursed by the Authority for the reasonable cost of such removal or relocation. Such orders, to the extent specified therein, shall be deemed a revocation of the right or license to maintain such pipes, conduits, wires, poles or other property in such public ways or places, and the owner of any such structures in public ways or lands shall comply with such orders. If any such owner shall fail to comply with any such order of the Authority within a reasonable time, to be fixed in the order, the Authority may discontinue and remove such conduits, pipes, wires, poles or other property, and may relocate the same. No such discontinuance, removal or relocation shall entitle the owner of the property thus affected to any damages on account thereof, except for the reimbursement of cost provided for above. Any such structures in or upon private lands may be removed and relocated by the Authority, or, if removed and relocated by the owner thereof, the reasonable expense shall be repaid to him by the Authority.

Any gas or electric company shall shut off the gas or current from any pipes or wires affected by any acts done hereunder, so far and for such time as may be necessary to prevent the escape or explosion of gas, or other public danger.

The commonwealth hereby consents to the use of all lands owned by it, including lands lying under water, which are deemed by the Authority to be necessary for the construction or operation of the Common garage project.

History—
1958, 606, § 6.

§ 7. City authorized to convey Necessary Interest in Common, etc.

Notwithstanding any contrary provision of general or special law, the city of Boston, by its mayor shall convey to the Authority, without consideration, such interest in the lands constituting Boston Common and in Commonwealth avenue, Arlington street, the Public Garden, Charles street and any other public street as the Authority may deem necessary for carrying out the provisions of this act; provided, that the parks and recreation commission of the city shall, by vote at a regular or special meeting of said commission, assent to such conveyance; and provided, further, that such conveyance is authorized, after two separate readings, by two separate votes of the city council of the city, the second of said readings and votes to be had not less than fourteen days after the first.

History—
1958, 606, § 7.

§ 8.   Common Garage Revenue Bonds.

The Authority is hereby authorized to provide by resolution, at one time or from time to time, for the issuance of Common garage revenue bonds of the Authority for the purpose of paying all or any part of the cost of the project or any part or parts thereof. The principal of and the interest on such bonds shall be payable solely from the funds herein provided for such payment. The bonds shall be dated, shall bear interest at such rate or rates and mature at such time or times, not exceeding forty years from their date or dates, all as may be determined by the Authority, and may be made redeemable before maturity, at the option of the Authority, at such price or prices and under such terms and conditions as may be fixed by the Authority prior to the issuance of the bonds. The Authority shall determine the form of the bonds, including any interest coupons to be attached thereto, and shall fix the denomination or denominations of the bonds and the place or places of payment of principal and interest which may be at any bank or trust company within or without the commonwealth. The bonds shall be signed by the chairman of the Authority or shall bear his facsimile signature, and shall bear a facsimile of the official seal of the Authority, attested by the Secretary-Treasurer of the Authority, and any coupons attached thereto shall bear the facsimile signature of the chairman of the Authority. In case any officer whose signature or a facsimile of whose signature shall appear on any bonds or coupons shall cease to be such officer before the delivery of such bonds, such signature or such facsimile shall nevertheless be valid and sufficient for all purposes the same as if he had remained in office until such delivery. All bonds issued under the provisions of this act shall have and are hereby declared to have all the qualities and incidents of negotiable instruments under the negotiable instruments law of the commonwealth. The bonds may be issued in coupon or in registered form, or both, as the Authority may determine, and provision may be made for the registration of any coupon bonds as to principal alone and also as to both principal and interest, for the reconversion into coupon bonds of any bonds registered as to both principal and interest, and for the interchange of registered and coupon bonds. The Authority may sell such bonds in such manner, either at public or at private sale, and for such price, as it may determine to be for the best interests of the Authority.

The proceeds of the bonds shall be used solely for the payment of the cost of the project, and shall be disbursed in such manner and under such restrictions, if any, as the Authority may provide in the resolution authorizing the issuance of such bonds or in the trust agreement hereinafter mentioned securing the same. If the proceeds of the bonds initially issued, by error of estimates or otherwise, shall be less than such cost, additional bonds may in like manner be issued to provide the amount of such deficit, and, unless otherwise provided in the resolution authorizing the issuance of such bonds or in the trust agreement securing the same shall be deemed to be of the same issue and shall be entitled to payment from the same fund without preference or priority of the bonds first issued. If the proceeds of the bonds shall exceed such cost, the surplus shall be deposited to the credit of the sinking fund for such bonds.

Prior to the preparation of definitive bonds, the Authority may, under like restrictions, issue interim receipts or temporary bonds, with or without coupons, exchangeable for definitive bonds when such bonds shall have been executed and are available for delivery:—The Authority may also provide for the replacement of any bonds which shall become mutilated or shall be destroyed or lost. Bonds and interim receipts may be issued by the Authority under the provisions of this act without obtaining the consent of any department, division, commission, board, bureau or agency of the Commonwealth or of the city, and without any other proceedings or the happening of any other conditions or things than those proceedings, conditions or things which are specifically required by this act.

History—
1958, 606, § 8.

§ 9.   Trust Agreement.

In the discretion of the Authority, the bonds issued under the provisions of this act may be secured by a trust agreement by and between the Authority and a corporate trustee, which shall be any trust company or bank having the powers of a trust company within the commonwealth. Such trust agreement or the resolution providing for the issuance of such bonds may pledge or assign the fees and other revenues to be received, but shall not convey or mortgage the project or any part thereof. Such trust agreement or resolution providing for the issuance of such bonds may contain such provisions for protecting and enforcing the rights and remedies of the bondholders as may be reasonable and proper and not in violation of law, including covenants setting forth the duties of the Authority in relation to the acquisition of property and the construction, improvement, maintenance, operation, leasing, repair and insurance of the project, the rates of fees to be charged, and the custody, safeguarding and application of all moneys, and may contain provisions for the employment of consulting engineers in connection with the construction and operation of the project. It shall be lawful for any bank or trust company incorporated under the laws of the commonwealth which may act as depositary of the proceeds of the bonds or of revenues to furnish such indemnifying bonds or to pledge such securities as may be required by the Authority. Such trust agreement or resolution shall set forth the rights and remedies of the bondholders and of the trustee, and may restrict the individual right of action by bondholders. In addition to the foregoing, such trust agreement or resolution may contain such other provisions as the Authority may deem reasonable and proper for the security of the bondholders. All expenses incurred in carrying out the provisions of such trust agreement or resolution may be treated as a part of the cost of operation of the project.

History—
1958, 606, § 9.

§ 10.   Revenues.

The Authority is hereby authorized to fix, revise, charge and collect fees for the use of the project and the different parts or sections thereof, and for the servicing of motor vehicles including the making of minor repairs, and to contract with any person, partnership, association or corporation as to the lease of the project for the parking and servicing of motor vehicles including the making of minor repairs and as to the sale of gasoline, and other motor vehicle fuels, oils and accessories. Such fees and the proceeds of such lease and contracts shall be so fixed and adjusted in respect of the aggregate of revenue from the project as to provide a fund sufficient to pay (a) the administrative expenses of the Authority and the cost of insuring, repairing, maintaining, operating or leasing the project and all extensions and improvements thereto, and (b) the principal of and the interest on bonds issued under this act as the same shall become due and payable, and (c) to create reserves for such purposes. Such fees and such lease and contract shall not be subject to supervision or regulation by any department, division, commission, board, bureau or agency of the commonwealth or any political subdivision thereof. The fees and all revenues derived from leases and contracts, except such part thereof as may be necessary to pay such current expenses and to provide such reserves therefor as may be provided for in the resolution authorizing the issuance of such bonds or in the trust agreement securing the same, and as may be necessary to meet any sinking fund requirements for the outstanding bonds, shall be set aside at such regular intervals as may be provided in such resolution or such trust agreement in a sinking fund which is hereby pledged to and charged with the payment of (1) The interest on such Common garage revenue bonds as such interest shall fall due; (2) The principal of such bonds as the same shall fall due; and (3) The redemption price or the purchase price of bonds retired by call or purchase as therein provided. Such pledge shall be valid and binding from the time when the pledge is made; the fees and other revenues or other moneys so pledged and thereafter received by the Authority shall immediately be subject to the lien of such pledge without any physical delivery thereof or further act, and the lien of any such pledge shall be valid and binding as against all parties having claims of any kind in tort, contract, or otherwise against the Authority, irrespective of whether such parties have notice thereof. Neither the resolution nor any trust agreement by which a pledge is created need be filed or recorded except in the records of the Authority. The use and disposition of moneys to the credit of such sinking fund shall be subject to the provisions of the resolution authorizing the issuance of such bonds or of such trust agreement. Except as may otherwise be provided in such resolution or trust agreement, such sinking fund shall be a fund for all such bonds without distinction or priority of one over another.

History—
1958, 606, § 10.

§ 11.   Trust Funds.

All moneys received pursuant to the authority of this act, whether as proceeds from the sale of Common garage revenue bonds or as revenues, shall be deemed to be trust funds to be held and applied solely as provided in this act. The resolution authorizing the issuance of bonds or the trust agreement securing such bonds shall provide that any officer with whom, or any bank or trust company with which, such moneys shall be deposited shall act as trustee of such moneys and shall hold and apply the same for the purposes hereof, subject to such regulations as this act and such resolution or trust agreement may provided.

History—
1958, 606, § 11.

§ 12.   Remedies.

Any holder of bonds issued under the provisions of this act or of any of the coupons appertaining thereto, and the trustee under any trust agreement or resolution, except to the extent the rights herein given may be restricted by such trust agreement or resolution, may, either at law or in equity, by suit, action, mandamus or other proceeding, protect and enforce any and all rights under the laws of the commonwealth or granted hereunder or under such trust agreement or resolution authorizing the issuance of such bonds, and may enforce and compel the performance of all duties required by this act or by such trust agreement or resolution to be performed by the Authority or by any officer thereof, including the fixing, charging and collecting of fees.

History—
1958, 606, § 12.

§ 13.   Bonds Eligible for Investment.

Bonds issued by the Authority under the provisions of this act are hereby made securities in which all public officers and public bodies of the commonwealth and its political subdivisions, all insurance companies, trust companies in their commercial departments and within the limits set by section fourteen of chapter one hundred and sixty-seven E of the General Laws, banking associations, investment companies, executors, trustees and other fiduciaries, and all other persons whatsoever who are now or may hereafter be authorized to invest in bonds or other obligations of a similar nature, may properly and legally invest funds, including capital in their control or belonging to them, and such bonds are hereby made obligations which may properly and legally be made eligible for the investment of savings deposits and the income thereof in the manner provided by section fifteen B of chapter one hundred and sixty-seven of the General Laws. Such bonds are hereby made securities which may properly and legally be deposited with and received by any state or municipal officer or any agency or political subdivision of the commonwealth for any purpose for which the deposit of bonds or other obligations of the commonwealth is now or may hereafter be authorized by law.

History—

1958, 606, § 13; 1983, 371, § 100.

Editorial Note—

The 1983 amendment rewrote the section to conform statutory references therein to changes occasioned by the recent reorganization of banking laws.

§ 14.   Miscellaneous.

The Common garage project, when constructed, shall be maintained and kept in good condition and repair by and at the expense of the Authority.

The city and all public agencies and commissions of the Commonwealth, notwithstanding any contrary provision of law, are hereby authorized and empowered to lease, lend, grant or convey to the Authority at its request and without cost and without the necessity for any advertisement, order of court or other action or formality, other than the regular and formal action of the authorities concerned any real property which may be necessary or convenient to the effectuation of the authorized purposes of the Authority under this act, including public roads and other real property already devoted to public use.

The Authority may call upon the state department of public works, the metropolitan district commission, the Boston city planning board, and the parks and recreation commission of the city and such other state or city boards, boards, authorities, commissions or divisions as may be deemed advisable for the purpose of assisting in making investigations and in effecting the design, construction and operation of the project, and the Authority may arrange for payment for such services and expenses of said agencies in connection therewith.

The Common garage project shall be policed and operated by such force of police, collectors, and other operating employees as the Authority or its lessee may in its discretion employ.

Until the project shall have been transferred to the city under the provisions of section fifteen of this act, the Authority or its lessee shall be liable to any person sustaining bodily injury or damage in his property by reason of a defect or want of repair therein or thereupon to the same extent as though the project were a way within the meaning of sections fifteen, eighteen and nineteen of chapter eighty-four of the General Laws, and shall be liable for the death of any person caused by such defect or want of repair to the same extent as is provided in chapter two hundred and twenty-nine of the General Laws. Any notice of such injury, damage or death required by law shall be given to any member of the Authority or to the secretary-treasurer.

Any operator of a vehicle using the project who refuses to pay the fee prescribed, or who evades or attempts to evade payment of the fee prescribed may be arrested without a warrant; and in addition thereto the Authority or its lessee shall have a lien upon the vehicle driven by such person for the amount of such fee and may take and retain possession thereof until the amount of such fee and all charges in connection therewith shall have been paid.

On or before the thirtieth day of January in each year the Authority shall make an annual report of its activities for the preceding calendar year to the governor, the general court and the mayor of the city. Each such report shall set forth a complete operating and financial statement covering its operations during the year. The Authority shall cause an audit of its books and accounts to be made at least once in each year by certified public accountants, and the cost thereof may be treated as a part of the cost of construction and operation of the project. Such audits shall be deemed to be public records within the meaning of chapter sixty-six of the General Laws.

History—
1958, 606, § 14.

§ 14A.   Auctioning of Unclaimed Property.

Notwithstanding the provisions of any general or special law to the contrary, if money, goods or other property which has been abandoned, mislaid or lost on the premises of the Authority comes into the possession of said Authority and remains unclaimed in its possession for a period of one hundred and twenty days, the Authority may sell same, excepting money so unclaimed, at public auction after notice of such sale has been published in a newspaper, for three consecutive weeks, in the city or town where such sale is to take place; provided, however, that if the Authority can identify the owner by examining such property, the Authority shall send notice of its possession of such property to said person at his last known address at least sixty days prior to said public auction. The net proceeds of such sale, after deducting the cost of storage and the expenses of the sale, and all money so unclaimed, shall be paid into and become the property of the Authority. If, in the opinion of the Authority, any property so abandoned, mislaid or lost which comes into the possession of the Authority and remains for a period of one hundred and twenty days, is the value of three dollars or less, the Authority may donate same to a charitable organization.

History—
1977, 197.

§ 15.　Transfer to City.

When all bonds and interim receipts issued under the provisions of this act and the interest thereon shall have been paid, or a sufficient amount for the payment of all such bonds and interim receipts and the interest thereon to the maturity thereof shall have been set aside in trust for the benefit of the bondholders, the project, if then in good condition and repair to the satisfaction of the board or officer then having power to lease public off-street parking facilities acquired under chapter four hundred and seventy-four of the acts of nineteen hundred and forty-six, as from time to time amended, shall become the property of the city and shall be held, leased and disposed of as if acquired under said chapter four hundred and seventy-four.

History—
1958, 606, § 15.

§ 16.　Exemption from Taxation.

The exercise of the powers granted by this act will be in all respects for the benefit of the people of the commonwealth, for the increase of their commerce and prosperity, and for the improvement of their health and living conditions, and as the operation and maintenance of the project will constitute the performance of essential governmental functions, the Authority shall not be required to pay any taxes or assessments upon the project or any property acquired or used by the Authority under the provision of this act or upon the income therefrom, and the bonds and interim receipts issued under the provisions of this act, their transfer and the income therefrom (including any profit made on the sale thereof) shall at all times be free from taxation within the commonwealth. The Authority is hereby authorized to enter into an agreement with the mayor of the city of Boston under which the Authority will undertake to make annual payments in lieu of taxes in connection with any real property acquired and owned by the Authority, the amounts of such payments to be reasonable sums stipulated in such agreement or agreements or determined in accordance with a reasonable formula so stipulated. Criteria to be employed by the parties to such agreement or agreements in agreeing upon the amount of such sums or upon any such formula shall include (i) the general level or property taxation in effect in the municipality, (ii) the effect of the facilities and activities of the Authority on the municipality and (iii) the needs of the Authority to maintain or improve its facilities.

No person, partnership, association or corporation which enters into a lease of the project or part thereof with the Authority for the parking and servicing of motor vehicles including the making of minor repairs and the sale of gasoline and other motor vehicle fuels, oils and accessories or for any of the foregoing purposes, or the sub-lessee or the assignee of such lessee, shall be assessed any tax upon any real estate, garage, underground passageway or tunnel of which it is lessee, sublessee or assignee or upon any structure or facilities constructed under any contract or lease while such lease is in force, the provisions of any general or special law to the contrary notwithstanding.

History—
1958, 606, § 16; 1982, 190 § 44.

Editorial Note—
The 1982 amendment added two sentences to the first paragraph, authorizing the Authority to make annual payments in lieu of taxes and establishing criteria for determination of such payments.

§ 17.   Common Garage Revenue Refunding Bonds.

The Authority is hereby authorized to provide by resolution for the issuance of its Common garage revenue refunding bonds for the purpose of refunding any bonds then outstanding which shall have been issued under the provisions of this act, including the payment of any redemption premium thereon and any interest accrued or to accrue to the date of redemption of such bonds, and, if deemed advisable by the Authority, for the additional purpose of constructing improvements, extensions or enlargements of the project. The issuance of such bonds, the maturities and other details thereof, and the rights, duties and obligations of the Authority in respect of the same, shall be governed by the provisions of this act insofar as the same may be applicable. The issuance of Common garage revenue bonds or Common garage revenue refunding bonds under the provisions of this act need not comply with the requirements of any other law applicable to the issuance of bonds.

History—
1958, 606, § 17.

§ 18.   Preliminary Expenses.

To provide for the preliminary expenses of the Authority in carrying out the provisions of this act, the sum of two hundred thousand dollars is hereby appropriated, which sum shall be paid to the Authority, and, simultaneously with the delivery of the bonds, the sum so paid shall be reimbursed by the Authority to the commonwealth out of the proceeds of any bonds which may be issued under the provisions of this act.

The Authority is hereby authorized and directed to make such surveys and studies of the project as may be necessary to effect the financing authorized by this act at the earliest practicable time and for this purpose to employ such consulting engineers, traffic engineers, legal and financial experts and such other employees and agents as it may deem necessary. To effect the purposes of this act, the city and the state department of public works and all other departments, boards, authorities, agencies, commissions and instrumentalities of the commonwealth and the city shall make available to the Authority all maps, plans, and data in their possession which may be useful to the Authority in making such plans and studies and in constructing the project. The state department of public works may furnish such assistance in making investigations and in preparing designs for the project as may be called for by the Authority and the cost thereof shall be paid by the Authority.

History—
1958, 606, § 18.

§ 19.   Construction of Tunnel, etc., not obligatory.

Nothing contained in this act shall be construed to require the Authority to construct either the underground passageway defined in section 2 (j) or the two-lane traffic tunnel defined in section 2 (h).

History—
1958, 606, § 19.

§ 20.   Act Liberally Construed.

This act, being necessary for the welfare of the commonwealth and its inhabitants, shall be liberally construed to effect the purposes thereof.

History—
1958, 606, § 20.

§ 21.   Constitutional Construction.

The provisions of this act are severable, and if any of its provisions shall be held unconstitutional by any court of competent jurisdiction, the decision of such court shall not affect or impair any of the remaining provisions.

History—
1958, 606, § 21.

§ 22.   Labor Relations Policy.

It is hereby declared to be the policy of the Authority to eliminate the causes of certain substantial obstructions to the free flow of industry and trade, and to mitigate and eliminate these obstructions when they have occurred by encouraging the practice and procedure of collective bargaining, and by protecting the exercise by workers of full freedom of association, self-organization, and designation of representatives of their own choosing, for the purpose of negotiating the terms and conditions of their employment or other mutual aid or protection.

The Authority shall have authority to bargain collectively with labor organizations representing employees of the Authority, and to enter into agreements with such organizations relative to wages, salaries, hours, working conditions, health benefits, pensions and retirement allowances and grievances and arbitration of disputes of such employees.

The provisions of sections twenty-six to twenty-seven D inclusive of chapter one hundred and forty-nine of the General Laws shall apply to the Authority.

History—
1958, 606, § 22.

Cross References—
Retirement systems and pensions, see ALM GL c 32 §§ 1 et seq.
Group insurance for employees and their dependents, see ALM GL c 32 §§ 2, 8.

§ 23.   Repeal of Statutes, Other Laws Inapplicable.

Chapter two hundred and ninety-four of the acts of nineteen hundred and forty-six, chapter six hundred and fifty-four of the acts of nineteen hundred and forty-eight, chapter three hundred and fifty-five of the acts of nineteen hundred and fifty-one, chapter five hundred and twenty-nine of the acts of nineteen hundred and fifty-five and chapter seven hundred and one of the acts of nineteen hundred and fifty-seven except section eleven thereof are hereby repealed.

History—
1958, 606, § 23; 1971, 693, § 3.

§ 24.   [1958, 606, § 24 amended **ALM GL** c 63 § 12.]

§ 25.   Effective Date.

This act shall take effect upon its passage.

History—
  1958, 606, § 25.

CHAPTER S73

Massachusetts Port Authority

(Acts 1956, Ch. 465)

> **Auto-Cite®:** Cases and annotations referred to herein can be further researched through the Auto-Cite® computer-assisted research service. Use Auto-Cite to check citations for form, parallel references, prior and later history, and annotation references.

§ 1. Definitions.

As used in this act, the following words and terms shall have the following meanings, unless the context shall indicate another or different meaning or intent:—

(a) The term "airport properties" shall include the General Edward Lawrence Logan International Airport, hereinafter called Logan Airport, and Lawrence G. Hanscom field, together with all buildings and other facilities and all equipment, appurtenances, property, rights, easements and interests formerly acquired or leased by the commonwealth in connection with the construction or the operation thereof and which were in the charge of the state airport management board on February seventeenth, nineteen hundred and fifty-nine, and together with all the land and buildings thereon at Logan Airport formerly owned, used or controlled by the military division of the commonwealth for purposes of the Air National Guard, including a certain parcel of land and the buildings thereon, new or formerly owned, used or controlled by said military division at the Logan Airport, bounded and described as follows:—

Beginning at a point at the intersection of the major and minor axis of the General Edward Lawrence Logan International Airport in latitude three thousand five hundred sixty-four and forty-six hundredths (N3564.46) feet north and longitude ten thousand nine hundred thirty-one and fifty-three hundredths (E10931.53) feet east; thence north fifty-eight degrees thirty-five minutes and thirty-two seconds west (N 58° 35′ 32 ″ W), six hundred forty-four and forty-one hundredths (644.41′) feet to a point; thence south thirty-one degrees, twenty-four minutes, and twenty-eight seconds west (S 31° 24′ 28″ W) fifty and fifty hundredths (50.50) feet to the point of beginning, point A; thence continuing south thirty-one degrees twenty-four minutes and twenty-eight seconds west (S 31° 24′ 28″ W) six hundred forty-seven and sixty hundredths (647.60′) feet to point B; thence turning and running north sixty-nine degrees forty-seven minutes and two seconds west (N 69° 47′ 02″ W), six hundred twenty-four and twenty-eight hundredths (624.28′) feet to point C; thence turning and running south thirty-one degrees, twenty-seven minutes and fifty-eight seconds west (S 31° 27′ 58″ W) twelve and seventy-five hundredths (12.75′) feet to point D, thence turning and running north fifty-eight degrees, thirty-two minutes and two seconds west (N 58° 32′ 02″ W) four hundred seventy-one and thirty-three hundredths (471.33) feet to point E, thence turning and running north forty degrees three minutes and twenty-six seconds east (N 40° 03′ 26″ E), two hundred ninety-seven and eleven hundredths (297.11) feet to point F; thence turning and running south forty-nine degrees thirty-six minutes and two seconds east (S 49° 36′ 02″ E) twenty-nine and forty hundredths (29.40′) feet to point G; thence curving in an easterly direction with a radius of one hundred thirty-five and no hundredths (R 135.00′) feet and length of arc of one hundred eighty-nine and fifty hundredths (L 189.50′) feet to point H; thence running north forty-nine degrees, fifty-nine minutes, and thirty-six seconds east (N 49° 59′ 36″ E), twenty-six and sixty hundredths (26.60′) feet to point J; thence turning and running south forty degrees, no minutes and twenty-four seconds east (S 40° 00′ 24″ E) six and twenty hundredths (6.20′) feet to point K; thence turning and running north forty-nine degrees, fifty-nine minutes and thirty-six seconds east (N 49 minutes and thirty-six seconds east (N 49° 59′ 36″ E) three hundred ninety-three and no hundredths (393.00′) feet to point L; thence turning and running south seventy-nine degrees, twenty-eight minutes and forty seconds east (S 79° 28′ 40″ E), sixty-one and thirty-eight hundredths (61.38′) feet to point M; thence turning and running south fifty-seven degrees, thirty-five minutes and thirty-two seconds east (S 57° 35′

32" E), six hundred sixty-two and no hundredths (622.00') feet, to point A, the point of beginning. The location of the intersection of the major and minor axis is fixed by a distance, called longitude, in feet, from a meridian passing through the center of the apex of the dome of the State House in Boston, and by a distance called latitude, in feet, from a line at right angles to said meridian and passing through the said center of the apex of the State House dome and the bearings refer to the true meridian.

(b) The word "Authority" shall mean the Massachusetts Port Authority created by section two or, if said Authority shall be abolished, the board, body or commission succeeding to the principal functions thereof or to whom the powers given by this act to the Authority shall be given by law.

(c) The word "city" shall mean the city of Boston.

(d) The word "cost", as applied to any additional facility financed under the provisions of this act or any extensions, enlargements or improvements of any project, shall embrace the cost of construction or acquisition, the cost of all labor, materials, machinery and equipment, the cost of all lands, property, rights, easements and interests acquired by the Authority in connection with the project, financing charges, interest prior to and during construction and for one year after completion of construction, cost of removal or relocation of any public utilities facilities, cost of traffic estimates and of engineering and legal services, plans, specifications, surveys, estimates of cost and of revenues, other expenses necessary or incident to determining the feasibility or practicability of the project, administrative expense, and such other expense as may be necessary or incident to the construction or acquisition of such additional facility or such extensions, enlargements or improvements, the financing thereof and the issuance of revenue bonds under the provisions of this act and placing the project in operation. Any obligation or expense hereafter incurred at the request of the Authority by the department of public works, the metropolitan district commission or by the public works department of the city or by any other governmental agency for engineering and legal services in connection with the construction of a project and the financing thereof shall be regarded as a part of the cost of the project and shall be assumed and paid by the Authority, or reimbursed to the commonwealth or to the city or to such agency out of the proceeds of the revenue bonds hereinafter authorized.

(e) The term "current expenses" shall mean the Authority's reasonable and necessary current expenses of maintaining, repairing and operating the projects and shall include, without limiting the generality of the foregoing, all administrative expenses, insurance premiums, fees and expenses of the Trustee, engineering expenses relating to operation and maintenance, legal expenses, charges of the paying agents, any taxes which may be lawfully imposed on the Authority or its income or operations or the property under its control and reserves for such taxes, any payments made by the Authority in lieu of taxes pursuant to section seventeen and reserves for such payments, ordinary and usual expenses of maintenance and repair, which may include expenses not annually recurring, and any other expenses required to be paid by the Authority under the provisions of the trust agreement hereinafter mentioned or by-law, but shall not include any reserves for operation, maintenance or repair, whether current or nonannually recurring, or any allowance for depreciation of transfers to the credit of the sinking fund for the revenue bonds.

(f) The term "fiscal year" shall be deemed to be the period commencing on the first day of July and ending on the last day of June of the following year.

(g) The words "Mystic River bridge" shall mean the bridge heretofore constructed and financed by the Mystic River Bridge Authority under the provisions of chapter five hundred and sixty-two of the acts of nineteen hundred and forty-six, as amended by chapter six hundred and twenty-six of the acts of nineteen hundred and forty-seven and by chapter four hundred and thirty-two of the acts of nineteen hundred and fifty-four, together with its approaches and approach facilities and all buildings and other facilities constructed, and all equipment, appurtenances, property, rights, easements and interests acquired or leased, by the Mystic River Bridge Authority in connection with the construction or the operation thereof.

(h) The term "Mystic River Bridge Revenue Bonds" shall mean the bonds, dated September first, nineteen hundred and forty-seven, and designated "Mystic River Bridge Authority Bridge Revenue Bonds (Boston — Chelsea Bridge)", which were issued by the Mystic River Bridge Authority under the provisions of said chapter five hundred and sixty-two of the acts of nineteen hundred and forty-six, as amended, for paying the cost of the Mystic River bridge.

(i) The term "port properties" shall embrace all lands, piers and other structures and facilities and all equipment, appurtenances, property, rights, easements and interests acquired or leased by the commonwealth in the port of Boston and in charge of the port of Boston commission.

The term "port of Boston" shall mean all of the tidewater lying westerly of the following described line: Point Allerton to the northeasterly side of Green island, thence to the southerly point of Deer island, thence to the northeasterly corner of President Roads anchorage basin, thence along the northerly side of said anchorage basin, thence along the westerly end of said anchorage basin and a line in extension thereof to the northerly line of the thirty-five-foot main ship channel, thence along the northerly line of the main ship channel to the Bird island anchorage basin, thence along the easterly end and northerly side of said Bird island anchorage basin to an intersection of the southeasterly side line of Jeffries street extended southwesterly, thence northeasterly along said line extended and the southeasterly side line of Jeffries street to Maverick street, excepting therefrom all of the tidewater now or formerly in the cities of Somerville, Cambridge, and Boston bounded on the seaward side by a line beginning at a point in the Charlestown section of the city of Boston having co-ordinates X =718,435.88 and Y =499,894.43 on the Massachusetts Co-ordinate System (Mainland Zone) as established by chapter forty-seven of the acts of nineteen hundred and forty-one, and extending thence, crossing the Charles river by a line bearing south 27° 50' 17" east, parallel to and approximately sixty feet easterly from the center line of the Charlestown bridge to the northerly street line of Commercial street; thence following said street line northeasterly, easterly and southeasterly to the easterly street line of Atlantic avenue; thence following said line of Atlantic avenue and an extension thereof southerly to a point on the extension of a line parallel to the center line of the Northern avenue bridge and approximately fifty feet distant southwesterly therefrom; thence following said line parallel to the center line of Northern avenue bridge south 61° 23' 02" east to the intersection of said line and the harbor line of the westerly side of Fort Point channel as established by section two of chapter one hundred and seventy of the acts of eighteen hundred and eighty; thence southwesterly by said harbor line to point I of the harbor line established by section two of said chapter one hundred and seventy; thence southwesterly by the harbor line by the arc of a circle having a radius of three hundred and thirty-eight feet about one hundred and fifty-seven feet to point H' as established by section one of chapter two hundred and seventy-eight of the acts of nineteen hundred and twenty-nine; thence by the harbor line to the left by the arc of a circle having a radius of seven hundred and fifty feet to a point G', said G' being the intersection of said arc and the harbor line as established by section one of chapter two hundred and thirty-two of the acts of eighteen hundred and seventy-three.

Neither the term "port properties" nor the term "port of Boston" shall include the trade and transportation center or any part thereof authorized by this act.

(j) The word "project" shall mean the Mystic River bridge, the airport properties, the port properties, or any additional facility, including the trade and transportation center, financed or acquired under the provisions of this act, together with all property, rights, easements and interests pertaining thereto or acquired for the construction or the operation thereof.

(k) The word "series" shall apply to any revenue bonds or revenue refunding bonds issued serially under the provisions of sections eight, nine or nineteen, or to any additional bonds of the same series issued under the provisions of section ten.

(l) The word "treasurer" shall mean the treasurer and receiver-general of the commonwealth.

(m) The word "Trustee" shall mean the bank or trust company acting as trustee under the trust agreement hereinafter mentioned.

(n) The term "trust agreement" shall mean the trust agreement made and entered into by and between the Authority and the Trustee under the provisions of section twelve.

(o) The term "South Station Area" shall mean the area of the city bounded generally by Summer Street, by Atlantic Avenue as extended to the Fort Point Channel, and by said Channel.

(p) The term "trade and transportation center" shall mean a project consisting of one or more areas, buildings, structures, improvements and accommodations necessary, convenient or desirable in the opinion of the Authority for the development and improvement of commerce in the city and the metropolitan area surrounding the city and for the more expeditious handling of such commerce, including, but not limited to, terminal and related facilities for ground transportation of all kinds, heliport facilities, off street parking facilities, offices, storage, warehouse marketing, display, and exhibition facilities, custom houses, custom stores, inspection and appraisal facilities, and hotel and motel accommodations.

In no event shall the Authority be permitted to operate or manage directly any hotel or motel accommodation, retail store, restaurant, or off-street parking facility forming a part of the trade and transportation center.

Nothing in this act shall authorize the constructing or leasing of any facility of a multi-commodity retail establishment of the type commonly known as a department store, and in no event may more than an aggregate of fifteen per cent of the total floor area of the trade and transportation center be used for retail and service activities not directly related to trade and transportation or customs functions.

History—
1956, 465, § 1; 1958, 599, § 1; 1967, 719, §§ 1–4; 1967, 869, § 4.

Code of Massachusetts Regulations—
Logan Airport–Minimum standards for aviation services, 740 CMR 26.01 et seq.

§ 2.   Massachusetts Port Authority.

There is hereby created and placed in the department of public words a body politic and corporate to be known as the Massachusetts Port Authority, which shall not be subject to the supervision or regulation of the department of public works or of any department, commission, board, bureau or agency of the commonwealth except to the extent and in the manner provided in this act. The Authority is hereby constituted a public instrumentality and the exercise by the Authority of the powers conferred by this act shall be deemed and held to be the performance of an essential governmental function.

The Authority shall consist of seven members all of whom shall be appointed by the governor by and with the advice and consent of the council, and shall be residents of the commonwealth. Not more than four of such members shall be of the same political party, and shall include persons with extensive experience in the fields of engineering, finance and commerce, and shall include a bona fide representative of a national or international labor organization, free of communist influence or domination which organization shall have the nature of its interests and employment directly and continually related to the scope of the activity of the Authority. The members of the Authority first appointed shall continue in office for terms expiring on June thirtieth, nineteen hundred and sixty, June thirtieth, nineteen hundred and sixty-one, June thirtieth, nineteen hundred and sixty-two, June thirtieth, nineteen hundred and sixty-three, June thirtieth nineteen hundred and sixty-four, June thirtieth, nineteen hundred and sixty-five, and June thirtieth, nineteen hundred and sixty-six, respectively, the term of each such member to be designated by the governor and to continue until his successor shall be duly appointed and qualified. The successor of each such member shall be appointed for a term of seven years and until his successor shall be duly appointed and qualified, except that any person appointed to fill a vacancy shall serve only for the unexpired term. Any member of the Authority shall be eligible for reappointment. Each member of the Authority may be removed by the governor, with the advice and consent of the council, for misfeasance, malfeasance or willful neglect of duty but only after reasonable notice and a public hearing unless the same are in writing expressly waived.

Each member of the Authority before entering upon his duties shall take an oath before the governor to administer the duties of his office faithfully and impartially, and a record of such oaths shall be filed in the office of the secretary of the commonwealth.

The governor shall designate one of the members as chairman of the Authority who shall serve as such chairman during his term of office as a member. Upon the expiration of the term of office of any such chairman, the governor shall designate one of the members as chairman, who shall serve as such chairman during his term or the remainder of his term of office as a member. The Authority shall annually elect one of its members as vice-chairman and shall also elect a secretary-treasurer who need not be a member of the Authority.

The secretary-treasurer shall keep a record of the proceedings of the Authority and shall be custodian of all books, documents and papers, filed with the Authority and of the minute book or journal of the Authority and of its official seal. He shall have authority to cause copies to be made of all minutes and other records and documents of the Authority and to give certificates under the official seal of the Authority to the effect that such copies are true copies, and all persons dealing with the Authority may rely upon such certificates.

Four members of the Authority shall constitute a quorum and the affirmative vote of four members shall be necessary for any action taken by the Authority. No vacancy in the membership of the Authority shall impair the right of a quorum to exercise all the rights and perform all the duties of the Authority.

Before the issuance of any revenue bonds under the provisions of this act the secretary-treasurer of the Authority shall execute a surety bond in the penal sum of one hundred thousand dollars, such surety bond to be conditioned upon the faithful performance of the duties of his office, to be executed by a surety company authorized to transact business in the commonwealth as surety and to be approved by the attorney general and filed in the office of the secretary of the commonwealth.

The members of the Authority shall serve without compensation, but each member shall be reimbursed for all necessary travel and other expenses incurred by him in the discharge of his official duties.

History—

1956, 465, § 2.

Cross References—

Agencies within Transportation and Construction Executive Office, see ALM GL c 6A § 19.

Authority's structures defined as public buildings, see ALM GL c 22 § 13A.

Appoinment of employees of Port of Boston authority as special state police officers, see ALM GL c 22C § 58.

Chairman as member of metropolitan area planning council, see ALM GL c 40B, § 24.

Code of Massachusetts Regulations—

Logan Airport–Minimum standards for aviation services, 740 CMR 26.01 et seq.

CASE NOTES

Under former ALM GL c 6 § 59B, commissioner of airport management is appointed by State Airport Management Board with approval of Governor and council, and he is responsible for general supervision of all state-owned airports. Commonwealth v Diaz (1950) 326 Mass 525, 95 NE2d 666.

To subject the Massachusetts Port Authority to the small business purchasing program established under Ch 484, Acts 1976, would conflict with the intent of §§ 2, 8, and 14 of Ch 465, Acts 1956 that the authority be independent in character; therefore, the authority is not a "purchasing agency" within the meaning of the small business purchasing program, and is not subject to the requirements of such program. 1976/1977 Op AG, No. 25.

§ 3.   General Grant of Powers.

The Authority is hereby authorized and empowered—

(a) To adopt by-laws for the regulation of its affairs and the conduct of its business, and to fix penalties for the violation thereof; provided, however, that no penalty shall be in excess of two thousand dollars.

(b) To adopt an official seal and alter the same at pleasure;

(c) To maintain offices at such place or places, either within or without the commonwealth, as it may determine;

(d) To sue and be sued in its own name, plead and be impleaded;

(e) To construct or acquire additional facilities;

(f) Except as provided in chapter three hundred and fifty-four of the acts of nineteen hundred and fifty-two, as amended from time to time, to investigate the necessity for additional facilities for the development and improvement of commerce in the city and in the metropolitan area surrounding the city and for the more expeditious handling of such commerce, including but not limited to, additional traffic facilities, bus and truck terminals, off-street parking facilities, and facilities for the handling, storage, loading or unloading of freight or passengers at steamship, railroad or motor terminals or airports, and to make such studies, surveys and estimates as may be necessary to determine the feasibility of any such facility; and further to investigate the operations, financing and traffic of the Metropolitan Transit Authority, to make such studies, surveys and estimates as may be necessary in addition to or in connection with those made by other public or private agencies to determine the feasibility of acquiring the properties of said authority as a facility of the Authority, and to report thereon to the governor and general court not later than two years from the effective date of this act;

(g) To extend, enlarge, improve, rehabilitate, lease as lessor or as lessee, maintain, repair and operate the projects under its control, and to establish rules and regulations for the use of any such project; provided, however, that no such rules or regulations shall conflict with the rules and regulations of any state or federal regulatory body having jurisdiction over the operation of aircraft; and provided, further, that in the enforcement of such rules and regulations the police appointed or employed by the Authority under section twenty-three shall have within the boundaries of all projects all the powers of police officers and constables of the towns of the commonwealth except the power of serving and executing civil process;

(h) To issue its revenue bonds, payable solely from revenues, and in anticipation of an issue of its revenue bonds to borrow money, all as hereinafter provided.

(i) To fix and revise from time to time and charge and collect tolls, rates, fees, rentals and other charges for the use of any project under its control; provided, however, that in revising or fixing the tolls for the use of the Mystic River bridge, the Authority shall give at least ten days' notice of the new schedule of tolls by publishing at least once in a daily newspaper of general circulation in the city; and provided, further, that no toll or charge for the use of any highway, bridge or tunnel of the Authority shall be collected for the passage of vehicles of the Metropolitan Transit Authority;

(j) To acquire, hold and dispose of real and personal property in the exercise of its powers and the performance of its duties under this act;

(k) To acquire in its own name by purchase or otherwise, on such terms and conditions and in such manner as it may deem proper, or by the exercise of the power of eminent domain in accordance with the provisions of chapter seventy-nine of the General Laws or any other alternative method now or hereafter provided by law, in so far as such provisions may be applicable, such public or private lands, or parts thereof or rights therein, and public or private ways as it may deem necessary for carrying out the provisions of this act;

provided, that the Authority shall act in its name and on its behalf in exercising its functions under this clause; and, provided, further, that before taking any private property the Authority shall give security to the treasurer, in such amount and in such form as may be determined by the department of public works, for the payment of such damages as may be awarded in accordance with law for such taking, and that the provisions of section forty of said chapter seventy-nine, in so far as the same may be applicable, shall govern the rights of the Authority and of any person whose property is so taken.

(l) To employ consulting engineers, accountants, attorneys, construction, financial and other experts, superintendents, managers, and such other employees and agents as may be necessary in its judgment, and to fix their compensation; provided, that all such expenses shall be payable solely from funds provided under the authority of this act;

(m) To appear in its own behalf before boards, commissions, departments or other agencies of the federal government and other states and international conferences and before committees of the congress of the United States and the general court of the commonwealth in all matters relating to its powers and purposes;

(n) To make application for, receive and accept from any federal agency grants for or in aid of the planning, construction or financing of any project or any additional facility, and to receive and accept contributions from any source of either money, property, labor or other things of value, to be held, used and applied only for the purposes for which such grants and contributions may be made;

(o) To make and enter into all contracts and agreements necessary or incidental to the performance of its duties and the execution of its powers under this act;

(p) To do all acts and things necessary or convenient to carry out the powers expressly granted in this act.

(q) To apply for, establish, operate and maintain or lease to others to operate and maintain, subject to the approval of the local municipality, a foreign trade zone and subzones in the commonwealth in accordance with the Foreign Trade Zones Act of 1934 (Title 19 U.S.C. Sections 81a–81u). Land acquired by the Authority after the effective date of this act which was subject to taxation on the assessment date next preceding the acquisition thereof and used by the Authority for a foreign trade zone shall not be exempt from local real estate taxes, and any such land leased by the Authority to others for said purpose shall be taxed by the city or town in which the land is situated to the lessees thereof in the same manner as if they were the owners.

(r) To make such studies, surveys and estimates as may be necessary in addition to or in connection with those made by other public or private agencies to determine the feasibility of acquiring necessary facilities and vessels to be operated by existing private marine carriers of passengers for hire, with or without such federal and or other aid as may be available, and to take whatever action necessary to implement such passenger carrier service.

(s) To indemnify its members, officers or employees from personal expense or damages incurred, arising out of any claim, suit, demand or judgment which arose out of any act or omission of the individual including the violation of the civil rights of any person under any federal law, if at the time of such act or omission the member, officer or employee was acting within the scope of his official duties or employment. The defense or settlement of any such claim against a member, officer or employee shall be made by the chief counsel of the Authority, by an attorney retained for such purpose by the Authority, or by an attorney provided by an insurer obligated under the terms of a policy of insurance to defend against such claims.

History—

1956, 465, § 3; 1958, 599, § 2; 1967, 869, § 5; 1968, 449, § 1; 1971, 771; 1972, 198; 1974, 208; 1977, 660, § 2.

Editorial Note—

Acts 1979, ch. 703, § 1, entitled "An act prohibiting the Massachusetts Port Authority from implementing certain rules and regulations relative to the towing or pushing of certain aircraft", provides as follows:

SECTION 1. Notwithstanding the provisions of paragraph (g), of section 3 of chapter 465 of the acts of 1956, or any other general or special law to the contrary, the Massachusetts Port Authority is hereby prohibited from adopting or enforcing any rule or regulation which would have the effect of requiring the towing or pushing of any aircraft for any part of a movement on the ground to or from a runway or taxiway in connection with a takeoff or landing, or which would have the effect of requiring the enplaning or deplaning of passengers at places other than fixed passenger terminal facilities.

Acts 1983, ch. 234, § 1, entitled "An act regulating the use of commonwealth pier commonly known as pier 5", provides as follows:

SECTION 1. *Whereas,* Pursuant to the grant of powers under chapter four hundred and sixty-five of the acts of nineteen hundred and fifty-six as heretofore amended, the Massachusetts Port Authority is authorized to lease all or any portion of Commonwealth Pier, commonly known as Pier 5, upon such terms and conditions as it may deem to be necessary or appropriate for the rehabilitation of said Pier, including provision of such uses and public purposes as a passenger ship terminal, a computer and communications industry market center, and related hotel, restaurant, and hospitality facilities.

§ 3A.   Flight Patterns; Public Hearings.

The authority, no less than thirty days prior to requesting from the Federal Aviation Administration any significant alteration of flight patterns arriving or departing from any airport owned by the authority, shall advertise in a newspaper or newspapers of general circulation in any city or town which would be affected by such alteration.

If the authority receives, within thirty days of said advertising, a petition signed by no fewer than fifty persons who are residents of the affected cities and towns, the authority, prior to requesting said alteration, shall hold a public hearing in the city or town where the greatest number of petitioners reside.

The authority shall, after considering the testimony at said public hearing, and at least seven days prior to requesting said alteration, issue a report, which shall be a public record, maintaining its intent to request said alteration, or making modifications thereto, and the reasons therefor.

For the purposes of this section significant alteration of flight patterns shall be those alterations proposed to be effective for a period of thirty days or longer, and shall not include any alterations necessitated by weather, equipment failure, or other emergency conditions.

History—
1979, 709.

§ 3B.   Ineligibility of Smokers for Certain Positions at Logan International Airport.

Subsequent to January first, nineteen hundred and eighty-eight, no person who smokes any tobacco product shall be eligible for appointment as a permanent crash crewman, crash boatman, fire controlman, or assistant fire controlman at the General Edward Lawrence Logan International Airport, and no person so appointed after said date shall continue in such office or position if such person thereafter smokes any tobacco products. The personnel administrator of the commonwealth shall promulgate regulations for the implementation of this section.

History—
1988, 199, § 43; 1989, 341, § 106, approved, with emergency preamble, August 15, 1989.

Editorial Note—
The 1988 amendment redesignated this section from § 3A to § 3B.
The 1989 amendment purported to redesignate this section from § 3A to § 3B; however, such redesignation was executed by 1988, 199, § 43.

§ 4.   Acquisition of Property.

The Authority is hereby authorized and empowered to acquire by purchase, whenever it shall deem such purchase expedient, any land, property, rights, rights of way, franchises, easements and other interests in lands as it may deem necessary or convenient for the construction or for the operation of any project, upon such terms and at such price as may be considered by it to be reasonable and can be agreed upon between the Authority and the owner thereof, and to take title thereto in the name of the Authority.

The Authority may, for the purposes of this act, acquire in its own name by purchase or otherwise, or may take by eminent domain under chapter seventy-nine of the General Laws or any other alternative method now or hereafter provided by law, lands in fee including buildings thereon, and easements, estates and rights in land, including the right to go under the surface thereof, or through or under buildings or parts of buildings thereon, or any leasehold rights, or other rights therein, or relative thereto; such takings in fee or otherwise may be made, whether the lands or other rights taken or otherwise affected are held under or by title derived by eminent domain or otherwise, and the Authority may, for such purposes, acquire in its own name by purchase or otherwise, or may take any property and rights of any kind deemed by it essential for the construction or for the operation of any project. A taking or purchase under this section of an easement or other estate air right or other right in a particular parcel of real estate, or any right taken, whether such parcel or other right taken consists of unimproved land or of land and buildings or rights of any nature, may be confined to a portion or section of such parcel or right fixed by planes of division, or otherwise, below or above or at the surface of the soil, and in such case no taking need be made of upper or lower portions, or other parts or section thereof, except of such easements therein, if any, as the Authority may deem necessary. The Authority shall, so far as may be practicable, notify all known owners of such taking, but the validity thereof shall not be affected by want of such notice.

The Authority may sell the buildings or other structures upon any lands taken by it, or may remove the same, and may sell, if a sale be practicable, or if not, may lease, if a lease be practicable, any lands or rights or interest in lands or other property taken or purchased for the purposes of this act, whenever the same shall, in the opinion of the Authority, cease to be needed for such purpose. The proceeds of any such sale or lease shall be applied toward the cost of the project or deposited to the credit of the sinking fund for the revenue bonds issued under the provisions of this act; provided, however, that no airport or port properties acquired from the commonwealth under the provisions of this act shall be sold without the prior approval of the governor and council; and provided, further, that the proceeds of any such sale shall be paid to the treasurer and shall be credited as provided in paragraph (a) of section seven.

The Authority may order the removal or relocation of any surface tracks, and the removal or relocation of any conduits, pipes, wires, poles or other property located in public ways or places, or in or upon private lands, which it deems to interfere with the laying out, construction or operation of any project, and the proper authorities shall grant new locations for any such structure so removed or relocated, and the owner thereof shall be reimbursed by the Authority for the reasonable cost of such removal or relocation. Such orders, to the extent specified therein, shall be deemed a revocation of the right or license to maintain such tracks, pipes, conduits, wires, poles or other property in such public ways or places, and the private owner of any such structures in public ways or lands shall comply with such orders. If any such owner shall fail to comply with any such order of the Authority relating to any such structure in public ways and places within a reasonable time, to be fixed in the order, the Authority may discontinue and remove such tracks, conduits, pipes, wires, poles or other property, and may relocate the same, and the cost of such discontinuance, removal or relocation shall be repaid to the Authority by the owner. No such discontinuance, removal or relocation shall entitle the owner of the property thus affected to any damages on account thereof, except for the reimbursement of cost provided for above. Any such structure in or upon private lands may be removed and relocated by the Authority, or, if removed and relocated by the owner thereof, the reasonable expense shall be repaid to him by the Authority. This section shall not apply to facilities on property of the commonwealth under the control of the department of public works or the metropolitan district commission or installed under licenses or permits granted by said department or commission, except with its approval.

The Authority and its authorized agents and employees may enter upon any lands, waters and premises in the commonwealth for the purpose of making surveys, soundings, drillings and examinations as it may deem necessary or convenient for the purposes of this act, and such entry shall not be deemed a trespass, nor shall an entry for such purposes be deemed an entry under any condemnation proceedings which may be then pending. The Authority shall make reimbursement for any actual damages resulting to such lands, waters and premises as a result of such activities.

The commonwealth hereby consents to the use of all lands owned by it, including lands lying under water, which are deemed by the Authority to be necessary for the construction or operation of any project; provided, however, that any such use shall require the prior approval of the governor and council, except as otherwise specifically provided in this act.

History—
1956, 465, § 4; 1958, 599, § 3; 1967, 869, § 6.

§ 4A.   Trade and Transportation Center.

In addition to and not in any way limiting the powers granted the Authority elsewhere in this act, the Authority is hereby authorized and empowered to acquire from the Boston Redevelopment Authority, by agreement therewith, any real property within the South Station Area and to acquire, construct, establish, own, lease, develop, maintain, operate, improve and rehabilitate as an additional facility (as that term is defined in section nine) a trade and transportation center to be located within the South Station Area and is hereby further authorized and empowered to operate and maintain the trade and transportation center or any part thereof either directly or indirectly through agents, lessees, concessionaries or others, but only in accordance with the provisions of section one.

History—
1967, 719, § 5.

§ 4B.   Financing of Project.

The Authority is hereby authorized and empowered to finance the trade and transportation center and in accordance with section nine to provide by resolution for the issuance at one time or from time to time of revenue bonds of the Authority for the purpose of providing funds for paying the cost of acquiring and constructing the trade and transportation center or any part thereof. The Authority is further authorized, subject to such conditions, limitations and restrictions as may be set forth in the trust agreement, to apply the tolls, rates, fees, rentals and other charges from all projects under the control of the Authority to the payment of such cost of acquiring and constructing the trade and transportation center.

History—
1967, 719, § 5.

113

§ 4C.   Agreements with Authority.

Any department, division, commission, public body, authority, board, bureau or agency of the commonwealth or the city is authorized and empowered to cooperate with the Authority and to enter into any agreement or agreements (and from time to time to enter into agreements amending or supplementing the same) with the Authority (a) for and in connection with or relating to the development of the South Station Area for purposes of the trade and transportation center, (b) for the purpose of providing for the construction, operation and maintenance of vehicular and pedestrian access facilities for the trade and transportation center, or any part thereof, to and from areas and public ways in the vicinity of the South Station Area, and (c) for any of the purposes of this act. All such agreements shall be upon such reasonable terms and conditions as may be determined by the Authority and by such department, division, commission, public body, authority, board, bureau or agency having jurisdiction in the premises.

History—

1967, 719, § 5.

§ 5.   Airport Properties.

Title to the airport properties shall be vested in the Authority upon the payment to the treasurer on the date of such transfer of; (a) a sum equal to the aggregate principal amount of all bonds of the commonwealth issued under the provisions of chapter three hundred and eighty-three of the acts of nineteen hundred and forty-five, chapter five hundred and sixteen of the acts of nineteen hundred and forty-six, chapter six hundred and seventy-six of the acts of nineteen hundred and forty-seven, chapter six hundred and fifty-two of the acts of nineteen hundred and forty-eight, chapter seven hundred and forty-five of the acts of nineteen hundred and forty-nine, chapter seven hundred and sixty of the acts of nineteen hundred and fifty and chapters seven hundred and thirty-one and seven hundred and thirty-three of the acts of nineteen hundred and fifty-one and outstanding on April thirtieth, nineteen hundred and fifty-six, which sum shall be certified by the treasurer; and (b) as of the date of transfer by the commonwealth a sum equal to the aggregate cash payments under the provisions of chapter seven hundred and fifty-six of the acts of nineteen hundred and fifty-one, chapter six hundred and four of the acts of nineteen hundred and fifty-two, chapter six hundred and sixty of the acts of nineteen hundred and fifty-three, chapter four hundred and seventy-one of the acts of nineteen hundred and fifty-four, and chapters one hundred and seventy-five, seven hundred and thirty-eight and seven hundred and sixty-nine of the acts of nineteen hundred and fifty-five for the development of or improvements to the airport properties, which sum ˚shall have been warranted and certified by the state comptroller.

Thereupon, the possession of the airport properties shall be transferred to the Authority and there shall be vested in the Authority the control, operation and maintenance of the airport properties and all rents, tolls, charges and revenues pertaining thereto, provided, however, that the Authority shall assume all of the obligations and have the benefit of all of the rights of the commonwealth in and to all leases, contracts and agreements relating to the airport properties and existing on the date of the transfer. The treasurer shall pay to the Authority, upon certification by the state comptroller, a sum equal to the unexpended cash balances of the proceeds of the bonds referred to in (a) above available on the date of the transfer. The treasurer shall collect for the commonwealth all accounts receivable as certified by the state airport management board outstanding on the date of transfer. Upon title to the airport properties becoming vested in the Authority, the state airport management board shall be dissolved.

History—
1956, 465, § 5.

§ 6.   Port Properties.

Upon the issuance of revenue bonds under the provisions of section eight and the application of the proceeds of said bonds as provided in said section eight (1) and (2), title to the port properties shall be vested in the Authority and the possession of the port properties shall be transferred to the Authority; provided, however, that the Authority shall pay to the treasurer within the first ninety days of each fiscal year the net revenues of the preceding fiscal year, if any, of the port properties, including any extensions, enlargements and improvements thereof, after deducting therefrom an amount equal to the principal and interest requirements of such preceding fiscal year as computed by the authority for all bonds issued under the provisions of section eight (c) and section nine for the purpose of constructing any extensions, enlargements or improvements of said properties, together with a sum which represents the amount of the overhead costs of the Authority allocated to the port properties by the Authority. The term "net revenues" as applied to this section shall mean the revenues of said properties over and above the current expenses for said properties, reserves for such purposes, the cost of renewals and replacements and the cost of acquiring and installing equipment.

The above payments shall continue until there shall have been paid to the treasurer (a) a sum equal to the aggregate cash payments by the commonwealth, as of the date of transfer of the title to the port properties, under the provisions of chapter four hundred and seventy-one of the acts of nineteen hundred and fifty-four and chapter seven hundred and thirty-eight of the acts of nineteen hundred and fifty-five for improvements to the port properties which shall have been warranted and certified by the state comptroller, and (b) a sum equal to the aggregate principal amount of all bonds of the commonwealth issued under the provisions of chapter six hundred and nineteen of the acts of nineteen hundred and forty-five, chapter five hundred and thirty-two of the acts of nineteen hundred and forty-seven, chapter seven hundred and seventy-one of the acts of nineteen hundred and fifty-one, chapter five hundred and five of the acts of nineteen hundred and fifty-two, chapter six hundred and forty-nine of the acts of nineteen hundred and fifty-three and chapter five hundred and seventy-five of the acts of nineteen hundred and fifty-four for the port properties and outstanding upon the date of the transfer and the interest paid thereon after said transfer, which sum shall be certified by the treasurer, less the unexpended cash balances of the proceeds of such bonds available upon said date of transfer, which balances shall be certified by the state comptroller and transferred to the Logan Airport and Port of Boston Bond Redemption Account established by section seven.

Upon transfer of the port properties there shall be vested in the Authority the control, operation and maintenance of the port properties and all rents, tolls, charges and revenues pertaining thereto, provided, however, that the Authority shall assume all of the obligations and have the benefit of all of the rights of the commonwealth in and to all leases, contracts and agreements relating to the port properties and existing on the date of the transfer. The treasurer shall collect for the commonwealth all accounts receivable of the Port of Boston Commission outstanding on the date of transfer. Upon title to the port properties becoming vested in the Authority, the Port of Boston Commission shall be dissolved.

Upon transfer of the port properties the Authority shall make all necessary plans for the development of the port of Boston. The Authority shall concern itself with the condition and location of piers, switching, floatage, lighterage, rates, rules, regulations and practices, dockage, wharfage, water front labor conditions, grain elevator and warehouse facilities within the port of Boston.

Upon transfer of the port properties the Authority may initiate or participate in any rate proceedings, or any hearings or investigations concerning the port of Boston, before any other body or official.

Upon transfer of the port properties, all the rights, powers and duties pertaining to the Port of Boston Commission in respect to lands, rights in lands, flats, shores, waters and rights belonging to the commonwealth in tidewaters and in lands under water, within the port of Boston, and any other rights and powers vested by the laws of the commonwealth in the Port of Boston Commission in respect to the port of Boston not heretofore in this act expressly vested in or imposed upon the Authority are hereby transferred to and hereafter shall be vested in and exercised by the Authority; provided, however, the department of public works, acting through the division of waterways, may, in accordance with such plans as it may adopt, not in conflict with the purposes, powers and plans for the development of the port of Boston or the Authority, excavate and dredge mooring basins for yachts and small craft, dredge channels, construct shore protection, remove hulks and wrecks, issue licenses and permits for filling, dredging, building of structures or excavating within the port of Boston, as defined in section one, provided no such license or permit shall be required to be obtained by the Authority.

History—
1956, 465, § 6; 1958, 599, § 4.

§ 7.   Application of Airport and Port Payments.

(a) The proceeds received by the treasurer for the airport properties under clause (a) of section five shall be credited on the books of the commonwealth to an account to be known as the Logan Airport and Port of Boston Bond Redemption Account. Such proceeds shall be invested in securities maturing not later than the several earliest maturities of the then outstanding bonds of the commonwealth which have been issued for the airport properties and the port properties. The income from such investments, together with the payments received by the commonwealth in accordance with section four of this act shall be credited to the Logan Airport and Port of Boston Bond Redemption Account. The principal and interest on said bonds of the commonwealth falling due after the title to the airport properties and port properties shall have vested in the Authority in accordance with the terms of this act shall be paid without appropriation from the Logan Airport and Port of Boston Bond Redemption Account. Upon retirement of said bonds of the commonwealth any balance then remaining in the Logan Airport and Port of Boston Bond Redemption Account shall be transferred to the General Fund and said account shall be abolished and any payments received thereafter by the treasurer in accordance with sections four and six shall be credited to the General Fund.

(b) The proceeds received by the commonwealth for the airport properties under clause (b) of section five shall be credited on the books of the commonwealth to the General Fund.

(c) The payments received by the commonwealth on account of the port properties under section six shall be credited on the books of the commonwealth to the General Fund.

History—
1956, 465, § 7.

§ 8.   Issuance of Revenue Bonds.

The Authority is hereby authorized and empowered to provide by resolution for the issuance of revenue bonds of the Authority, at one time or from time to time, for the purpose of providing funds for:—

(a) Refunding the Mystic River Bridge Revenue Bonds then outstanding, including the payment of the redemption premium thereon;

(b) Making the payments to the treasurer which are provided for in section five and making the payments required to be made by chapters four hundred and eighty-four and seven hundred and twelve of the acts of nineteen hundred and fifty-seven;

(c) Paying the cost of constructing such extensions, enlargements and improvements of the airport properties and the port properties as may be authorized by said resolution; and

(d) Providing funds for paying the current expenses of the Authority prior to the time when the revenues of the projects will be available for such purposes and for reimbursing the commonwealth for sums paid the Authority under section twenty-six.

The proceeds of such bonds shall be deposited with the Trustee and applied as follows:—

(1) Such amount of the proceeds as may be required for paying the principal of and the redemption premium on the Mystic River Bridge Revenue Bonds then outstanding shall be deposited with the trustee under the trust agreement securing said bonds in trust for the sole and exclusive purpose of paying such principal and redemption premium, and said bonds shall thereupon be called for redemption at the earliest practicable date. The amount required for paying

118

the interest which will accrue on said bonds from the last interest payment date to the date designated for the redemption of said bonds shall be withdrawn from the Mystic River bridge interest and sinking fund, a special fund created under the provisions of said trust agreement, and applied to the payment of such interest;

(2) There shall be paid to the treasurer the sums provided in section five and the payments required by chapters four hundred and eighty-four and seven hundred and twelve of the acts of nineteen hundred and fifty-seven shall be made;

(3) The Trustee shall set aside from such proceeds such amount as may be provided in the trust agreement for paying the current expenses of the Authority prior to the time when the revenues of the projects will be available for such purpose;

(4) The balance of such proceeds shall be deposited with the Trustee to the credit of a special fund or funds to be used solely for the payment of the cost of the extensions, enlargements and improvements of the airport and port properties which shall be authorized by said resolution and shall be disbursed in such manner and under such restrictions as may be provided in the trust agreement.

History—
1956, 465, § 8; 1958, 599, § 5.

CASE NOTES

To subject the Massachusetts Port Authority to the small business purchasing program established under Ch 484, Acts 1976, would conflict with the intent of §§ 2, 8, and 14 of Ch 465, Acts 1956 that the authority be independent in character; therefore, the authority is not a "purchasing agency" within the meaning of the small business purchasing program, and is not subject to the requirements of such program. 1976/1977 Op AG, No. 25.

§ 9.   Additional Revenue Bonds.

In addition to the bonds issued under the provisions of section eight, the Authority is authorized and empowered, subject to such conditions, limitations and restrictions as may be set forth in the trust agreement, to provide by resolution for the issuance at one time or from time to time of revenue bonds of the Authority or the borrowing of money in anticipation of the issuance of such revenue bonds for the purpose of providing funds for paying the cost of acquiring or constructing any additional revenue producing facility, the acquisition or construction and the financing of which by the Authority under the provisions of this act may hereafter be authorized by the general court (any such facility being herein called "additional facility"), or of acquiring or constructing any extensions, enlargements or improvements of any project then under the control of the Authority or, in the case of revenue bonds, of paying and discharging notes theretofore issued in anticipation of the issuance of such bonds, or any combination of the foregoing; provided, however, that no such additional facility, extension or enlargement shall be constructed which will impair the revenues to be derived from facilities constructed pursuant to chapter three hundred and fifty-four of the acts of nineteen hundred and fifty-two, as from time to time amended.

History—
1956, 465, § 9; 1968, 449, § 2; 1969, 869, § 1.

§ 10.   Provisions Applicable to All Bonds.

The principal of and the interest on all bonds issued under the provisions of this act shall be payable solely from the funds provided therefor from revenues as herein provided. The bonds may be of one or more series but all bonds issued by the Authority shall be dated, shall bear interest at such rate or rates per annum as the Authority shall determine, shall mature at such time or times not exceeding forty years from their date, as may be determined by the Authority and may be made redeemable before maturity, at the option of the Authority at such price or prices and under such conditions as may be fixed by the Authority prior to the issuance of the bonds. The Authority shall determine the form and the manner of execution of the bonds, including any interest coupons to be attached thereto, and shall fix the denomination or denominations of the bonds and the place or places of payment of principal and interest, which may be at any bank or trust company within or without the commonwealth. In case any officer whose signature or a facsimile of whose signature shall appear on any bonds or coupons shall cease to be such officer before the delivery of such bonds, such signature or such facsimile shall nevertheless be valid and sufficient for all purposes the same as if he had remained in office until such delivery. Notwithstanding any other provision of this act or any recitals in any bonds issued under the provisions of this act, all such bonds shall be deemed to be negotiable instruments under the laws of the commonwealth, subject only to any provisions for registration contained in any such bond. The bonds may be issued in coupon or in registered form or both, as the Authority may determine, and provision may be made for the registration of any coupon bonds as to principal alone and also as to both principal and interest, for the reconversion into coupon bonds or any bonds registered as to both principal and interest, and for the interchange of coupon and registered bonds. The Authority may sell such bonds in such manner, either at public or private sale, and for such price as it may determine to be for the best interests of the Authority.

If proceeds of the bonds of any series initially issued, by reason of increased construction costs or error in estimates or otherwise, shall be less than the amount required for the purpose for which such bonds are authorized, additional bonds may in like manner be issued to provide the amount of such deficiency and shall be deemed to be of the same series and shall be entitled to payment from the same fund or funds as the bonds first issued without preference or priority of the bonds first issued. If the proceeds of such bonds shall exceed the amount so required, such excess shall be deposited to the credit of the sinking fund for such bonds or, if so provided in the trust agreement, may be applied to the payment of any other project.

Prior to the preparation of definitive bonds, the Authority may, under like restrictions, issue interim receipts or temporary bonds, with or without coupons, exchangeable for definitive bonds when such bonds shall have been executed and are available for delivery. The Authority may also provide for the replacement of any bonds which shall become mutilated or shall be destroyed or lost. Bonds may be issued by the Authority under the provisions of this act without obtaining the consent of any department, division, commission, board, bureau or agency of the commonwealth or the city, and without any other proceedings or the happening of any other conditions or things than those proceedings, conditions or things which are specifically required by this act.

History—
1956, 465, § 10; 1958, 599, § 6; 1968, 449, §§ 3, 4; 1969, 869, § 2.

§ 10A.   Provisions Applicable to Money Borrowed.

Money borrowed by the Authority in anticipation of the issuance of revenue bonds shall be evidenced by notes or other obligations of the Authority. The aggregate principal amount so borrowed by the Authority and evidenced by such notes or other obligations (but excluding the aggregate principal amount borrowed which is contemporaneously to be repaid from the proceeds of notes then to be issued) shall not exceed ten per centum of the aggregate principal amount of revenue bonds of the Authority outstanding at the time such borrowing is made. The principal and interest of all notes or other obligations of the Authority so issued under the provisions of this act shall be payable no later than the fourth anniversary of the date of issue thereof, shall in no event, except as herein specifically provided, be payable from revenues of the Authority but shall be payable solely (i) from the proceeds of revenue bonds subsequently issued, or (ii) from the proceeds of subsequent borrowings which comply with the provisions hereof, or (iii), if the notes or other obligations evidencing such borrowings so provide, from moneys held for the credit of the maintenance reserve fund or the improvement and extension fund established by the trust agreement dated as of July first, nineteen hundred and sixty-four relating to revenue bonds of the Authority or any similar fund or funds established in any subsequent trust agreement, if such moneys, to the extent permitted thereby, are pledged by the Authority to the payment of the principal of and interest on such notes or other obligations and if such notes or other obligations were issued by the Authority for any purpose for which the moneys held for the credit of such fund or funds may be disbursed, or (iv) from revenues but only to the extent of the claim or charge provided in the following sentence. If and to the extent then permitted by any trust agreement relating to revenue bonds of the Authority and to the extent set forth in such notes or other obligations or the resolutions of the Authority authorizing the same, such notes may be secured by a claim or charge upon the revenues of the Authority which may be equal and proportionate with, but not superior to, that securing all bonds then outstanding or subsequently issued under said trust agreement. Notwithstanding any other provisions of this act or any recitals in any notes issued under the provisions of this act, all such notes shall be deemed to be negotiable instruments under the laws of the commonwealth, subject only to any provisions for registration contained in any such notes. Such notes or other obligations or any issue thereof shall be in such form and contain such other provisions as the Authority may determine and such notes or other obligations or any issue thereof and any resolution or resolutions authorizing such notes or other obligations or any issue thereof may contain, in addition to any provisions, conditions, covenants or limitations authorized by this act, any provisions, conditions, covenants or limitations which the Authority is authorized to include in any resolution or resolutions authorizing revenue bonds of the Authority, in such bonds or in the trust agreement relating thereto. The Authority may issue such notes or other obligations in such manner either publicly or privately and on such terms as it may determine to be in the best interests of the Authority. Such notes or other obligations may be issued by the Authority under the provisions of this act without obtaining the consent of any department, division, commission, board, bureau or agency of the commonwealth or the city and without any other proceedings or the happening of any other conditions or things than those proceedings, conditions or things which are specifically required by this act.

History—

1968, 449, § 5; 1969, 869, § 3.

§ 11. Credit of Commonwealth or Any Political Subdivision Thereof Not Pledged.

Revenue bonds or notes issued under the provisions of this act shall not be deemed to constitute a debt of the commonwealth or of any political subdivision thereof or a pledge of the faith and credit of the commonwealth or of any political subdivision, but such bonds or notes shall be payable solely from the funds herein provided therefor from revenues or, in the case of notes, from the proceeds of bonds as herein provided. All such revenue bonds or notes shall contain on the face thereof a statement to the effect that neither the Authority nor the commonwealth nor any political subdivision thereof shall be obligated to pay the same or the interest thereon except from revenues or, in the case of notes, from the proceeds of bonds as herein provided and that neither the faith and credit nor the taxing power of the commonwealth or any political subdivision thereof is pledged to the payment of the principal of or the interest on such bonds or notes.

All expenses incurred in carrying out the provisions of this act shall be payable solely from funds provided under the authority of this act and no liability or obligation shall be incurred by the Authority hereunder beyond the extent to which moneys shall have been provided under the provisions of this act.

History—
1956, 556, § 11; 1968, 449, § 6.

§ 12. Trust Agreement.

The bonds issued under the provisions of this act shall be secured by a trust agreement by and between the Authority and a corporate trustee, which shall be located within the commonwealth and shall be a trust company or bank having the powers of a trust company. The Authority shall appoint a financial advisor, whose appointment shall be subject to approval by the governor. Such advisor shall be an individual, firm or corporation of established reputation in the field of finance and investment who, before any trust agreement is executed by the Authority, shall certify in a writing filed with the commissioner of administration and with the Authority that such trust agreement fully protects the public interest affected by its provisions. The governor's approval of such advisor shall be conclusively evidenced by a writing to that effect filed with the commissioner or administration and with the Authority. Such trust agreement may pledge or assign the tolls and other revenues of the projects on account of which the bonds secured by such trust agreement shall be issued, but shall not convey or mortgage any project or any part thereof. Such trust agreement shall contain such provisions for protecting and enforcing the rights and remedies of the bondholders as may be reasonable and proper and not in violation of law, including covenants setting forth the duties of the Authority in relation to the acquisition or construction of any project and the extension, enlargement, improvement, maintenance, operation, repair and insurance of the projects and the custody, safeguarding and application of all moneys and may contain provisions for the employment of consulting engineers in connection with any such construction and the operation of such projects. It shall be lawful for any bank or trust company incorporated under the laws of the commonwealth which may act as depository of the proceeds of the bonds or of revenues to furnish such indemnifying bonds or to pledge such securities as may be required by the Authority. Such trust agreement shall set forth the rights and remedies of the bondholders and of the Trustee, and may restrict the individual right of action by bondholders. In addition to the foregoing, such trust agreement may contain such other provisions as the Authority may deem reasonable and proper for the security of the bondholders. All expenses incurred in carrying out the provisions of such trust agreement may be treated as an item of current expenses.

History—
1956, 465, § 12; 1958, 599, § 7.

§ 13.   Operation of Bridge.

Upon the issuance of revenue bonds under the provisions of section eight and the application of the proceeds of said bonds as provided in said section eight (1), title to the Mystic River bridge shall be vested in the Authority, said bridge shall thereafter be maintained, repaired and operated by the Authority, the trustee under the trust agreement securing the outstanding Mystic River Bridge Revenue Bonds shall deposit with the Trustee for the credit of the appropriate funds all moneys then in its hands which pertain to the Mystic River bridge and the Mystic River Bridge Authority shall be dissolved.

History—
1956, 465, § 13; 1958, 599, § 8.

§ 14.   Revenues.

The Authority is hereby authorized to fix, revise, charge and collect tolls, rates, fees, rentals and other charges for the use of each project, and to contract with any person, partnership, association or corporation desiring the use of any part of a project and its approaches and appurtenances for any proper purpose, and to fix the terms, conditions, rents and rates or charges for such use including such commutation rate of a uniform nature for the users of the bridge facilities as the Authority may deem desirable. Such tolls, rates, fees, rentals and other charges shall be so fixed and adjusted in respect of the aggregate thereof from the projects under the control of the Authority as to provide a fund sufficient with other revenues, if any, (a) to pay the current expenses of the Authority, (b) to pay the principal of and the interest on all bonds issued under the provisions of this act as the same become due and payable, (c) to create reserves for such purposes, (d) to make any payments which may be required under the provisions of section six, (e) to provide funds for making the investigations, studies, surveys and estimates authorized in section three, and (f) to provide funds for paying the cost of renewals or replacements, the cost of acquiring or installing equipment and the cost of enlarging, extending, reconstructing or improving any project or projects. Such tolls, rates, fees, rentals and other charges shall not be subject to supervision or regulation by any department, division, commission, board, bureau or agency of the commonwealth or any political subdivision thereof.

The Authority is further authorized to pledge such amount of such tolls and other revenues, over and above the amounts necessary to pay such current expenses and to provide such reserves therefor as may be provided for in the trust agreement, to the payment of the interest on and the principal of the bonds issued under the provisions of this act. The moneys so pledged shall be set aside at such regular intervals and in such amounts as may be provided in the trust agreement in a sinking fund for the payment of such interest, principal and the redemption price or purchase price of such bonds. Such pledge shall be valid and binding from the time when the pledge is made; the tolls or other revenues or other moneys so pledged and thereafter received by the Authority shall immediately be subject to the lien of such pledge without any physical delivery thereof or further act, and the lien of any such pledge shall be valid and binding as against all parties having claims of any kind in tort, contract or otherwise against the Authority, irrespective of whether such parties have notice thereof. The balance of such tolls and other revenues not needed for such sinking fund requirements shall be applied to the purposes set forth in clauses (d), (e) and (f) of this section as may be provided in the trust agreement.

No trust agreement by which a pledge is created need be filed or recorded except in the records of the Authority. The use and disposition of moneys to the credit of such sinking fund shall be subject to the provisions of the trust agreement. Except as may otherwise be provided in the trust agreement, such sinking fund shall be a fund for all such bonds without distinction or priority of one over another.

The word "bonds" as used in this section and in sections fourteen, sixteen, seventeen, eighteen and twenty-five shall be deemed to include all obligations of the Authority issued under the provisions of this act, including, without limitation, notes of the Authority.

History—
1956, 465, § 14; 1958, 599, § 9; 1969, 869, § 4.

CASE NOTES

To subject the Massachusetts Port Authority to the small business purchasing program established under Ch 484, Acts 1976, would conflict with the intent of §§ 2, 8, and 14 of Ch 465, Acts 1956 that the authority be independent in character; therefore, the authority is not a "purchasing agency" within the meaning of the small business purchasing program, and is not subject to the requirements of such program. 1976/1977 Op AG, No. 25.

§ 15.   Trust Funds.

All moneys received pursuant to the authority of this act, whether as proceeds from the sale of revenue bonds, notes or as revenues, shall be deemed to be trust funds, to be held and applied solely as provided in this act. The trust agreement shall provide that any officer to whom, or any bank or trust company to which, any such moneys shall be paid shall act as trustee of such moneys and shall hold and apply the same for the purposes hereof, subject to such regulations as this act and the trust agreement may provide.

History—
1956, 465, § 15; 1968, 449, § 7.

§ 16.   Remedies.

Any holder of bonds issued under the provisions of this act or of any of the coupons appertaining thereto, and the Trustee, except to the extent the rights herein given may be restricted by the trust agreement, may either at law or in equity, by suit, action, mandamus or other proceeding, protect and enforce any and all rights under the laws of the commonwealth or granted hereunder or under the trust agreement, and may enforce and compel the performance of all duties required by this act or by the trust agreement to be performed by the Authority or by any officer thereof, including the fixing, charging and collecting of tolls, rates, fees, rentals and other charges for the use of the projects.

History—
1956, 465, § 16.

§ 17.   Exemption from Taxation.

The exercise of the powers granted by this act will be in all respects for the benefit of the people of the commonwealth, for the increase of their commerce and prosperity, and for the improvement of their health and living conditions, and as the operation and maintenance of the projects by the Authority will constitute the performance of essential governmental functions, the Authority shall not be required to pay any taxes or assessments upon any project or any property acquired or used, by the Authority under the provisions of this act or upon the income therefrom and the bonds issued under the provisions of this act, their transfer and the income therefrom, including any profit made on the sale thereof, shall at all times be free from taxation within the commonwealth, and no property of the Authority shall be taxed to a lessee thereof under section three A of chapter fifty-nine of the General Laws; provided, however, that anything herein to the contrary notwithstanding, lands of the Authority, except lands acquired by the commonwealth under the provisions of chapter seven hundred and five of the acts of nineteen hundred and fifty-one situated in that part of the city called South Boston and constituting a part of the Commonwealth Flats, and lands acquired by the Authority which were subject to taxation on the assessment date next preceding the acquisition thereof, shall, if leased for business purposes, be taxed by the city or by any city or town in which the said land may be situated to the lessees thereof, respectively, in the same manner as the lands and the buildings thereon would be taxed to such lessees if they were the owners of the fee, except that the payment of the tax shall not be enforced by any lien upon or sale of the lands, but a sale of the leasehold interest therein and of the buildings thereon may be made by the collector of the city in the manner provided by law in case of nonpayment of taxes for selling real estate, for the purpose of enforcing the payment of the taxes by such lessees to the city or town assessed under the provisions hereof. The Authority is hereby authorized and empowered to enter into an agreement or agreements with the Boston Redevelopment Authority, with the approval of the mayor of the city, where the Authority will undertake to make the city annual payments in lieu of taxes in connection with any real property acquired and owned by the Authority as a part of the trade and transportation center, the amounts of such payments to be reasonable sums stipulated in such agreement or agreements or determined in accordance with a reasonable formula so stipulated. No such property shall be taxed to a lessee thereof from the Authority regardless of the date of acquisition of such property by the Authority. No revenue bonds of the Authority shall be issued pursuant to section four B of this act until the Authority shall have entered into such agreement or agreements with the Boston Redevelopment Authority, which agreement or agreements shall be conclusively deemed to comply with the provisions hereof if executed by the Boston Redevelopment Authority and the mayor of the city of Boston.

In addition to and without limitation of the foregoing, and notwithstanding any contrary provisions of this act or any other general or special law, the Authority is authorized and directed to enter into agreements with the cities of Chelsea and Boston and the town of Winthrop whereby the Authority will make to each such city and town annual payments in lieu of taxes. Any such agreement shall provide for annual payments for a period extending at least five years from the date thereof. Such agreements may be amended by the mutual agreement of the respective city and the Authority and shall be extended each year to incorporate an additional year or years to the term of the agreement. In arriving at the agreed upon level of such annual payments or any amendments thereto, the respective city and the Authority shall consider (1) the general level of property taxation in effect in such city; (2) the effect of the projects, facilities or activities of the Authority on such city; (3) the general economic condition of the users or other persons who pay the tolls, rates, fees, rentals, or other charges of the Authority; and (4) the needs of the Authority to maintain or improve its facilities or projects; provided, that no such annual payments as agreed upon or any amendments thereto shall exceed in the aggregate for any fiscal year of the Authority the balance of revenues remaining for such fiscal year after payment of all other current expenses of the Authority, any payments to the state treasurer which may be required under the provisions of section six hereof and the deposits to the credit of any maintenance reserve or like fund and the interest and sinking fund provided for in the trust agreement referred to in section twelve as from time to time in effect. Notwithstanding the provisions of clause (e) of section 1 hereof, any moneys set aside or payable or paid under such agreements with the cities of Chelsea and Boston and the town of Winthrop shall not constitute current expenses for the purposes of the second paragraph of section fourteen hereof, and notwithstanding any provision of section twelve hereof, such trust agreement may provide that such amounts shall be set aside or payable or paid only after the Authority has set aside or paid all other current expenses of the Authority, any payments to the state treasurer which may be required under the provisions of section six hereof and the deposits to the credit of any maintenance reserve or like fund and the interest and sinking fund provided for in said trust agreement, as from time to time in effect.

There shall be added to the equalized valuations of the cities of Chelsea and Boston and the town of Winthrop as calculated by the department of revenue, a value equivalent to that which would produce the amount of tax revenues accruing to said cities and town under the agreement authorized herein.

History—

1956, 465, § 17; 1967, 719, § 6; 1977, 949, § 8; 1978, 332, §§ 2, 3; 1980, 497, §§ 1–3.

Editorial Note—

Section 4 of the 1978 amending act, provides as follows:

SECTION 4. The supreme judicial court is hereby granted exclusive original jurisdiction to hear and settle disputes arising under the provisions of this act.

The **1980 amendment** rewrote the first sentence of the second paragraph and the third paragraph authorizing the Massachusetts Port Authority to make payments in lieu of taxes to the town of Winthrop.

§ 18.   Bonds Eligible for Investment.

Bonds issued under the provisions of this act are hereby made securities in which all public officers and public bodies of the commonwealth and its political subdivisions, all insurance companies, trust companies in their commercial departments and within the limits set by section fourteen of chapter one hundred and sixty-seven E of the General Laws, banking associations, investment companies, executors, trustees and other fiduciaries, and all other persons whatsoever who are now or may hereafter be authorized to invest in bonds or other obligations of the commonwealth may properly and legally invest funds, including capital in their control or belonging to them, and such bonds are hereby made obligations which may properly and legally be made eligible for the investment of savings deposits and the income thereof in the manner provided by section fifteen B of chapter one hundred and sixty-seven of the General Laws. Such bonds are hereby made securities which may properly and legally be deposited with and received by any state or municipal officer or any agency or political subdivision of the commonwealth for any purpose for which the deposit of bonds or other obligations of the commonwealth now or may hereafter be authorized by law.

History—

1956, 465, § 18; 1983, 371, § 99.

Editorial Note—

The **1983 amendment** rewrote the section to conform statutory references therein to changes occasioned by the reorganization of banking laws by Acts 1982 ch 155.

§ 19.   Revenue Refunding Bonds.

The Authority is hereby authorized to provide by resolution for the issue of its revenue refunding bonds for the purpose of refunding any bonds then outstanding which shall have been issued under the provisions of this act, including the payment of any redemption premium thereon and any interest accrued to the date of redemption of such bonds, and, if deemed advisable by the Authority, for any one or more of the following purposes:—(a) constructing improvements, extension or enlargements of any project or projects or, (b) paying all or any part of the cost of any additional facility or facilities or, (c) in the case of revenue bonds, of paying and discharging notes theretofore issued in anticipation of the issuance of such bonds, or any combination of the foregoing. The issuance of such bonds, the maturities and other details thereof, the rights of the holders thereof, and the rights, duties and obligations of the Authority in respect of the same, shall be governed by the provisions of this act in so far as the same may be applicable.

History—
1956, 465, § 19; 1968, 449, § 8.

§ 20.   Freedom from Competition.

After the effective date of this act and so long as any bonds issued under the provisions thereof shall be outstanding, no bridge, tunnel or ferry, for vehicular traffic, shall be constructed by the commonwealth or any political subdivision thereof or by any public instrumentality, over, under or across the Mystic river between its junction with the Chelsea creek and a point one mile upstream from the location of the bridge authorized by chapter five hundred and sixty-two of the acts of nineteen hundred and forty-six and no franchise shall be granted for the construction or operation of such a bridge, tunnel or ferry.

History—
1956, 465, § 20; 1958, 599, § 9A.

§ 21.   Annual Reports.

On or before the thirtieth day of November in each year the Authority shall make an annual report of its activities for the preceding fiscal year to the governor and to the general court. Each such report shall set forth a complete operating and financial statement covering its operations during the year. The Authority shall cause an audit of its books and accounts to be made at least once in each fiscal year by certified public accountants and the cost thereof shall be treated as an item of current expenses. The state auditor shall likewise audit said books and accounts at least once in each fiscal year. Such audits shall be deemed to be public records within the meaning of chapter sixty-six of the General Laws.

History—

1956, 465, § 4; 1961, 384, § 1.

Editorial Note—

Section 2 of the 1961 amending act provides as follows: "Such audit shall be made by the state auditor without any additional appropriation."

§ 22.   Transfer of Employees.

Upon the control of the Mystic River bridge, the airport properties or the port properties becoming vested in the authority, the employees of said projects whose work is directly related to such projects shall be transferred to the Authority and shall continue to perform the same duties at a salary not less than theretofore and every employee so transferred who immediately prior to such transfer was subject to section nine A of chapter thirty or to chapter thirty-one of the General Laws under a permanent appointment and who has served a probationary period shall continue to serve subject to the provisions of said section nine A of chapter thirty or to sections sixteen A, forty-three and forty-five of said chapter thirty-one as the case may be, whether or not thereafter reclassified, and shall retain all rights to holidays, sick leave and vacations in effect on the effective date of this act; provided, that any person transferred who was not subject to said section nine A or said chapter thirty-one and persons appointed after the effective date of this act shall not be subject to said section nine A of chapter thirty or to any provisions of said chapter thirty-one.

Every employee who upon transfer to the Authority is covered by the group insurance provided by chapter thirty-two A of the General Laws shall continue in uninterrupted coverage and all other employees of the authority are hereby likewise made eligible for said group insurance to the same extent as if they were employees of the commonwealth; provided, that the share of the commonwealth of the cost of such insurance shall, with respect to the employees of the Authority, be borne by said Authority. The Authority shall forward its contribution, together with all amounts withheld from the salaries or wages of its employees as provided in paragraph (a) of section eight of said chapter thirty-two A and all amounts paid by an employee as provided in paragraph (b) of said section, to the state employees group insurance commission at such time and in such manner as said commission may prescribe.

Each employee of the Authority as of January first, nineteen hundred and seventy-nine, and each employee of the Authority thereafter shall become a member of the Massachusetts Port Authority employees' retirement system. All others who are members of the state employees' retirement system on account of employment by the Authority shall continue to be members thereof and subject to the laws applicable thereto. The Massachusetts Port Authority employees' retirement system shall reimburse the commonwealth for the Authority's proportionate share of any amounts expended by the commonwealth under the provisions of chapter thirty-two of the General Laws for retirement allowances to or on account of the Authority's employees.

Whenever a person who is a member of the state employees' retirement system on account of employment by the Massachusetts Port Authority shall become a member of the Massachusetts Port Authority employees' retirement system pursuant to this section, that employee shall be entitled to all creditable service and all rights and benefits to which he was entitled as a member of the state employees' retirement system. Within ninety days of such transfer by a member of the state employees' retirement system to the Massachusetts Port Authority employees' retirement system, the amount of the accumulated total deductions credited to his account in the annuity savings fund of the state employees' retirement system shall be transferred and credited to the annuity savings fund of the Massachusetts Port Authority employees' retirement system.

Anything to the contrary in section twenty-two of chapter thrity-two of the General Laws notwithstanding, the amount to be appropriated by the Massachusetts Port Authority for any fiscal year for the pension fund as described in subparagraph (3) of said section 22 shall be the sum of (a) the normal pension cost, as hereinafter defined, incurred by the authority for that year plus (b) the amount necessary to amortize in equal annual installments over a period of twenty years the unfunded past service liability of the authority as of July first, nineteen hundred and seventy-eight. For purposes of this section the term "past service liability" of the Authority shall mean the excess of the present value of all future pension benefits payable by the Massachusetts Port Authority employees' retirement system as determined under the entry age normal actuarial cost method with frozen initial liability over the present value of all future normal costs. The terms "unfunded past service liability" shall mean the past service liability less the assets of the system. The term "normal pension cost" as applied to the authority for any year shall mean the amount, as determined under the entry age normal actuarial cost method with frozen initial liability, required to finance pension benefits earned by Authority employees during that year as members of the Massachusetts Port Authority employees' retirement system.

Any funds paid into the Massachusetts Port Authority employees' retirement system pursuant to this section or any provision of chapter thirty-two of the General Laws shall be used solely for the purpose of paying the costs of operation of the system. The provisions of this paragraph shall be deemed to constitute a contractual right and benefit on behalf of members of the system who are or may be retired pursuant to said chapter thirty-two, and no amendment or alteration shall be made which would result in a diversion of said fund for other purposes.

Every person who immediately prior to being transferred to the authority was subject to the provisions of sections fifty-six to sixty, inclusive, of chapter thirty-two of the General Laws, shall continue subject to the provisions of said sections; provided, however, that the words "retiring authority", as used in said sections shall mean the members of said Authority; and provided further, that the amount of all retirement allowances payable under said sections by virtue of this act shall be paid by the Authority, and the commonwealth shall reimburse the Authority for its proportionate share of any amounts so paid. Upon the retirement of any such person under said sections fifty-six to sixty, inclusive, the Massachusetts Port Authority employees' retirement board shall refund to the person so retired the amount of his accumulated deductions.

History—
1956, 465, § 22; 1958, 599, § 10; 1959, 476; 1960, 525; 1978, 487, § 20.

Editorial Note—
Section 2, of the 1960 amending act provides that no person who was an employee of the Mystic River Bridge Authority on the date of the acquisition of said Authority by the Massachusetts Port Authority, shall be excluded from membership in the state employees retirement system if he was under the maximum age for his group on said date.

Section 23 of the 1978 amending act provides as follows:

SECTION 23. Nothing in this act shall be deemed to repeal, decrease, abridge or in any way change the annuities, pensions, retirement allowances, refunds of accumulated total deductions or any other right or benefit to which a person transferred to the Massachusetts Port Authority employees' retirement system pursuant to this act would have been entitled had he remained a member of the state employees' retirement system.

§ 22A. Deferred Compensation Contracts Authorized for Funding Life Insurance Contracts, Mutual Funds or Bank Investment Trusts.

The secretary-treasurer of the Massachusetts Port Authority, on behalf of the authority, may contract with an employee to defer a portion of that employee's compensation and may, for the purpose of funding a deferred compensation program for said employee, established in accordance with the U.S. Internal Revenue Code, (the "Code"), invest the deferred portion of the employee's income in a life insurance or annuity contract, mutual fund, or a bank investment trust. The secretary-treasurer shall, before making any such investment, solicit bids from insurance companies authorized to conduct business within the commonwealth pursuant to chapter one hundred and seventy-five of the General Laws, mutual fund managers, and banks, which bids shall be sealed, and opened at a time and place designated by the secretary-treasurer. Any bid submitted by an insurance company, mutual fund, or bank investment trust to fund the deferred compensation program shall, where applicable, clearly indicate the interest rate which shall be paid on the deferred funds, any commissions which will be paid to the salesmen, any load imposed for the purpose of administering the funds, mortality projections, expected payouts, tax implications for participating employees and such other information as the secretary-treasurer may require. Any contract entered into between an employee and the Authority pursuant to this section shall include all such information in terms the employee can reasonably be expected to understand.

As used in this section, the word "employee" shall have the same meaning as "employee" in section one of chapter thirty-two of the General Laws and shall also include consultants and independent contractors who are natural persons paid by the Authority.

Notwithstanding any provisions herein to the contrary, the secretary-treasurer shall not be required to solicit bids to invest the deferred portion of an employee's income provided: (a) the secretary-treasurer elects to invest such funds in the same investment products as provided through the deferred compensation plan for employees of the commonwealth administered by the state treasurer, provided such plan resulted from the solicitation of bids in accordance with bidding requirements comparable to those required under this section; or (b) the secretary-treasurer elects to invest such funds in the investment products offered pursuant to a plan developed through a competitive selection process, provided that such plan resulted from the solicitation of bids by a group of any combination of three or more city, town, county or public authority treasurers acting as a "Common Group" for purposes of soliciting such proposals in accordance with bidding requirements comparable to those required under this section.

An employee may defer compensation so long as such deferral is the lesser of seven thousand five hundred dollars or thirty-three and one-third per cent of his includible compensation for a taxable year, except that for one or more of the last three taxable years ending before he attains normal retirement age under the plan the employee may defer the lesser of fifteen thousand dollars or the sum of (1) seven thousand five hundred dollars or thirty-three and one-third per cent of his includible compensation for a such year, plus (2) a sum not more than the total deferrable compensation for prior taxable years that had not in fact been deferred in such years.

Such deferred compensation program shall be in addition to and not a part of the retirement program or pension system as provided under said chapter thirty-two and any other benefit program provided by law for such employee. Any compensation deferred under such a plan shall continue to be included as regular compensation, as defined in section one of said chapter thirty-two, for the purpose of computing the retirement and pension benefits earned by any such employee, but any compensation so deferred shall not be included in the computation of any taxes withheld on behalf of any such employee.

History—
1981, 731, § 6.

§ 22B. Deferred Compensation Contracts Authorized for Funding Individual Retirement Accounts.

The secretary-treasurer of the Massachusetts Port Authority, on behalf of the authority, may contract with an employee to make contributions for and in the name of such employee, from amounts otherwise payable to the employee as current compensation, to an Individual Retirement Account ("IRA") by such employee established in accordance with the U. S. Internal Revenue Code, (the "Code"). The participating employee may invest that portion of his income so contributed to an IRA in an annuity contract, mutual fund, bank investment trust or other investment authorized by the Code. Before making such deduction, the secretary-treasurer shall be required to solicit bids from insurance companies authorized to conduct business within the commonwealth pursuant to chapter one hundred and seventy-five of the General Laws, mutual fund managers, and banks which bids shall be sealed, and opened at a time and place designated by the secretary-treasurer. Any bid submitted by an insurance company, mutual fund, or bank investment trust seeking investment of the IRA contribution shall, where applicable, clearly indicate the interest rate which shall be paid on the invested funds, any commissions which will be paid to the salesmen, any load imposed for the purpose of administering the funds, expected payouts, tax implications for participating employees and such other information as the secretary-treasurer may require. Upon the treasurer's determining which provider offers the product or products most beneficial to the employee in each category for which bids were solicited, the secretary-treasurer may offer such employee the opportunity to establish an IRA with one or more such providers. The employee who wishes to invest his IRA funds with any such provider, or combination of providers, may authorize the secretary-treasurer to deduct from amounts otherwise payable to the employee, at one time or on a periodic basis, amounts to be paid into the employee's IRA. If the employee so elects, the secretary-treasurer shall pay to the providers the amount designated by the employee, in the name of the employee, to the employee's IRA. Amounts so paid to the providers for the employee's IRA account shall belong exclusively to the employee. Except as otherwise provided herein, the secretary-treasurer may restrict an employee's right to contract to have contributions made to an IRA through deductions and payments by the secretary-treasurer, to those providers selected as the result of the competitive bidding process outlined herein, but the authority conferred upon the secretary-treasurer shall not be construed to restrict or limit the right of any employee to establish one or more IRAs with such banks, insurance companies, or similar authorized institutions as the employee may choose in any manner other than through an authorized deduction by the secretary-treasurer of a portion of the employees compensation as outlined herein. Any contract entered into between an employee and the authority pursuant to this section shall include all information in terms the employee can reasonably be expected to understand.

As used in this section the word "employee" shall have the same meaning as "employee" in section one of chapter thirty-two of the General Laws and shall also include consultants and independent contractors who are natural persons paid by the Authority.

An employee may contribute a portion of his compensation to an IRA under the program outlined herein so long as such contribution, for an employee who is single, is the lesser of two thousand dollars or one hundred per cent of his compensation for a taxable year, and, for an employee who is married, the contribution is the lesser of two thousand two hundred and fifty dollars or one hundred per cent of his compensation for a taxable year. If an employee has any compensation deferred under a deferred compensation plan for employees of the Authority, if one is established by the treasurer under section twenty-two A, then the aggregate amount of such deferred compensation deduction and amounts contributed to such employee's IRA shall not exceed the limits imposed upon such combined deduction and contribution by the Code.

Notwithstanding any provisions to the contrary, the secretary-treasurer shall not be required to solicit bids to invest the contributed portion of an employee's income into the employee's IRA provided: (a) the secretary-treasurer is authorized by the employee to pay that portion of the employee's compensation into the employee's IRA in the same investment products as provided through a deferred compensation or IRA plan for employees of the commonwealth administered by the state treasurer, or a deferred compensation plan for employees of the Authority administered by the secretary-treasurer, provided such plan resulted from the solicitation of bids in accordance with bidding requirements comparable to those required under this section; or (b) the secretary-treasurer is authorized by the employee to pay that portion of the employee's compensation into the employee's IRA in the investment products offered pursuant to a deferred compensation plan or an IRA investment option program developed through a competitive selection process, provided that such plan or program resulted from the solicitation of bids by a group of any combination of three or more city, town, county or public authority treasurers acting as a "Common Group" for purposes of soliciting such proposals in accordance with bidding requirements comparable to those required under this section.

Such IRA plan shall be in addition to and not a part of the retirement program or pension system as provided under said chapter thirty-two and any other benefit program provided by law for such employee. Any compensation contributed by the employee to his IRA under such a plan shall continue to be included as regular compensation, as defined in section one of said chapter thirty-two, for the purpose of computing the retirement and pension benefits earned by any such employee, but any compensation so contributed shall not be included in the computation of federal taxes but shall be included in the computation of state taxes withheld on behalf of any such employee.

History—
1981, 731, § 6.

§ 23.   Miscellaneous.

Any member, agent or employee of the Authority who contracts with the Authority or is interested, either directly or indirectly, in any contract with the Authority or in the sale or lease of any property, either real or personal, to, or in the purchase or lease of any property from the Authority, shall be punished by a fine of not more than one thousand dollars or by imprisonment for not more than one year, or both.

The Authority may call upon the department of public works, the metropolitan district commission, the department of commerce, the department of public safety, the planning board of the city, and such other state or city boards, commissions, divisions or agencies as may be deemed advisable for the purposes of assisting in making investigations, studies, surveys and estimates, and in policing the projects, and the Authority may arrange for payment for such services and expenses of said agencies in connection therewith.

All maps, charts, plans, records and all other related documents and equipment pertaining to the acquisition, construction, maintenance and operation of the airport properties and the port properties which are in the possession of the division of building construction of the commission on administration and finance, the state airport management board and the Port of Boston Commission upon the transfer of those properties to the Authority shall be transferred and delivered to the Authority.

Any action taken by the Authority under the provisions of this act may be authorized by resolution at any regular or special meeting, and each such resolution shall take effect immediately and need not be published or posted.

Each project shall be maintained and kept in good condition and repair by the Authority. Each such project shall also be policed and operated by such force of police, tolltakers and other operating employees as the Authority may in its discretion employ.

Any person who uses any project and fails or refuses to pay the toll provided therefor shall be punished by a fine of not more than one hundred dollars to be paid to the Authority or by imprisonment for not more than thirty days or both, and in addition thereto the Authority shall have a lien upon the vehicle driven by such person for the amount of such toll and may take and retain possession thereof until the amount of such toll and all charges in connection therewith shall have been paid.

Until the projects of the Authority shall have come under the control of the general court under the provisions of section twenty-five, the Authority shall be liable to any persons sustaining bodily injury or damage in or on its property by reason of a defect or want of repair of ways in or on said projects to the same extent as though said ways were ways within the meaning of sections fifteen, eighteen, and nineteen of chapter eighty-four of the General Laws, and shall be liable for the death of any person caused by such defect or want of repair to the same extent as is provided in chapter two hundred and twenty-nine of the General Laws. Any notice of such injury, damage or death required by law shall be given to any member of the Authority or to the secretary-treasurer of the Authority.

History—
1956, 465, § 23; 1958, 599, § 11; 1960, 328; 1967, 869, § 7.

CASE NOTES

It is unclear whether Massachusetts Port Authority's liability, which under Acts 1956, Ch. 465 § 23 is the same for defect or want of repair of ways as for municipal corporations under GL c 84, § 15, would be limited in regard to plaintiff who slipped and fell on icy sidewalk at airport, but in any event the limitation would be affirmative defense which would be waived if not pleaded. Jakobsen v Massachusetts Port Authority (CA1 Mass) 520 F2d 810, 21 FR Serv 2d 855.

§ 24.   Labor Relations Policy.

It is hereby declared to be the policy of the Authority to eliminate the causes of certain substantial obstructions to the free flow of industry and trade and to mitigate and eliminate these obstructions when they have occurred by encouraging the practice and procedure of collective bargaining and by protecting the exercise by workers of full freedom of association, self-organization, and designation of representatives of their own choosing, for the purpose of negotiating the terms and conditions of their employment or other mutual aid or protection.

The Authority shall have authority to bargain collectively with labor organizations representing employees of the Authority and to enter into agreements with such organizations relative to wages, salaries, hours, working conditions, health benefits, pensions and retirement allowances of such employees. The employees of the Authority shall submit all grievances and disputes to arbitration pursuant to the arbitration provisions in agreements existing at the time of this act or subsequently entered into with the Authority, or in the absence of such provisions to the state board of conciliation and arbitration, or other board or body having similar powers and duties, whose decision shall be final and binding.

The provisions of sections twenty-six to twenty-seven D, inclusive, sections forty-four A to forty-four E, inclusive, of chapter one hundred and forty-nine of the General Laws, shall apply to the Authority. The provisions of sections twenty-six to twenty-nine, inclusive, and of sections forty-four A to forty-four L, inclusive, of chapter one hundred and forty-nine of the General Laws, and the provisions of sections thirty-nine F to thirty-nine M, inclusive, of chapter thirty of the General Laws shall apply to the Authority in regard to the trade and transportation center.

History—
1956, 465, § 24; 1967, 719, § 7.

Cross References—
Retirement systems and pensions, see ALM GL c 32 §§ 1 et seq.

§ 25.   Transfer to Commonwealth.

(a) When all payments due on account of the port properties, as provided in section six, shall have been made, and when all bonds issued under the provisions of this act and the interest thereon shall have been paid or a sufficient amount of the payment of all such bonds and the interest thereon to the maturity thereof shall have been set aside in trust for the benefit of the bondholders, and contributions shall have been made to the several funds of the Massachusetts Port Authority employees' retirement system established under sections one to twenty-eight, inclusive, of chapter thirty-two of the General Laws such as are sufficient, in the opinion of the actuary, as defined in section one of said chapter thirty-two, to provide for the payment of all amounts payable by the system after that date with respect to all persons then receiving allowances from the Massachusetts Port Authority employees' retirement system and with respect to all persons who are then employees, as defined in said section one, of the Authority, whether or not any such amount is or becomes payable to any such person or the spouse or other beneficiary of any such person, such opinion to be based upon the assumption, among others, that such persons who are then employees are then or thereafter become entitled to receive retirement allowances in the amounts then provided by sections five, six and seven of said chapter thirty-two on the basis of the regular compensation received by, and the years of creditable service of, such persons at such date, all projects then under the control of the Authority shall be operated and maintained in such manner as may be provided by the general court.

(b) Should the general court dissolve the Authority under the provisions of subparagraph (a) the members of the Massachusetts Port Authority employees' retirement system on the effective date of the dissolution of the authority who do not then transfer to or enter service in a governmental unit in which a contributory retirement system established under the provisions of sections one to twenty-eight, inclusive, of said chapter thirty-two, or under corresponding provisions of earlier laws or of any special law, shall continue to be members of the Massachusetts Port Authority employees' retirement system and shall then be entitled to apply for and receive retirement allowances from such system in the amounts, upon the terms, subject to the conditions and with all of the related rights provided by and under sections six, seven, ten and twelve of said chapter thirty-two.

(c) Effective upon the date of dissolution of the Authority (1) the Massachusetts Port Authority employees' retirement system shall continue under the provisions of sections 1 to 28 inclusive of said chapter 32; (2) the management of the Massachusetts Port Authority employees' retirement system shall be transferred to the state board of retirement provided for in section eighteen of chapter ten of the General Laws which board shall have with respect thereto the general powers and duties set forth in subdivision (5) of section twenty of said chapter thirty-two; (3) all data, files, papers and records and other materials of the retirement board provided for in paragraph (b) of subdivisions (4^7/8) of said section twenty shall be transferred to and held by the state board of retirement; (4) the funds of the Massachusetts Port Authority employees' retirement system in the custody of the secretary-treasurer of the Authority shall be transferred to the state treasurer who shall thereafter be and perform the duties of the treasurer-custodian of such funds which shall then be held by him for the exclusive benefit and use of the members of the Massachusetts Port Authority employees' retirement system and their beneficiaries; and (5) the retirement board provided for in said paragraph (b) of subdivision (4^7/8) shall be abolished; provided, however, that the members and officers thereof shall continue to be authorized to do all such things and take all such action as may be necessary or desirable to be done or taken by them to effectuate the transfers to be made pursuant to this section.

(d) Effective upon the date of dissolution of the Massachusetts Port Authority or a default in its obligations under chapter thirty-two of the General Laws, the payment of all annuities, pensions, retirement allowances and refunds of accumulated total deductions and of any other benefits granted under the provisions of sections one to twenty-eight, inclusive, of said chapter thirty-two are hereby made obligations of the commonwealth in the case of any such payments from funds of the Massachusetts Port Authority employees' retirement system.

History—
1956, 465, § 25; 1978, 487, § 21.

Editorial Note—
Section 23 of the 1978 amending act provides as follows:
SECTION 23. Nothing in this act shall be deemed to repeal, decrease, abridge or in any way change the annuities, pensions, retirement allowances, refunds of accumulated total deductions or any other right or benefit to which a person transferred to the Massachusetts Port Authority employees' retirement system pursuant to this act would have been entitled had he remained a member of the state employees' retirement system.

§ 26.　Appropriation.

To provide for the expenses of the Authority in carrying out the provisions of this act, the sum of seven hundred and fifty thousand dollars is hereby appropriated from the General Fund of the commonwealth, which sum shall be paid to the Authority, and any sum so paid shall be reimbursed by the Authority to the commonwealth out of the proceeds of any revenue bonds which may be issued under the provisions of section eight.

History—
1956, 465, § 26.

§ 27.   Act Liberally Construed.

This act, being necessary for the welfare of the commonwealth and its inhabitants, shall be liberally construed to effect the purposes thereof.

History—
1956, 465, § 27.

§ 28.   Constitutional Construction.

The provisions of this act are severable, and if any of its provisions shall be held unconstitutional by any court of competent jurisdiction, the decision of such court shall not affect or impair any of the remaining provisions.

History—
1956, 465, § 28.

§ 29.   Inconsistent Laws Inapplicable.

All other general or special laws, or parts thereof, inconsistent herewith are hereby declared to be inapplicable to the provisions of this act, excepting section fifty-one M of chapter ninety of the General Laws, and chapter three hundred and fifty-four of the acts of nineteen hundred and fifty-two as from time to time amended.

History—
1956, 465, § 29.

§ 30.   [1956, 465, § 30 amended ALM GL c 63 § 12.]

§ 31.   [1956, 465, § 31 repealed Acts 1950, ch. 741.]

§ 32.   Other Laws Inoperative Upon Vesting of Title to Airport Properties in Authority.

Upon title to the airport properties becoming vested in the Author-

ity under the provisions of section five of this act, sections fifty-nine A
to fifty-nine C, inclusive, of chapter six of the General Laws and
sections fifty A to fifty L, inclusive, of chapter ninety of the General
Laws shall be inoperative and cease to be effective, and no bonds of the
commonwealth shall thereafter be issued under the provisions of
chapters four hundred and eighty-four and seven hundred and twelve
of the acts of nineteen hundred and fifty-seven.

History—
1956, 465, § 32; 1958, 599, § 12.

§ 33. Other Laws Inoperative Upon Vesting of Title to Port Properties in Authority.

Upon title to the port properties becoming vested in the Authority
under the provisions of section six of this act, sections fifty-three to
fifty-five, inclusive, of chapter six of the General Laws, chapter ninety-
one A of the General Laws and sections five, six and eight of chapter
six hundred and nineteen of the acts of nineteen hundred and forty-five
and sections thirteen to sixteen, inclusive, of chapter six hundred and
eight of the acts of nineteen hundred and fifty-three shall be inoperative and cease to be effective.

History—
1956, 465, § 33.

§ 34. Other Laws Inoperative Upon Vesting of Title to Mystic River Bridge in Authority.

Upon title to the Mystic River bridge becoming vested in the
Authority under the provisions of section thirteen of this act, chapter
five hundred and sixty-two of the acts of nineteen hundred and forty-
six, as amended by chapter six hundred and twenty-six of the acts of
nineteen hundred and forty-seven and chapter four hundred and
thirty-two of the acts of nineteen hundred and fifty-four shall be
inoperative and cease to be effective.

History—
1956, 465, § 34.

§ 34A. Authority to Reimburse Commonwealth for Retirement Costs Associated with Department of Public Safety Employees; Rate to be Set by Commissioner of Administration.

The Authority is hereby authorized and directed to reimburse the commonwealth for the amount of retirement costs incurred by the commonwealth on behalf of employees of the department of public safety for the time such employees are assigned by the commissioner of said department to duty with the Authority. Said amount shall be the retirement cost portion of the cost of fringe benefits as determined by the commissioner of administration pursuant to section six B of chapter twenty-nine of the General Laws. Said amount shall be reimbursed annually to the commonwealth for fiscal years beginning after June thirtieth, nineteen hundred and eighty-seven.

History—
1987, 199, § 146.

§ 35.   [Repealed, 1958, 599, § 13.]

CHAPTER S75

Massachusetts Turnpike Authority

(Acts 1952, Ch. 354)

> **Auto-Cite®:** Cases and annotations referred to herein can be further researched through the Auto-Cite® computer-assisted research service. Use Auto-Cite to check citations for form, parallel references, prior and later history, and annotation references.

§ 1.   Massachusetts Turnpike.

The Massachusetts Turnpike Authority (hereinafter created) is hereby authorized and empowered, subject to the provisions of this act, to construct, maintain, repair and operate at such location as may be approved by the state department of public works a toll express highway, to be known as the "Massachusetts Turnpike", from a point in the vicinity of the city of Boston or from a point or points within said city to a point at or near the boundary line between the Commonwealth and the State of New York or such part or parts thereof as it may determine, and to issue turnpike revenue bonds of the Authority, payable solely from revenues, to finance such turnpike.

History—
1952, 354, § 1; 1955, 47.

Code of Massachusetts Regulations—
Massachusetts Turnpike Authority regulations, generally, 730 CMR 2.01 et seq.

§ 2.   Credit of Commonwealth not Pledged.

Turnpike revenue bonds issued under the provisions of this act shall not constitute a debt of the commonwealth or of any political subdivision thereof or a pledge of the faith and credit of the commonwealth or of any such political subdivision, but such bonds shall be payable solely from the funds herein provided therefor from revenues. All such turnpike revenue bonds shall contain on the face thereof a statement to the effect that neither the commonwealth nor the Authority shall pay the same or the interest thereon except from revenues of the turnpike and that neither the faith and credit nor the taxing power of the commonwealth or of any political subdivision thereof is pledged to the payment of the principal of or the interest on such bonds.

All expenses incurred in carrying out the provisions of this act shall be payable solely from funds provided under the authority of this act and no liability or obligation shall be incurred by the Authority hereunder beyond the extent to which moneys shall have been provided under the provisions of this act.

History—
1952, 354, § 2.

§ 3.   Massachusetts Turnpike Authority.

There is hereby created and placed in the state department of public works a body politic and corporate to be known as the "Massachusetts Turnpike Authority", which shall not be subject to the supervision and regulation of the department of public works or of any other department, commission, board, bureau or agency of the commonwealth except to the extent and in the manner provided in this act. The Authority is hereby constituted a public instrumentality, and the exercise by the Authority of the powers conferred by this act in the construction, operation and maintenance of the turnpike shall be deemed and held to be the performance of an essential governmental function.

The Massachusetts Turnpike Authority shall consist of three members, to be appointed by the governor, who shall be residents of the commonwealth, not more than two of whom shall be of the same political party. The members of the Authority first appointed shall continue in office for terms expiring on July first, nineteen hundred and fifty-eight, July first, nineteen hundred and fifty-nine and July first, nineteen hundred and sixty, respectively, the term of each such member to be designated by the governor, and until their respective successors shall be duly appointed and qualified. The governor shall designate one of the members as chairman who shall serve as such during his term of office. Upon the expiration of the term of office of such chairman, the governor shall appoint one of the members as his successor as chairman. The successor of each member shall be appointed for a term of eight years, except that any person appointed to fill a vacancy shall serve only for the unexpired term. Any member of the Authority shall be eligible for reappointment. Each member of the Authority before entering upon his duties shall take an oath before the governor to administer the duties of his office faithfully and impartially, and a record of such oaths shall be filed in the office of the secretary of the commonwealth.

The Authority shall elect one of the members as vice chairman thereof and shall also elect a secretary-treasurer who need not be a member of the Authority. Two members of the Authority shall constitute a quorum and the affirmative vote of two members shall be necessary for any action taken by the Authority. No vacancy in the membership of the Authority shall impair the right of a quorum to exercise all the rights and perform all the duties of the Authority.

Before the issuance of any turnpike revenue bonds under the provisions of this act, each member of the Authority shall execute a surety bond in the penal sum of twenty-five thousand dollars, and the secretary-treasurer shall execute a surety bond in the penal sum of fifty thousand dollars, each such surety bond to be conditioned upon the faithful performance of the duties of his office, to be executed by a surety company authorized to transact business in the commonwealth as surety and to be approved by the attorney general and filed in the office of the secretary of the commonwealth. In addition to the salary provided in the last paragraph of section four of chapter five hundred and ninety-eight of the acts of nineteen hundred and fifty-eight, the chairman of the authority shall receive an annual salary of forty-one thousand seven hundred and thirty dollars and the other members shall receive an annual salary of twenty-two thousand and eighty dollars. Each member shall be reimbursed for his actual expenses necessarily incurred in the performance of his duties. All expenses incurred in carrying out the provisions of this act shall be paid solely from funds provided under the authority of this act and no liability or obligation shall be incurred by the Authority hereunder beyond the extent to which moneys shall have been provided under the authority of this act.

The Authority may indemnify any member, officer or employee from personal expense or damages incurred, arising out of any claim, suit, demand or judgment which arose out of any act or omission of the individual including the violation of the civil rights of any person under any federal law, if at the time of such act or omission the member, officer or employee was acting within the scope of his official duties or employment; provided that the defense or settlement of such claim shall have been made by the resident counsel of the Authority, by an attorney retained for such purpose by the Authority, or by an attorney provided by an insurer obligated under the terms of a policy of insurance to defend against such claims.

History—

1952, 354, § 3; 1963, 801, § 84; 1969, 688, § 1; 1969, 786, § 1; 1972, 300, § 40A; 1973, 426, § 44; 1974, 422, § 49; 1977, 234, § 196A; 1977, 234, § 196B; 1977, 234, § 196C; 1977, 660, § 1; 1977, 872, § 197; 1977, 872, § 198; 1977, 872, § 199; 1980, 354, § 18.

Editorial Note—

The **1980 amendment** amended the second sentence of the fourth paragraph increasing, from $38,384 to $41,730, the salary of the chairman of the Massachusetts Turnpike Authority.

Acts 1981, ch. 699, § 93A, entitled "An act further regulating the personnel system of the commonwealth" provides as follows:

SECTION 93A. Notwithstanding any special or general law to the contrary, the chairman of the Massachusetts Turnpike Authority may receive such salary increase as the governor may determine. Any such increase shall be filed with the house and senate committees on ways and means at least thirty days prior to the effective date of such increase.

Cross References—

Agencies within Transportation and Construction Executive Office, see ALM GL c 6A § 19.

Authority's structures defined as public buildings, see ALM GL c 22 § 13A.

Appoinment of employees of authority as special state police officers, see ALM GL c 22C § 61.

Chairman as member of metropolitan area planning council, see ALM GL c 40B § 24.

Penalty for dropping or throwing objects from bridges or overpasses, see ALM GL c 265 § 35.

Disposition of fines paid to Authority, see ALM GL c 280 § 2.

Code of Massachusetts Regulations—

Rules for adopting administrative regulations, 730 CMR 2.00 et seq.

Use of Summer and Callahan Tunnels, 730 CMR 3.00 et seq.

FORMS

Complaint for Injuries from Defective Guard rail[1]

[Title of Court and Cause]

1. The plaintiff, __1____ resides at __2____ *[address]*, City of __3_____, State of __4____.

2. The defendant, Massachusetts Turnpike Authority, is a body politic incorporate, having a principal place of business at __5____ *[address]*, in the City of __6____, County of __7____, Commonwealth of Massachusetts.

3. On or about __8____, 19_9_, the plaintiff, __10____, was operating a motor vehicle on the Massachusetts Turnpike, Westbound, in the City of __11____, County of __12____, Commonwealth of Massachusetts, when that motor vehicle was caused to come in contact with a guard rail at the edge of the roadway. The motor vehicle then went down the embankment next to the roadway, causing the plaintiff to sustain severe and permanent personal injuries.

4. The cause of the plaintiff's personal injuries as described above was as a result of the carelessness and negligence of the defendant, Massachusetts Turnpike Authority, its servants, agents, or employees, resulting in the existence of a defect and/or want of repair and/or want of a sufficient railing in or upon the above-described roadway, thereby causing and/or permitting the motor vehicle operated by the plaintiff to go through or over the guard rail.

5. As a result of the injuries sustained by the plaintiff as described above, she was caused to suffer great pain of body and anguish of mind, h__13__ earning capacity has been and will be impaired for a long period of time, and _14_ he

---

[1] Adapted from form provided by W. Thomas Smith of Sugarman and Sugarman, P.C., Boston.

has incurred and will incur large sums of money for medical care and attendance.

6. All notices, including notice pursuant to M.G.L., Ch. 84, § 18, to the extent that any such notices are required by law in the incident action, have been duly given and conditions precedent, if any, have been complied with.

CAUSE OF ACTION

7. This is an action by the plaintiff, ___15_____, against the defendant, Massachusetts Turnpike Authority, for negligence resulting in personal injuries.

DEMAND FOR RELIEF

8. The plaintiff, ___16_____, demands judgment against the defendant, Massachusetts Turnpike Authority, in the amount of $___17_____, with interest and costs, on h__18__ Cause of Action.

JURY CLAIM

The plaintiff claims a trial by jury.
Dated: ___19_____, 19_20_.

[Signature]

§ 4.   Definitions.

As used in this act, the following words and terms shall have the following meanings, unless the context shall indicate another or different meaning or intent:—

(a) The word "Authority" shall mean the Massachusetts Turnpike Authority, created by section three of this act, or, if said Authority shall be abolished, the board, body or commission succeeding to the principal functions thereof or to whom the powers given by this act to the Authority shall be given by law.

(b) The word "turnpike" shall mean the express toll highway or such part or parts thereof as may be constructed under the provisions of this act, together with and including all bridges, tunnels, overpasses, underpasses, interchanges, entrance plazas, approaches, connecting highways, service stations, restaurants and administration, storage and other buildings and facilities which the Authority may deem necessary for the operation of the turnpike, together with all property, rights, easements and interests which may be acquired by the Authority for the construction or the operation of the turnpike.

(c) The term "cost of the turnpike" shall embrace the cost of construction, the cost of the acquisition of all land, rights-of-way, property, rights, easements and interests acquired by the Authority for such construction, the cost of demolishing or removing any buildings or structures on land so acquired, including the cost of acquiring any lands to which such buildings or structures may be moved, the cost of all machinery and equipment, financing charges, interest prior to and during construction, and, if deemed advisable by the Authority, for one year after completion of construction, cost of traffic estimates and of engineering and legal expenses, plans, specifications, surveys, estimates of cost and of revenues, other expenses necessary or incident to determining the feasibility or practicability of constructing the turnpike, administrative expenses, and such other expenses as may be necessary or incident to the construction of the turnpike, the financing of such construction and the placing of the turnpike in operation. Any obligation or expense hereafter incurred by the state department of public works with the approval of the Authority for traffic surveys, borings, preparation of plans and specifications, and other engineering services in connection with the construction of the turnpike shall be regarded as a part of the cost of the turnpike and shall be reimbursed to the commonwealth to the credit of the Highway Fund.

History—
1952, 354, § 4.

§ 5.   General Grant of Powers.

The Authority is hereby authorized and empowered—

(a) To adopt by-laws for the regulation of its affairs and the conduct of its business;

(b) To adopt an official seal and alter the same at pleasure;

(c) To maintain an office or offices at such place or places within the commonwealth as it may determine;

(d) To sue and be sued in its own name, plead and be impleaded;

(e) To construct, reconstruct, maintain, repair and operate the turnpike or any part or parts thereof as it may determine, and the provisions of chapter ninety-one of the General Laws shall not apply to the construction by the Authority of structures in, on or over rivers, streams and waterways; provided, that for drainage areas greater than one thousand acres the said structures shall be designed to pass a rare flood as computed by the Kinnison-Colby formula, and for drainage areas of one thousand acres or less, the said structures shall be designed to meet the requirements of the "Massachusetts Turnpike Drainage Standards" dated June fourth, nineteen hundred and fifty-four.

(f) To acquire sites abutting on the turnpike and to construct or contract for the construction of buildings and appurtenances for gasoline stations, restaurants and other services and to lease the same for the above purposes in such manner and under such terms as it may determine;

(g) To issue turnpike revenue bonds of the Authority for any of its corporate purposes, payable solely from the tolls and revenues pledged for their payment, and to refund its bonds, all as provided in this act;

(h) To fix and revise from time to time and charge and collect tolls for transit over the turnpike, and it shall upon request furnish a user of the turnpike a toll receipt showing the amount of toll paid, the classification of the vehicle and the date and place of exit from said turnpike.

(i) To establish rules and regulations for the use of the turnpike not repugnant to the provisions of the General Laws made applicable thereto by section fifteen, and to provide penalties for the violation of said rules and regulations in which, except as provided in section fifteen C, shall not exceed five hundred dollars for each offense, which may be recovered by indictment or by complaint before a district court eighty per cent of which shall be accounted for and paid to the Authority.

(j) To acquire, hold and dispose of real and personal property in the exercise of its powers and the performance of its duties under this act;

(k) To acquire in the name of the Authority by purchase or otherwise, on such terms and conditions and in such manner as it may deem proper, or by the exercise of the power of eminent domain in accordance with the provisions of chapter seventy-nine of the General Laws or any alternative method now or hereafter provided by general law, in so far as such provisions may be applicable, such public lands, parks, playgrounds, reservations, cemeteries, highways or parkways, or parts thereof or rights therein, and any fee simple absolute or any lesser interest in such private property as it may deem necessary for carrying out the provisions of this act, including any fee simple absolute in, easements upon, or the benefit of restrictions upon, abutting property to preserve and protect the turnpike; provided, however, that whenever a parcel of private property so taken is used in whole or part for residential purposes, the owner or owners of said parcel may, within thirty days of the date of the Authority's notice to vacate such parcel, appeal to the Authority for a postponement of the date set for vacating, whereupon the Authority shall grant to the owner or owners of the property a postponement of three months from the date of such appeal; provided, however, that the appeal for such postponement shall be in the form of a written request to the Authority sent by registered mail, return receipt requested; and provided, further, that the Authority shall give security to the state treasurer, in such amount and in such form as may be determined by the state department of public works, for the payment of such damages as may be awarded in accordance with law for such taking, and that the provisions of section forty of said chapter seventy-nine, in so far as the same may be applicable, shall govern the rights of the Authority and of any person whose property shall be so taken;

(l) To designate the locations, and establish, limit and control such points of ingress to and egress from the turnpike as may be necessary or desirable in the judgment of the Authority to insure the proper operation and maintenance of the turnpike, and to prohibit entrance to the turnpike from any point or points not so designated;

(m) To make and enter into all contracts and agreements necessary or incidental to the performance of its duties and the execution of its powers under this act; provided, that sections twenty-six to twenty-nine, inclusive, and sections forty-four A to forty-four L, inclusive, of chapter one hundred and forty-nine of the General Laws and sections thirty-nine F to thirty-nine M, inclusive, of chapter thirty of the General Laws shall apply to contracts of the Authority to the same extent and in the same manner as they are applicable to the commonwealth. All general or special laws, or parts thereof, inconsistent herewith, are hereby declared to be inapplicable to the provisions of this act. Notwithstanding the provisions of this clause, the Authority may, with the approval of the secretary of transportation and construction or his designee, without competitive bids and notwithstanding any general or special law, award a contract, otherwise subject to this section, limited to the performance of emergency repairs necessary to preserve the safety of persons or property.

(n) To employ consulting engineers, attorneys, accountants, construction and financial experts, superintendents, managers, and such other employees and agents as may be necessary in its judgment, and to fix their compensation;

(o) To receive and accept from any federal agency grants for or in aid of the construction of the turnpike, and to receive and accept aid or contributions from any source of either money, property, labor or other things of value, to be held, used and applied only for the purposes for which such grants and contributions may be made; and

(p) To do all acts and things necessary or convenient to carry out the powers expressly granted in this act.

(q) Any sale of real property shall be awarded, after advertisement for bids, to the bidder who is the highest responsible bidder. The authority shall have the right to reject all bids and to readvertise for bids. Before any real property shall be so sold or conveyed notice that such real property is for sale shall be publicly advertised in two daily newspapers published in the city of Boston, and, if such real property is located in any other city or town, in a newspaper published in such other city or town, once a week for three successive weeks. Such advertisements shall state the time and place where all pertinent information relative to the real property to be sold or conveyed may be obtained, and the time and place of opening the bids in answer to said advertisements, and that the authority reserves the right to reject any or all such bids. All bids in response to advertisements shall be sealed and shall be publicly opened by the authority. The authority may require, as evidence of good faith, that a deposit of a reasonable sum, to be fixed by the authority, accompany the proposals. This clause shall not be applicable to any sale of real property by the Authority to the commonwealth or any city, town or public instrumentality nor to a sale of real property which is determined by the Authority to have a fair market value of five thousand dollars or less.

History—
1952, 354, § 5; 1955, 213; 1955, 653, § 1; 1957, 728, § 4; 1971, 660, §§ 1, 2; 1972, 632, § 4; 1975, 843, § 1; 1976, 491, § 1; 1979, 377, § 1; 1980, 49.

Editorial Note—
The **1979 amendment** rewrote paragraph (i) adding language exempting § 15C, dealing with overweight vehicles on Massachusetts Turnpike, from the maximum fine of $500 for each violation of the rules and regulations governing the use of the turnpike.

The **1980 amendment** rewrote clause (m), allowing the Massachusetts Turnpike Authority to award contracts for certain emergency repairs without the submission of competitive bids.

Cross References—
Police as employees of Massachusetts Turnpike Authority, see ALM GL c 22, §§ 9G, 9H.

Police as employees of Massachusetts Turnpike Authority, see ALM GL c 147, § 10D.

Code of Massachusetts Regulations—
Massachusetts Turnpike Authority regulations, generally, 730 CMR 2.01 et seq.

§ 6.   State Highways.

The Authority may, with the approval of the state department of public works, incorporate in the turnpike any existing state highway or part thereof or any partially completed state highway or any bridge which it may deem necessary for a proper alignment of the turnpike, and the actual cost thereof shall be reimbursed to the commonwealth to the credit of the Highway Fund from the proceeds of its turnpike revenue bonds.

History—
1952, 354, § 6.

Cross References—
State highways, generally, see ALM GL c 91.

§ 7.   Incidental Powers.

The Authority shall have power to construct grade separations at intersections of the turnpike with public highways and to change and adjust the lines and grades of such highways so as to accommodate the same to the design of such grade separation. The cost of such grade separations and any damage incurred in changing and adjusting the lines and grades of such highways shall be ascertained and paid by the Authority as a part of the cost of the turnpike.

If the Authority shall find it necessary to change the location of any portion of any public highway, it shall reconstruct the same at such location as the Authority shall deem most favorable, with the approval of the state department of public works, and of substantially the same type and in as good condition as the original highway. The cost of such reconstruction and any damage incurred in changing the location of any such highway shall be ascertained and paid by the Authority as a part of the cost of the turnpike. In exercising the power herein granted, the Authority may take private property in the name of a city or town by exercise of the power of eminent domain as provided in chapter seventy-nine of the General Laws.

Any public highway affected by the construction of the turnpike may be vacated or relocated by the Authority and any damages awarded on account thereof shall be paid by the Authority as a part of the cost of the turnpike.

In addition to the foregoing powers the Authority and its authorized agents and employees may enter upon any lands, waters and premises in the commonwealth for the purpose of making surveys, soundings, drillings and examinations as they may deem necessary or convenient for the purposes of this act, and such entry shall not be deemed a trespass, nor shall an entry for such purposes be deemed an entry under any condemnation proceedings which may be then pending. The

Authority shall make reimbursement for any actual damage resulting to such lands, waters and premises as a result of such activities.

The Authority shall also have power to make reasonable regulations including the authority to grant easements for the installation, construction, maintenance, repair, renewal, relocation and removal of tracks, pipes, pipelines, mains, conduits, cables, wires, towers, poles and other equipment and appliances of any public utility, or of any corporation or person owning or operating pipelines in, on, along, over or under the turnpike. Whenever the Authority shall determine that it is necessary that any such facilities which now are, or hereafter may be located in, on, along, over or under the turnpike should be relocated in the turnpike, or should be removed from the turnpike, the public utility, corporation or person owning or operating such facilities shall relocate or remove the same in accordance with the order of the Authority. In case of any such relocation or removal of facilities, the public utility, corporation or person owning or operating the same, its successors or assigns, may maintain and operate such facilities, with the necessary appurtenances, in the new location or new locations, for as long a period, and upon the same terms and conditions, as it had the right to maintain and operate such facilities in their former location or locations.

The Authority shall have power, in the process of constructing or reconstructing all or any part of the turnpike or any extension thereof or additions thereto, to take by eminent domain pursuant to chapter seventy-nine of the General Laws, such land abutting the turnpike as it may deem necessary or desirable for the purposes of removing or relocating all or any part of the facilities of any public utility, including rail lines, and may thereafter lease the same or convey an easement or any other interest therein to such utility company upon such terms as it, in its sole discretion, may determine. The relocation of the facilities of any public utility, including rail lines, in accordance with the provisions of this section shall be valid upon the filing of the plans thereof with the department of public utilities, and no general laws or other special laws, or parts thereof, shall be applicable to such relocation.

The commonwealth hereby consents to the use of all lands owned by it, including lands lying under water, which are deemed by the Authority to be necessary for the construction or operation of the turnpike.

The Authority may sell the buildings or other structures upon any lands taken by it, or may remove the same, and shall sell, if a sale be practicable, or if not, shall lease, if a lease be practicable, any lands or rights or interest in lands or other property taken or purchased for the purposes of this act, whenever the same shall, in the opinion of the

Authority, cease to be needed for such purpose. The proceeds of any such sale or lease shall be applied toward the cost of the turnpike or deposited to the credit of the sinking fund for the turnpike revenue bonds issued under the provisions of this act.

The Authority may place and maintain or may grant permission by easement or otherwise to any corporation or person to place and maintain on or under or within the turnpike ducts, pipes, pipelines, wires or other structures, to be so located as not to interfere with the safe and convenient operation and maintenance of the turnpike, and may contract with any such person or corporation for such permission on such terms and conditions as may be fixed by the Authority. The construction, maintenance and repairs of any such ducts, pipes, pipelines, wires or other structures shall be subject to such directions and regulations as the Authority may impose.

History—

1952, 354, § 7; 1958, 384, §§ 1–3.

§ 8. Turnpike Revenue Bonds.

The Authority is hereby authorized to provide by resolution, at one time or from time to time, for the issuance of turnpike revenue bonds of the Authority for the purpose of paying all or any part of the cost of the turnpike or any part or parts thereof. The principal of and the interest on such bonds shall be payable solely from the funds herein provided for such payment. The bonds shall be dated, shall bear interest at such rate or rates, shall mature at such time or times not exceeding forty years from their date or dates, all as may be determined by the Authority, and may be made redeemable before maturity, at the option of the Authority, at such price or prices and under such terms and conditions as may be fixed by the Authority prior to the issuance of the bonds. The authority shall determine the form of the bonds, including any interest coupons to be attached thereto, and shall fix the denomination or denominations of the bonds and the place or places of payment of principal and interest, which may be at any bank or trust company within or without the commonwealth. The bonds shall be signed by the chairman of the Authority or shall bear his facsimile signature, and shall bear a facsimile of the official seal of the Authority, attested by the secretary-treasurer of the Authority, and any coupons attached thereto shall bear the facsimile signature of the chairman of the Authority. In case any officer whose signature or a facsimile of whose signature shall appear on any bonds or coupons shall cease to be such officer before the delivery of such bonds, such signature or such facsimile shall nevertheless be valid and sufficient for all purposes the same as if he had remained in office until such delivery. All bonds issued under the provisions of this act shall have and are hereby declared to have all the qualities and incidents of negotiable instruments, including negotiability of investment securities, under the Uniform Commercial Code. The bonds may be issued in coupon or in registered form, or both, as the Authority may determine, and provision may be made for the registration of any coupon bonds as to principal alone and also as to both principal and interest, for the reconversion into coupon bonds of any bonds registered as to both principal and interest, and for the interchange of registered and coupon bonds. The Authority may sell such bonds in such manner, either at public or at private sale, and for such price or prices, as it may determine to be in the best interest of the Authority.

The proceeds of the bonds shall be used solely for the payment of the cost of the turnpike, and shall be disbursed in such manner and under such restrictions, if any, as the Authority may provide in the resolution authorizing the issuance of such bonds or in the trust agreement hereinafter mentioned securing the same. If the proceeds of the bonds initially issued, by error of estimates or otherwise, shall be less than such cost, additional bonds may in like manner be issued to provide the amount of such deficit, and, unless otherwise provided in the resolution authorizing the issuance of such bonds or in the trust agreement securing the same shall be deemed to be of the same issue and shall be entitled to payment from the same fund without preference or priority of the bonds first issued. If the proceeds of the bonds shall exceed such cost, the surplus shall be deposited to the credit of the sinking fund for such bonds.

Prior to the preparation of definitive bonds, the Authority may, under like restrictions, issue interim receipts or temporary bonds, with or without coupons, exchangeable for definitive bonds when such bonds shall have been executed and are available for delivery. The Authority may also provide for the replacement of any bonds which shall become mutilated or shall be destroyed or lost. Bonds may be issued under the provisions of this act without obtaining the consent of any department, division, commission, board, bureau or agency of the commonwealth, and without any other proceedings or the happening of any other conditions or things than those proceedings, conditions or things which are specifically required by this act.

History—
1952, 354, § 8; 1968, 757; 1969, 688, § 2; 1985, 811, § 37A.

Editorial Note—
The 1985 amendment, in the first paragraph, deleted from the third sentence ", not exceeding six percent per annum", and rewrote the last

sentence of the first paragraph relative to the manner of sale of bonds, deleting language which provided that no such sale shall be made at a price so low as to require the payment of interest on the money received therefor at more than six percentum per annum, computed with relation to the absolute maturity of the bonds in accordance with standard tables of bond values, excluding, however, from such computation the amount of any premium to be paid on redemption of any bonds prior to maturity.

Cross References—
Investment securities under the Uniform Commercial Code, see ALM GL c 106, §§ 8-101 et seq.

§ 9.   Trust Agreement.

In the discretion of the Authority the bonds issued under the provisions of this act may be secured by a trust agreement by and between the Authority and a corporate trustee, which may be any trust company or bank having the powers of a trust company within or without the commonwealth. Such trust agreement or the resolution providing for the issuance of such bonds may pledge or assign the tolls and other revenues to be received, but shall not convey or mortgage the turnpike or any part thereof. Such trust agreement or resolution providing for the issuance of such bonds may contain such provisions for protecting and enforcing the rights and remedies of the bondholders as may be reasonable and proper and not in violation of law, including covenants setting forth the duties of the Authority in relation to the acquisition of property and the construction, improvement, maintenance, repair, operation and insurance of the turnpike, the rates of toll to be charged, and the custody, safeguarding and application of all moneys. It shall be lawful for any bank or trust company incorporated under the laws of the commonwealth which may act as depositary of the proceeds of bonds or of revenues to furnish such indemnifying bonds or to pledge such securities as may be required by the Authority. Such trust agreement may set forth the rights and remedies of the bondholders and of the trustee, and may restrict the individual right of action by bondholders. In addition to the foregoing, such trust agreement or resolution may contain such other provisions as the Authority may deem reasonable and proper for the security of the bondholders. All expenses incurred in carrying out the provisions of such trust agreement or resolution may be treated as a part of the cost of the operation of the turnpike.

History—
1952, 354, § 9.

§ 10.   Revenues.

The Authority is hereby authorized to fix, revise, charge and collect tolls for the use of the turnpike and the different parts or sections thereof, and to contract with any person, partnership, association or corporation desiring the use of any part thereof, including the right of way adjoining the paved portion, for placing thereon telephone, telegraph, electric light or power lines, gas stations, garages and restaurants, or for any other purpose, and to fix the terms, conditions, rents and rates of charges for such use. Such tolls shall be so fixed and adjusted in respect of the aggregate of tolls from the turnpike as to provide a fund sufficient with other revenues, if any, to pay (a) the cost of maintaining, repairing and operating the turnpike and (b) the principal of and the interest on such bonds as the same shall become due and payable, and to create reserves for such purposes. Such tolls shall not be subject to supervision or regulation by any department, division, commission, board, bureau or agency of the commonwealth or any political subdivision thereof. The tolls and all other revenues derived from the turnpike, except such part thereof as may be necessary to pay such cost of maintenance, repair and operation and to provide such reserves therefor as may be provided for in the resolution authorizing the issuance of such bonds or in the trust agreement securing the same, shall be set aside at such regular intervals as may be provided in such resolution or such trust agreement in a sinking fund which is hereby pledged to, and charged with, the payment of the principal of and the interest on such bonds as the same shall become due, and the redemption price or the purchase price of bonds retired by call or purchase as therein provided. Such pledge shall be valid and binding from the time when the pledge is made; the tolls or other revenues or other moneys so pledged and thereafter received by the Authority shall immediately be subject to the lien of such pledge without any physical delivery thereof or further act, and the lien of any such pledge shall be valid and binding as against all parties having claims of any kind in tort, contract or otherwise against the Authority, irrespective of whether such parties have notice thereof. Neither the resolution nor any trust agreement by which a pledge is created need be filed or recorded except in the records of the Authority. The use and disposition of moneys to the credit of such sinking fund shall be subject to the provisions of the resolutions authorizing the issuance of such bonds or of such trust agreement. Except as may otherwise be provided in such resolution or such trust agreement, such sinking fund shall be a fund for all such bonds without distinction or priority of one over another.

History—
1952, 354, § 10; 1958, 384, § 4.

§ 11.   Trust Funds.

All moneys received pursuant to the authority of this act, whether as proceeds from the sale of bonds or as revenues, shall be deemed to be trust funds to be held and applied solely as provided in this act. The resolution authorizing the bonds or the trust agreement securing such bonds shall provide that any officer with whom, or any bank or trust company with which, such moneys shall be deposited shall act as trustee of such moneys and shall hold and apply the same for the purposes hereof, subject to such regulations as this act and such resolution or trust agreement may provide.

History—
1952, 354, § 11.

§ 12.   Remedies.

Any holder of bonds issued under the provisions of this act or any of the coupons appertaining thereto, and the trustee under any trust agreement, except to the extent the rights herein given may be restricted by such trust agreement, may, either at law or in equity, by suit, action, mandamus or other proceeding, protect and enforce any and all rights under the laws of the commonwealth or granted hereunder or under such trust agreement or resolution authorizing the issuance of such bonds, and may enforce and compel the performance of all duties required by this act or by such trust agreement or resolution to be performed by the Authority or by any officer thereof, including the fixing, charging and collecting of tolls.

History—
1952, 354, § 12.

§ 13.   Exemption from Taxation.

The exercise of the powers granted by this act will be in all respects for the benefit of the people of the commonwealth, for the increase of their commerce and prosperity, and for the improvement of their health and living conditions, and as the operation and maintenance of the turnpike by the Authority will constitute the performance of essential governmental functions, the Authority shall not be required to pay any taxes or assessments upon the turnpike or any property acquired or used by the Authority under the provisions of this act or upon the income therefrom, and the bonds issued under the provisions of this act, their transfer and the income therefrom (including any profit made on the sale thereof), shall at all times be free from taxation within the commonwealth.

§ 14.   Bonds Eligible for Investment.

Bonds issued by the Authority under the provisions of this act are hereby made securities in which all public officers and public bodies of the commonwealth and its political subdivisions, all insurance companies, and savings banks, co-operative banks and trust companies in their banking departments and within the limits set by section fourteen of chapter one hundred and sixty-seven E of the General Laws, banking associations, investment companies, executors, trustees and other fiduciaries, and all other persons whatsoever who are now or may hereafter be authorized to invest in bonds or other obligations of a similar nature, may properly and legally invest funds, including capital in their control or belonging to them, and such bonds are hereby made obligations which may properly and legally be made eligible for the investment of savings deposits and the income thereof in the manner provided by section fifteen B of chapter one hundred and sixty-seven of the General Laws. Such bonds are hereby made securities which may properly and legally be deposited with and received by any state or municipal officer or any agency or political subdivision of the commonwealth for any purpose for which the deposit of bonds or other obligations of the commonwealth is now or may here after be authorized by law.

History—
1952, 354, § 14; 1969, 688, § 3; 1983, 371, § 98; 1986, 92.

Editorial Note—
The 1983 amendment, while purporting to replace the entire first sentence, in the opinion of the editor, revises just the first part of said sentence, adding the words "and savings banks, co-operative banks and", deleting the word "commercial" from before the word "department" and inserting in place thereof the word "banking", and changing the initial statutory reference therein from "section fifty-four of chapter one hundred and seventy-two" to "section fourteen of chapter one hundred and sixty-seven E".

The 1986 amendment replaced the first sentence, adding, after "sixty-seven E of the General Laws," all the language beginning with "banking associations, investment companies, executors, . . ."

Cross References—
Investments authorized for savings banks, see ALM GL c 167F, § 2.

§ 15.   Miscellaneous.

The turnpike when constructed and open to traffic shall be maintained and kept in good condition and repair by the Authority. The turnpike shall also be policed and operated by such force of police, toll-takers and other operating employees as the Authority may in its discretion employ.

All private property damaged or destroyed in carrying out the powers granted by this act shall be restored or repaired and placed in its original condition as nearly as practicable, or adequate compensation made therefor, out of funds provided under the authority of this act.

All counties, cities, towns and other political subdivisions and all public agencies and commissions of the commonwealth, notwithstanding any contrary provision of law, are hereby authorized and empowered to lease, lend, grant or convey to the Authority at its request upon such terms and conditions as the proper authorities of such counties, cities, towns, political subdivisions, agencies or commissions of the commonwealth may deem reasonable and fair and without the necessity for any advertisement, order of court or other action or formality, other than the regular and formal action of the authorities concerned, any real property which may be necessary or convenient to the effectuation of the authorized purposes of the Authority, including public roads and other real property already devoted to public use.

Until the turnpike shall have become a part of the state highway system under the provisions of section seventeen of this act, the Authority shall be liable to any person sustaining bodily injury or damage in his property by reason of a defect or want of repair therein or thereupon to the same extent as though the turnpike were a way within the meaning of sections fifteen, eighteen and nineteen of chapter eighty-four of the General Laws, and shall be liable for the death of any person caused by such defect or want of repair to the same extent as is provided in chapter two hundred and twenty-nine of the General Laws. Any notice of such injury, damage or death required by law shall be given to any member of the Authority or to the secretary-treasurer.

Until the turnpike shall have become a part of the state highway system, it shall be deemed to be a way within the meaning and purport of sections two, four A, four B and five of chapter eighty-nine of the General Laws, and sections three A, three B, three C, six, seven, nine, ten, eleven, twelve, thirteen, fourteen, fourteen B, sixteen, the first sentence of section seventeen, section twenty, the first sentence of section twenty-one, sections twenty-three, twenty-four, twenty-five, twenty-six and thirty-four J of chapter ninety of the General Laws.

Any operator of a vehicle using the turnpike who refuses to pay the toll prescribed by the Authority, or who evades or attempts to evade payment of the toll prescribed by the Authority, may be arrested without a warrant.

Any person damaged in his property by the exercise of any of the powers granted by this act may recover his damages from the Authority under chapter seventy-nine of the General Laws.

On or before the first day of April in each year, the Authority shall make an annual report of its activities for the preceding calendar year to the governor and to the general court. Each such report shall set forth a complete operating and financial statement covering its operations during the year. The Authority shall cause an audit of its books and accounts to be made at least once in each year by certified public accountants, and the cost thereof may be treated as a part of the cost of construction or operation of the turnpike. Such audits shall be deemed to be public records within the meaning of chapter sixty-six of the General Laws.

Notwithstanding the provisions of chapters one hundred and thirty-four and one hundred and forty-seven of the General Laws, if money, goods or other property which has been abandoned, mislaid or lost on the premises of the Massachusetts Turnpike Authority comes into the possession of said Authority and remains unclaimed in its possession for a period of one hundred and twenty days, the Authority may sell the same, excepting money so unclaimed, at public auction after notice of such sale has been published for three successive weeks in a newspaper published in the city or town where such sale is to take place. The net proceeds of such sale, after deducting the cost of storage and the expenses of the sale, and all money so unclaimed, shall be paid into and become the property of the Authority. If, in the opinion of the Authority any property so abandoned, mislaid or lost which comes into the possession of the Authority and remains unclaimed in its possession for a period of one hundred and twenty days, is of the value of three dollars or less, the Authority may donate the same to a charitable organization.

Whoever, for the purpose of soliciting a ride on the turnpike, displays a sign, signals a moving vehicle, causes the stopping of a vehicle, or stands on property of the Authority in view of a ramp or roadway of the turnpike may be arrested without a warrant and shall be punished by a fine of not more than fifty dollars.

History—

1952, 354, § 15; 1955, 653, § 2; 1957, 292; 1958, 290; 1966, 270, § 1; 1968, 280, § 1; 1984, 47, § 1.

Editorial Note—

The 1984 amendment rewrote the eighth paragraph changing from the first day of March to the first day of April the time at which the Authority shall make its annual report of its activities.

§ 15A.   Utilization of Air Rights.

In addition to any other power the Authority may have to make leases, the Authority may, on behalf of itself and the commonwealth, lease at one time, or from time to time for a term or terms not to exceed ninety-nine years, upon such terms and conditions as the Authority in its discretion deems advisable, air rights over land owned or held by the Authority in connection with the Massachusetts Turnpike, including the Boston Extension thereof, including rights for support, access, utilities, light and air, for such nonturnpike purposes as, in the opinion of the Authority, will not impair the construction, full use, safety, maintenance, repair, operation or revenues of the Massachusetts Turnpike; provided, however, that any such lease for a period of forty years or more shall be subject to the approval of the governor. Any lease granted under this section may, with the consent of the Authority, be assigned, pledged or mortgaged and the lien of such pledge or mortgage may be foreclosed by appropriate action. The proceeds from any such lease, after payment of all expenses in connection therewith, shall, before the Massachusetts Turnpike becomes part of the state highway system in accordance with section seventeen, be applied toward the cost of operation of the turnpike or be deposited to the credit of the sinking fund for the appropriate Turnpike Revenue Bonds issued under the provisions of this act, and thereafter be paid into the treasury of the commonwealth for credit to the Highway Fund.

Use of air rights leased under this section respecting land within the territorial limits of the city of Boston and the construction and occupancy of buildings or other things erected or affixed pursuant to any such lease shall be subject to the provisions of the state building code relative to the safety of persons in buildings, but shall not be subject to any other building, fire, garage, health or zoning law or any building, fire, garage, health or zoning ordinance, rule or regulation applicable in the city of Boston. The Authority shall include in any lease of such air rights a requirement that buildings or other things shall be erected or affixed pursuant to such lease in accordance with the provisions of the National Building Code, Edition of 1955 (as amended in December, 1957 and January, 1963) and such other requirements as the Authority deems necessary or advisable to promote the public health, convenience and the safety of persons and property.

The Authority shall not lease any air rights in a particular location unless it shall find that the construction and use of buildings or other things to be erected or affixed pursuant to any such lease will be in no way detrimental to the maintenance, use and operation of the Massachusetts Turnpike, including the Boston Extension; and, in the city of Boston, unless the Authority shall also find, after consultation with the mayor, that the construction and use of such buildings or other things will preserve and increase the amenities of the community.

The construction or occupancy of any building, or other thing erected or affixed under any lease under this section of air rights respecting land outside the territorial limits of the city of Boston shall be subject to the building, fire, garage, health or zoning laws and the building, fire, garage, health and zoning ordinances, by-laws, rules and regulations applicable in the city or town in which such building or other thing is located.

A copy of all leases granted by the Authority under this section, attested by the secretary-treasurer, shall be filed by the Authority with the governor and with the mayor or chairman of the board of selectmen of the city or town concerned and such leases shall be deemed to be public records within the meaning of chapter sixty-six of the General Laws.

Neither such air rights nor any buildings or other things erected or affixed pursuant to any such lease nor the proceeds from any such lease shall be taxed or assessed to the Authority under any general or special law; but buildings and other things erected or affixed pursuant to any such lease shall be taxed to the lessee thereof or his assigns in the same manner and to the same extent as if such lessee or his assigns were the owners of the land in fee; provided, that no part of the value of the land shall be included in any such assessment; and provided, further, that payment of any such taxes shall not be enforced by any lien upon or sale or taking of said land except that the leasehold estate may be sold or taken by the collector of taxes of the city or town in which the real estate is situated for the non-payment of any tax assessed as aforesaid in the manner provided by law for the sale or taking of real estate for non-payment of local taxes. Said collector shall have for the collection of taxes assessed under this section all other remedies provided by the General Laws for the collection of taxes by collectors of cities and towns.

The Authority shall include in any lease of such air rights a provision whereby the lessee agrees, in the event that the foregoing tax provision is determined by any court of competent jurisdiction to be inapplicable, to pay annually to the city or town in which the building or other thing leased is located, a sum of money in lieu of taxes which would otherwise be assessed for such year.

History—
    1963, 505, § 1; 1965, 446, § 1; 1968, 528; 1969, 688, § 4; 1970, 774, §§ 1, 2; 1972, 802, § 65.

State building code, generally, see ALM GL c 143 §§ 1 et seq.

Savings bank mortgage loans on leasehold interests on air rights over land held by Massachusetts Turnpike Authority, see ALM GL c 167E § 2.

§ 15B.   Utilization of Excess Land.

In addition to any other power the Authority may have to make leases, the Authority may on behalf of itself and the commonwealth, for nonturnpike purposes, lease at one time, or from time to time for a term or terms not to exceed ninety-nine years, upon such terms and conditions as the Authority in its discretion deems advisable, land owned by the Authority and no longer required for the maintenance, repair or operation of the Massachusetts Turnpike, including the Boston Extension; provided, however, that any such lease for a period of forty years or more shall be subject to the approval of the governor. Any lease granted under this section may, with the consent of the Authority, be assigned, pledged or mortgaged and the lien of such pledge or mortgage may be foreclosed by appropriate action. The proceeds from any such lease, after payment of all expenses in connection therewith, shall, before the Massachusetts Turnpike becomes part of the state highway system in accordance with section seventeen, be applied by the Authority in accordance with the appropriate trust agreement applicable to the leased land and thereafter be paid into the treasury of the commonwealth for credit to the Highway Fund.

The construction or occupancy of any building or other thing erected or affixed under any lease of land under this section shall be subject to the building, fire and zoning laws, ordinances or by-laws applicable in the city or town where such building or other thing is located.

A copy of all leases granted by the Authority under this section, attested by its secretary-treasurer, shall be filed by the Authority with the governor and with the mayor or chairman of the board of selectmen of the city or town concerned and such leases shall be deemed to be public records within the meaning of chapter sixty-six of the General Laws.

Neither such land nor any buildings or other things erected or affixed pursuant to any such lease nor the proceeds from any such lease shall be taxed or assessed to the Authority under any general or special law; but such land and buildings and other things erected or affixed pursuant to any such lease shall be taxed to the lessee thereof or his assigns in the same manner and to the same extent as if such lessee or his assigns were the owners of the land in fee; this tax provision shall apply to any project constructed pursuant to chapter 21D of the General Laws provided, that payment of any such taxes shall not be enforced by any lien upon or sale or taking of said land except that the leasehold estate may be sold or taken by the collector of taxes of the city or town in which the land is situated for the nonpayment of any tax assessed as aforesaid in the manner provided by law for the sale or taking of real estate for nonpayment of local taxes. Said collector shall have for the collection of taxes assessed under this section all other remedies provided by the General Laws for the collection of taxes by collectors of cities and towns.

The Authority shall include in any lease of such land a provision whereby the lessee agrees, in the event that the foregoing tax provision is determined by any court of competent jurisdiction to be inapplicable, to pay annually to the city or town in which such leased land is located a sum of money in lieu of taxes which would otherwise be assessed for such year.

History—
1970, 773, § 1; 1983, 540, § 1.

Editorial Note—
The 1983 amendment, in the fourth paragraph, inserted the words "this tax provision shall apply to any project constructed pursuant to chapter 21D of the General Laws" after the word "fee"; in the opinion of the editor, these added words, as inserted at the designated location, are grammatically incorrect and probably should constitute a separate sentence.

Cross References—
Trust company's mortgage loans on leasehold interest on land held by Massachusetts Turnpike Authority, see ALM GL c 167E § 2.

§ 15C.   Overweight Vehicles.

No motor vehicle, trailer, semi-trailer or semi-trailer unit, hereinafter in this section called a motor vehicle, shall be operated on the Massachusetts Turnpike, including the Boston extension thereof, hereinafter in this section called the turnpike, nor shall the owner or bailee thereof require or permit such operation when the gross weight of such motor vehicle exceeds the weight provided in the rules and regulations adopted by the Authority pursuant to paragraph (i) of section five or that specified in a special hauling permit issued by the Authority for such motor vehicle pursuant to Appendix B of said rules and regulations, whichever is greater; nor shall any person load or cause to be loaded such motor vehicle in excess of such weights; provided, however, that the authority shall not adopt or enforce any rule or regulation which prohibits any motor vehicle from traveling on the turnpike without a permit if said motor vehicle may travel on a public way of the commonwealth, without a permit, under the provisions of section nineteen A of chapter ninety of the General Laws, or which prohibits the issuance of a permit by the Authority for travel on the turnpike by a motor vehicle if said motor vehicle may travel on a public way of the commonwealth with a permit under the provisions of section thirty A of chapter eighty-five of the General Laws.

In the weighing of any motor vehicle under this section, portable scales may be used, provided that such scales have been approved by the director of standards under section twenty-nine of chapter ninety-eight of the General Laws; and provided, further, that such scales shall be inspected at least once each year by the director of standards or his inspectors.

Enforcement of this section shall be by members of the division of state police assigned to the Authority who have been appointed as weighers and measurers of motor vehicles and of the loads of such motor vehicles pursuant to section eighty-seven A of chapter forty-one of the General Laws. In any prosecution for a violation of this section, a signed certificate on oath of a member of the division of state police assigned and appointed as a weigher and measurer of motor vehicles in accordance with this paragraph shall be admissible in evidence without further proof, and shall constitute prima facie evidence of the weight of the motor vehicle described in such certificate. Said certificate shall be in such form as the registrar of motor vehicles shall prescribe pursuant to section nineteen A of chapter ninety of the General Laws and shall be signed and sworn to by a member of the division of state police assigned and appointed as a weigher and measurer of motor vehicles in accordance with this paragraph and present at the weighing of such motor vehicle, and the court shall take judicial notice of the signature of such person and that he is so assigned and appointed.

In any claim for bodily injuries including death or for damage to property arising out of such weighing, any member of the division of the state police, assigned and appointed as a weigher and measurer of motor vehicles in accordance with the preceding paragraph, to enforce the provisions of this section may file a written request with the Authority that it defend him against such claim and the Authority shall indemnify such member of the division of state police from personal expenses or damages incurred and arising out of such claim, provided, that the defense or settlement of such claim shall have been made by the resident counsel of the Authority, by an attorney retained for such purpose by the Authority, or by an attorney provided by an insurer obligated under the terms of a policy of insurance to defend against such claims.

Any person convicted of a violation of this section shall be punished by a fine of not less than thirty dollars for each one thousand pounds of weight or fraction thereof by which the gross weight of the motor vehicle as operated, exceeds the weight provided in the rules and regulations adopted by the Authority pursuant to paragraph (i) of section five or that specified in a special hauling permit issued by the Authority for such motor vehicle pursuant to Appendix B of said rules and regulations, whichever is greater; provided, however, that if the total of such excess weight is greater than ten thousand pounds, the fine shall be not less than sixty dollars for each one thousand pounds or faction thereof over said ten thousand pounds.

Any person convicted of a violation of the provisions of the first sentence of section seventeen of chapter ninety of the General Laws while operating a vehicle which is also in violation of the first paragraph of this section shall be punished by a fine of not more than fifty dollars for a first offense nor less than fifty nor more than seventy-five dollars for a second offense committed in any twelve month period, and not less than seventy-five nor more than one hundred and fifty dollars for subsequent offenses committed in any twelve month period, and complaints of such violations shall not be placed on file by the court.

History—
1979, 377, § 2.

§ 15D. Deferred Compensation.

The secretary-treasurer, on behalf of the Authority, may contract with an employee to defer a portion of that employee's compensation and may, for the purpose of funding a deferred compensation program for said employee, established in accordance with the U.S. Internal Revenue Code, (the "Code"), invest the deferred portion of the employee's compensation in a life insurance or annuity contract, mutual fund, or bank investment trust. The secretary-treasurer shall, before making any such investment, solicit bids from insurance companies authorized to conduct business within the commonwealth pursuant to chapter one hundred and seventy-five of the General Laws, mutual fund managers and banks, which bids shall be sealed and opened at a time and place designated by the secretary-treasurer. Any bid submitted by an insurance company, mutual fund or bank investment trust to fund the deferred compensation program, where applicable, shall clearly indicate the interest rate which shall be paid on the deferred funds, any commissions which will be paid to salesmen, any load imposed for the purpose of administering the funds, mortality projections, expected

170

payouts, tax implications for participating employees, and such other information as the secretary-treasurer may require. Any contract entered into between an employee and the Authority pursuant to this section shall include all such information in terms the employee can reasonably be expected to understand.

As used in this section, the word "employee" shall have the same meaning as "employee" in section one of chapter thirty-two of the General Laws and shall also include consultants and independent contractors who are natural persons paid by the Authority.

An employee may defer compensation so long as such deferral is the lesser of seven thousand five hundred dollars or thirty-three and one-third per cent of his includible compensation for a taxable year; except that for one or more of the last three taxable years ending before he attains normal retirement age, an employee may defer the lesser of fifteen thousand dollars or the sum of (1) seven thousand five hundred dollars or thirty-three and one-third per cent of his includible compensation for such year, plus (2) a sum not more than the total deferrable compensation for prior taxable years that had not in fact been deferred in such years.

Such deferred compensation program shall be in addition to, and not part of, the retirement or pension system as provided under said chapter thirty-two and any other benefit program provided by law for such employee. Any compensation deferred under such program shall continue to be included as regular compensation, as defined in section one of said chapter thirty-two, for the purpose of computing the retirement and pension benefits earned by any such employee, but any compensation so deferred shall not be included in the computation of any taxes withheld on behalf of any such employee.

History—
1980, 176; 1981, 731, § 5.

Editorial Note—
The 1981 amendment rewrote this section making numerous changes, including the addition, in the first sentence, after the phrase "for the purpose of funding a deferred compensation program for said employee", of the phrase "established in accordance with the US Internal Revenue Code", and also a change in the amount which may be invested from an amount not to exceed the total annual salary or compensation under the existing salary schedule or classification plan to the less of $7,500 or 33$^{1}/_{3}$ percent of the employee's compensation for any taxable year, except that for one or more of the last 3 taxable years ending before the employee attains normal retirement age under the plan, he may defer the lesser of $15,000 of the sum of (1) $7,500 or 33$^{1}/_{3}$ percent of his compensation, plus (2) a sum not more than the total deferrable compensation for prior taxable years that had not in fact been deferred in such years.

§ 15E.　Deferred Compensation Contracts Authorized for Funding Individual Retirement Accounts.

The secretary-treasurer on behalf of the Authority, may contract with an employee to make contributions for and in the name of such employee, from amounts otherwise payable to the employee as current compensation, to an Individual Retirement Account ("IRA") by such employee established in accordance with the U.S. Internal Revenue Code, (the "Code"). The participating employee may invest that portion of his income so contributed to an IRA in an annuity contract, mutual fund, bank investment trust or other investment authorized by the Code. Before making such deduction, the secretary-treasurer shall be required to solicit bids from insurance companies authorized to conduct business within the commonwealth pursuant to chapter one hundred and seventy-five of the General Laws, mutual fund managers, and banks which bids shall be sealed, and opened at a time and place designated by the secretary-treasurer. Any bid submitted by an insurance company, mutual fund, or bank investment trust seeking investment of the IRA contribution shall, where applicable, clearly indicate the interest rate which shall be paid on the invested funds, any commissions which will be paid to the salesmen, any load imposed for the purpose of administering the funds, expected payouts, tax implications for participating employees and such other information as the secretary-treasurer may require. Upon the secretary-treasurer's determining which provider offers the product or products most beneficial to the employee in each category for which bids were solicited, the secretary-treasurer may offer such employee the opportunity to establish an IRA with one or more such providers. The employee who wishes to invest his IRA funds with any such provider, or combination of providers, may authorize the secretary-treasurer to deduct from amounts otherwise payable to the employee, at one time or on a periodic basis, amounts to be paid into the employee's IRA. If the employee so elects, the secretary-treasurer shall pay to the providers the amount designated by the employee, in the name of the employee, to the employee's IRA. Amounts so paid to the providers for the employee's IRA account shall belong exclusively to the employee. Except as otherwise provided herein, the secretary-treasurer may restrict an employee's right to contract to have contributions made to an IRA through deductions and payments by the secretary-treasurer, to those providers selected as the result of the competitive bidding process outlined herein, but the authority conferred upon the secretary-treasurer shall not be construed to restrict or limit the right of any employee to establish one or more IRAs with such banks, insurance companies, or similar authorized institutions as the employee may choose in any manner other than through an authorized deduction by the secretary-treasurer of a portion of the employees compensation as outlined herein. Any contract entered into between an employee and the Authority pursuant to this section shall include all information in terms the employee can reasonably be expected to understand.

As used in this section the word "employee" shall have the same meaning as "employee" in section one of chapter thirty-two of the General Laws and shall also include consultants and independent contractors who are natural persons paid by the Authority.

An employee may contribute a portion of his compensation to an IRA under the program outlined herein so long as such contribution, for an employee who is single, is the lesser of two thousand dollars or one hundred per cent of his compensation for a taxable year, and, for an employee who is married, the contribution is the lesser of two thousand two hundred and fifty dollars or one hundred per cent of his compensation for a taxable year. If an employee has any compensation deferred under a deferred compensation plan for employees of the authority, if one is established by the treasurer under section fifteen D, then the aggregate amount of such deferred compensation deduction and amounts contributed to such employee's IRA shall not exceed the limits imposed upon such combined deduction and contribution by the Code.

Notwithstanding any provisions to the contrary, the secretary-treasurer shall not be required to solicit bids to invest the contributed portion of an employee's income into the employee's IRA provided: (a) the secretary-treasurer is authorized by the employee to pay that portion of the employee's compensation into the employee's IRA in the same investment products as provided through a deferred compensation or IRA plan for employees of the commonwealth administered by the state treasurer, or a deferred compensation plan for employees of the Authority administered by the secretary-treasurer, provided such plan resulted from the solicitation of bids in accordance with bidding requirements comparable to those required under this section; or (b) the secretary-treasurer is authorized by the employee to pay that portion of the employee's compensation into the employee's IRA in the investment products offered pursuant to a deferred compensation or IRA plan developed through a competitive selection process, provided that such plan resulted from the solicitation of bids by a group of any combination of three or more city, town, county or public authority treasurers acting as a "Common Group" for purposes of soliciting such proposals in accordance with bidding requirements comparable to those required under this section.

Such IRA plan shall be in addition to and not a part of the retirement program or pension system as provided under said chapter thirty-two and any other benefit program provided by law for such employee. Any compensation contributed by the employee to his IRA under such a plan shall continue to be included as regular compensation, as defined in section one of said chapter thirty-two, for the purpose of computing the retirement and pension benefits earned by any such employee, but any compensation so contributed shall not be included in the computation of federal taxes but shall be included in the computation of state taxes withheld on behalf of any such employee.

History—
1981, 731, § 5.

§ 16.   Turnpike Revenue Refunding Bonds.

The Authority is hereby authorized to provide by resolution for the issuance of turnpike revenue refunding bonds of the Authority for the purpose of refunding any bonds then outstanding which shall have been issued under the provisions of this act, including the payment of any redemption premium thereon and any interest accrued or to accrue to the date of redemption of such bonds, and, if deemed advisable by the Authority, for the additional purpose of constructing any additional portion or portions of the turnpike or improvements, extensions, or enlargements thereof. The issuance of such bonds, the maturities and other details thereof, the rights of the holders thereof, and the rights, duties and obligations of the Authority in respect of the same, shall be governed by the provisions of this act in so far as the same may be applicable. The issuance of turnpike revenue bonds or turnpike revenue refunding bonds under the provisions of this act need not comply with the requirements of any other law applicable to the issuance of bonds.

History—
1952, 354, § 16.

§ 17.   Transfer to Commonwealth.

When the last of the following to occur, namely: (a) all bonds issued under the provisions of this act and the interest thereon shall have been paid or a sufficient amount for the payment of all such bonds and the interest thereon to the maturity thereof shall have been set aside in trust for the benefit of the bondholders, (b) the tunnels owned and operated by the authority under and pursuant to Chapter 598 of the acts of 1958 have become a part of the state highway system pursuant to section 16 of said chapter 598, and (c) the Authority has contributed to the pension and expense funds of the Massachusetts Turnpike Authority employees' retirement system established under sections 1 to 28 inclusive of chapter 32 of the General Laws amounts sufficient, in the opinion of the actuary as defined in section 1 of said chapter 32, to cause the amounts then on deposit in said funds to be adequate to provide benefits from said system to persons then and thereafter entitled thereto, as determined under and pursuant to said chapter 32, and to pay or provide for the payment of all future expenses of administration of said system, the turnpike, if then in good condition and repair to the satisfaction of the state department of public works, shall become a part of the state highway system and shall thereafter be maintained and operated by said department free of tolls as may be provided by law, and thereupon the Authority shall be dissolved, all remaining funds of the Authority shall be paid into the treasury of the commonwealth for the credit of the Highway Fund and all machinery, equipment and other property belonging to the Authority shall be vested in the commonwealth and delivered to the state department of public works.

History—

1952, 354, § 17; 1978, 566, § 1.

Editorial Note—

Sections §§ 2–6 of the 1978 amending act, entitled "An act providing for the funding of the retirement system of the Massachusetts Turnpike Authority" provide as follow:

SECTION 2. Anything to the contrary in section 22 of said chapter 32 notwithstanding, the amount to be paid by the Massachusetts Turnpike Authority for any fiscal year for the pension fund of the Massachusetts Turnpike Authority employees' retirement system shall be the sum of (a) the normal pension cost, as hereinafter defined, incurred by the Authority for that year plus (b) not less than the following percentages of the unfunded past service liability of the Authority calculated in the amount of twenty-one million four hundred eighty-seven thousand and seven hundred dollars as of December thirty-first, nineteen hundred and seventy-seven: for the years nineteen hundred and seventy-nine through nineteen hundred and eighty-three, twenty-seven per cent; for the years nineteen hundred and eighty-four through nineteen hundred and eighty-eight, fifty-three per cent; for the year nineteen hundred and eighty-nine until the Authority is dissolved, one hundred and thirty-three per cent; provided, however, that the amount paid in the year in which the Authority shall be dissolved shall be an amount which, in the opinion of the actuary, when added to all other amounts theretofore paid for such purpose, shall be sufficient to amortize the unfunded past service liability of the Authority calculated in such year.

For purposes of this section the term "past service liability" of the authority shall mean the excess of the present value of all future pension benefits payable by the Massachusetts Turnpike Authority employees' retirement system as determined under the entry age normal actuarial cost method with frozen initial liability over the present value of all future normal costs. The term "unfunded past service liability" shall mean the past service liability less the assets of the system. The term "normal pension cost" for any year shall mean the amount, as determined under the entry age normal actuarial cost method with frozen initial liability, required to finance pension benefits earned by employees of the Authority during that year as members of the Massachusetts Turnpike Authority employees' retirement system.

Any balance of the pension fund above the past service liability at the close of business on December thirty-first of any year shall be applied to reduce the payments required in subsequent years pursuant to this section.

SECTION 3. In the fiscal period of the Massachusetts Turnpike Authority ending on the date of dissolution of the Authority, the Authority shall pay for the expense fund of the Massachusetts Turnpike Authority employees' retirement system an amount, in addition to all other amounts payable by the Authority in said period for such fund, sufficient in the opinion of the actuary, as defined in section one of chapter thirty-two, when added to the amount then on deposit in said fund and with the proceeds of investment thereof, to pay or provide for the payment of the expenses of administration of said system thereafter to be incurred. This sum shall become a separate account within the expense fund of the Massachusetts State Employee Retirement System.

SECTION 4. The employees of the Massachusetts Turnpike Authority who are members of the Massachusetts Turnpike Authority employees' retirement system on the effective date of the dissolution of the Authority and who do not then transfer to service in a governmental unit in which a contributory retirement system is established under the provisions of sections one to twenty-eight, inclusive, of said chapter thirty-two, or under corresponding provisions of earlier laws or of any special law, shall continue to be members of the Massachusetts Turnpike Authority employees' retirement system and shall then be entitled to apply for and receive retirement allowances from such system in the amounts, upon the terms, subject to the conditions and with all of the related rights provided by and under said chapter thirty-two.

SECTION 5. Effective upon the date of dissolution of the Massachusetts Turnpike Authority (a) the Massachusetts Turnpike Authority employees' retirement system shall continue under the provisions of said chapter thirty-two, (b) the management of the Massachusetts Turnpike Authority employees' retirement system shall be transferred to the state board of retirement provided for in section eighteen of chapter ten of the General Laws which board shall have respect thereto the general powers and duties set forth in subdivision (5) of section twenty of said chapter thirty-two, (c) all data, files, papers and records and other materials of the retirement board provided for in paragraph (4-1/2) (b) of said section twenty shall be transferred to and held by the state board of retirement, (d) the funds of the Massachusetts Turnpike Authority employees' retirement system in the custody of the secretary-treasurer of the Authority and treasurer-custodian of the retirement system shall be transferred to the state treasurer who shall thereafter be and perform the duties of the treasurer-custodian of such funds, which shall be held, administered, invested and maintained as an account separate and apart from all other funds and accounts in his custody or possession as treasurer-custodian of any other retirement system, and (e) the retirement board provided for in said paragraph (41/2) (b) shall be abolished; provided, however, that the members and officers thereof shall continue to be authorized to do all such things and take all such action as may be necessary or desirable to be done or taken by them to effectuate the transfers to be made pursuant to this section.

SECTION 6. Effective upon the date of dissolution of the Massachusetts Turnpike Authority, said chapter thirty-two shall be amended as follows:

(1) Section 11 of subdivision (3) shall be amended by striking out the second paragraph of subdivision (3) and inserting in place thereof the following:- No check which has been issued by the state treasurer in payment of any obligation of the state board of retirement, the teachers' retirement board or the Massachusetts Turnpike Authority employees' retirement system under authority of sections 1 to 28, inclusive, or which is issued by any county, city or town treasurer or by the secretary-treasurer of the Massachusetts Turnpike Authority or by the treasurer of Massachusetts Housing Finance Agency in payment of any obligation of any retirement system established under this chapter shall be payable later than six years after its date, and the obligation of the commonwealth or of any county, city, town, the Massachusetts Turnpike Authority or the Massachusetts Housing Finance Agency represented by any such check shall not be enforceable if such check is not presented for payment within such period. The amount represented by such check shall thereupon be transferred to the pension fund of the retirement system under whose authority the check was originally issued, or its successor in interest.

(2) Section 20 shall be amended by striking out paragraphs (4½) (b), (4¹ /2) (c), (4¹ /2) (d), (4¹ /2) (e) and (4¹ /2) (f) thereof.

(3) Section 20 shall be further amended by striking out the third and sixth sentences of paragraph (5) (i) and by inserting in place of such third sentence the following:- The state retirement board shall file a copy of its report, which shall include the Massachusetts Turnpike Authority employees' retirement system as a separate item, with the governor, and with the state treasurer for publication in his annual report.

(4) Section 21 shall be amended by striking out of the third sentence of paragraph (1) (c) the words:— the Massachusetts Turnpike Authority.

(5) Section 21 shall be further amended by striking out the fourth sentence of subdivision (2) and inserting in place thereof the following:— The pension fund of the Massachusetts Turnpike Authority employees' retirement system shall be charged with, and the treasurer-custodian thereof shall pay therefrom to the commonwealth, such proportion of such expenses attributable to such system as shall be determined just and proper by the commissioner, which sum shall be paid to the state treasurer upon notice from the commissioner.

(6) Section 22 shall be further amended by striking out paragraph (7) (e).

(7) Section 23 shall be amended by striking out the first sentence of paragraph (1) (a) and inserting in place thereof the following:— There shall be an unpaid investment committee which shall have general supervision of the investment and reinvestment of the funds of the state employees' retirement system, the funds of the teachers' retirement system and the funds of the Massachusetts Turnpike Authority employees' retirement system.

(8) Section 23 shall be further amended by striking out of the heading of subdivision (2) the words "the Massachusetts Turnpike Authority" and by striking out of the first sentence of paragraph (2) (a) the words "the secretary-treasurer of the Massachusetts Turnpike Authority" and the words "the Massachusetts Turnpike Authority."

(9) Section 24 shall be amended by striking out of the first sentence of subdivision (1) the words "the Massachusetts Turnpike Authority."

(10) Section 25 shall be amended by striking out subdivision (4) and inserting in place thereof the following:— The payment of all annuities, pensions, retirement allowances and refunds of accumulated total deductions and of any other benefits granted under the provisions of sections 1 to 28, inclusive, are hereby made obligations of the commonwealth in the case of any such payments from funds of the state employees' retirement system, of the teachers' retirement system or of the Massachusetts Turnpike Authority employees' retirement system and obligations of the governmental unit in which the system is established in the case of payments from funds of any system established in any county, city or town or in the Massachusetts Bay Transportation Authority or the Massachusetts Housing Finance Agency.

Cross References—

Retirement systems and pensions, see ALM GL c 32 §§ 1 et seq.

Reimbursement for tax paid on fuel used for other than highway operation, see ALM GL c 64A 7; 64E, § 5.

§ 17A.   Authority to Reimburse Commonwealth for Retirement Costs Associated with Department of Public Safety Employees; Rate to be Set by Commissioner of Administration.

The Authority is hereby authorized and directed to reimburse the commonwealth for the amount of retirement costs incurred by the commonwealth on behalf of employees of the department of public safety for the time such employees are assigned by the commissioner of said department to duty with the Authority. Said amount shall be the retirement cost portion of the cost of fringe benefits as determined by the commissioner of administration pursuant to section six B of chapter twenty-nine of the General Laws. Said amount shall be reimbursed annually to the commonwealth for fiscal years beginning after June thirtieth, nineteen hundred and eighty-seven.

History—

1987, 199, § 145.

§ 18.   Preliminary Expenses.

To provide for the preliminary expenses of the Authority in carrying out the provisions of this act the sum of five hundred thousand dollars is hereby appropriated from the Highway Fund, which sum shall be paid to the Authority and, simultaneously with the delivery of the bonds, the sum so paid shall be reimbursed by the Authority to the commonwealth for the credit of the Highway Fund out of the proceeds of any bonds which may be issued by the Authority under the provisions of this act.

The Authority is hereby authorized and directed to make such surveys and studies of the turnpike as may be necessary to effect the financing authorized by this act at the earliest practicable time, and for this purpose to employ such consulting engineers, traffic engineers, legal and financial experts and such other employees and agents as it may deem necessary. To effect the purposes of this act the state department of public works shall make available to the Authority all data in the possession of the department which may be useful to the Authority in making such surveys and studies and the department may furnish such assistance in making investigations and in preparing designs for the turnpike project as may be agreed upon between the department and the Authority, the cost of such surveys and expenses incurred by the department to be paid by the Authority.

History—
1952, 354, § 18.

§ 19.   Act Liberally Construed.

This act, being necessary for the welfare of the commonwealth and its inhabitants, shall be liberally construed to effect the purposes thereof.

History—
1952, 354, § 19.

§ 20.   Constitutional Construction.

The provisions of this act are severable, and if any of its provisions shall be held unconstitutional by any court of competent jurisdiction, the decision of such court shall not affect or impair any of the remaining provisions.

History—
1952, 354, § 20.

§ 21.   Inconsistent Laws Inapplicable.

All other general or special laws, or parts thereof, inconsistent herewith are hereby declared to be inapplicable to the provisions of this act.

History—
1952, 354, § 21.

CHAPTER S77

Woods Hole, Martha's Vineyard and Nantucket
Steamship Authority

(Acts 1960, Ch. 701)

> **Auto-Cite®:** Cases and annotations referred to herein can be further researched through the Auto-Cite® computer-assisted research service. Use Auto-Cite to check citations for form, parallel references, prior and later history, and annotation references.

§ 1.   The Woods Hole, Martha's Vineyard and Nantucket Steamship Line.

As used in this act the word "Authority" unless the context shall indicate another or different meaning or intent, shall mean the Woods Hole, Martha's Vineyard and Nantucket Steamship Authority created by section three of this act, or if said Authority shall be abolished, the board, body or commission succeeding to the principal functions thereof, or to whom the powers given by this act to the Authority shall be given by law.

In order to provide adequate transportation of persons and necessaries of life for the islands of Nantucket and Martha's Vineyard, the Authority is hereby authorized and empowered to purchase, construct, maintain and operate necessary vessels, docks, wharves, other vessels, equipment, furniture and supplies and to issue its revenue bonds payable solely from revenues, or funds as hereinafter authorized in section nine of this act.

History—
1960, 701, § 1.

§ 2.   Credit of the Commonwealth not Pledged.

Steamship bonds issued under the provisions of this act shall not be deemed to constitute a debt of the commonwealth, nor a pledge of the faith and credit of the commonwealth, but the bonds shall be payable solely from the funds herein provided therefor. All such bonds shall contain on the face thereof a statement to the effect that neither the Authority nor the commonwealth shall be obligated to pay the same, or the interest thereon except as herein provided, and that the faith and credit of the commonwealth are not pledged to the payment of the principal or of the interest on such bonds.

History—
1960, 701, § 2.

§ 3.   The Woods Hole, Martha's Vineyard and Nantucket Steamship Authority.

There is hereby created a body corporate to be known as the Woods

Hole, Martha's Vineyard and Nantucket Steamship Authority, which shall be deemed to be a public instrumentality for the purpose of this act, and by that name the Authority may sue and be sued, plead and be impleaded, contract and be contracted with, and shall have an official seal and may alter the same at pleasure.

The Woods Hole, Martha's Vineyard and Nantucket Steamship Authority shall consist of four persons to be appointed as follows:— one resident of the town of Nantucket by the selectmen thereof; one resident of the county of Dukes County by the county commissioners thereof; and one resident of the town of Falmouth by the selectmen thereof, each of whom shall serve for a term of three years and until his successor has been appointed and qualified; and one resident of the town of Barnstable by the town council thereof, which shall be a nonvoting member of the authority and who shall serve at the pleasure of said town council. The successor of each member from the town of Nantucket, the county of Dukes County, and the town of Falmouth shall be appointed in a like manner for a like term, except that any person appointed to fill a vacancy shall serve only for the period of the unexpired term. A member from the town of Nantucket, the county of Dukes County or the town of Falmouth may be removed for cause by the selectmen of the town or the commissioners of the county of which he was a resident at the time of his appointment.

The chairmanship of said Authority shall rotate every year in the following order: first, the member from Nantucket; second, the member from the county of Dukes county; and third the member from the town of Falmouth.

The authority shall elect one of the voting members as vice-chairman and as secretary and shall also elect a treasurer who need not be a member of the authority. Two voting members of the authority shall constitute a quorum, and the vote of two members shall be necessary for any action taken by the authority. No vacancy in the membership of the authority shall impair the right of a quorum to exercise all the rights and perform all the duties of the authority. Before the issuance of any steamship bonds under the provisions of this act, each voting member of the authority shall execute a surety bond to the commonwealth with a surety company authorized to transact business in this commonwealth as surety in the penal sum of ten thousand dollars, and the treasurer shall execute such a bond in the penal sum of twenty thousand dollars conditioned upon the faithful performance of the duties of his office. Each surety bond shall be approved by the attorney general and filed in the office of the state secretary. The members of the authority shall serve without compensation. Each member shall be reimbursed for his actual expenses necessarily incurred in the performance of his duties. All expenses incurred in carrying out the provisions of this act shall be paid solely from funds provided under the authority of this act, and no liability or obligation shall be incurred by the authority hereunder beyond the extent to which monies shall have been provided under authority of this act.

History—

1960, 701, § 3; 1991, 33, §§ 102, 103, approved, with emergency preamble, May 10, 1991.

Editorial Note—

The **1991 amendment,** rewrote the second and fourth paragraphs.

Acts 1981, ch. 223, entitled "An act exempting the Woods Hole, Martha's Vineyard and Nantucket Steamship Authority from regulation by the Martha's Vineyard Commission", provides as follows:

Notwithstanding any general or special law to the contrary, the Woods Hole, Martha's Vineyard and Nantucket Steamship Authority, established by chapter seven hundred and one of the acts of nineteen hundred and sixty, its operation, management, any water under its care, control or custody, and all property real and personal shall be exempt from any control or regulation by the Martha's Vineyard Commission established by chapter eight hundred and thirty-one of the acts of nineteen hundred and seventy-seven.

§ 4.   General Grant of Powers.

The Authority is hereby authorized and empowered—

(a) to acquire, maintain, repair and operate a boat line.

(b) To issue bonds of the Authority payable solely from the funds herein provided for such payment for the purpose of paying for replacements and new construction or acquisition of vessels and other facilities required to provide adequate service; the total amount to be outstanding at any one time, including refunding bonds but excluding the bonds to be refunded thereby, not to exceed fifty million dollars.

(c) To fix, from time to time, such rates of fare and charges for service furnished or operated as in the judgment of its members are best adapted to insure sufficient income to meet the cost of the service, as hereinafter defined. Rates so fixed shall be and remain in effect until changed by the Authority unless the department of public utilities shall upon petition and after a public hearing disapprove them. Such disapproval, if any, shall not be retroactive in effect.

The cost of the service shall include (1) operating expenses, (2) taxes, (3) rentals, (4) interest on all indebtedness of the Massachusetts Steamship Lines, Incorporated and the New Bedford, Woods Hole, Martha's Vineyard and Nantucket Steamship Authority, created by section three of chapter five hundred and forty-four of the acts of nineteen hundred and forty-eight, if any, (including amortization of discount or premium) assumed by the Authority and still outstanding, (5) interest and amortization (including amortization of discount or premium) on bonds or notes of the Authority issued under this act, (6) such allowance as the Authority may deem necessary or advisable for depreciation of property and for obsolescence and losses in respect to property sold, destroyed or abandoned, (7) salaries and wages of all officers and employees appointed or employed by or subject to the supervision of the Authority, and, to the extent authorized by the Authority, pensions and retirement allowances, if any, to present and former employees of said Massachusetts Steamship Lines, Incorporated and said New Bedford, Woods Hole, Martha's Vineyard and Nantucket Steamship Authority and employees of the Authority, (8) all other expenditures and charges which are properly chargeable against income or surplus.

(d) To adopt by-laws for the regulation of its affairs and the conduct of its business.

(e) To acquire, hold and dispose of real and personal property, including additional vessels and fixtures, for its corporate purposes; provided, however, that no acquisition of real property or capital improvement in excess of fifty thousand dollars shall be undertaken by the authority within the town of Barnstable unless written notice of said real property acquisition or capital improvement is forwarded by registered mail and subsequently approved by the Barnstable town council, a majority of the members thereof present and voting. Said notice shall include, but not be limited to, a detailed description of the proposed real property acquisition or capital improvement and any other documents relevant or pertinent to said proposal. Failure on the part of said town council to render a vote on said real property acquisition or capital improvement within ninety days of the receipt of said notice shall constitute approval of said town council; to lease or charter any of its vessels when in the opinion of the Authority they are not required for the purposes of this act; and to contract by license, lease, charter or other arrangement for the provision of excursion service by other persons to and from the islands of Martha's Vineyard and Nantucket from any point on the mainland of the commonwealth, when it shall be deemed necessary or desirable to serve the purposes of this act.

(f) To make and enter into all contracts and agreements necessary or incidental to the performance of its duties and the execution of its powers under this act, and to employ consulting engineers, superintendents, managers, accounting experts, attorneys and such other employees and agents as may be necessary in its judgment, and to fix their compensation, provided that all such expenses shall be solely from the proceeds of bonds issued under the provisions of this act or of chapter five hundred and forty-four of the acts of nineteen hundred and forty-eight, as amended, or from the revenues of the operation of the steamship line.

(g) To receive and accept from any federal agency grants for any purpose for or in aid of the acquisition or operation of the steamship line, or any vessels, equipment and facilities thereof, and to receive and to accept contributions from any source of either money, property, labor or other things of value, to be held, used and applied only for the puposes for which such grants and contributions may be made; and further, to be authorized as a designated agency to receive directly federal participation under Section 139 of Title 23 of the United States Code, notwithstanding the provisions of section one of chapter seven hundred and sixty-eight of the acts of nineteen hundred and sixty-nine and to be further authorized to match directly any such federal funds as required under such federal participation; and to do all acts and things necessary or convenient to carry out the powers expressly granted in this act.

(h) To employ, in so far as may be practicable, the regular employees of said New Bedford, Woods Hole, Martha's Vineyard and Nantucket Steamship Authority, and to recognize such seniority and pension benefits as the said employees currently enjoy under any health, sickness or retirement program.

(i) To insure its employees under the provisions of the Employment Security Law and to become liable for payments instead of contributions as provided in subsection (o) of section fourteen of chapter one hundred and fifty-one A of the General Laws.

(j) To provide by resolution at one time or from time to time for the issue of interest bearing or discounted notes for the purposes and in the amounts that bonds may be issued. The notes shall be payable within three years from their dates, but the principal of and interest on notes issued for a shorter period may be renewed or paid from time to time by the issue of other notes hereunder maturing within the required time from the date of the original loan being refunded. When bonds are issued for the purposes for which the notes were issued, the proceeds of the bonds shall be used to repay the notes and interest on the notes will be charged to current expense. The notes may be secured by the provisions of a resolution, as in the case of bonds. Bond anticipation notes may be issued either before or after the authorization of the bonds being anticipated.

History—
1960, 701, § 4; 1965, 437; 1963, 528; 1968, 317; 1969, 779; 1976, 517; 1978,

524; 1985, 460, §§ 1, 2; 1991, 33, §§ 104, 105, approved, with emergency preamble, May 10, 1991.

Editorial Note—

The **1985 amendment** rewrote clause (b) by changing the maximum amount of outstanding bonds from twenty million dollars to twenty-five million dollars, and rewrote the first two sentences of clause (j) by deleting "in an amount not to exceed five hundred thousand dollars outstanding", and changing the time in which the notes shall be payable from two years to three years.

The **1991 amendment**, in clause (b), substituted "fifty" for "twenty-five", and in clause (e), after the first appearance of "purposes" inserted words relative to providing for an accelerated transportation development and improvement program for the commonwealth.

Acts 1985, ch. 579, § 1, entitled "An act relative to the operation of the Woods Hole, Martha's Vineyard and Nantucket Steamship Authority", provides as follows:

SECTION 1. The provisions of chapter four hundred and sixty of the acts of nineteen hundred and eighty-five are hereby ratified and confirmed.

§ 5.   Steamship Bonds.

The Authority is hereby authorized to provide by resolution at one time or from time to time for the issuance of bonds of the Authority for the purpose of paying for replacements and new construction or acquisition of vessels and other facilities required to provide adequate service. The principal and interest of such bonds shall be payable solely from the funds herein provided for such payment. The bonds of each issue shall be dated, shall bear interest at such rates, shall mature at such time or times not exceeding forty years from their date or dates as may be determined by the Authority, and may be made redeemable before maturity at the option of the Authority, at such price or prices and under such terms and conditions as may be fixed by the Authority prior to the issuance of the bonds. The Authority shall determine the form of the bonds, including any interest coupons to be attached thereto, and the manner of execution of the bonds, and shall fix the denomination or denominations of the bonds and the place or places of payment of principal and interest, which may be at any bank or trust company within the commonwealth. In case any officer whose signature or a facsimile of whose signature shall appear on any bonds or coupons shall cease to be such officer before the delivery of such bonds, such signature or such facsimile shall nevertheless be valid and sufficient for all purposes, the same as if he had remained in office until such delivery. All bonds issued under the provisions of this act shall have and are hereby declared to have all the qualities and incidents of negotiable instruments under the Uniform Commercial Code. The bonds may be issued in coupon or in registered form, or both, as the

Authority may determine, and provision may be made for the registration of any coupon bonds as to principal alone, and also as to both principal and interest, and for the reconversion into coupon bonds of any bonds registered as to both principal and interest. The Authority may sell such bonds in such manner, either at public or at private sale, and for such price, as it may determine to be for the best interests of the Authority.

The proceeds of such bonds shall be used solely for replacements and new construction or acquisition of vessels and other facilities required to provide adequate service and shall be disbursed in such manner and under such restrictions, if any, as the Authority may provide. The Authority may also provide for the replacement of any bonds which shall become mutilated or shall be destroyed or lost. Bonds may be issued under the provisions of this act without obtaining the consent of any department, division, commission, board, bureau or agency of the commonwealth, and without any other proceedings or the happening of any other conditions or things than those proceedings, conditions or things which are specifically required by this act.

The Authority is hereby authorized to provide by resolution for the issuance of refunding bonds of the Authority for the purpose of refunding any bonds that are outstanding and issued under the provisions of this act or of said chapter five hundred and forty-four of the acts of nineteen hundred and forty-eight, as amended, including payment of any redemption premium thereon and any interest accrued or to accrue to the date of redemption of such bonds, and, if deemed advisable by the Authority, for the additional purpose of purchasing additional vessels or equipment. The issuance of such bonds, the maturities and other details thereof, and the duties of the Authority in respect to the same, shall be governed by the provisions of this act in so far as the same may be applicable.

While any bonds issued by the Authority or by said New Bedford, Woods Hole, Martha's Vineyard and Nantucket Steamship Authority remain outstanding, the powers, duties or existence of the Authority shall not be diminished or impaired in any way that will affect adversely the interests and rights of the holders of such bonds.

Except as provided in this act, no person shall operate a vessel with a Coast Guard approved capacity rating in excess of forty passengers or a vessel of more than seventy-five gross tons for the carriage of passengers for hire by water between the mainland and the island of Martha's Vineyard or the island of Nantucket or between said islands unless licensed or permitted in writing to do so by the Authority. Except as provided in this act, no person shall operate a vessel for the carriage of vehicles or freight for hire or resale by water between the mainland and the island of Martha's Vineyard or the island of Nantucket or between said islands unless licensed or permitted in writing to do so by the Authority. The superior court shall have jurisdiction, on a petition in equity by the Authority, to enjoin any such operation. This section shall not apply to continuance of existing services by vessels or a replacement of similar capacity thereof, which were in service on a daily seasonal basis on or before May thirtieth, nineteen hundred and seventy-three, or which were under contract for construction or purchase therefor executed on or before May thirtieth, nineteen hundred and seventy-three. The foregoing exclusion, however, shall not be applicable to vessels operating on a charter basis from a nonfinancial institution.

The provisions of the foregoing paragraph shall not apply to the continuance of the existing service from the port of New Bedford to the island of Martha's Vineyard by the motor vessel Manisee or a replacement of similar capacity, nor shall said provisions be construed to prohibit the operation of another motor vessel for a period of twenty days, in the event that the motor vessel Manisee or a replacement is unable to operate because of a breakdown or an emergency situation.

History—
1960, 701, § 5; 1962, 675; 1973, 942; 1981, 584.

Editorial Note—
The 1981 amendment struck out the first sentence of the fifth paragraph, and inserted in place thereof two sentences, separating provisions for the carriage of passengers and the carriage of vehicles or freight.

Cross References—
Investment securities under the Uniform Commercial Code, see ALM GL c 106, §§ 8-101 et seq.

§ 6.   Exemption from Taxation.

The exercise of the powers granted by this act will be in all respects for the benefit of the people of the commonwealth, for the increase of their commerce and prosperity, and for the improvement of their health and living conditions, and as the operation and maintenance of the steamship line by the Authority will constitute the performance of essential governmental functions, the Authority shall not be required to pay any taxes or assessments upon any property acquired or used by the Authority under the provisions of this act or upon the income therefrom, and the bonds and refunding bonds issued under the provisions of this act, their transfer and the income therefrom (including any profit made on the sale thereof), shall at all times be free from taxation within the commonwealth.

History—
1960, 701, § 6.

§ 7.   [1960, 701, § 7 amended ALM GL c 63 § 12.]

§ 8.   Trust Agreement.

In the discretion of the Authority such bonds or refunding bonds shall be secured by a trust agreement by and between the Authority and a corporate trustee, which may be any trust company or bank having the powers of a trust company within the commonwealth. Such trust agreement may pledge or assign the revenues to be received, but shall not convey or mortgage the vessels, equipment or property. Either the resolution providing for the issuance of bonds or such trust agreement may contain such provisions for protecting and enforcing the rights and remedies of the bondholders as may be reasonable and proper and not in violation of law, including covenants setting forth the duties of the Authority in relation to the acquisition, improvement, maintenance, operation, repair and insurance of the project, and the custody, safeguarding and application of all moneys.

It shall be lawful for any bank or trust company incorporated under the laws of the commonwealth to act as depository of the proceeds of bonds or of revenues and to furnish such indemnifying bonds or to pledge such securities as may be required by the Authority. Such trust agreement may set forth the rights and remedies of the bondholders and of the trustee, and may restrict the individual right of action by bondholders as is customary in trust agreement or trust indentures securing bonds and debentures of corporations. In addition to the foregoing, such trust agreement may contain such other provisions, including a provision for a sinking fund, as the Authority may deem reasonable and proper for the security of the bondholders. All expenses incurred in carrying out the provisions of such trust agreement may be treated as a part of the cost of the operation of the steamship line.

History—
1960, 701, § 8.

§ 9.   Revenues.

The revenues derived from the operation of the steamship line shall be set aside at regular intervals in the following order, in the following amounts and for the following purposes:

First: to an operations fund, an amount sufficient to pay the cost of maintenance, repair and operation of the steamship line for the current month and the next ensuing month, and to maintain working capital for such purposes in an amount not exceeding one thirty-sixth of the operating budget for the then current fiscal year;

Second: to a sinking fund, an amount sufficient to provide for the payment of the interest on and for the amortization and payment of the principal of all bonds as the same shall become due and payable;

Third: to a replacement fund, if so provided in the resolution authorizing the issuance of bonds, such amount, if any, as the Authority may deem necessary or advisable for depreciation of property and for obsolescence and losses in respect to property sold, destroyed or abandoned, and for improvements to and acquisitions of real and personal property, provided that accumulated amounts not needed for the foregoing purposes may from time to time be transferred to the sinking fund to be used for purchase or redemption of bonds;

Fourth: to a reserve fund, an amount sufficient to maintain said fund at a level equal to five per cent of the principal amount of all bonds outstanding or six hundred thousand dollars, whichever is greater; and

Fifth: to the sinking fund, all of the remaining revenues, to be used within a reasonable time for the purchase or redemption of bonds or, in the Authority's discretion, to be transferred to the replacement fund or to the capital improvement fund to be used for any purposes for which bonds may be issued.

Whenever the income of the Authority is insufficient to meet the cost of the service, as defined in section four, the reserve fund shall be used as far as necessary to make up said deficiency.

If as of the last day of December in any year the amount remaining in the reserve fund shall be insufficient to meet the deficiency hereinbefore referred to, the Authority shall notify the state treasurer of the amount of such deficiency, less the amount, if any, in the reserve fund applicable thereto, and the commonwealth shall thereupon pay over to the Authority the amount so ascertained and the Authority shall apply the amount so received from the commonwealth in payment of such deficiency. Pending such payment, the Authority shall borrow such amount of money as may be necessary to enable it to make all payments as they become due.

If as of the last day of December in any year the reserve fund shall exceed the amount established therefor, the Authority shall deposit such excess in the sinking fund, to be used within a reasonable time for the purchase or redemption of bonds outstanding. When there are no such bonds outstanding to be redeemed, then such excess funds shall be first paid to the commonwealth for any amounts which it may have paid to the Authority under the provisions hereof and the commonwealth shall thereupon distribute the amounts so received to the towns assessable for a deficiency, as provided in this section in proportion to the amounts for which they may be so assessed.

In order to meet any payment required of the commonwealth under this section, the state treasurer may borrow at any time, in anticipation of the assessments to be levied upon the towns hereinafter specified, such sums of money as may be necessary to make said payments and he shall repay any sums so borrowed as soon after said assessments are paid as is expedient.

In case the commonwealth shall be called upon in the calendar year nineteen hundred and sixty-one to pay the Authority any amount under this section on account of any such deficiency for the calendar year nineteen hundred and sixty, such amount with interest or other charges incurred in borrowing the money for the purpose, except such amounts as may be appropriated by the general court therefor, shall be assessed on the city of New Bedford and the towns of Falmouth and Nantucket and the county of Dukes county, in the following proportions, viz.: forty per cent on the city of New Bedford; ten per cent on the town of Falmouth; twenty per cent on the town of Nantucket; and thirty per cent on the county of Dukes county. The county commissioners of the county of Dukes county shall allocate such assessment upon said county to be paid severally by the towns in said county, excepting the town of Gosnold, in the same proportions as in the assessment of the county tax.

In case the commonwealth shall be called upon in the calendar year nineteen hundred and sixty-two or in any subsequent calendar year to pay the Authority any amount under this section on account of any such deficiency for the calendar year nineteen hundred and sixty-one or any subsequent calendar year, such amount with interest or other charges incurred in borrowing the money for the purpose, except such amounts as may be appropriated by the general court therefor, shall be assessed on the towns of Falmouth and Nantucket and the county of Dukes county, in the following proportions: ten per cent on the town of Falmouth; forty per cent on the town of Nantucket; and fifty per cent on the county of Dukes county. The county commissioners of the county of Dukes county shall allocate such assessment upon said county to be paid severally by the towns in said county, excepting the town of Gosnold, in the same proportions as in the assessment of the county tax.

If at any time the Authority has not sufficient cash to make the payments required in the course of its management and operation of the steamship line and other properties under its control, the Authority may temporarily borrow money and issue notes of the Authority therefor.

If at any time any principal or interest is due or about to become due on any bond or note issued or assumed by the Authority, and funds to pay the same are not available, the Authority shall certify to the state treasurer the amount required to meet such obligations, and the commonwealth shall thereupon pay over to the Authority the amount so certified. If the commonwealth shall not make such payment within a reasonable time, the Authority or any holder of an unpaid bond or note issued or assumed by the Authority, acting in the name of and on behalf of the Authority, shall have the right to require the commonwealth to pay the Authority the amount remaining unpaid, which right shall be enforceable as a claim against the commonwealth. The Authority or any such holder of an unpaid bond or note may file a petition in the superior court of Suffolk county to enforce such claim or intervene in any such proceeding already commenced, and the provisions of chapter two hundred and fifty-eight of the General Laws shall apply to such petition insofar as it relates to the enforcement of a claim against the commonwealth. Any such holder who shall have filed such a petition may apply for an order of said court requiring the Authority to apply funds received by the Authority on its claim against the commonwealth to the payment of the petitioner's unpaid bond or note, and said court, if it finds such amount to be due, shall issue such an order.

History—

1960, 701, § 9; 1965, 779; 1969, 654; 1971, 1038, § 2; 1975, 717, § 1; 1978, 502; 1985, 460 § 3.

Editorial Note—

The **1985 amendment** rewrote the first paragraph, making the following changes: (1) in clause "First", following the words "steamship line", added the words "for the current month and the next ensuing month," deleted "in an amount not exceeding two hundred thousand dollars" and inserted therein "in an amount not exceeding one thirty-sixth of the operating budget for the then current fiscal year", (2) in clause "Third", deleted the words following the word "abandoned" "and for improvement expenditures, not in excess of twenty-five thousand dollars in any one year, and not in excess of fifty thousand dollars in the accumulated account, with a limit of twenty thousand dollars for the improvement expenditure on any one project," and inserted therein "and for improvements to and acquisitions of real and personal property, provided that accumulated amounts not needed for the foregoing purposes may from time to time be transferred to the sinking fund to be used for the purchase or redemption of bonds," (3) in clause "Fourth", deleted the words "at the amount of six hundred thousand dollars," and inserted therein "at a level equal to five per cent of the principal amount of all bonds outstanding or six hundred thousand dollars, whichever is greater," and (4) in clause "Fifth", added to the clause following the word "bonds" the words "or, in the Authority's discretion, to be transferred to the replacement fund or to the capital improvement fund to be used for any purposes for which bonds may be issued".

Acts 1985, ch. 579, § 1, entitled "An act relative to the operation of the Woods Hole, Martha's Vineyard and Nantucket Steamship Authority", provides as follows:

SECTION 1. The provisions of chapter four hundred and sixty of the acts of nineteen hundred and eighty-five are hereby ratified and confirmed.

§ 9A.   Contracts With Commonwealth for Reimbursement.

Notwithstanding any other provisions of this act, the authority is hereby authorized to enter into a contract or contracts with the commonwealth, and the commonwealth, acting by and through the executive office for administration and finance, may enter into a contract or contracts with the authority whereby the commonwealth agrees to reimburse the authority for an amount equal to ninety per cent of the debt service on any bonds issued in respect to any vessels, equipment or facility for mass transportation purposes acquired by the authority after the establishment of the Massachusetts Bay Transportation Authority, less the amounts available from revenues or any reserve fund or sinking fund for such debt service. Such contract shall also provide that in the event that the reserve fund provided in section nine in any year shall exceed the amount established therefor, then the amount of excess paid the commonwealth for distribution to the towns shall first be reduced by any amount previously advanced by the commonwealth for the purposes of this section and not otherwise repaid to it. Such sum shall be returned to the cigarette tax fund for mass transportation purposes, as set forth in paragraph (b) of section twenty-eight of chapter sixty-four C of the General Laws.

History—
1964, 563, § 17.

Cross References—
Payment from cigarette excise proceeds certain reimbursement for mass transportation, see ALM GL c 58 § 25B(b).

§ 10.   Trust Funds.

All moneys received pursuant to the authority of this act, whether as proceeds from the sale of bonds or as revenues, shall be deemed to be trust funds, to be held and applied solely as provided in this act. The Authority shall, in the resolution authorizing the issuance of bonds or in the trust agreement, provide for the payment of the proceeds of the sale of such bonds, and all revenues to be received, to any officer who, or to any agency, bank or trust company which, shall act as trustee of such funds and shall hold and apply the same to the purposes hereof, subject to such regulations as this act and such resolution or trust agreement may provide.

History—
1960, 701, § 10.

§ 11.   Bonds Eligible for Investment.

Bonds and refunding bonds issued under the provisions of this act are hereby made securities in which all public officers and public bodies of the commonwealth and its political subdivisions, all insurance companies, trust companies in their commercial departments and within the limits set by section fourteen of chapter one hundred and sixty-seven E of the General Laws, banking associations, investment companies, executors, trustees and other fiduciaries, and all other persons whatsoever who are now or may hereafter be authorized to invest in bonds or other obligations of a similar nature may properly and legally invest funds, including capital in their control or belonging to them, and such bonds are hereby made obligations which may properly and legally be made eligible for the investment of savings deposits and the income thereof in the manner provided by paragraph 2 of section fifteen B of chapter one hundred and sixty-seven of the General Laws. Such revenue bonds are hereby made securities which may properly and legally be deposited with and received by any state or municipal officer or any agency or political subdivision of the commonwealth for any purpose for which the deposit of bonds or other obligations of the commonwealth now or may hereafter be authorized by law.

History—
1960, 701, § 11; 1983, 371, § 101.

Editorial Note—
The **1983 amendment** rewrote the section to conform statutory references therein to changes occasioned by the recent reorganization of banking laws.

§ 12.   Remedies.

Any holder of bonds or refunding bonds issued under the provisions of this act or of any of the coupons appertaining thereto, and the trustee under the trust agreement, if any, except to the extent the rights herein given may be restricted by such resolution or trust agreement, may, either at law or in equity, by suit action, mandamus or other proceeding, protect and enforce any and all rights under the laws of the commonwealth or granted hereunder or under such resolution or trust agreement, and may enforce and compel the performance of all duties required by this act or by such resolution or trust agreement to be performed by the Authority or by any officer thereof, including the fixing, charging and collecting of tolls and charges for the use of the project.

History—
1960, 701, § 12.

§ 13.   Report.

On or before the first day of April in each year, the Authority shall make an annual report of its activities for the preceding calendar year to the governor and to the general court. Each such report shall set forth a complete operating and financial statement covering its operations during the year. The state auditor shall cause an audit of the books of the Authority to be made at least once each year. The cost of such audit shall not be borne by the Authority. Such audits made by the state auditor shall be conducted on a completely independent basis from the Authority and shall be deemed to be public records within the meaning of chapter sixty-six of the General Laws.

History—
1960, 701, § 13; 1962, 276; 1967, 575.

§ 14.   Finance Advisory Board.

There is hereby created and established a board to be known as the finance advisory board of the Woods Hole, Martha's Vineyard and Nantucket Steamship Authority which shall consist of three members; one member to be elected by the voters of the town of Falmouth for a term of one year; one member to be elected by the voters of the county of Dukes county for a term of two years; one member to be elected by the voters of the town of Nantucket for a term of three years. In the event of a vacancy on said board from whatever cause, such vacancy shall be filled for the remainder of the term in the case of the county of Dukes County by appointment by the county commissioners thereof, and in the case of said towns, by appointment by the select-men. Upon the expiration of the term of a member from either the town of Falmouth or Nantucket, his successor shall be elected in like manner for a term of two years. Upon the expiration of the term of the member elected by the voters of the county of Dukes County his successor shall be appointed by the county commissioners of the county of Dukes County for a term of two years, and thereafter each such member shall be appointed in like manner for a term of two years. In the event of a vacancy on said board from whatever cause, such vacancy shall be filled for the remainder of the term in the case of the county of Dukes County by appointment by the county commissioners thereof, and in the case of said towns, by appointment by the select-men. It shall have access to such books, records and files of the Authority it may deem necessary or desirable for the exercise of its powers. The members of the board shall serve without compensation but shall be reimbursed from the funds of the Authority for any actual expenses necessarily incurred in the performance of their duties.

History—
     1960, 701, § 14; 1964, 313; 1979, 316; 1980, 48.

Editorial Note—
     The **1979 amendment** rewrote the former second, third and fourth sentences of this section by combining them into two sentences relative to the election of certain persons to the finance advisory board of the Woods Hole, Martha's Vineyard and Nantucket Steamship Authority.

     The **1980 amendment** rewrote the second and third sentences, inserting in their place three sentences relative to the membership of the Finance Advisory Board of the Woods Hole, Martha's Vineyard and Nantucket Steamship Authority.

§ 15.   Miscellaneous.

If transportation of passengers on the steamship line of the Authority is interrupted by reason of any group of employees calling a strike or going out on strike, or causing any such stoppage or slow down, or by reason of any other labor dispute, the provisions of chapter one hundred and fifty B of the General Laws shall apply, in so far as they are applicable.

Any member, agent or employee of the Authority who contracts with the Authority or is interested, either directly or indirectly in any contract with the Authority, other than a contract relating to labor or wages, shall be punished by a fine of not more than one thousand dollars or by imprisonment for not more than one year or both.

No member of the Authority shall be in the employ of, or be in any way, directly or indirectly, financially interested in any person, partnership, corporation or association having any business or financial transactions with the Authority, or which is furnishing any transportation of freight or passengers in the area of the Authority, or rendering any service similar to that performed by the Authority.

No contract shall be awarded by the Authority for construction work or for the purchase of equipment, supplies or materials, whether for repairs or original construction, the estimated cost of which amounts to one thousand dollars or more, except in cases of special emergency involving the health, convenience or safety of the people using the facilities of the Authority, unless proposals for the same have been invited by advertisements in at least one newspaper published in each of the towns of Falmouth and Nantucket and the county of Dukes County once a week for at least two consecutive weeks, the last publication to be at least one week before the time specified for the opening of said proposals. Such advertisements shall state the time and place where plans and specifications of proposed work or supplies may be had and the time and place for opening the proposals in answer to said advertisements. Every such contract shall be awarded to the lowest responsible and eligible bidder, provided, however, the Authority may reject any such proposal if it is in the public interest. Nothing hereinbefore contained shall be construed as requiring the invitation of proposals for engineering or architectural work in connection with a proposed project.

The Authority may indemnify any member, officer or employee from personal expense or damages incurred, arising out of any claim, suit, demand or judgment which arose out of any act or omission of the individual, including the violation of the civil rights of any person under any federal law, if at the time of such act or omission the member, officer or employee was acting within the scope of his official duties or employment; provided, that the defense or settlement of such claim shall have been made by counsel for the Authority, by an attorney retained for such purpose by the Authority, or by an attorney provided by an insurer obligated under the terms of a policy of insurance to defend against such claims.

History—
1960, 701, § 15; 1964, 278; 1978, 427.

§ 15A.   Schedule Changes; Notice.

The Authority shall post and advertise in at least one newspaper published in each of the towns of Falmouth and Nantucket and the county of Dukes county all proposed schedule changes no later than sixty days prior to the effective date of said proposed changes. In the event that the Authority shall receive, within thirty days of said posting and advertising, a petition signed by no fewer than fifty persons who are residents of the towns of Falmouth, Nantucket or the county of Dukes county requesting a public hearing on said proposed changes. The Authority shall, within fourteen days of receiving said petition, conduct said public hearing.

The location of said hearing shall be either on Martha's Vineyard, Nantucket, or in Falmouth, wherever the greatest number of petitioners reside.

The Authority shall, after considering the testimony at said public hearing, and at least seven days prior to the effective date of the proposed changes issue a report either maintaining its original proposed schedule changes, or making modifications thereto, and explaining their reasons therefor. In the event that modifications are made to a proposed schedule change as a result of a public hearing, said modifications may take effect on the original proposed effective date.

For the purposes of this section, proposed schedule changes shall not include any changes necessitated by weather, equipment failure, or other emergency conditions, but shall include all seasonal schedule changes of said Authority.

History—
1979, 102.

§ 15B.   Public Hearings.

The Authority shall annually hold at least one public hearing on each of the islands of Martha's Vineyard and Nantucket. Each such hearing shall be advertised in a newspaper or newspapers of general circulation on the island where said hearing is to be located at least seven days prior to said hearing.

History—
1979, 140.

§ 16.   Abolition of New Bedford, Woods Hole, Marth'a Vineyard and Nantucket Steamship Authority and transfer of its assets and liabilities to Woods Hole, Martha's Vineyard and Nantucket Steamship Authority.

Said New Bedford, Woods Hole, Martha's Vineyard and Nantucket Steamship Authority is hereby abolished; and all its assets, including its real property, shall, without further conveyance and by virtue of this act, be and become vested in said Woods Hole, Martha's Vineyard and Nantucket Steamship Authority; and all its outstanding indebtedness and liabilities shall, without further action and by virtue of this act, be assumed by said Woods Hole, Martha's Vineyard and Nantucket Steamship Authority. When used in any instrument acknowledging indebtedness or other obligation the words "New Bedford, Woods Hole, Martha's Vineyard and Nantucket Steamship Authority" shall mean said Woods Hole, Martha's Vineyard and Nantucket Steamship Authority.

All books, records and papers in the possession of the said New Bedford, Woods Hole, Martha's Vineyard and Nantucket Steamship Authority shall, upon the effective date of this act, be turned over to said Woods Hole, Martha's Vineyard and Nantucket Steamship Authority.

Except as provided herein, nothing contained in this act or in said chapter five hundred and forty-four of the acts of nineteen hundred and forty-eight, as amended by chapter one hundred and forty-two of the acts of nineteen hundred and forty-nine, chapter four hundred and forty-nine of the acts of nineteen hundred and fifty-four, chapter six hundred and twenty-two of the acts of nineteen hundred and fifty-four and chapter seven hundred and forty-seven of the acts of nineteen hundred and fifty-six, shall be deemed or construed to require that said Woods Hole, Martha's Vineyard and Nantucket Steamship Authority provide ferry runs or such transportation of passengers, vehicles or freight to or from any point on the mainland of the commonwealth to or from any other such point or to and from the islands of Martha's Vineyard or Nantucket; provided, however, that except in cases of emergency or necessity, said ferry runs or such transportation shall be provided to and from the port of Woods Hole to and from the island of Martha's Vineyard; provided, further, that except in cases of emergency or necessity, said ferry runs or such transportation shall be provided to and from the mainland to and from the island of Nantucket; and provided, further, that for no less than the period of April first to December thirty-first of each year said ferry runs or such transportation shall be provided to and from inner Lewis Bay, in the town of Barnstable, to and from the island of Nantucket.

The Authority may, in its discretion, provide ferry runs or such transportation annually from May first to September thirtieth to and from the port of New Bedford, via the port of Woods Hole to and from said islands, and throughout the year may also provide ferry service to and from inner Lewis bay, in the town of Barnstable, to and from the islands of Martha's Vineyard and Nantucket, and may acquire any business enterprise necessary or convenient for such purposes.

History—
    1960, 701 § 16; 1965, 413; 1969, 573; 1974, 392; 1979, 133, § 1.

Editorial Note—

The 1979 amendment, although reciting that it affected the fourth paragraph, apparently rewrote the third paragraph, adding a provision for service to Nantucket in emergencies, and service between Barnstable and Nantucket from April 1 through December 31.

§ 17.　Act Liberally Construed.

This act, being necessary for the welfare of the commonwealth and its inhabitants, shall be liberally construed to effect the purposes thereof.

History—
1960, 701, § 17.

§ 18.　Constitutional Construction.

The provisions of this act are severable, and if any of its provisions shall be held unconstitutional by any court of competent jurisdiction, the decision of such court shall not affect or impair any of the remaining provisions.

History—
1960, 701, § 18.

§ 19.　Inconsistent Laws Inapplicable.

All other general or special laws, or parts thereof, inconsistent herewith are hereby declared to be inapplicable to the provisions of this act.

History—
1960, 701, § 19.

§ 20.　Effective Date.

This act shall take effect on January first, nineteen hundred and sixty-one.

History—
1960, 701, § 20.

CHAPTER S79

Local-aid Transportation Bond Authorization to Assist Highway and Transit Development in Cities and Towns Throughout the Commonwealth

(Acts 1973, Ch. 1140)

Auto-Cite®: Cases and annotations referred to herein can be further researched through the Auto-Cite® computer-assisted research service. Use Auto-Cite to check citations for form, parallel references, prior and later history, and annotation references.

---

§§ 1–15. [1973, 1140, §§ 1–15 amended ALM GL c 44, § 6A, and ALM GL c 161A, §§ 1, 3, 5–8, and 23.]

§ 16. Commonwealth to Enter Into Contracts of Assistance with MBTA to Pay Portion of Net Cost of Service.

In addition to any contract assistance provided in section twenty-eight of chapter one hundred and sixty-one A of the General Laws and by chapter six hundred and eighty-one of the acts of nineteen hundred and seventy-two, the commonwealth, acting by and through the executive office for administration and finance, shall prior to December thirty-first, nineteen hundred and seventy-five, enter into an additional contract or contracts with the Massachusetts Bay Transportation Authority providing that an additional thirty-five million dollars of the net cost of service of the authority for calendar years nineteen hundred and seventy-three shall be paid by the commonwealth from the General Fund and shall not be assessed upon the cities and towns constituting said authority; provided however, that the total state contract assistance in calendar year 1973, shall not exceed fifty-five million dollars.

Said thirty-five million dollars in additional contract assistance shall not be assessed upon the cities and towns, and shall be so applied that for assessment purposes, the total contract assistance provided by the commonwealth to the Massachusetts Bay Transportation Authority for calendar year nineteen hundred and seventy-three shall result in proportionally equal reductions in all cost items comprising the Massachusetts Bay Transportation Authority net cost of service.

In any calendar year after calendar year nineteen hundred and seventy-three, the commonwealth, acting by and through the executive office for administration and finance, shall enter into a contract or contracts with the authority providing that a portion of the net cost of service shall be paid by the commonwealth, and shall not be assessed upon the cities and towns constituting the authority. The portion of the net cost of service not to be so assessed, hereinafter called contract assistance, shall not in any one calendar year be less than the contract assistance provided in calendar year nineteen hundred and seventy-three under section twenty-eight of chapter one hundred and sixty-one A and under chapter six hundred and eighty-one of the acts of nineteen hundred and seventy-two. Additional contract assistance provided by the Commonwealth to the Massachusetts Bay Transportation Authority under this paragraph shall, for assessment purposes, be applied so as to result in proportionally equal reductions to all cost items comprising the Massachusetts Bay Transportation Authority net cost of service.

History—

1973, 1140, § 16; 1975, 746, § 3.

§ 17.   [1973, 1140, § 17 added ALM GL c 180, § 17H.]

§ 18.   MBTA Program for Transportation.

The program for mass transportation provided for in paragraph (g) of section five of chapter one hundred and sixty-one A of the General Laws, as existing immediately prior to the effective date of this act, shall continue to serve as the authority's program for mass transportation until such time as a program is prepared, developed or revised pursuant to said paragraph (g) of said section five of said chapter one hundred and sixty-one A, as appearing in section seven of this act.

History—
1973, 1140, § 18.

§ 19.   Transfer of Officers and Employees of MBTA.

All officers and employees of the Massachusetts Bay Transportation Authority whose powers and duties are transferred pursuant to this act shall continue to be employees of said authority with all the rights, benefits and privileges which they enjoyed immediately prior to the effective date of this act, including but not limited to, those related to wages, salaries, hours, working conditions, health benefits, pensions, and retirement allowances; provided, however, that such officers and employees shall exercise all powers and perform all duties so transferred subject to the directions, control and supervision of the department of transportation and construction. Nothing contained herein shall be construed to limit or restrict in any way any rights or obligations of the authority or any such employees or officers which may exist under agreements entered into pursuant to section nineteen of chapter one hundred and sixty-one A of the General Laws.

History—
1973, 1140, § 19.

§ 20.   Apportionment of Sums; Use of Sums.

The department of public works is hereby authorized and directed to apportion the sum of fifteen million dollars among the following cities and towns in the amounts indicated:

Abington	44,293
Acton	59,845
Acushnet	35,980

Adams	49,271
Agawam	89,342
Alford	7,853
Amesbury	51,740
Amherst	74,894
Andover	128,311
Ashburnham	35,010
Ashby	24,941
Ashfield	29,716
Athol	72,338
Attleboro	196,769
Auburn	64,055
Avon	24,703
Ayer	26,714
Barnstable	159,568
Barre	47,410
Becket	24,354
Belchertown	50,737
Bellingham	53,483
Berkley	20,335
Berlin	18,591
Bernardston	18,011
Billerica	115,382
Blackstone	24,472
Blandford	26,520
Bolton	25,874
Bourne	55,475
Boxborough	10,815
Boxford	31,938
Boylston	18,310
Brewster	20,130
Bridgewater	52,852
Brimfield	29,082
Brockton	315,364
Brookfield	19,680
Buckland	19,161
Carlisle	22,277
Carver	29,014
Charlemont	17,347
Charlton	51,038
Chatham	30,803
Chelmsford	114,512
Cheshire	21,971
Chester	22,905
Chesterfield	21,811

Chicopee	249,369
Chilmark	6,255
Clarksburg	8,699
Clinton	62,260
Colrain	36,088
Conway	25,060
Cummington	20,802
Dalton	28,607
Dartmouth	96,923
Deerfield	38,250
Dennis	58,749
Dighton	40,091
Douglas	34,104
Dracut	72,351
Dudley	42,718
Dunstable	15,232
East Bridgewater	39,155
East Brookfield	11,121
East Longmeadow	63,206
Eastham	17,882
Easthampton	61,160
Easton	50,620
Edgartown	20,552
Egremont	16,700
Erving	15,633
Essex	13,777
Fairhaven	61,436
Fall River	394,389
Falmouth	104,204
Fitchburg	209,100
Florida	15,899
Foxborough	66,270
Franklin	68,372
Freetown	33,908
Gardner	94,558
Gay Head	3,452
Georgetown	26,043
Gill	14,609
Gloucester	108,989
Goshen	13,112
Gosnold	919
Grafton	56,951
Granby	29,920
Granville	27,474
Great Barrington	49,964

Greenfield	94,269
Groton	40,653
Groveland	22,969
Hadley	31,162
Halifax	23,117
Hampden	26,299
Hancock	10,903
Hanson	32,074
Hardwick	39,143
Harvard	40,366
Harwich	47,179
Hatfield	23,710
Haverhill	196,088
Hawley	18,485
Heath	21,320
Hinsdale	17,568
Holden	60,679
Holland	15,845
Holliston	47,823
Holyoke	214,239
Hopedale	26,621
Hopkinton	38,868
Hubbardston	30,592
Hudson	63,678
Huntington	16,156
Ipswich	50,844
Kingston	28,676
Lakeville	28,193
Lancaster	30,324
Lanesborough	22,225
Lawrence	269,738
Lee	38,688
Leicester	45,012
Lenox	32,762
Leominster	152,370
Leverett	14,457
Leyden	14,670
Littleton	34,628
Longmeadow	60,065
Lowell	361,101
Ludlow	68,719
Lunenburg	39,605
Mansfield	48,009
Marion	18,764
Marlborough	103,448

Mashpee	18,640
Mattapoisett	21,582
Medway	34,340
Mendon	18,036
Merrimac	18,411
Methuen	114,280
Middleborough	89,518
Middlefield	14,836
Milford	69,789
Millbury	51,232
Millville	9,890
Monroe	7,519
Monson	53,755
Montague	54,304
Monterey	21,501
Montgomery	12,249
Mount Washington	6,810
Nantucket	64,812
New Ashford	4,875
New Bedford	435,435
New Braintree	19,897
New Marlborough	34,347
New Salem	15,407
Newbury	22,280
Newburyport	57,230
North Adams	89,085
North Andover	115,618
North Attleborough	78,728
North Brookfield	37,728
Northampton	127,493
Northborough	40,057
Northbridge	39,183
Northfield	29,450
Norton	44,499
Oak Bluffs	15,772
Oakham	19,507
Orange	47,067
Orleans	25,977
Otis	17,831
Oxford	46,429
Palmer	68,416
Paxton	18,735
Pelham	9,877
Pepperell	36,679
Peru	13,372

Petersham	27,058
Phillipston	17,943
Pittsfield	275,190
Plainfield	18,238
Plainville	29,613
Plymouth	108,913
Plympton	14,173
Princeton	30,948
Provincetown	14,210
Raynham	34,229
Rehoboth	55,009
Richmond	16,599
Rochester	22,822
Rockport	24,357
Rowe	14,932
Rowley	17,954
Royalston	27,368
Russell	11,211
Rutland	34,264
Salisbury	19,985
Sandisfield	30,742
Sandwich	36,958
Savoy	19,482
Seekonk	52,469
Sheffield	36,652
Shelburne	24,101
Shirley	26,643
Shrewsbury	75,544
Shutesbury	15,581
Somerset	60,915
South Hadley	62,208
Southhampton	27,418
Southborough	33,089
Southbridge	91,635
Southwick	37,015
Spencer	52,201
Springfield	705,622
Sterling	37,187
Stockbridge	20,249
Stoughton	82,005
Stow	24,289
Sturbridge	45,668
Sunderland	16,508
Sutton	39,001
Swansea	52,572

Taunton	177,439
Templeton	40,997
Tewksbury	79,560
Tisbury	15,916
Tolland	14,594
Townsend	33,448
Truro	15,151
Tyngsborough	23,993
Tyringham	10,516
Upton	29,160
Uxbridge	47,177
Wales	10,184
Ware	54,504
Wareham	61,445
Warren	37,373
Warwick	24,090
Washington	20,215
Webster	68,450
Wellfleet	18,406
Wendell	23,063
West Boylston	29,959
West Bridgewater	31,716
West Brookfield	26,229
West Newbury	18,945
West Springfield	128,627
West Stockbridge	16,116
West Tisbury	6,429
Westborough	60,007
Westfield	154,001
Westford	56,192
Westhampton	16,866
Westminister	42,780
Westport	56,506
Whately	16,024
Whitman	48,066
Wilbraham	55,246
Williamsburg	19,575
Williamstown	38,049
Winchendon	51,818
Windsor	24,806
Worcester	750,607
Worthington	23,581
Wrentham	36,717
Yarmouth	80,175

The department shall certify said apportionment to the comptroller, and such sums approved by the department not exceeding fifteen million dollars shall be made available for distribution on or before December thirty-first, nineteen hundred and seventy-three. The sums received by each city and town hereunder shall be used only for the purposes for which said city or town may borrow money within its debt limit under clause (5) of section seven of chapter forty-four of the General Laws, or for the construction under section thirty-four of chapter ninety of the General Laws of town highways of a type equal to that currently used by said town as approved by the department, or for the erection or maintenance of traffic safety devices; provided, however, that such sums shall not be available for the construction, surfacing or resurfacing of off-street parking areas.

Said sums may be expended by a city or town for the aforesaid purposes in addition to any federal funds allocated to such city or town and available for such expenditure; provided, that such city or town may elect to expend any part of the sum allocated to it at any time prior to June thirtieth, nineteen hundred and seventy-seven. Any unexpended balances remaining on said June thirtieth shall be refunded to the department forthwith, to be applied as refunds of amounts expended under this section.

History—
1973, 1140, § 20; 1974, 825, § 10.

§ 21.   Apportionment of Sums; Use of Sums.

The department of public works is hereby authorized and directed to apportion the sum of two million five hundred thousand dollars among the following cities and towns in the amounts indicated:

Ashland	55,382
Bedford	67,866
Beverly	76,000
Braintree	67,000
Burlington	78,766
Canton	59,938
Cohasset	19,400
Concord	48,200
Danvers	49,000
Dover	19,200
Duxbury	42,000
Framingham	170,400
Hamilton	22,000
Hanover	26,000
Hingham	50,000

Holebrook	21,400
Hull	23,000
Lincoln	24,000
Lynnfield	25,000
Manchester	14,000
Marshfield	42,000
Maynard	21,000
Medfield	55,952
Middleton	37,550
Millis	46,418
Natick	103,500
Needham	59,400
Norfolk	49,066
North Reading	54,830
Norwell	30,684
Norwood	51,800
Peabody	72,000
Pembroke	65,458
Randolph	38,600
Reading	45,600
Rockland	36,000
Scituate	42,400
Sharon	43,200
Sherborn	46,744
Stoneham	37,000
Sudbury	90,600
Topsfield	48,982
Walpole	45,000
Wayland	54,000
Wellesley	61,000
Wenham	15,000
Weston	32,600
Westwood	30,000
Weymouth	98,600
Wilmington	86,464

The department shall certify said apportionment to the comptroller, and such sums approved by the department not exceeding two million five hundred thousand dollars shall be made available for distribution on or before December thirty-first, nineteen hundred and seventy-three. The sums received by each city and town hereunder shall be used only for the purposes for which said city or town may borrow money within its debt limit under clause (5) of section seven of chapter forty-four of the General Laws, or for the construction under section thirty-four of chapter ninety of the General Laws of town highways of a type equal to that currently used by said town as approved by the department, or for the erection or maintenance of traffic safety devices; provided, however, that such sums shall not be available for the construction, surfacing or resurfacing of off-street parking areas.

Said sums may be expended by a city or town for the aforesaid purposes in addition to any federal funds allocated to such city or town and available for such expenditure, provided, that such city or town may elect to expend any part of the sum allocated to it at any time prior to June thirtieth, nineteen hundred and seventy-seven. Any unexpended balances remaining on said June thirtieth shall be refunded to the department forthwith, to be applied as refunds of amounts expended under this section.

History—
1973, 1140, § 21; 1974, 825, § 11.

§ 22.   Apportionment of Sums; Use of Sums.

The department of public works is hereby authorized and directed to apportion the sum of twenty-five million dollars, in addition to the amount apportioned as provided in section twenty among the following cities and towns and in the amounts indicated:

Abington	73,822
Acton	99,742
Acushnet	59,966
Adams	82,118
Agawam	148,903
Alford	13,089
Amesbury	86,233
Amherst	124,823
Andover	213,852
Ashburnham	58,349
Ashby	41,569
Ashfield	49,527
Athol	120,564
Attleboro	327,948
Auburn	106,758
Avon	41,172
Ayer	44,523
Barnstable	265,947
Barre	79,071
Becket	40,589
Belchertown	84,562
Bellingham	89,139
Berkley	33,891

Berlin	30,985
Bernardston	30,018
Billerica	192,303
Blackstone	40,787
Blandford	44,201
Bolton	43,123
Bourne	92,459
Boxborough	18,026
Boxford	53,230
Boylston	30,516
Brewster	33,550
Bridgewater	88,086
Brimfield	48,469
Brockton	525,607
Brookfield	32,800
Buckland	31,934
Carlisle	37,128
Carver	48,356
Charlemont	28,912
Charlton	85,064
Chatham	51,338
Chelmsford	190,854
Cheshire	36,619
Chester	38,175
Chesterfield	36,352
Chicopee	415,615
Chilmark	10,425
Clarksburg	14,498
Clinton	103,767
Colrain	60,147
Conway	41,767
Cummington	34,670
Dalton	47,679
Dartmouth	161,359
Deerfield	63,749
Dennis	97,915
Dighton	66,818
Douglas	56,839
Dracut	120,584
Dudley	71,197
Dunstable	25,387
East Bridgewater	65,259
East Brookfield	18,536
East Longmeadow	105,343
Eastham	29,803

Easthampton	101,933
Easton	84,366
Edgartown	34,253
Egremont	27,833
Erving	26,055
Essex	22,962
Fairhaven	102,393
Fall River	657,316
Falmouth	173,673
Fitchburg	348,500
Florida	26,498
Foxborough	110,450
Franklin	113,954
Freetown	56,513
Gardner	157,597
Gay Head	5,753
Georgetown	43,405
Gill	24,348
Gloucester	181,648
Goshen	21,853
Gosnold	1,531
Grafton	94,919
Granby	49,867
Granville	45,789
Great Barrington	83,274
Greenfield	157,114
Groton	67,754
Groveland	38,282
Hadley	51,936
Halifax	38,529
Hampden	43,831
Hancock	18,172
Hanson	53,457
Hardwick	65,238
Harvard	67,277
Harwich	78,631
Hatfield	39,517
Haverhill	326,814
Hawley	30,808
Heath	35,533
Hinsdale	29,281
Holden	101,132
Holland	26,409
Holliston	79,706
Holyoke	357,064

Hopedale	44,368
Hopkinton	64,780
Hubbardston	50,986
Hudson	106,130
Huntington	26,927
Ipswich	84,739
Kingston	47,793
Lakeville	46,989
Lancaster	50,540
Lanesborough	37,041
Lawrence	449,564
Lee	64,479
Leicester	75,019
Lenox	54,604
Leominister	253,949
Leverett	24,096
Leyden	24,450
Littleton	57,713
Longmeadow	100,109
Lowell	601,835
Ludlow	114,531
Lunenburg	66,009
Mansfield	80,015
Marion	31,273
Marlborough	172,413
Mashpee	31,067
Mattapoisett	35,970
Medway	57,234
Mendon	30,060
Merrimac	30,686
Methuen	190,466
Middleborough	149,197
Middlefield	24,726
Milford	116,315
Millbury	85,387
Millville	16,484
Monroe	12,532
Monson	89,592
Montague	90,507
Monterey	35,835
Montgomery	20,415
Mount Washington	11,350
Nantucket	108,020
New Ashford	8,126
New Bedford	725,726

New Braintree	33,161
New Marlborough	57,245
New Salem	25,678
Newbury	37,133
Newburyport	95,383
North Adams	148,475
North Andover	192,696
North Attleborough	131,214
North Brookfield	62,881
Northampton	212,489
Northborough	66,762
Northbridge	65,306
Northfield	49,083
Norton	74,165
Oak Bluffs	26,286
Oakham	32,511
Orange	78,445
Orleans	43,294
Otis	29,719
Oxford	77,382
Palmer	114,027
Paxton	31,225
Pelham	16,461
Pepperell	61,132
Peru	22,287
Petersham	45,097
Phillipston	29,905
Pittsfield	458,650
Plainfield	30,397
Plainville	49,354
Plymouth	181,521
Plympton	23,621
Princeton	51,580
Provincetown	23,683
Raynham	57,049
Rehoboth	91,681
Richmond	27,664
Rochester	38,037
Rockport	40,594
Rowe	24,886
Rowley	29,923
Royalston	45,613
Russell	18,684
Rutland	57,107
Salisbury	33,309

Sandishfield	51,237
Sandwich	61,596
Savoy	32,471
Seekonk	87,448
Sheffield	61,087
Shelburne	40,168
Shirley	44,404
Shrewsbury	125,906
Shutesbury	25,968
Somerset	101,526
South Hadley	103,681
Southhampton	45,697
Southborough	55,148
Southbridge	152,725
Southwick	61,691
Spencer	87,002
Springfield	1,176,038
Sterling	61,979
Stockbridge	33,749
Stoughton	136,675
Stow	40,482
Sturbridge	76,113
Sunderland	27,513
Sutton	65,001
Swansea	87,619
Taunton	295,732
Templeton	68,328
Tewksbury	132,600
Tisbury	26,526
Tolland	24,324
Townsend	55,746
Truro	25,252
Tyngsborough	39,988
Tyringham	17,526
Upton	48,600
Uxbridge	78,628
Wales	16,973
Ware	90,840
Wareham	102,408
Warren	62,288
Warwick	40,151
Washington	33,691
Webster	114,084
Wellfleet	30,677
Wendell	38,438

West Boylston	49,932
West Bridgewater	52,860
West Brookfield	43,715
West Newbury	31,574
West Springfield	214,379
West Stockbridge	26,860
West Tisbury	10,714
Westborough	100,012
Westfield	256,668
Westford	93,653
Westhampton	28,109
Westminster	71,300
Westport	94,176
Whately	26,707
Whitman	80,111
Wilbraham	92,077
Williamsburg	32,625
Williamstown	63,414
Winchendon	86,363
Windsor	41,343
Worcester	1,251,014
Worthington	39,302
Wrentham	61,194
Yarmouth	133,626
	$25,000,000

The sum payable to each city and town as provided in this section shall be used only to reimburse such city or town for funds expended for the purpose of reconstruction, maintenance, and repair of public highways and bridges, and of the enforcement of traffic laws, and shall not exceed the amount so expended by such city or town on or before June thirtieth, nineteen hundred and seventy-five.

The department shall certify said apportionment to the comptroller and such sums approved by the department not exceeding twenty-five million dollars shall be made available for distribution on or before January thirty-first, nineteen hundred and seventy-four; provided, that the mayor of each city and selectmen of each town shall notify the department in writing of the amount that will be expended by their respective cities and towns for the reconstruction, maintenance and repair of highways and bridges and for the enforcement of traffic laws on or before June thirtieth, nineteen hundred and seventy-five.

History—

1973, 1140, § 22; 1974, 825, §§ 12, 13.

§ 23.   Issuance and Sale of Bonds Designated Highway Improvement Loan Act of 1973.

To meet the expenditures necessary in carrying out the provisions of sections twenty and twenty-one of this act, the state treasurer shall, upon request of the governor, issue and sell at public or private sale bonds of the commonwealth, registered or with interest coupons attached, as he may deem best, to an amount to be specified by the governor from time to time, but not exceeding in the aggregate, the sum of seventeen million five hundred thousand dollars. All bonds issued by the commonwealth, as aforesaid, shall be designated on their face, Highway Improvement Loan, Act of 1973, and shall be on the serial payment plan for such maximum term of years, not exceeding twenty years, as the governor may recommend to the general court pursuant to Section 3 of Article LXII of the Amendments to the Constitution of the Commonwealth, the maturities thereof to be so arranged that the amounts payable in the several years of the period of amortization, other than the final year, shall be as nearly equal as in the opinion of the state treasurer it is practicable to make them. Said bonds shall bear interest semiannually at such rate as the state treasurer, with the approval of the governor shall fix. The initial maturities of such bonds shall be payable not later than one year from the date of issue thereof, and the entire issue not later than June thirtieth, nineteen hundred and ninety-seven. All interest payments and payments on account of principal on such bonds shall be payable from the Highway Fund; provided that notwithstanding the foregoing, such bonds shall be general obligations of the commonwealth.

History—
1973, 1140, § 23.

§ 24.   Appropriations from Highway Fund Debt Service.

To meet the expenditures authorized by section twenty-two of this act there is hereby appropriated from the Highway Fund debt service amount the sum of twenty-five million dollars.

History—
1973, 1140, § 24.

§ 25.   [1973, 1140, § 25 amended Acts 1972, ch. 765, § 1.]

§ 26.   MBTA May Alter or Change Power Source for Generators.

Notwithstanding any special or general law to the contrary, or any provisions of this act, the Massachusetts Bay Transportation Authority shall not be prohibited from altering or changing the source of power for its generators.

History—
1973, 1140, § 26.

§ 27. Massachusetts Aeronautics Commission's Expenditures for Airport Systems Planning and Reimbursements to Cities and Towns.

The Massachusetts aeronautics commission is hereby authorized and directed to expend a sum not exceeding two million dollars for airport systems planning in the commonwealth and for reimbursements to cities, towns, excluding the town of Norwood, and counties for planning, design and construction of airports pursuant to sections thirty-nine F and fifty-one K of chapter ninety of the General Laws. The town of Norwood shall, pursuant to said sections thirty-nine F and fifty-one K, be so reimbursed for the cost of the repair of existing runways, taxiways and parking aprons, made at its airport with the approval of said town and the Massachusetts aeronautics commission. Funds provided in this section shall be in addition to any prior appropriations authorized for the purposes of this section, and, ninety per cent of such bond proceeds shall be expended only for projects for which the federal government has provided grants averaging fifty per cent of the estimated eligible cost of such projects or for expenditures which are preliminary to the obtaining of federal grants.

History—
1973, 1140, § 27; 1976, 493.

Cross References—
Massachusetts Aeronautics Commission, generally, see ALM GL c 90 §§ 39 et seq.

§ 28. Issuance and Sale of Bonds Designated Airport Outlay Loan Act of 1973.

To meet the expenditures necessary in carrying out the provisions of section twenty-seven of this act, the state treasurer shall, upon request of the governor, issue and sell at public or private sale, bonds of the commonwealth, registered or with interest coupons attached, as he may deem best, to an amount to be specified by the governor from time to time, but not exceeding in the aggregate the sum of two million dollars. All bonds, issued by the commonwealth, as aforesaid, shall be designated on their face, Airport Capital Outlay Loan, Act of 1973, and shall be on the serial payment plan for such maximum term of years, not exceeding twenty years, as the governor may recommend to the general court pursuant to Section 3 of Article LXII of the Amendments to the Constitution of the Commonwealth the maturities thereof to be so arranged that the amounts payable in the several years of the period of amortization, other than the final year, shall be as nearly equal as in the opinion of the state treasurer it is practicable to make them. Said bonds shall bear interest semiannually at such rate as the state treasurer, with the approval of the governor shall fix. The initial maturities of such bonds shall be payable not later than one year from the date of issue thereof, and the entire issue not later than June thirtieth, nineteen hundred and ninety-seven. All interest payments and payments on account of principal on such bonds shall be payable from the General Fund; provided that notwithstanding the foregoing, such bonds shall be general obligations of the commonwealth.

History—
1973, 1140, § 28.

Editorial Note—
Acts 1981, ch. 13, § 39, entitled "An act relative to the terms of certain bonds and notes to be issued by the Commonwealth, provides as follows:

SECTION 39. Notwithstanding any provision of law to the contrary, the bonds which the state treasurer is authorized to issue under section twenty-eight of chapter one thousand one hundred and forty of the acts of nineteen hundred and seventy-three, if issued after January first, nineteen hundred and eighty-one, shall be issued for a term not to exceed twenty years, provided, however, that all such bonds shall be payable by June thirtieth, nineteen hundred and ninety-seven, as recommended by the governor in a message to the general court dated January twenty-sixth, nineteen hundred and eighty-one, in pursuance of Section 3 of Article LXII of the Amendments to the Constitution of the Commonwealth.

§ 29.   Expenditures Based on Federal Support.

The proceeds of ninety per cent of the additional forty million dollars in bond authorizations authorized by section 23 of chapter 161A of the general laws as amended by section 14 of this act, shall be expended only for projects for which the authority has agreement with the federal government providing for grants averaging four-fifths of the estimated eligible costs of such projects or for expenditures which are preliminary to the obtaining of federal grants.

History—
1973, 1140, § 29.

§ 30.   Effective Date; Termination of Terms of Office.

Sections five, six, seven, ten, eighteen, and nineteen of this act shall take effect on January first, nineteen hundred and seventy-five. The members of the board of directors appointed under section six of chapter 161A of the general laws, as existing immediately prior to the effective date of section 10, shall serve until the end of their respective terms; provided, however, that the term of the director designated as chairman by the governor pursuant to the provisions of section 6 of chapter 161A of the general laws, as existing immediately prior to the effective date of section 10 of this act, shall terminate upon the effective date of said section 10. On October 15, 1975, section three of this act shall take effect, and the appointment and employment of the general manager pursuant to paragraph (d) of section three of said chapter one hundred and sixty-one A of the General Laws shall be terminated and all of the powers and duties of said general manager shall thereafter be exercised by the chairman.

History—
1973, 1140, § 30.

CHAPTER S81

Nantucket Regional Transit Authority

(Acts 1986, Ch. 304)

> **Auto-Cite®**: Cases and annotations referred to herein can be further researched through the Auto-Cite® computer-assisted research service. Use Auto-Cite to check citations for form, parallel references, prior and later history, and annotation references.

§ 1. Nantucket Regional Transit Authority.

There is hereby established the Nantucket Regional Transit Authority. The territory of the town of Nantucket and the inhabitants of said town shall constitute said Authority and shall be a body politic and corporate and a political subdivision of the commonwealth.

History—
1986, 304, § 1.

§ 2. Advisory Board Established; Powers.

There is hereby established an advisory board to said Authority consisting of the five members of the board of selectmen of said town. Said Authority shall have the power to provide funding for Nantucket's elderly van services in view of the need to replace and expand existing equipment and services, and in view of cutbacks in traditional funding sources; to improve parking opportunities for downtown employees by making physical improvements to existing satellite parking lots and by acquiring and improving additional sites; and to fund and conduct a professionally prepared island-wide transportation study to address the problems of traffic congestion, parking, elderly transportation services, and transit.

Said Authority shall have all the powers granted to a "Transit Authority" under the provisions of chapter one hundred and sixty-one B of the General Laws.

All the provisions of said chapter one hundred and sixty-one B, not inconsistent with the provisions of this act, shall be applicable to the Nantucket Regional Transit Authority.

History—

1986, 304, § 2.

TITLE IX

INTERSTATE COMPACTS AND AGREEMENTS

CHAPTER S91

Compact with Other New England States Relative to Military Aid in an Emergency

(Acts 1957, Ch. 650)

Auto-Cite®: Cases and annotations referred to herein can be further researched through the Auto-Cite® computer-assisted research service. Use Auto-Cite to check citations for form, parallel references, prior and later history, and annotation references.

Form of Compact

Whereas, The deferred operation of this act would tend to defeat its purpose, which is to provide forthwith, with the consent of Congress, for mutual military aid between the commonwealth and the other New England states in certain cases of emergency, therefore it is hereby declared to be an emergency law necessary for the immediate preservation of the public convenience and safety.

The governor is hereby authorized and requested to execute, on behalf of the commonwealth, with the states of Connecticut, Maine, New Hampshire, Rhode Island and Vermont, or with such of said states as may join therein, a compact for the purpose of providing for mutual military aid, and matters incidental thereto, in the event of an emergency caused or brought about by invasion or other hostile action, disaster or insurrection, or imminent danger thereof, said compact to be in the form substantially as follows:

AN INTERSTATE COMPACT FOR MUTUAL MILITARY AID IN
AN EMERGENCY

ARTICLE I

1. The purposes of this compact are:

(a) To provide for mutual military aid and assistance in an emergency by the military forces of a signatory state to the military forces of the other signatory states or of the United States, including among other military missions, the protection of interstate bridges, tunnels, ferries, pipe lines, communications facilities and other vital installations, plants and facilities; and the military support of civil defense agencies;

(b) To provide for the fresh pursuit in case of an emergency, by the military forces or any part or member thereof of a signatory state into another state, of insurrectionists, saboteurs, enemies or enemy forces or persons seeking or appearing to seek to overthrow the government of the United States or of a signatory state;

(c) To make provision for the powers, duties, rights, privileges and immunities of the members of the military forces of a signatory state while so engaged outside of their own state.

2.(a) "Emergency" as used in this compact shall mean and include invasion or other hostile action, disaster or insurrection, or imminent danger thereof.

(b) "State" as used in this compact shall include any signatory state.

(c) "Military forces" as used in this compact shall include the organized militia, or any force thereof, of a signatory state.

ARTICLE II

This compact shall become effective as to the signatory states when the legislatures thereof have approved it and when the Congress has given its consent either before or after the date hereof. Any state not a party to this compact at the date hereof may become a party hereto.

ARTICLE III

The governor of each signatory state or his designated military representative shall constitute the Committee for Mutual Military Aid for the signatory states. It shall be the duty of the Committee for Mutual Military Aid to make joint plans for the employment of the military forces of the signatory states for mutual military aid and assistance in case of emergency.

ARTICLE IV

[1.] It shall be the duty of each signatory state to integrate its plan for the employment of its military forces in case of emergency with the joint plans recommended by the Committee for Mutual Military Aid and with the emergency plans of the armed forces of the United States.

2. In case of emergency, upon the request of the Governor of a signatory state, the Governor of each signatory state, to the extent consistent with the needs of his own state, shall order its military forces or such part thereof as he, in his discretion, may find necessary, to assist the military forces of the requesting state in order to carry out the purposes set forth in this compact. In such case, it shall be the duty of the Governor of each signatory state receiving such a request to issue the necessary orders for such use of the military forces of his state without the borders of his state and to direct the commander of such forces to place them under the operational control of the commander of the forces of the requesting

229

state or of the United States which may be engaged in meeting the emergency.

3. The Governor of any signatory state, in his discretion, may recall the military forces of his state serving without its borders or any part or any member of such forces.

ARTICLE V

In case of an emergency, any unit or member of the military forces of a signatory state which has been ordered into active service by the Governor may upon order of the officer in immediate command thereof continue beyond the borders of his own state into another signatory state in fresh pursuit of insurrectionists, saboteurs, enemies or enemy forces or persons seeking or appearing to seek to overthrow the government of the United States or of any one of the signatory states, until they are apprehended by such unit or member. Any such person who shall be apprehended or captured in a signatory state by a unit or member of the military forces of another signatory state shall without unnecessary delay be surrendered to the military or police forces of the state in which he is taken or to the forces of the United States. Such surrender shall not constitute a waiver by the state of the military forces making the capture, of its right to extradite or prosecute such persons for any crime committed in that state.

ARTICLE VI

1. Whenever the military forces or any part thereof of any signatory state are engaged outside of their own state in carrying out the purposes of this compact, the individual members of such military forces so engaged shall not be liable, civilly or criminally, for any act or acts done by them in the performance of their duty.

2. The individual members of such forces shall have the same powers, duties, rights, privileges and immunities as the members of the military forces of the state in which they are engaged, but in any event,

3. Each signatory state shall save harmless any member of its military forces wherever serving and any member of the military forces of any other signatory state serving within its borders for any act or acts done by them in the performance of their duty while engaged in carrying out the purposes of this compact.

ARTICLE VII

1. Each signatory state shall provide, in the same amounts and manner as if they were on duty within their own state, for the pay and allowances of the personnel of its military forces, and for the

medical and hospital expenses, disability and death benefits, pensions and funeral expenses of wounded, injured or sick personnel and of dependents or representatives of deceased personnel of its military forces, in case such personnel shall suffer wounds, injuries, disease, disability or death while engaged without the state pursuant to this compact and while going to and returning from such other signatory state. Each signatory state shall provide in the same amounts and manner as if they were on duty within their own state for the logistical support and for other costs and expenses of its military forces while engaged without the state pursuant to this compact and while going to and returning from such other signatory state.

2. Any signatory state rendering outside aid in case of insurrection or disaster not the result of invasion or hostile action, shall, if it so elects, be reimbursed by the signatory state receiving such aid for the pay and allowances of its personnel, logistical support and all other costs and expenses referred to in section one of this Article and incurred in connection with the request for aid. Such election shall be exercised by the Governor of the aiding state presenting a statement and request for reimbursement of such costs and expenses to the Governor of the requesting state.

ARTICLE VIII

Nothing in this compact shall be construed to limit or restrict the power of any signatory state in case of an emergency affecting that state only, to provide for the internal defense of any part of the territory of said state or for the protection and control of any bridge, tunnel, ferry, installation, plant or facility or any part thereof within the borders of such state or to prohibit the enforcement of any laws, rules and regulations or the execution of any plan with regard thereto.

ARTICLE IX

This compact shall continue in force and remain binding on each signatory state until the legislature or the Governor of such state gives notice of withdrawal therefrom. Such notice of withdrawal shall not be effective until six months after said notice has been given to the Governor of each of the other statutory states.

History—
1957, 650.

Cross References—
When Armed Forces may be ordered outside of commonwealth, see ALM GL c 33 § 39.
Call of militia in case of invasion, insurrection, etc., see ALM GL c 33 § 40.

Call of militia in case of tumult, riot, etc., see ALM GL c 33 § 41.

No liability for acts under certain orders, see ALM GL c 33 § 53.

Pay and allowances for militia, see ALM GL c 33 §§ 83 et seq.

Claims for personal injury and property damage, see ALM GL c 33 §§ 88 et seq.

CHAPTER S93

Compact with New York for Military Aid in an Emergency

(Acts 1957, Ch 707)

Auto-Cite®: Cases and annotations referred to herein can be further researched through the Auto-Cite® computer-assisted research service. Use Auto-Cite to check citations for form, parallel references, prior and later history, and annotation references.

Form of Compact

For the purpose of providing for mutual military aid, and matters incidental thereto, in the event of an emergency caused or brought about by invasion or other hostile action, disaster, insurrection or imminent danger thereof, the governor is hereby authorized and requested to execute, on behalf of the commonwealth, with the State of New York an agreement making the commonwealth a party to the pertinent compact for said purpose as consented to and authorized by the Act of July 1, 1952, Public Law 435 of the 82nd Congress (66 Stat. 315), as amended by the Act of June 4, 1956, Public Law 564 of the 84th Congress.

The compact referred to in the preceding paragraph reads as follows:—

AN INTERSTATE COMPACT FOR MUTUAL MILITARY AID IN AN EMERGENCY

ARTICLE I.

1. The purposes of this compact are:

(a) To provide for mutual military aid and assistance in an emergency by the military forces of a signatory state to the military forces of the other signatory states or of the United States, including among other military missions, the protection of interstate bridges, tunnels, ferries, pipe lines, communications facilities and other vital installations, plants and facilities; and the military support of civil defense agencies;

(b) To provide for the fresh pursuit in case of an emergency, by the military forces or any part or member thereof of a signatory state into another state, of insurrectionists, saboteurs, enemies or enemy forces or persons seeking or appearing to seek to overthrow the government of the United States or of a signatory state;

(c) To make provision for the powers, duties, rights, privileges and immunities of the members of the military forces of a signatory state while so engaged outside of their own state.

2.(a) "Emergency" as used in this compact shall mean and include invasion or other hostile action, disaster, insurrection or imminent danger thereof.

(b) "State" as used in this compact shall include any signatory state.

(c) "Military forces" as used in this compact shall include the organized militia, or any force thereof, of a signatory state.

ARTICLE II.

This compact shall become effective as to the signatory states when the legislatures thereof have approved it and when the Congress has given its consent either before or after the date hereof. Any state not a party to this compact at the date hereof may become a party hereto.

ARTICLE III.

The governor of each signatory state or his designated military representative shall constitute the Committee for Mutual Military Aid for the signatory states. It shall be the duty of the Committee for Mutual Military Aid to make joint plans for the employment of the military forces of the signatory states for mutual military aid and assistance in case of emergency.

ARTICLE IV.

1. It shall be the duty of each signatory state to integrate its plan for the employment of its military forces in case of emergency with the joint plans recommended by the Committee for Mutual Military Aid and with the emergency plans of the armed forces of the United States.

2. In case of emergency, upon the request of the Governor of a signatory state, the Governor of each signatory state, to the extent consistent with the needs of his own state, shall order its military forces or such part thereof as he, in his discretion, may find necessary, to assist the military forces of the requesting state in order to carry out the purposes set forth in this compact. In such case, it shall be the duty of the governor of each signatory state receiving such a request to issue the necessary orders for such use of the military forces of his state without the borders of his state and to direct the commander of such forces to place them under the operational control of the commander of the forces of the requesting state or of the United States which may be engaged in meeting the emergency.

3. The governor of any signatory state, in his discretion, may recall the military forces of his state serving without its borders or any part or any member of such forces.

ARTICLE V.

In case of an emergency, any unit or member of the military forces of a signatory state which has been ordered into active service by the Governor may upon order of the officer in immediate command thereof continue beyond the borders of his own state into another signatory state in fresh pursuit of insurrectionists, saboteurs, enemies or enemy forces or persons seeking or appearing to seek to overthrow the government of the United States or of any one of the signatory states, until they are apprehended by such unit or member. Any such person who shall be apprehended or captured in a signatory state by a unit or member of the military forces of another signatory state shall without unnecessary delay be surrendered to the military or police forces of the state in which he is taken or to the forces of the United States. Such surrender shall not constitute a waiver by the state of the military forces making the capture, of its right to extradite or prosecute such persons for any crime committed in that state.

ARTICLE VI.

1. Whenever the military forces or any part thereof of any signatory state are engaged outside of their own state in carrying out the purposes of this compact, the individual members of such military forces so engaged shall not be liable, civilly or criminally, for any act or acts done by them in the performance of their duty.

2. The individual members of such forces shall have the same powers, duties, rights, privileges and immunities as the members of the military forces of the state in which they are engaged, but in any event,

3. Each signatory state shall save harmless any member of its military forces wherever serving and any member of the military forces of any other signatory state serving within its borders for any act or acts done by them in the performance of their duty while engaged in carrying out the purposes of this compact.

ARTICLE VII.

1. Each signatory state shall provide, in the same amounts and manner as if they were on duty within their own state, for the pay and allowances of the personnel of its military forces, and for the medical and hospital expenses, disability and death benefits, pensions and funeral expenses of wounded, injured or sick personnel and of dependents or representatives of deceased personnel of its military

forces, in case such personnel shall suffer wounds, injuries, disease, disability or death while engaged without the state pursuant to this compact and while going to and returning from such other signatory state. Each signatory state shall provide in the same amounts and manner as if they were on duty within their own state for the logistical support and for other costs and expenses of its military forces while engaged without the state pursuant to this compact and while going to and returning from such other signatory state.

2. Any signatory state rendering outside aid in case of insurrection or disaster not the result of invasion or hostile action, shall, if it so elects, be reimbursed by the signatory state receiving such aid for the pay and allowances of its personnel, logistical support and all other costs and expenses referred to in section 1 of this Article and incurred in connection with the request for aid. Such election shall be exercised by the Governor of the aiding state presenting a statement and request for reimbursement of such costs and expenses to the Governor of the requesting state.

ARTICLE VIII.

Nothing in this compact shall be construed to limit or restrict the power of any signatory state in case of an emergency affecting that state only, to provide for the internal defense of any part of the territory of said state or for the protection and control of any bridge, tunnel, ferry, installation, plant or facility or any part thereof within the borders of such state or to prohibit the enforcement of any laws, rules and regulations or the execution of any plan with regard thereto.

ARTICLE IX.

This compact shall continue in force and remain binding on each signatory state until the legislature or the Governor of such state gives notice of withdrawal therefrom. Such notice of withdrawal shall not be effective until six months after said notice has been given to the Governor of each of the other signatory states.

History—
1957, 707.

Cross References—
When Armed Forces may be ordered outside of commonwealth, see ALM GL c 33 § 39.

Call of militia in case of invasion, insurrection, etc., see ALM GL c 33 § 40.

Call of militia in case of tumult, riot, etc., see ALM GL c 33 § 41.

No liability for acts under certain orders, see ALM GL c 33 § 53.

Pay and allowances for militia, see ALM GL c 33 §§ 83 et seq.

Claims for personal injury and property damage, see ALM GL c 33 §§ 88 et seq.

CHAPTER S95

Interstate Compact on the Placement of Children

(Acts 1963, Ch. 452)

Auto-Cite®: Cases and annotations referred to herein can be further researched through the Auto-Cite® computer-assisted research service. Use Auto-Cite to check citations for form, parallel references, prior and later history, and annotation references.

---

§ 1.   Form of Compact.

A compact is hereby entered into with all jurisdictions legally joining therein in substantially the following form:—

INTERSTATE COMPACT ON THE PLACEMENT OF CHILDREN

ARTICLE I. PURPOSE AND POLICY.

It is the purpose and policy of the party states to co-operate with each other in the interstate placement of children to the end that:

(a) Each child requiring placement shall receive the maximum opportunity to be placed in a suitable environment and with persons or institutions having appropriate qualifications and facilities to provide a necessary and desirable degree and type of care.

(b) The appropriate authorities in a state where a child is to be placed may have full opportunity to ascertain the circumstances of the proposed placement, thereby promoting full compliance with applicable requirements for the protection of the child.

(c) The proper authorities of the state from which the placement is made may obtain the most complete information on the basis of which to evaluate a projected placement before it is made.

(d) Appropriate jurisdictional arrangements for the care of children will be promoted.

ARTICLE II. DEFINITIONS.

As used in this compact:

(a) "Child" means a person who, by reason of minority, is legally subject to parental guardianship or similar control.

(b) "Sending agency" means a party state, officer or employee thereof; a subdivision of a party state, or officer or employee thereof; a court of a party state; a person, corporation, association, charitable agency or other entity which sends, brings or causes to be sent or brought any child to another party state.

(c) "Receiving state" means the state to which a child is sent, brought or caused to be sent or brought, whether by public authorities or private persons or agencies, and whether for placement with state or local public authorities or for placement with private agencies or persons.

(d) "Placement" means the arrangement for the care of a child in a family free or boarding home or in a child-caring agency or institution but does not include any institution caring for the mentally ill, mentally defective or epileptic or any institution primarily educational in character, and any hospital or other medical facility.

ARTICLE III. CONDITIONS FOR PLACEMENT.

(a) No sending agency shall send, bring or cause to be sent or brought into any other party state any child for placement in foster care or as a preliminary to a possible adoption unless the sending agency shall comply with each and every requirement set forth in this article and with the applicable laws of the receiving state governing the placement of children therein.

(b) Prior to sending, bringing or causing any child to be sent or brought into a receiving state for placement in foster care or as a preliminary to a possible adoption, the sending agency shall furnish the appropriate public authorities in the receiving state written notice of the intention to send, bring or place the child in the receiving state. The notice shall contain:

(1) The name, date and place of birth of the child.

(2) The identity and address or addresses of the parents or legal guardian.

(3) The name and address of the person, agency or institution to or with which the sending agency proposes to send, bring or place the child.

(4) A full statement of the reasons for such proposed action and evidence of the authority pursuant to which the placement is proposed to be made.

(c) Any public officer or agency in a receiving state which is in receipt of a notice pursuant to paragraph (b) of this article may request of the sending agency, or any other appropriate officer or agency of or in the sending agency's state, and shall be entitled to receive therefrom, such supporting or additional information as it may deem necessary under the circumstances to carry out the purpose and policy of this compact.

(d) The child shall not be sent, brought or caused to be sent or brought into the receiving state until the appropriate public authorities in the receiving state shall notify the sending agency, in writing, to the effect that the proposed placement does not appear to be contrary to the interests of the child.

ARTICLE IV. PENALTY FOR ILLEGAL PLACEMENT.

The sending, bringing or causing to be sent or brought into any receiving state of a child in violation of the terms of this compact shall constitute a violation of the laws respecting the placement of children of both the state in which the sending agency is located or from which it sends or brings the child and of the receiving state. Such violation may be punished or subjected to penalty in either jurisdiction in accordance with its laws. In addition to liability for any such punishment or penalty, any such violation shall constitute full and sufficient grounds for the suspension or revocation of any license, permit or other legal authorization held by the sending agency which empowers or allows it to place or care for children.

ARTICLE V. RETENTION OF JURISDICTION.

(a) The sending agency shall retain jurisdiction over the child sufficient to determine all matters in relation to the custody, supervision, care, treatment and disposition of the child which it would have had if the child had remained in the sending agency's state, until the child is adopted, reaches majority, becomes self-supporting or is discharged with the concurrence of the appropriate authority in the receiving state. Such jurisdiction shall also include the power to effect or cause the return of the child or its transfer to another location and custody pursuant to law. The sending agency shall continue to have financial responsibility for support and maintenance of the child during the period of the placement. Nothing contained herein shall defeat a claim of jurisdiction by a receiving state sufficient to deal with an act of delinquency or crime committed therein.

(b) When the sending agency is a public agency, it may enter into an agreement with an authorized public or private agency in the receiving state providing for the performance of one or more services in respect of such case by the latter as agent for the sending agency.

(c) Nothing in this compact shall be construed to prevent a private charitable agency authorized to place children in the receiving state from performing services or acting as agent in that state for a private charitable agency of the sending state; nor to prevent the agency in the receiving state from discharging financial responsibility for the support and maintenance of a child who has been placed on behalf of the sending agency without relieving the responsibility set forth in paragraph (a) hereof.

ARTICLE VI. INSTITUTIONAL CARE OF DELINQUENT CHILDREN.

A child adjudicated delinquent may be placed in an institution in another party jurisdiction pursuant to this compact, but no such placement shall be made unless the child is given a court hearing on notice to the parent or guardian with opportunity to be heard, prior to his being sent to such other party jurisdiction for institutional care and the court finds that:

1. Equivalent facilities for the child are not available in the sending agency's jurisdiction; and

2. Institutional care in the other jurisdiction is in the best interest of the child and will not produce undue hardship.

ARTICLE VII. COMPACT ADMINISTRATOR.

The executive head of each jurisdiction party to this compact shall designate an officer who shall be general co-ordinator of activities under this compact in his jurisdiction and who, acting jointly with like officers of other party jurisdictions, shall have power to promulgate rules and regulations to carry out more effectively the terms and provisions of this compact.

ARTICLE VIII. LIMITATIONS.

This compact shall not apply to:

(a) The sending or bringing of a child into a receiving state by his parent, stepparent, grandparent, adult brother or sister, adult uncle or aunt, or his guardian and leaving the child with any such relative or non-agency guardian in the receiving state.

(b) Any placement, sending or bringing of a child into a receiving state pursuant to any other interstate compact to which both the state from which the child is sent or brought and the receiving state are party, or to any other agreement between said states which has the force of law.

ARTICLE IX. ENACTMENT AND WITHDRAWAL.

This compact shall be open to joinder by any state, territory or possession of the United States, the District of Columbia, the Commonwealth of Puerto Rico, and, with the consent of Congress, the Government of Canada or any province thereof. It shall become effective with respect to any such jurisdiction when such jurisdiction has enacted the same into law. Withdrawal from this compact shall be by the enactment of a statute repealing the same, but shall not take effect until two years after the effective date of such statute and until written notice of the withdrawal has been given by the withdrawing state to the governor of each other party jurisdiction. Withdrawal of a party state shall not affect the rights, duties and obligations under this compact of any sending agency therein with respect to a placement made prior to the effective date of withdrawal.

ARTICLE X. CONSTRUCTION AND SEVERABILITY.

The provisions of this compact shall be liberally construed to effectuate the purposes thereof. The provisions of this compact shall be severable and if any phrase, clause, sentence or provision of this compact is declared to be contrary to the constitution of any party state or of the United States or the applicability thereof to any government, agency, person or circumstances is held invalid, the validity of the remainder of this compact and the applicability thereof to any government, agency, person or circumstance shall not be affected thereby. If this compact shall be held contrary to the constitution of any state party thereto, the compact shall remain in full force and effect as to the remaining states and in full force and effect as to the state affected as to all severable matters.

History—
1963, 452, § 1.

Cross References—
Protection and care of children, see ALM GL c 119.

CASE NOTES

When child who is subject to ongoing care and protection case is placed with agreement and participation of Commonwealth in another state, Interstate Compact on Placement of Children (St. 1963, c 452, § 1) should be followed to assure that services and treatment continue until they are determined to be no longer necessary. Custody of Quincy (1990) 29 Mass App 981, 562 NE2d 94.

§ 2. Law Inapplicable to Compact.

The provisions of section thirty-six of chapter one hundred and nineteen of the General Laws shall not apply to a public sending agency of, or in, another state party to said compact.

History—
1963, 452, § 2.

§ 3. Financial Responsibility for Child.

Financial responsibility for any child placed pursuant to the provisions of the interstate compact on the placement of children shall be determined in accordance with the provisions of Article V thereof in the first instance. However, in the event of partial or complete default of performance thereunder, the provisions of said section thirty-six also may be invoked.

History—
1963, 452, § 3.

§ 4. Appropriate Authority in the Receiving State, Defined.

As used in Articles III (b) and V (a) of the interstate compact on the placement of children, the phrase "appropriate authority in the receiving state" with reference to the Commonwealth of Massachusetts shall mean the state department of public welfare.

History—
1963, 452, § 4.

§ 5. Agreements With Officers or Agencies of Other States Relating to Placement.

The officers and agencies of the commonwealth and its political subdivisions having authority to place children are hereby empowered to enter into agreements with appropriate officers or agencies of or in other party states pursuant to Article V (b) of the interstate compact on the placement of children. Any such agreement which contains a financial commitment or imposes a financial obligation on the commonwealth or a political subdivision or agency thereof shall not be binding unless it has the approval in writing of the commissioner of administration in the case of the commonwealth and of the chief local fiscal officer in the case of a political subdivision thereof.

History—
1963, 452, § 5.

§ 6.   Requirements for Visitation, Inspection or Supervision of Children, Homes or Institutions in Another Party State.

Any requirements for visitation, inspection or supervision of children, homes, institutions or other agencies in another party state which may apply under sections fourteen, fifteen and sixteen of said chapter one hundred and nineteen, shall be deemed to be met if performed pursuant to an agreement entered into by appropriate officers or agencies of the commonwealth or a political subdivision thereof as contemplated by Article V (b) of the interstate compact on the placement of children.

History—
1963, 452, § 6.

§ 7.   Jurisdiction of Courts to Place Delinquent Children.

Any court having jurisdiction to place delinquent children may place a delinquent child in an institution of or in another state pursuant to Article VI of the interstate compact on the placement of children, and shall retain jurisdiction as provided in Article V thereof.

History—
1963, 452, § 7.

Cross References—
Delinquent children, see ALM GL c 119, §§ 52 et seq.

§ 8.   Executive Head, Defined.

As used in Article VII of the interstate compact on the placement of children, the term "executive head" means the governor.

History—
1963, 452, § 8.

CHAPTER S97

Compact Relative to the Supervision, Care and Assistance to Juveniles

(Acts 1955, Ch 687)

Auto-Cite®: Cases and annotations referred to herein can be further researched through the Auto-Cite® computer-assisted research service. Use Auto-Cite to check citations for form, parallel references, prior and later history, and annotation references.

---

§ 1. Form of Compact.

The governor is hereby authorized and directed to execute a compact on behalf of this commonwealth with any other state or states legally joining therein in the form substantially as follows:

INTERSTATE COMPACT ON JUVENILES

The contracting states solemnly agree:

ARTICLE I.—FINDINGS AND PURPOSES

That juveniles who are not under proper supervision and control, or who have absconded, escaped or run away, are likely to endanger their own health, morals and welfare, and the health, morals and welfare of others. The co-operation of the states party to this compact is therefore necessary to provide for the welfare and protection of juveniles and of the public with respect to (1) co-operative supervision of delinquent juveniles on probation or paroled; (2) the return, from one state to another, of delinquent

245

juveniles who have escaped or absconded; (3) the return, from one state to another, of non-delinquent juveniles who have run away from home; and (4) additional measures for the protection of juveniles and of the public, which any two or more of the party states may find desirable to undertake co-operatively. In carrying out the provisions of this compact the party states shall be guided by the non-criminal, reformative and protective policies which guide their laws concerning delinquent, neglected or dependent juveniles generally. It shall be the policy of the states party to this compact to co-operate and observe their respective responsibilities for the prompt return and acceptance of juveniles and delinquent juveniles who become subject to the provisions of this compact. The provisions of this compact shall be reasonably and liberally construed to accomplish the foregoing purposes.

ARTICLE II.—EXISTING RIGHTS AND REMEDIES

That all remedies and procedures provided by this compact shall be in addition to and not in substitution for other rights, remedies and procedures, and shall not be in derogation of parental rights and responsibilities.

ARTICLE III.—DEFINITIONS

That, for the purposes of this compact, "delinquent juvenile" means any juvenile who has been adjudged delinquent, and who, at the time the provisions of this compact are invoked, is still subject to the jurisdiction of the court that has made such adjudication or to the jurisdiction or supervision of an agency or institution pursuant to an order of such court; "probation or parole" means any kind of conditional release of juveniles authorized under the laws of the states party hereto; "court" means any court having jurisdiction over delinquent, neglected or dependent children; "state" means any state, territory or possession of the United States, the District of Columbia, and the Commonwealth of Puerto Rico; and "residence" or any variant thereof means a place at which a home or regular place of abode is maintained.

ARTICLE IV.—RETURN OF RUNAWAYS

(a) That the parent, guardian, person or agency entitled to legal custody of a juvenile who has not been adjudged delinquent, but who has run away without the consent of such parent, guardian, person or agency, may petition the appropriate court in the demanding state for the issuance of a requisition for his return. The petition shall state the name and age of the juvenile, the name of the petitioner, and the basis of entitlement to the juvenile's custody, the circumstances of his running away, his location if known at the time application is made, and such other facts as may tend to show that the juvenile who has run away is endangering his own welfare or the welfare of others and is not an emancipated minor. The petition shall be verified by affidavit, shall be executed in duplicate, and shall be accompanied by two certified copies of the document or documents on which the petitioner's entitlement to the juvenile's custody is based, such as birth certificates, letters of guardianship, or custody decrees. Such further affidavits and other documents as may be deemed proper may be submitted with such petition. The judge of the court to which such petition is addressed may hold a hearing thereon to determine whether for the purposes of this compact the petitioner is entitled to the legal custody of the juvenile, whether or not it appears that the juvenile has in fact run away without consent, whether or not he is an emancipated minor, and whether or not it is in the best interest of the juvenile to compel his return to the state. If the judge determines, either with or without a hearing, that the juvenile should be returned, he shall present to the appropriate court or to the executive authority of the state where the juvenile is alleged to be located a written requisition for the return of such juvenile. Such requisition shall set forth the name and age of the juvenile, the determination of the court that the juvenile has run away without the consent of a parent, guardian, person or agency entitled to his legal custody, and that it is in the best interest and for the protection of such juvenile that he be returned. In the event that a proceeding for the adjudication of the juvenile as a delinquent, neglected or dependent juvenile is pending in the court at the time when such juvenile runs away, the court may issue a requisition for the return of such juvenile upon its own motion, regardless of the consent of the parent, guardian, person or agency entitled to legal custody, reciting therein the nature and circumstances of the pending proceeding. The requisition shall in every case be executed in duplicate and shall be signed by the judge. One copy of the requisition shall be filed with the compact administrator of the demanding state, there to remain on file subject to the provisions of law governing records of such court. Upon the receipt of a requisition demanding the return of a juvenile who has run away, the court or the executive authority to whom the requisition is addressed shall issue an order to any peace officer or other appropriate person directing him to take into custody and detain such juvenile. Such detention order shall substantially recite the facts necessary to the validity of its issuance hereunder. No juvenile detained upon such order shall be delivered over to the officer whom the court demanding him shall have appointed to receive him, unless he shall first be taken forthwith before a judge of a court in the state, who shall inform him of the demand made for his return, and who may appoint counsel or guardian ad litem for him. If the judge of such court shall find that the requisition is in order, he shall deliver such juvenile over to the officer whom the court demanding him shall have appointed to receive him. The judge, however, may fix a reasonable time to be allowed for the purpose of testing the legality of the proceeding.

Upon reasonable information that a person is a juvenile who has run away from another state party to this compact without the consent of a parent, guardian, person or agency entitled to his legal custody, such juvenile may be taken into custody without a requisition and brought forthwith before a judge of the appropriate court who may appoint counsel or guardian ad litem for such juvenile, and who shall determine after a hearing whether sufficient cause exists to hold the person, subject to the order of the court, for his own protection and welfare, for such a time not exceeding ninety days as will enable his return to another state party to this compact pursuant to a requisition for his return from a court of that state. If, at the time when a state seeks the return of a juvenile who has run away, there is pending in the state wherein he is found any criminal charge, or any proceeding to have him adjudicated a delinquent juvenile for an act committed in such state, or if he is suspected of having committed within such state a criminal offense or an act of juvenile delinquency, he shall not be returned without the consent of such state until discharged from prosecution or other form of proceeding, imprisonment, detention or supervision for such offense or juvenile delinquency. The duly accredited officers of any state party to this compact, upon the establishment of their authority and the identity of the juvenile being returned, shall be permitted to transport such juvenile through any and all states party to this compact, without interference. Upon his return to the state from which he ran away, the juvenile shall be subject to such further proceedings as may be appropriate under the laws of that state.

(b) That the state to which a juvenile is returned under this Article shall be responsible for payment of the transportation costs of such return.

(c) That "juvenile" as used in this Article means any person who is a minor under the law of the state of residence of the parent, guardian, person or agency entitled to the legal custody of such minor.

ARTICLE V.—RETURN OF ESCAPEES AND ABSCONDERS

(a) That the appropriate person or authority from whose probation or parole supervision a delinquent juvenile has absconded or from whose institutional custody he has escaped shall present to the appropriate court or to the executive authority of the state where the delinquent juvenile is alleged to be located a written requisition for the return of such delinquent juvenile. Such requisition shall state the name and age of the delinquent juvenile, the particulars of his adjudication as a delinquent juvenile, the circumstances of the breach of the terms of his probation or parole or of his escape from an institution or agency vested with his legal custody or supervision, and the location of such delinquent juvenile, if known, at the time the requisition is made. The requisition shall be verified by affidavit, shall be executed in duplicate, and shall be accompanied by two certified copies of the judgment, formal adjudication, or order of commitment which subjects such delinquent juvenile to probation or parole or to the legal custody of the institution or agency concerned. Such further affidavits and other documents as may be deemed proper may be submitted with such requisition. One copy of the requisition shall be filed with the compact administrator of the demanding state, there to remain on file subject to the provisions of law governing records of the appropriate court. Upon the receipt of a requisition demanding the return of a delinquent juvenile who has absconded or escaped, the court or the executive authority to whom the requisition is addressed shall issue an order to any peace officer or other appropriate person directing him to take into custody and detain such delinquent juvenile. Such detention order must substantially recite the facts necessary to the validity of its issuance hereunder. No delinquent juvenile detained upon such order shall be delivered over to the officer whom the appropriate person or authority demanding him shall have appointed to receive him, unless he shall first be taken forthwith before a judge of an appropriate court in the state, who shall inform him of the demand made for his return and who may appoint counsel or guardian ad litem for him. If the judge of such court shall find that the requisition is in order, he shall deliver such delinquent juvenile over to the officer whom the appropriate person or authority demanding him shall have appointed to receive him. The judge, however, may fix a reasonable time to be allowed for the purpose of testing the legality of the proceeding.

Upon reasonable information that a person is a delinquent juvenile who has absconded while on probation or parole, or escaped from an institution or agency vested with his legal custody or supervision in any state party to this compact, such person may be taken into custody in any other state party to this compact without a requisition. But in such event, he must be taken forthwith before a judge of the appropriate court, who may appoint counsel or guardian ad litem for such person and who shall determine, after a hearing, whether sufficient cause exists to hold the person subject to the order of the court for such a time, not exceeding ninety days, as will enable his detention under a detention order issued on a requisition pursuant to this Article. If, at the time when a state seeks the return of a delinquent juvenile who has either absconded while on probation or parole or escaped from an institution or agency vested with his legal custody or supervision, there is pending in the state wherein he is detained any criminal charge or any proceeding to have him adjudicated a delinquent juvenile for an act committed in such state, or if he is suspected of having committed within such state a criminal offense or an act of juvenile delinquency, he shall not be returned without the consent of such state until discharged from prosecution or other form of proceeding, imprisonment, detention or supervision for such offense or juvenile delinquency. The duly accredited officers of any state party to this compact, upon the establishment of their authority and the identity of the delinquent juvenile being returned, shall be permitted to transport such delinquent juvenile through any and all states party to this compact, without interference. Upon his return to the state from which he escaped or absconded, the delinquent juvenile shall be subject to such further proceedings as may be appropriate under the laws of that state.

(b) That the state to which a delinquent juvenile is returned under this Article shall be responsible for payment of the transportation costs of such return.

ARTICLE VI.—VOLUNTARY RETURN PROCEDURE

That any delinquent juvenile who has absconded while on probation or parole, or escaped from an institution or agency vested with his legal custody or supervision in any state party to this compact, and any juvenile who has run away from any state party to this compact, who is taken into custody without a requisition in another state party to this compact under the provisions of Article IV (a) or of Article V (a), may consent to his immediate return to the state from which he absconded, escaped or ran away. Such consent shall be given by the juvenile or delinquent juvenile and his counsel or guardian ad litem if any, by executing or subscribing a writing, in the presence of a judge of the appropriate court, which states that the juvenile or delinquent juvenile and his counsel or guardian ad litem, if any, consent to his return to the demanding state. Before such consent shall be executed or subscribed, however, the judge, in the presence of counsel or guardian ad litem, if any, shall inform the juvenile or delinquent juvenile of his rights under this compact. When the consent has been duly executed, it shall be forwarded to and filed with the compact administrator of the state in which the court is located and the judge shall direct the officer having the juvenile or delinquent juvenile in custody to deliver him to the duly accredited officer or officers of the state demanding his return, and shall cause to be delivered to such officer or officers a copy of the consent. The court may, however, upon the request of the state to which the juvenile or delinquent juvenile is being returned, order him to return unaccompanied to such state and shall provide him with a copy of such court order; in such event a copy of the consent shall be forwarded to the compact administrator of the state to which said juvenile or delinquent juvenile is ordered to return.

ARTICLE VII.—CO-OPERATIVE SUPERVISION OF PROBATIONERS AND PAROLEES

(a) That the duly constituted judicial and administrative authorities of a state party to this compact, herein called "sending state", may permit any delinquent juvenile within such state, placed on probation or parole, to reside in any other state party to this compact, herein called "receiving state", while on probation or parole, and the receiving state shall accept such delinquent juvenile, if the parent, guardian or person entitled to the legal custody of such delinquent juvenile is residing or undertakes to reside within the receiving state. Before granting such permission, opportunity shall be given to the receiving state to make such investigations as it deems necessary. The authorities of the sending state shall send to the authorities of the receiving state copies of pertinent court orders, social case studies and all other available information which may be of value to and assist the receiving state in supervising a probationer or parolee under this compact. A receiving state, in its discretion, may agree to accept supervision of a probationer or parolee in cases where the parent, guardian or person entitled to the legal custody of the delinquent juvenile is not a resident of the receiving state, and if so accepted the sending state may transfer supervision accordingly.

(b) That each receiving state will assume the duties of visitation and of supervision over any such delinquent juvenile and in the exercise of those duties will be governed by the same standards of visitation and supervision that prevail for its own delinquent juveniles released on probation or parole.

(c) That, after consultation between the appropriate authorities of the sending state and of the receiving state as to the desirability and necessity of returning such a delinquent juvenile, the duly accredited officers of a sending state may enter a receiving state and there apprehend and retake any such delinquent juvenile on probation or parole. For that purpose, no formalities will be required, other than establishing the authority of the officer and the identity of the delinquent juvenile to be retaken and returned. The decision of the sending state to retake a delinquent juvenile on probation or parole shall be conclusive upon and not reviewable within the receiving state, but if, at the time the sending state seeks to retake a delinquent juvenile on probation or parole, there is pending against him within the receiving state any criminal charge or any proceeding to have him adjudicated a delinquent juvenile for any act committed in such state, or if he is suspected of having committed within such state a criminal offense or an act of juvenile delinquency, he shall not be returned without the consent of the receiving state until discharged from prosecution or other form of proceeding, imprisonment, detention or supervision for such offense or juvenile delinquency. The duly accredited officers of the sending state shall be permitted to transport delinquent juveniles being so returned through any and all states party to this compact, without interference.

(d) That the sending state shall be responsible under this Article for paying the costs of transporting any delinquent juvenile to the receiving state or of returning any delinquent juvenile to the sending state.

ARTICLE VIII.—RESPONSIBILITY FOR COSTS

(a) That the provisions of Articles IV (b), V (b) and VII (d) of this compact shall not be construed to alter or affect any internal relationship among the departments, agencies and officers of and in the government of a party state, or between a party state and its subdivisions, as to the payment of costs, or responsibilities therefor.

(b) That nothing in this compact shall be construed to prevent any party state or subdivision thereof from asserting any right against any person, agency or other entity in regard to costs for which such party state or subdivision thereof may be responsible pursuant to Articles IV (b), V (b) or VII (d) of this compact.

ARTICLE IX.—DETENTION PRACTICES

That, to every extent possible, it shall be the policy of states party to this compact that no juvenile or delinquent juvenile shall be placed or detained in any prison, jail or lockup nor be detained or transported in association with criminal, vicious or dissolute persons.

ARTICLE X.—SUPPLEMENTARY AGREEMENTS

That the duly constituted administrative authorities of a state party to this compact may enter into supplementary agreements with any other state or states party hereto for the co-operative care, treatment and rehabilitation of delinquent juveniles whenever they shall find that such agreements will improve the facilities or programs available for such care, treatment and rehabilitation. Such care, treatment and rehabilitation may be provided in an institution located within any state entering into such supplementary agreement. Such supplementary agreements shall (1) provide the rates to be paid for the care, treatment and custody of such delinquent juveniles, taking into consideration the character of facilities, services and subsistence furnished; (2) provided that the delinquent juvenile shall be given a court hearing prior to his being sent to another state for care, treatment and custody; (3) provide that the state receiving such a delinquent juvenile in one of its institutions shall act solely as agent for the state sending such delinquent juvenile; (4) provide that the sending state shall at all times retain jurisdiction over delinquent juveniles sent to an institution in another state; (5) provide for reasonable inspection of such institutions by the sending state; (6) provide that the consent of the parent, guardian, person or agency entitled to the legal custody of said delinquent juvenile shall be secured prior to his being sent to another state; and (7) make provision for such other matters and details as shall be necessary to protect the rights and equities of such delinquent juveniles and of the co-operating states.

ARTICLE XI.—ACCEPTANCE OF FEDERAL AND OTHER AID

That any state party to this compact may accept any and all donations, gifts and grants of money, equipment and services from the federal or any local government, or any agency thereof and from any person, firm or corporation, for any of the purposes and functions of this compact, and may receive and utilize the same subject to the terms, conditions and regulations governing such donations, gifts and grants.

ARTICLE XII.—COMPACT ADMINISTRATORS

That the governor of each state party to this compact shall designate an officer who, acting jointly with like officers of other party states, shall promulgate rules and regulations to carry out more effectively the terms and provisions of this compact.

ARTICLE XIII.—EXECUTION OF COMPACT

That this compact shall become operative immediately upon its execution by any state as between it and any other state or states so executing. When executed it shall have the full force and effect of law within such state, the form of execution to be in accordance with the laws of the executing state.

ARTICLE XIV.—RENUNCIATION

That this compact shall continue in force and remain binding upon each executing state until renounced by it. Renunciation of this compact shall be by the same authority which executed it, by sending six months' notice in writing of its intention to withdraw from the compact to the other states party hereto. The duties and obligations of a renouncing state under Article VII hereof shall continue as to parolees and probationers residing therein at the time of withdrawal until retaken or finally discharged. Supplementary agreements entered into under Article X hereof shall be subject to renunciation as provided by such supplementary agreements, and shall not be subject to the six months' renunciation notice of the present Article.

ARTICLE XV.—SEVERABILITY

That the provisions of this compact shall be severable and if any phrase, clause, sentence or provision of this compact is declared to be contrary to the constitution of any participating state or of the United States or the applicability thereof to any government, agency, person or circumstance is held invalid, the validity of the remainder of this compact and the applicability thereof to any government, agency, person or circumstance shall not be affected thereby. If this compact shall be held contrary to the constitution of any state participating therein, the compact shall remain in full force and effect as to the remaining states and in full force and effect as to the state affected as to all severable matters.

ARTICLE XVI.—RETURN OF JUVENILE DELINQUENTS

(a) All provisions and procedures of Articles V and VI of this compact shall be construed to apply to any juvenile charged with being a delinquent by reason of a violation of any criminal law. Any juvenile, charged with being a delinquent by reason of violating any criminal law may be returned to the requesting state upon a requisition to the state where the juvenile may be found. A petition in such case shall be filed in a court of competent jurisdiction in the requesting state where the violation of criminal law is alleged to have been committed. The petition may be filed regardless of whether the juvenile has left the state before or after the filing of the petition. The requisition described in Article V of this compact shall be forwarded by the judge of the court in which the petition has been filed.

(b) This Article shall provide additional remedies, and shall be binding only as among and between those party states which specifically execute the same.

ARTICLE XVII.—RETURN OF CERTAIN CHILDREN TO THEIR HOME STATE

(a) That when any child is brought before a court of a state of which he is not a resident, and such state is willing to permit the return of such a child to his home state, such home state, upon being so advised by the state in which such proceeding is pending, shall immediately institute proceedings to determine the residence and jurisdictional facts as to such child in such home state, and upon finding that such child is in fact a resident thereof and subject to the jurisdiction of the courts thereof, shall, within five days, authorize the return of such child to his home state, and to the parent or custodial agency legally authorized to accept such custody in such home state, and at the expense of such home state, to be paid from such funds as such home state may procure, designate, or provide, prompt action being of the essence.

(b) This Article shall provide additional remedies, and shall be binding only as among and between those party states which specifically execute the same.

For the purposes of this Article, "child" means any minor within the jurisdictional age limits of any court in the home state.

History—
1955, 687, § 1; 1958, 92, 362.

Cross References—
Delinquent children, see ALM GL c 119 §§ 52 et seq.
Protection and care of children, see ALM GL c 119.

§ 2. Compact Administrator Authorized to Promulgate Rules and Regulations; Term; Cooperation With Governmental Agencies and Departments.

Pursuant to said compact, the governor is hereby authorized and empowered to designate an officer who shall be the compact administrator and who, acting jointly with like officers of other party states, shall promulgate rules and regulations to carry out more effectively the terms of the compact. Said compact administrator shall serve subject to the pleasure of the governor. The compact administrator is hereby authorized, empowered and directed to co-operate with all departments, agencies and officers of and in the government of this state and its subdivisions in facilitating the proper administration of the compact or of any supplementary agreement or agreements entered into by this commonwealth thereunder.

History—
1955, 687, § 2.

§ 3.   Supplementary Agreements.

The compact administrator is hereby authorized and empowered to enter into supplementary agreements with appropriate officials of other states pursuant to the compact. In the event that such supplementary agreement shall require or contemplate the use of any institution or facility of this state or require or contemplate the provision of any service by this state, said supplementary agreement shall have no force or effect until approved by the head of the department or agency under whose jurisdiction said institution or facility is operated or whose department or agency will be charged with the rendering of such service.

History—
1955, 687, § 3.

§ 4.   Discharge of Financial Obligations.

The compact administrator, subject to the approval of the governor and council, may make or arrange for any payments necessary to discharge any financial obligations imposed upon this commonwealth by the compact or by any supplementary agreement entered into thereunder.

History—
1955, 687, § 4.

§ 5.   Fees Relating to Appointment of Counsel or Guardian Ad Litem.

Any judge of this commonwealth who appoints counsel or guardian ad litem pursuant to the provisions of the compact may, in his discretion, fix a fee to be paid out of funds available for disposition by the court.

History—
1955, 687, § 5.

§ 6.   Enforcement of Compact.

The courts, departments, agencies and officers of this commonwealth and its subdivisions shall enforce this compact and shall do all things appropriate to the effectuation of its purposes and intent which may be within their respective jurisdictions.

History—
1955, 687, § 6.

§ 7.   Cessation of Effectiveness of Compact.

Notwithstanding any provision of Article XIV hereof, this act shall cease to be in effect upon the adoption by both branches of the general court of a joint resolution stating that it is no longer necessary for the public good; or may be repealed.

History—
1955, 687, § 7.

CHAPTER S99

Compact for Education

(Acts 1967, Ch. 453)

> **Auto-Cite®:** Cases and annotations referred to herein can be further researched through the Auto-Cite® computer-assisted research service. Use Auto-Cite to check citations for form, parallel references, prior and later history, and annotation references.

§ 1. Form of Compact.

. A compact is hereby entered into with all jurisdictions legally joining therein in substantially the following form:—

COMPACT FOR EDUCATION

ARTICLE I. PURPOSES AND POLICY

A. It is the purpose of this compact to:

1. Establish and maintain close cooperation and understanding among executive, legislative, professional, educational and lay leadership on a nationwide basis at the state and local levels.

2. Provide a forum for the discussion, development, crystalization and recommendation of public policy alternatives in the field of education.

3. Provide a clearing house of information on matters relating to educational problems and how they are being met in different places throughout the nation, so that the executive and legislative branches of state governments and of local communities may have ready access to the experience and record of the entire country, and so that both lay and professional groups in the field of education may have additional avenues for the sharing of experience and the interchange of ideas in the formation of public policy in education.

4. Facilitate the improvement of state and local educational systems so that all of them will be able to meet adequate and desirable goals in a society which requires continuous qualitative and quantitative advance in educational opportunities, methods and facilities.

B. It is the policy of this compact to encourage and promote state and local initiative in the development, maintenance, improvement and administration of educational systems and institutions in a manner which will accord with the needs and advantages of diversity among localities and states.

C. The party states recognize that each of them has an interest in the quality and quantity of education furnished in each of the other states, as well as in the excellence of its own educational systems and institutions, because of the highly mobile character of individuals within the nation, and because the products and services contributing to the health, welfare and economic advancement of each state are supplied in significant part by persons educated in other states.

ARTICLE II. STATE DEFINED

As used in this Compact, "State" means a state, territory or possession of the United States, the District of Columbia, or the Commonwealth of Puerto Rico.

ARTICLE III. THE COMMISSION

A. The Education Commission of the States, hereinafter called the Commission, is hereby established. The commission shall consist of seven members representing each party state. The seven members representing the Commonwealth of Massachusetts shall be appointed by and served at the pleasure of the governor. In addition to any other principles or requirements which a state may establish for the appointment and service of its members of the commission, the guiding principle for the composition of the membership of the commission from each party state shall be that the members representing such state shall, by virtue of their training, experience, knowledge or affiliations, be in a position collectively to reflect broadly the interests of the state government, higher education, the state education system, local education, lay and professional, public and nonpublic educational leadership. Of those appointees, one shall be the head of a state agency or institution, designated by the governor, having responsibility for one or more programs of public education. In addition to the members of the commission representing the party states, there may be not more than ten nonvoting commissioners selected by the steering committee for terms of one year. Such commissioners shall represent leading national organizations of professional educators or persons concerned with educational administration.

B. The members of the commission shall be entitled to one vote each on the commission. No action of the commission shall be binding unless taken at a meeting at which a majority of the total number of votes on the commission are cast in favor thereof. The commission may act only at a meeting at which a majority of the commissioners are present. The commission shall meet at least once a year. In its by-laws, and subject to such directions and limitations as may be contained therein, the commission may delegate the exercise of any of its powers to the steering committee or the executive director, except for the power to approve budgets or requests for appropriations, the power to make policy recommendations, and the adoption of the annual report pursuant to paragraph J of this Article.

C. The commission shall have a seal.

D. The commission shall elect annually, from among its members, a chairman, who shall be a governor, a vice chairman and a treasurer. The commission shall provide for the appointment of an executive director. Such executive director shall serve at the pleasure of the commission, and, together with the treasurer and such other personnel as the commission may deem appropriate shall be bonded in such amount as the commission shall determine. The executive director shall be secretary.

E. Irrespective of the civil service, personnel or other merit system laws of any of the party states, the executive director subject to the approval of the steering committee shall appoint, remove or discharge such personnel as may be necessary for the performance of the functions of the commission, and shall fix the duties and compensation of such personnel. The commission in its by-laws shall provide for the personnel policies and programs of the commission.

F. The commission may borrow, accept or contract for the services of personnel from any party jurisdiction, the United States, or any subdivision or agency of the aforementioned governments, or from any agency of two or more of the party jurisdictions or their subdivisions.

G. The commission may accept for any of its purposes and functions under this compact any and all donations, and grants of money, equipment, supplies, materials and services, conditional or otherwise, from any state, the United States, or any other governmental agency, or from any person, firm, association, foundation, or corporation, and may receive, utilize and dispose of the same. Any donation or grant accepted by the commission pursuant to this paragraph, or services borrowed pursuant to paragraph F of this Article, shall be reported in the annual report of the commission. Such report shall include the nature, amount and conditions, if any, of the donation, grant, or services borrowed, and the identity of the donor or lender.

H. The commission may establish and maintain such facilities as may be necessary for the transacting of its business. The commission may acquire, hold, and convey real and personal property and any interest therein.

I. The commission shall adopt by-laws for the conduct of its business and shall have the power to amend and rescind these by-laws. The commission shall publish its by-laws in convenient form and shall file a copy thereof and a copy of any amendment thereto, with the appropriate agency or officer in each party state.

J. The commission annually shall make to the governor and legislature of each party state a report covering the activities of the commission for the preceding year. The commission may make such additional reports as it may deem desirable.

ARTICLE IV. POWERS

In addition to authority conferred on the commission by other provisions of the compact, the commission shall have authority to:

1. Collect, correlate, analyze and interpret information and data concerning educational needs and resources.

2. Encourage and foster research in all aspects of education, but with special reference to the desirable scope of instruction, organization, administration, and instructional methods and standards employed or suitable for employment in public educational systems.

3. Develop proposals for adequate financing of education as a whole and at each of its many levels.

4. Conduct or participate in research of the types referred to in this Article in any instance where the commission finds that such research is necessary for the advancement of the purposes and policies of this compact, utilizing fully the resources of national associations, regional compact organizations for higher education, and other agencies and institutions, both public and private.

5. Formulate suggested policies and plans for the improvement of public education as a whole, or for any segment thereof, and make recommendations with respect thereto available to the appropriate governmental units, agencies and public officials.

6. Do such other things as may be necessary or incidental to the administration of any of its authority or functions pursuant to this compact.

ARTICLE V. COOPERATION WITH FEDERAL GOVERNMENT

A. If the laws of the United States specifically so provide, or if administrative provision is made therefor within the federal government, the United States may be represented on the commission by not more than ten representatives. Any such representative or representatives of the United States shall be appointed and serve in such manner as may be provided by or pursuant to federal law, and may be drawn from any one or more branches of the federal government, but no such representative shall have a vote on the commission.

B. The commission may provide information and make recommendations to any executive or legislative agency or officer of the federal government concerning the common educational policies of the states, and may advise with any such agencies or officers concerning any matter of mutual interest.

ARTICLE VI. COMMITTEES

A. To assist in the expeditious conduct of its business when the full commission is not meeting, the commission shall elect a steering committee of thirty-two members which, subject to the provisions of this compact and consistent with the policies of the commission, shall be constituted and function as provided in the by-laws of the commission. One fourth of the voting membership of the steering committee shall consist of governors, one fourth shall consist of legislators, and the remainder shall consist of other members of the commission. A federal representative on the commission may serve with the steering committee, but without vote. The voting members of the steering committee shall serve for terms of two years, except that members elected to the first steering committee of the commission shall be elected as follows: sixteen for one year and sixteen for two years. The chairman, vice chairman, and treasurer of the commission shall be members of the steering committee and, anything in this paragraph to the contrary notwithstanding, shall serve during their continuance in these offices. Vacancies in the steering committee shall not affect its authority to act, but the commission at its next regularly ensuing meeting following the occurrence of any vacancy shall fill it for the unexpired term. No person shall serve more than two terms as a member of the steering committee; provided that service for a partial term of one year or less shall not be counted toward the two term limitation.

B. The commission may establish advisory and technical committees composed of state, local, and federal officials, and private persons to advise it with respect to any one or more of its functions. Any advisory or technical committee may, on request of the states concerned, be established to consider any matter of special concern to two or more of the party states.

C. The commission may establish such additional committees as its by-laws may provide.

ARTICLE VII. FINANCE

A. The commission shall advise the governor or designated officer or officers of each party state of its budget and estimated expenditures for such period as may be required by the laws of that party state. Each of the commission's budgets of estimated expenditures shall contain specific recommendations of the amount or amounts to be appropriated by each of the party states.

B. The total amount of appropriation requests under any budget shall be apportioned among the party states. In making such apportionment, the commission shall devise and employ a formula which takes equitable account of the populations and per capita income levels of the party states.

C. The commission shall not pledge the credit of any party state. The commission may meet any of its obligations in whole or in part with funds available to it pursuant to paragraph G of Article III, provided that the commission takes specific action setting aside such funds prior to incurring an obligation to be met in whole or in part in such manner. Except where the commission makes use of funds available to it pursuant to said paragraph G of said Article III, the commission shall not incur any obligation prior to the allotment by the party states of funds adequate to meet the same.

D. The commission shall keep accurate accounts of all receipts and disbursements. The receipts and disbursements of the commission shall be subject to the audit and accounting procedures established by its by-laws. However, all receipts and disbursements of funds handled by the commission shall be audited yearly by a qualified public accountant, and the report of the audit shall be included in and become part of the annual reports of the commission.

E. The accounts of the commission shall be open at any reasonable time for inspection by duly constituted officers of the party states and by any persons authorized by the commission.

F. Nothing contained herein shall be construed to prevent the commission from complying with laws relating to audit or inspection of accounts by or on behalf of any government contributing to the support of the commission.

ARTICLE VIII. ELIGIBLE PARTIES; ENTRY INTO AND WITHDRAWAL

A. This compact shall have as eligible parties all states, territories and possessions of the United States, the District of Columbia, and the Commonwealth of Puerto Rico. In respect of any such jurisdiction not having a governor, the term "governor" as used in this compact shall mean the closest equivalent official of such jurisdiction.

B. Any state or other eligible jurisdiction may enter into this compact and it shall become binding thereon when it has adopted the same; provided that in order to enter into initial effect, adoption by at least ten eligible party jurisdictions shall be required.

C. Adoption of the compact may be either by enactment thereof or by adherence thereto by the governor; provided that in the absence of enactment, adherence by the governor shall be sufficient to make his state a party only until December 31, 1967. During any period when a state is participating in this compact through gubernatorial action, the governor shall appoint those persons who, in addition to himself, shall serve as the members of the commission from his state, and shall provide to the commission an equitable share of the financial support of the commission from any source available to him.

D. Except for a withdrawal effective on December 31, 1967 in accordance with paragraph C of this Article, any party state may withdraw from this compact by enacting a statute repealing the same, but no such withdrawal shall take effect until one year after the governor of the withdrawing state has given notice in writing of the withdrawal to the governors of all other party states. No withdrawal shall affect any liability already incurred by or chargeable to a party state prior to the time of such withdrawal.

ARTICLE IX. CONSTRUCTION AND SEVERABILITY

This compact shall be liberally construed so as to effectuate the purposes thereof. The provisions of this compact shall be severable and if any phrase, clause, sentence or provision of this compact is declared to be contrary to the constitution of any state or of the United States, or the application thereof to any government, agency, person or circumstance is held invalid, the validity of the remainder of this compact and the applicability thereof to any government, agency, person or circumstance shall not be affected thereby. If this compact shall be held contrary to the constitution of any state participating therein, the compact shall remain in full force and effect as to the state affected as to all severable matters.

History—
1967, 453, § 1.

Cross References—
Designation of persons to perform duties of members of boards or commissions appointed under interstate compacts, see ALM GL c 30 § 6A.
Entering into contracts with interstate compact agencies to promote objectives of University of Massachusetts, see ALM GL c 75 § 11.
Entering into contracts with interstate compact agencies to promote objectives of University of Lowell, see ALM GL c 75A § 8.
Entering into contracts with interstate compact agencies to promote objectives of Southeastern Massachusetts University, see ALM GL c 75B § 8.

§ 2.   Education Compact Council of Massachusetts.

There is hereby established the Education Compact Council of Massachusetts, composed of the members of the Education Commission of the States representing the commonwealth and twenty other persons who shall be appointed by the governor for terms coterminous with his. Such other persons shall be selected so as to be broadly representative of professional and lay interest within the commonwealth, having the responsibilities for, knowledge with respect to, and interest in educational matters. The chairman shall be designated by the governor from among its members. The council shall meet on the call of the chairman or at the request of a majority of its members, but in any event the council shall meet not less than three times in each year. The council may consider any and all matters relating to recommendations of the Education Commission of the States and the activities of the members representing the commonwealth thereon.

History—
1967, 453, § 2.

§ 3.   Filing of Bylaws and Amendments of Education Commission of the States.

Pursuant to the provisions of paragraph I of Article III of the Compact for Education, the Education Commission of the States shall file a copy of its by-laws and any amendments thereof with the state secretary of this commonwealth.

History—
    1967, 453, § 3.

CHAPTER S101

Compact for Establishment of New England Board of Higher Education

(Acts 1954, Ch. 589)

Auto-Cite®: Cases and annotations referred to herein can be further researched through the Auto-Cite® computer-assisted research service. Use Auto-Cite to check citations for form, parallel references, prior and later history, and annotation references.

---

§ 1. Form of Compact.

Whereas, The several New England states cooperatively deem it feasible to provide needed, acceptable, efficient, educational facilities to meet the needs of New England in the fields of medicine, dentistry, veterinary medicine, and other fields of technical, professional and graduate training;

Now, therefore, the Governor, on behalf of this Commonwealth, is hereby authorized to enter into a compact, substantially in the following form, with any one or more of the states of Connecticut, Maine, New Hampshire, Rhode Island and Vermont, and the general court hereby signifies in advance its approval and ratification of such a compact so entered into, such approval and ratification to be effective upon the filing of a copy of such compact in the office of the state secretary.

NEW ENGLAND HIGHER EDUCATION COMPACT

ARTICLE I.

The purposes of the New England Higher Education Compact shall be to provide greater educational opportunities and services through the establishment and maintenance of a co-ordinated educational program for the persons residing in the several states of New England parties to this compact, with the aim of furthering higher education in the fields of medicine, dentistry, veterinary medicine, public health and in professional, technical, scientific, literary and other fields.

ARTICLE II.

There is hereby created and established a New England board of higher education hereinafter known as the board, which shall be an agency of each state party to the compact. The board shall be a body corporate and politic, having the powers, duties and jurisdiction herein enumerated and such other and additional powers as shall be conferred upon it by the concurrent act or acts of the compacting states. The board shall consist of eight resident members from each compacting state, at least two of whom may be members of the general court, chosen in the manner and for the terms provided by law of the several states parties to this compact.

ARTICLE III.

This compact shall become operative immediately as to those states executing it whenever any two or more of the states of Maine, Vermont, New Hampshire, Massachusetts, Rhode Island and Connecticut have executed it in the form which is in accordance with the laws of the respective compacting states.

ARTICLE IV.

The board shall annually elect from its members a chairman and vice-chairman and shall appoint and at its pleasure remove or discharge said officers. It may appoint and employ an executive secretary and may employ such stenographic, clerical, technical or legal personnel as shall be necessary, and at its pleasure remove or discharge such personnel. It shall adopt a seal and suitable by-laws and shall promulgate any and all rules and regulations which may be necessary for the conduct of its business. It may maintain an office or offices within the territory of the compacting states and may meet at any time or place. Meetings shall be held at least once each year. A majority of the members shall constitute a quorum for the transaction of business, but no action of the board imposing any obligation on any compacting state shall be binding unless a majority of the members from such compacting state shall have voted in favor thereof. Where meetings are planned to discuss matters relevant to problems of education affecting only certain of the compacting states, the board may vote to authorize special meetings of the board members of such states. The board shall keep accurate accounts of all receipts and disbursements and shall make an annual report to the governor and the legislature of each compacting state, setting forth in detail the operations and transactions conducted by it pursuant to this compact, and shall make recommendations for any legislative action deemed by it advisable, including amendments to the statutes of the compacting states which may be necessary to carry out the intent and purpose of this compact. The board shall not pledge the credit of any compacting state without the consent of the legislature thereof given pursuant to the constitutional processes of said state. The board may meet any of its obligations in whole or in part with funds available to it under Article VII of this compact; provided, that the board takes specific action setting aside such funds prior to the incurring of any obligation to be met in whole or in part in this manner. Except where the board makes use of funds available to it under Article VII hereof, the board shall not incur any obligations for salaries, office, administrative, traveling or other expenses prior to the allotment of funds by the compacting states adequate to meet same. Each compacting state reserves the right to provide hereafter by law for the examination and audit of the accounts of the board. The board shall appoint a treasurer and assistant treasurer who may be empowered to perform any and all duties of the treasurer. Fiscal disbursements of the board shall be valid only when authorized by any two persons from among those authorized by the board to execute this authority, and when substantiated by vouchers signed and countersigned by any two members from among those authorized by the board to execute this authority. The executive secretary shall be custodian of the records of the board with authority to attest to and certify such records or copie' thereof.

ARTICLE V.

The board shall have the power to: (1) collect, correlate, and evaluate data in the fields of its interest under this compact; to publish reports, bulletins and other documents making available the results of its research; and, in its discretion, to charge fees for said reports, bulletins and documents; (2) enter into such contractual agreements or arrangements with any of the compacting states or agencies thereof and with educational institutions and agencies as may be required in the judgment of the board to provide adequate services and facilities in educational fields covered by this compact; provided, that it shall be the policy of the board in the negotiation of its agreements to serve increased numbers of students from the compacting states through arrangements with then existing institutions, whenever in the judgment of the board adequate service can be so secured in the New England region. Each of the compacting states shall contribute funds to carry out the contracts of the board on the basis of the number of students from such state for whom the board may contract. Contributions shall be at the rate determined by the board in each educational field. Except in those instances where the board by specific action allocates funds available to it under Article VII hereof, the board's authority to enter into such contracts shall be only upon appropriation of funds by the compacting states. Any contract entered into shall be in accordance with rules and regulations promulgated by the board and in accordance with the laws of the compacting states.

ARTICLE VI.

Each state agrees that, when authorized by the legislature pursuant to the constitutional processes, it will from time to time make available to the board such funds as may be required for the expenses of the board as authorized under the terms of this compact. The contribution of each state for this purpose shall be in the proportion that its population bears to the total combined population of the states who are parties hereto as shown from time to time by the most recent official published report of the Bureau of the Census of the United States of America, unless the board shall adopt another basis in making its recommendation for appropriation to the compacting states.

ARTICLE VII.

The board for the purposes of this compact is hereby empowered to receive grants, devises, gifts and bequests which the board may agree to accept and administer. The board shall administer property held in accordance with special trusts, grants and bequests, and shall also administer grants and devises of land and gifts or bequests of personal property made to the board for special uses, and shall execute said trusts, investing the proceeds thereof in notes or bonds secured by sufficient mortgages or other securities.

ARTICLE VIII.

The provisions of this compact shall be severable, and if any phrase, clause, sentence or provision of this compact is declared to be contrary to the constitution of any compacting state or of the United States the validity of the remainder of this compact and the applicability thereof to any government, agency, person or circumstance shall not be affected thereby; provided, that if this compact is held to be contrary to the constitution of any compacting state the compact shall remain in full force and effect as to all other compacting states.

ARTICLE IX.

This compact shall continue in force and remain binding upon a compacting state until the legislature or the governor of such state, as the laws of such state shall provide, takes action to withdraw therefrom. Such action shall not be effective until two years after notice thereof has been sent by the governor of the state desiring to withdraw to the governors of all other states then parties to the compact. Such withdrawal shall not relieve the withdrawing state from its obligations accruing hereunder prior to the effective date of withdrawal. Any state so withdrawing, unless reinstated, shall cease to have any claim to or ownership of any of the property held by or vested in the board or to any of the funds of the board held under the terms of the compact. Thereafter, the withdrawing state may be reinstated by application after appropriate legislation is enacted by such state, upon approval by a majority vote of the board.

ARTICLE X.

If any compacting state shall at any time default in the performance of any of its obligations assumed or imposed in accordance with the provisions of this compact, all rights and privileges and benefits conferred by this compact or agreement hereunder shall be suspended from the effective date of such default as fixed by the board. Unless such default shall be remedied within a period of two years following the effective date of such default, this compact may be terminated with respect to such defaulting state by affirmative vote of three fourths of the other member states. Any such defaulting state may be reinstated by (a) performing all acts and obligations upon which it has heretofore defaulted, and (b) application to and approval by a majority vote of the board.

History—

1954, 589, § 1; 1972, 664, §§ 1, 2.

Editorial Note—

Section 4 of the 1972 amending act, provides as follows:

SECTION 4. The amendments to said compact contained in this act shall become operative when they have been ratified by one or more states which are parties thereto.

Cross References—

Entering into contracts with interstate compact agencies to promote objectives of University of Massachusetts, see ALM GL c 75 § 11.

Entering into contracts with interstate compact agencies to promote objectives of University of Lowell, see ALM GL c 75A § 8.

Entering into contracts with interstate compact agencies to promote objectives of Southeastern Massachusetts University, see ALM GL c 75B § 8.

§ 2.   When Compact Becomes Operative and Effective; Responsibility of Governor.

When the governor shall have executed said compact on behalf of this state, and shall have caused a verified copy thereof to be filed with the state secretary, and when said compact shall have been ratified by one or more of the states named in section one of this act, then said compact shall become operative and effective as between this state and such other state or states. The governor is hereby authorized and directed to take such action as may be necessary to complete the exchange and filing of official documents as between this state and any other state ratifying said compact, and to take such steps as may be necessary to secure the consent of the Congress of the United States to the compact.

History—
1954, 589, § 2.

§ 3.   Gubernatorial Appointees to Board; Term of Office; Vacancies.

Eight persons shall represent the commonwealth as members of the board. The governor shall designate or appoint seven members, of whom at least one shall be a president of a public institution of higher education, at least one shall be a president of a private institution of higher education, at least one may be a member of the senate and at least one may be a member of the house of representatives. The chancellor of the board of higher education shall serve ex officio as a member of the board. Each of the members designated or appointed under this section shall serve for a term of six years. No more than two board members' terms shall expire in any single year and intitial designations or appointments of less than six years may be made as necessary for this purpose. Any person who is a member of the board on the effective date of this act shall continue to serve as a member for the remainder of his term and the number of persons initially appointed or designated under the provisions of this section shall be reduced accordingly. If a member of the board who is a member of the senate of the house of representatives ceases to be a member of the senate or the house of representatives, his membership on the board shall be terminated and his position shall be considered as vacant. Any vacancy among the designative or appointive positions on the board due to causes other than the expiration of term shall be filled for the unexpired portion of the term in the same manner as an original appointment or designation.

History—
1972, 664, § 3.

Editorial Note—
Section 4 of the inserting act, provides as follows:
SECTION 4. The amendments to said compact contained in this act shall become operative when they have been ratified by one or more states which are parties thereto.

§ 4.   Salaries of Appointees.

Each member designated or appointed by the governor who, while such member, holds no salaried state office, shall be paid by the commonwealth as compensation, the sum of thirty-seven dollars and fifty cents for each day's service performed in connection with his duties as such member, but not to exceed twenty-five hundred dollars in any fiscal year. Such compensation shall be paid by the state treasurer not oftener than once in two weeks, upon bills approved by the chairman or vice-chairman and the secretary of the board. All members shall be entitled to their actual expenses incurred in the performance of their duties as such.

History—
1954, 589, § 4.

§ 5.   Report of Receipts and Disbursements of Board; Recommendations for Legislation.

The board on the part of the commonwealth shall obtain accurate accounts of all the board's receipts and disbursements and shall report to the governor and the budget commissioner annually on or before the fifteenth day of September, setting forth in such detail as the budget commissioner may require the transactions of the board for the fiscal year ending on the preceding June thirtieth. They shall include in such report recommendations for any legislation to the commonwealth as may be necessary or desirable to carry out the intent and purposes of the New England Higher Education Compact among the states joining therein.

History—
1954, 589, § 5.

§ 6.   Payback by Service Under Health Profession Contract Programs; Penalty; Repayment; Default in Payment Schedule.

As used in this section, the following words shall have the following meanings:

"Payback by service", the practice of a health profession pursuant to the participant's contract for which each participant was trained under one of the health profession contract programs operated by the New England board of higher education.

There shall be a financial penalty for failure to perform payback by service within the commonwealth for all participants who are residents of the commonwealth in the regional medical, veterinary, and optometry student contract programs operated by the New England board of higher education. For residents of the commonwealth who participate in the contract programs graduating in nineteen hundred and eighty to nineteen hundred and eighty-five, inclusive, the penalty for failure to perform return service at the rate of six months for every one year of participation in one of the above contract programs shall be monetary payback to the commonwealth of that amount of contract funds credited against each participant's tuition while in school.

Participants shall have ten years, commencing from the date when all required internships, residencies, and fellowships are completed, to repay the total amount received. At least one-tenth of the total amount received shall be paid on November first in each year.

Payments shall be made payable to the commonwealth and forwarded to the New England board of higher education which shall in turn forward payments to the state treasurer.

Any default in the payment schedule shall be reported by the New England board of higher education to the attorney general who shall secure payment in the event of default. Any overdue payment shall bear interest at the annual rate of one per cent over the prime rate, and the attorney general may declare immediately due and payable the entire outstanding balance of principal and interest upon such default of payment.

History—
1987, 571.

CHAPTER S103

Interstate Library Compact

(Acts 1963, Ch. 693, as amended)

Auto-Cite®: Cases and annotations referred to herein can be further researched through the Auto-Cite® computer-assisted research service. Use Auto-Cite to check citations for form, parallel references, prior and later history, and annotation references.

---

§ 1. Form of Compact.

The interstate library compact is hereby entered into by the commonwealth with all states legally joining therein in the form substantially as follows:—

INTERSTATE LIBRARY COMPACT

ARTICLE I. POLICY AND PURPOSE.

Because the desire for the services provided by libraries transcends governmental boundaries and can most effectively be satisfied by giving such services to communities and people regardless of jurisdictional lines, it is the policy of the states party to this compact to co-operate and share their responsibilities; to authorize co-operation and sharing with respect to those types of library facilities and services which can be more economically or efficiently developed and maintained on a co-operative basis, and to authorize co-operation and sharing among localities, states and others in providing joint or co-operative library services in areas where the distribution of population or of existing and potential library resources make the provision of library service on an interstate basis the most effective way of providing adequate and efficient service.

ARTICLE II. DEFINITIONS.

As used in this campact:

(a) "Public library agency" means any unit or agency of local or state government operating or having power to operate a library.

(b) "Private library agency" means any non-governmental entity which operates or assumes a legal obligation to operate a library.

(c) "Library agreement" means a contract establishing an interstate library district pursuant to this compact or providing for the joint or co-operative furnishing of library services.

ARTICLE III. INTERSTATE LIBRARY DISTRICTS.

(a) Any one or more public library agencies in a party state in co-operation with any public library agency or agencies in one or more other party states may establish and maintain an interstate library district. Subject to the provisions of this compact and any other laws of the party states which pursuant hereto remain applicable, such district may establish, maintain and operate some or all of the library facilities and services for the area concerned in accordance with the terms of a library agreement therefor. Any private library agency or agencies within an interstate library district may co-operate therewith, assume duties, responsibilities and obligations thereto, and receive benefits therefrom as provided in any library agreement to which such agency or agencies become party.

(b) Within an interstate library district, and as provided by a library agreement, the performance of library functions may be undertaken on a joint or co-operative basis or may be undertaken by means of one or more arrangements between or among public or private library agencies for the extension of library privileges to the use of facilities or services operated or rendered by one or more of the individual library agencies.

(c) If a library agreement provides for joint establishment, maintenance or operation of library facilities or services by an interstate library district, such district shall have power to do any one or more of the following in accordance with such library agreement:

1. Undertake, administer and participate in programs or arrangements for securing, lending or servicing of books and other publications, any other materials suitable to be kept or made available by libraries, library equipment or for the dissemination

of information about libraries, the value and significance of particular items therein, and the use thereof.

2. Accept for any of its purposes under this compact any and all donations, and grants of money, equipment, supplies, materials, and services (conditional or otherwise), from any state or the United States or any subdivision or agency thereof, or interstate agency, or from any institution, person, firm or corporation, and receive, utilize and dispose of the same.

3. Operate mobile library units or equipment for the purpose of rendering bookmobile service within the district.

4. Employ professional, technical, clerical and other personnel and fix terms of employment, compensation and other appropriate benefits; and where desirable, provide for the in-service training of such personnel.

5. Sue and be sued in any court of competent jurisdiction.

6. Acquire, hold and dispose of any real or personal property or any interest or interests therein as may be appropriate to the rendering of library service.

7. Construct, maintain and operate a library, including any appropriate branches thereof.

8. Do such other things as may be incidental to or appropriate for the carrying out of any of the foregoing powers.

ARTICLE IV. INTERSTATE LIBRARY DISTRICTS, GOVERNING BOARD.

(a) An interstate library district which establishes, maintains or operates any facilities or services in its own right shall have a governing board which shall direct the affairs of the district and act for it in all matters relating to its business. Each participating public library agency in the district shall be represented on the governing board which shall be organized and conduct its business in accordance with provision therefor in the library agreement, but in no event shall a governing board meet less often than twice a year.

(b) Any private library agency or agencies party to a library agreement establishing an interstate library district may be represented on or advise with the governing board of the district in such manner as the library agreement may provide.

ARTICLE V. STATE LIBRARY AGENCY CO-OPERATION.

Any two or more state library agencies of two or more of the party states may undertake and conduct joint or co-operative library programs, render joint or co-operative library services, and enter into and perform arrangements for the co-operative or joint acquisition, use, housing and disposition of items or collections of materials which, by reason of expense, rarity, specialized nature, or infrequency of demand therefor would be appropriate for central collection and shared use. Any such programs, services or arrangements may include provision for the exercise on a co-operative or joint basis of any power exercisable by an interstate library district and an agreement embodying any such program, service or arrangement shall contain provisions covering the subjects detailed in Article VI of this compact for interstate library agreements.

ARTICLE VI. LIBRARY AGREEMENTS.

(a) In order to provide for any joint or co-operative undertaking pursuant to this compact, public and private library agencies may enter into library agreements. Any agreement executed pursuant to the provisions of this compact shall, as among the parties to the agreement:

1. Detail the specific nature of the services, programs, facilities, arrangements or properties to which it is applicable.

2. Provide for the allocation of costs and other financial responsibilities.

3. Specify the respective rights, duties, obligations and liabilities of the parties.

4. Set forth the terms and conditions for duration, renewal, termination, abrogation, disposal of joint or common property, if any, and all other matters which may be appropriate to the proper effectuation and performance of the agreement.

(b) No public or private library agency shall undertake to exercise itself, or jointly with any other library agency, by means of a library agreement any power prohibited to such agency by the constitution or statutes of its state.

(c) No library agreement shall become effective until filed with the compact administrator of each state involved, and approved in accordance with Article VII of this compact.

ARTICLE VII. APPROVAL OF LIBRARY AGREEMENTS.

(a) Every library agreement made pursuant to this compact shall, prior to and as a condition precedent to its entry into force, be submitted to the attorney general of each state in which a public library agency party thereto is situated, who shall determine whether the agreement is in proper form and compatible with the laws of his state. The attorneys general shall approve any agreement submitted to them unless they shall find that it does not meet the conditions set forth herein and shall detail in writing addressed to the governing bodies of the public library agencies concerned the specific respects in which the proposed agreement fails to meet the requirements of law. Failure to disapprove an agreement submitted hereunder within ninety days of its submission shall constitute approval thereof.

(b) In the event that a library agreement made pursuant to this compact shall deal in whole or in part with the provision of services or facilities with regard to which an officer or agency of the state government has constitutional or statutory powers of control, the agreement shall, as a condition precedent to its entry into force, be submitted to the state officer or agency having such power of control and shall be approved or disapproved by him or it as to all matters within his or its jurisdiction in the same manner and subject to the same requirements governing the action of the attorneys general pursuant to paragraph (a) of this article. This requirement of submission and approval shall be in addition to and not in substitution for the requirement of submission to and approval by the attorneys general.

ARTICLE VIII. OTHER LAWS APPLICABLE.

Nothing in this compact or in any library agreement shall be construed to supersede, alter or otherwise impair any obligation imposed on any library by otherwise applicable law, nor to authorize the transfer or disposition of any property held in trust by a library agency in a manner contrary to the terms of such trust.

ARTICLE IX. APPROPRIATIONS AND AID.

(a) Any public library agency party to a library agreement may appropriate funds to the interstate library district established thereby in the same manner and to the same extent as to a library wholly maintained by it and, subject to the laws of the state in which such public library agency is situated, may pledge its credit in support of an interstate library district established by the agreement.

(b) Subject to the provisions of the library agreement pursuant to which it functions and the laws of the states in which such district is situated, an interstate library district may claim and receive any state and federal aid which may be available to library agencies.

ARTICLE X. COMPACT ADMINISTRATOR.

Each state shall designate a compact administrator with whom copies of all library agreements to which his state or any public library agency thereof is party shall be filed. The administrator shall have such other powers as may be conferred upon him by the laws of his state and may consult and co-operate with the compact administrators of other party states and take such steps as may effectuate the purposes of this compact. If the laws of a party state so provide, such state may designate one or more deputy compact administrators in addition to its compact administrator.

ARTICLE XI. ENTRY INTO FORCE AND WITHDRAWAL.

(a) This compact shall enter into force and effect immediately upon its enactment into law by any two states. Thereafter, it shall enter into force and effect as to any other state upon the enactment thereof by such state.

(b) This compact shall continue in force with respect to a party state and remain binding upon such state until six months after such state has given notice to each other party state of the repeal thereof. Such withdrawal shall not be construed to relieve any party to a library agreement entered into pursuant to this compact from any obligation of that agreement prior to the end of its duration as provided therein.

ARTICLE XII. CONSTRUCTION AND SEVERABILITY.

This compact shall be liberally construed so as to effectuate the purposes thereof. The provisions of this compact shall be severable and if any phrase, clause, sentence or provision of this compact is declared to be contrary to the constitution of any party state or of the United States or the applicability thereof to any government, agency, person or circumstance is held invalid, the validity of the remainder of this compact and the applicability thereof to any government, agency, person or circumstance shall not be affected thereby. If this compact shall be held contrary to the constitution of any state party thereto, the compact shall remain in full force and effect as to the remaining states and in full force and effect as to the state affected as to all severable matters.

History—
1963, 693, § 1; 1982, 569.

Editorial Note—
The 1982 amendment rewrote the introductory sentence of this section, deleting references to specific states.

§ 2.　Compliance with Laws Governing Capital Outlays and Pledging of Credit of Political Subdivisions.

No political subdivision of the commonwealth shall be a party to a library agreement which provides for the construction or maintenance of a library pursuant to Article III, paragraph (c) 7, of the compact, nor pledge its credit in support of such a library, or contribute to the capital financing thereof, except after compliance with any laws applicable to such political subdivision relating to or governing capital outlays and the pledging of credit.

History—
1963, 693, § 2.

§ 3.　State Library Agency, Defined.

As used in this compact "state library agency", with reference to the commonwealth, means the board of library commissioners.

History—
1963, 693, § 3; 1977, 565, § 7.

Cross References—
Board of library commissioners, see ALM GL c 78, §§ 14 et seq.

§ 4.　Interstate Library Districts Lying Partially within Commonwealth.

An interstate library district lying partly within the commonwealth may claim and be entitled to receive state aid in support of any of its functions to the same extent and in the same manner as such functions are eligible for support when carried on by entities wholly within this state. For the purpose of computing and apportioning state aid to an interstate library district, the commonwealth will consider that portion of the district which lies within the commonwealth as an independent entity for the performance of the aided function or functions and compute and apportion the aid accordingly. Subject to any applicable laws of this state, such a district also may apply for and be entitled to receive any federal aid for which it may be eligible.

History—
1963, 693, § 4.

§ 5.   Appointment of Compact Administrator.

The governor, with the advice and consent of the council, shall appoint the compact administrator pursuant to Article X of the compact.

History—
1963, 693, § 5.

§ 6.   Withdrawal of Commonwealth from Compact.

In the event of withdrawal of the commonwealth from the compact the governor shall send and receive any notices required by Article XI of the compact.

History—
1963, 693, § 6.

CHAPTER S105

Interstate Agreement on Certification of Educational Personnel

(Acts 1968, Ch 748)

Auto-Cite®: Cases and annotations referred to herein can be further researched through the Auto-Cite® computer-assisted research service. Use Auto-Cite to check citations for form, parallel references, prior and later history, and annotation references.

---

§ 1. Form of Agreement.

An agreement is hereby entered into with all jurisdictions legally joining therein in substantially the following form:—

INTERSTATE AGREEMENT ON CERTIFICATION OF EDUCATIONAL PERSONNEL

ARTICLE I. *PURPOSE, FINDINGS AND POLICY.*

1. The States party to this Agreement, desiring by common action to improve their respective school systems by utilizing the teacher or other professional educational person wherever educated, declare that it is the policy of each of them, on the basis of cooperation with one another, to take advantage of the preparation and experience of such persons wherever gained, thereby serving the best interests of society, of education, and of the teaching profession. It is the purpose of this Agreement to provide for the development and execution of such programs of cooperation as will facilitate the movement of teachers and other professional educational personnel contracts to achieve that end.

2. The party States find that included in the large movement of population among all sections of the nation are many qualified educational personnel who move for family and other personal reasons but who are hindered in using their professional skill and

285

experience in their new locations. Variations from State to State in requirements for qualifying educational personnel discourage such personnel from taking the steps necessary to qualify in other States. As a consequence, a significant number of professionally prepared and experienced educators is lost to our school systems. Facilitating the employment of qualified educational personnel, without reference to their States of origin, can increase the available educational resources. Participation in this Agreement can increase the availability of educational manpower.

ARTICLE II. *DEFINITIONS.*

As used in this Agreement and contracts made pursuant to it, unless the context clearly requires otherwise:

1. "Educational personnel" means persons who must meet requirements pursuant to State law as a condition of employment in educational programs.

2. "Designated State official" means the education official of a State selected by that State to negotiate and enter into, on behalf of his State, contracts pursuant to his Agreement.

3. "Accept", or any variant thereof, means to recognize and give effect to one or more determinations of another State relating to the qualifications of educational personnel in lieu of making or requiring a like determination that would otherwise be required by or pursuant to the laws of a receiving State.

4. "State" means a State, territory or possession of the United States; the District of Columbia; or the Commonwealth of Puerto Rico.

5. "Originating State" means a State (and the subdivision thereof, if any) whose determination that certain educational personnel are qualified to be employed for specific duties in schools is acceptable in accordance with the terms of a contract made pursuant to Article III.

6. "Receiving State" means a State (and the subdivisions thereof) which accept educational personnel in accordance with the terms of a contract made pursuant to Article III.

ARTICLE III. *INTERSTATE EDUCATIONAL PERSONNEL CONTRACTS.*

1. The designated State official of a party State may make one or more contracts on behalf of his State with one or more other party States providing for the acceptance of educational personnel. Any such contract for the period of its duration shall be applicable to and

binding on the States whose designated state officials enter into it, and the subdivisions of those States, with the same force and effect as if incorporated in this Agreement. A designated state official may enter into a contract pursuant to this Article only with States in which he finds that there are programs of education, certification standards or other acceptable qualifications that assure preparation or qualification of educational personnel on a basis sufficiently comparable, even though not identical to that prevailing in his own State.

2. Any such contract shall provide for:

(a) Its duration.

(b) The criteria to be applied by an originating State in qualifying educational personnel for acceptance by a receiving State.

(c) Such waivers, substitutions and conditional acceptances as shall aid the practical effectuation of the contract without sacrifice of basic educational standards.

(d) Any other necessary matters.

3. No contract made pursuant to this Agreement shall be for a term longer than five years but any such contract may be renewed for like or lesser periods.

4. Any contract dealing with acceptance of educational personnel on the basis of their having completed an educational program shall specify the earliest date or dates on which originating state approval of the program or programs involved can have occurred. No contract made pursuant to this Agreement shall require acceptance by a receiving State of any persons qualified because of successful completion of a program prior to January 1, 1954.

5. The certification or other acceptance of a person who has been accepted pursuant to the terms of a contract shall not be revoked or otherwise impaired because the contract has expired or been terminated. However, any certificate or other qualifying document may be revoked or suspended on any ground which would be sufficient for revocation or suspension of a certificate or other qualifying document initially granted or approved in the receiving State.

6. A contract committee composed of the designated state officials of the contracting States or their representatives shall keep the contract under continuous review, study means of improving its administration and report not less frequently than once a year to the heads of the appropriate education agencies of the contracting States.

ARTICLE IV. [Reserved]

ARTICLE V. *INTERSTATE COOPERATION.*

The party States agree that:

1. They will, so far as practicable, prefer the making of multilateral contracts pursuant to Article III of this Agreement.

2. They will facilitate and strengthen cooperation in interstate certification and other elements of educational personnel qualification and for this purpose shall cooperate with agencies, organizations and associations interested in certification and other elements of educational personnel qualification.

ARTICLE VI. *AGREEMENT EVALUATION.*

The designated state officials of any party State may meet from time to time as a group to evaluate progress under the agreement and to formulate recommendations for changes.

ARTICLE VII. *OTHER ARRANGEMENTS.*

Nothing in this Agreement shall be construed to prevent or inhibit other arrangements or practices of any party State or States to facilitate the interchange of educational personnel.

ARTICLE VIII. *EFFECT AND WITHDRAWAL.*

1. This Agreement shall become effective when enacted into law by two States. Thereafter it shall become effective as to any State upon its enactment of this Agreement.

2. Any party State may withdraw from this Agreement by enacting a statute repealing the same, but no such withdrawal shall take effect until one year after the Governor of the withdrawing State has given notice in writing of the withdrawal to the Governors of all other party States.

3. No withdrawal shall relieve the withdrawing State of any obligation imposed upon it by a contract to which it is a party. The duration of contracts and the methods and conditions of withdrawal therefrom shall be those specified in their terms.

ARTICLE IX. *CONSTRUCTION AND SEVERABILITY.*

This Agreement shall be liberally construed so as to effectuate the purposes thereof. The provisions of this Agreement shall be severable and if any phrase, clause, sentence or provision of this Agreement is declared to be contrary to the constitution of any State or of the United States, or the application thereof to any Government, agency, person or circumstance is held invalid, the validity of the remainder of this Agreement and the applicability thereof to any Government, agency, person or circumstance shall not be affected thereby. If this Agreement shall be held contrary to the constitution of any State participating therein, the Agreement shall remain in full force and effect as to the State affected as to all severable matters.

History—
1968, 748, § 1.

Cross References—
Standards of certification of teachers, see ALM GL c 71 § 38G.

§ 2.   Educational Official Authorized to Negotiate and Enter Into Agreements.

2. Pursuant to the Interstate Agreement on Certification of Educational Personnel contained in section one of this act, the board of education is hereby authorized and empowered to designate the education official to negotiate, and, subject to the approval of the board in each instance, to enter into on behalf of the commonwealth agreements in accordance with this act.

History—
1968, 748, § 2.

§ 3.   Withdrawal Provisions in Agreements.

Any agreement entered into under this act shall contain provisions for withdrawal by the commonwealth following one year's notice pursuant to paragraph 2 of Article VIII of said Agreement.

History—
1968, 748, § 3.

CHAPTER S107

Interstate Compact on Mental Health

(Acts 1956, Ch. 441)

Auto-Cite®: Cases and annotations referred to herein can be further researched through the Auto-Cite® computer-assisted research service. Use Auto-Cite to check citations for form, parallel references, prior and later history, and annotation references.

---

§ 1. Form of Compact.

The interstate compact on mental health is hereby enacted into law and entered into by this commonwealth with all other states legally joining therein in the form substantially as follows:

INTERSTATE COMPACT ON MENTAL HEALTH

The contracting states solemnly agree that:—

ARTICLE I.

The party states find that the proper and expeditious treatment of the mentally ill and mentally deficient can be facilitated by co-operative action, to the benefit of the patients, their families and society as a whole. Further, the party states find that the necessity of and desirability for furnishing such care and treatment bears no primary relation to the residence or citizenship of the patient but that, on the contrary, the controlling factors of community safety and humanitarianism require that facilities and services be made available for all who are in need of them. Consequently, it is the purpose of this compact and of the party states to provide the necessary legal basis for the institutionalization or other appropriate care and treatment of the mentally ill and mentally deficient under a system that recognizes the paramount importance of patient welfare and to

291

establish the responsibilities of the party states in terms of such welfare.

ARTICLE II.

As used in this compact:—

(a) "Sending state" shall mean a party state from which a patient is transported pursuant to the provisions of the compact or from which it is contemplated that a patient may be so sent.

(b) "Receiving state" shall mean a party state to which a patient is transported pursuant to the provisions of the compact or to which it is contemplated that a patient may be so sent.

(c) "Institution" shall mean any hospital or other facility maintained by a party state or political subdivision thereof for the care and treatment of mental illness or mental deficiency.

(d) "Patient" shall mean any person subject to or eligible as determined by the laws of the sending state, for institutionalization or other care, treatment or supervision pursuant to the provisions of this compact.

(e) "After-care" shall mean care, treatment and services provided a patient, as defined herein, or convalescent status or conditional release.

(f) "Mental illness" shall mean mental disease to such extent that a person so afflicted requires care and treatment for his own welfare, or the welfare of others, or of the community.

(g) "Mental deficiency" shall mean mental deficiency as defined by appropriate clinical authorities to such extent that a person so afflicted is incapable of managing himself and his affairs, but shall not include mental illness as defined herein.

(h) "State" shall mean any state, territory or possession of the United States, the District of Columbia, and the Commonwealth of Puerto Rico.

ARTICLE III.

(a) Whenever a person physically present in any party state shall be in need of institutionalization by reason of mental illness or mental deficiency, he shall be eligible for care and treatment in an institution in that state irrespective of his residence, settlement or citizenship qualifications.

(b) The provisions of paragraph (a) of this article to the contrary notwithstanding, any patient may be transferred to an institution in another state whenever there are factors based upon clinical determinations indicating that the care and treatment of said patient would be facilitated or improved thereby. Any such institutionalization may be for the entire period of care and treatment or for any portion or portions thereof. The factors referred to in this paragraph shall include the patient's full record with due regard for the location of the patient's family, character of the illness and probable duration thereof, and such other factors as shall be considered appropriate.

(c) No state shall be obliged to receive any patient pursuant to the provisions of paragraph (b) of this article unless the sending state has given advance notice of its intention to send the patient; furnished all available medical and other pertinent records concerning the patient; given the qualified medical or other appropriate clinical authorities of the receiving state an opportunity to examine the patient if said authorities so wish; and unless the receiving state shall agree to accept the patient.

(d) In the event that the laws of the receiving state establish a system of priorities for the admission of patients, and interstate patient under this compact shall receive the same priority as a local patient and shall be taken in the same order and at the same time that he would be taken if he were a local patient.

(e) Pursuant to this compact, the determination as to the suitable place of institutionalization for a patient may be reviewed at any time and such further transfer of the patient may be made as seems likely to be in the best interest of the patient.

ARTICLE IV.

(a) Whenever, pursuant to the laws of the state in which a patient is physically present, it shall be determined that the patient should receive after-care or supervision, such care or supervision may be provided in a receiving state. If the medical or other appropriate clinical authorities having responsibility for the care and treatment of the patient in the sending state shall have reason to believe that after-care in another state would be in the best interest of the patient and would not jeopardize the public safety, they shall request the appropriate authorities in the receiving state to investigate the desirability of affording the patient such after-care in said receiving state, and such investigation shall be made with all reasonable speed. The request for investigation shall be accompanied by complete information concerning the patient's intended place of residence and the identity of the person in whose charge it is proposed to place the patient, the complete medical history of the patient, and such other documents as may be pertinent.

(b) If the medical or other appropriate clinical authorities having responsibility for the care and treatment of the patient in the sending state and the appropriate authorities in the receiving state find that the best interest of the patient would be served thereby, and if the public safety would not be jeopardized thereby, the patient may receive after-care or supervision in the receiving state.

(c) In supervising, treating or caring for a patient on after-care pursuant to the terms of this article, a receiving state shall employ the same standards of visitation, examination, care and treatment that it employs for similar local patients.

ARTICLE V.

Whenever a dangerous or potentially dangerous patient escapes from an institution in any party state, that state shall promptly notify all appropriate authorities within and without the jurisdiction of the escape in a manner reasonably calculated to facilitate the speedy apprehension of the escapee. Immediately upon the apprehension and identification of any such dangerous or potentially dangerous patient, he shall be detained in the state where found pending disposition in accordance with law.

ARTICLE VI.

The duly accredited officers of any state party to this compact, upon the establishment of their authority and the identity of the patient, shall be permitted to transport any patient being moved pursuant to this compact through any and all states party to this compact, without interference.

ARTICLE VII.

(a) No person shall be deemed a patient of more than one institution at any given time. Completion of transfer of any patient to an institution in a receiving state shall have the effect of making the person a patient of the institution in the receiving state.

(b) The sending state shall pay all costs of and incidental to the transportation of any patient pursuant to this compact, but any two or more party states may, by making a specific agreement for that purpose, arrange for a different allocation of costs as among themselves.

(c) No provision of this compact shall be construed to alter or affect any internal relationships among the departments, agencies and officers of and in the government of a party state, or between a party state and its subdivisions, as to the payment of costs, or responsibilities therefor.

(d) Nothing in this compact shall be construed to prevent any party state or subdivision thereof from asserting any right against any person, agency or other entity in regard to costs for which such party state or subdivision thereof may be responsible pursuant to any provision of this compact.

(e) Nothing in this compact shall be construed to invalidate any reciprocal agreement between a party state and a non-party state relating to institutionalization, care or treatment of the mentally ill or mentally deficient, or any statutory authority pursuant to which such agreements may be made.

ARTICLE VIII.

(a) Nothing in this compact shall be construed to abridge, diminish, or in any way impair the rights, duties and responsibilities of any patient's guardian on his own behalf or in respect of any patient for whom he may serve, except that where the transfer of any patient to another jurisdiction makes advisable the appointment of a supplemental or substitute guardian, any court of competent jurisdiction in the receiving state may make such supplemental or substitute appointment and the court which appointed the previous guardian shall upon being duly advised of the new appointment, and upon the satisfactory completion of such accounting and other acts as such court may by law require, relieve the previous guardian of power and responsibility to whatever extent shall be appropriate in the circumstances; provided, however, that in the case of any patient having settlement in the sending state, the court of competent jurisdiction in the sending state shall have the sole discretion to relieve a guardian appointed by it or continue his power and responsibility, whichever it shall deem advisable. The court in the receiving state may, in its discretion, confirm or reappoint the person or persons previously serving as guardian in the sending state in lieu of making a supplemental or substitute appointment.

(b) The term "guardian" as used in paragraph (a) of this article shall include any guardian, trustee, legal committee, conservator, or other person or agency however denominated who is charged by law with power to act for or responsibility for the person or property of a patient.

ARTICLE IX.

(a) No provision of this compact except Article V shall apply to any person institutionalized while under sentence in a penal or correctional institution or while subject to trial on a criminal charge, or whose institutionalization is due to the commission of an offense for which, in the absence of mental illness or mental deficiency, said person would be subject to incarceration in a penal or correctional institution.

(b) To every extent possible, it shall be the policy of states party to this compact that no patient shall be placed or detained in any prison, jail or lockup, but such patient shall, with all expedition, be taken to a suitable institutional facility for mental illness or mental deficiency.

ARTICLE X.

(a) Each party state shall appoint a "compact administrator" who, on behalf of his state, shall act as general coordinator of activities under the compact in his state and who shall receive copies of all reports, correspondence, and other documents relating to any patient processed under the compact by his state either in the capacity of sending or receiving state. The compact administrator or his duly designated representative shall be the official with whom other party states shall deal in any matter relating to the compact or any patient processed thereunder.

(b) The compact administrators of the respective party states shall have power to promulgate reasonable rules and regulations to carry out more effectively the terms and provisions of this compact.

ARTICLE XI.

The duly constituted administrative authorities of any two or more party states may enter into supplementary agreements for the provision of any service or facility or for the maintenance of any institution on a joint or co-operative basis whenever the states concerned shall find that such agreements will improve services, facilities, or institutional care and treatment in the fields of mental illness or mental deficiency. No such supplementary agreement shall be construed so as to relieve any party state of any obligation which it otherwise would have under other provisions of this compact.

ARTICLE XII.

This compact shall enter into full force and effect as to any state when enacted by it into law and such state shall thereafter be a party thereto with any and all states legally joining therein.

ARTICLE XIII.

(a) A state party to this compact may withdraw therefrom by enacting a statute repealing the same. Such withdrawal shall take effect one year after notice thereof has been communicated officially and in writing to the governors and compact administrators of all other party states. However, the withdrawal of any state shall not change the status of any patient who has been sent to said state or sent out of said state pursuant to the provisions of the compact.

(b) Withdrawal from any agreement permitted by Article VII (b) as to costs or from any supplementary agreement made pursuant to Article XI shall be in accordance with the terms of such agreement.

ARTICLE XIV.

This compact shall be liberally construed so as to effectuate the purposes thereof. The provisions of this compact shall be severable and if any phrase, clause, sentence or provision of this compact is declared to be contrary to the constitution of any party state or of the United States or the applicability thereof to any government, agency, person or circumstance is held invalid, the validity of the remainder of this compact and the applicability thereof to any government, agency, person or circumstance shall not be affected thereby. If this compact shall be held contrary to the constitution of any state party thereto, the compact shall remain in full force and effect as to the remaining states and in full force and effect as to the state affected as to all severable matters.

History—
1956, 441, § 1.

Cross References—
Treatment and commitment of mentally ill and mentally retarded persons, see ALM GL c 123.

§ 2. Compact Administrator Authorized to Promulgate Rules and Regulations; Supplementary Agreements; Cooperation with Commonwealth Departments and Agencies.

Pursuant to the terms of the foregoing compact the commissioner of mental health is designated compact administrator and acting jointly with like officers of other contracting states or the District of Columbia or the Commonwealth of Puerto Rico shall have the power to promulgate rules and regulations to carry out more effectively the terms of the compact to which the commonwealth is a party. The compact administrator is authorized to enter into supplementary agreements with the appropriate officials of other states pursuant to Articles VII and XI of the foregoing compact. If such supplementary agreements require or contemplate the use of any institution or facility of the commonwealth or the provision of any service by the commonwealth, no such agreement shall have force or effect until approved by the head of the department or agency under whose jurisdiction such institution or facility is operated or whose department or agency will be charged with the rendering of such service. The compact administrator is directed to co-operate with all the departments, agencies and officers of the commonwealth and its subdivisions in facilitating proper administration of the compacts or any supplementary agreement or agreements entered into by the compact administrator thereunder.

History—
1956, 441, § 2.

Cross References—
Duties of commissioner of mental health, generally, see ALM GL c 19 § 2.
Designation of persons to perform duties of members of boards or commissions appointed under interstate compacts, see ALM GL c 30 § 6A.

§ 3.　Compact Finances.

Any payments necessary to discharge any financial obligation imposed upon the commonwealth by the foregoing compact or by any supplementary agreement entered into thereunder shall be reported to the governor and the budget commissioner annually on or before the fifteenth day of September for inclusion in the budget of the department of mental health.

History—
1956, 441, § 3.

§ 4.　Copies of Act.

Copies of this act shall be transmitted by the secretary of the commonwealth to the governor of each state, and to the attorney general and the secretary of the state of the United States.

History—
1956, 441, § 4.

New England Compact on Radiological Health Protection

(Acts 1967, Ch. 801)

SEC.
1. Short Title.
2. Form of Compact.
3. Public Health Commissioner to Formulate Radiation Incident Plan.
4. Public Health Commissioner or Designee as Compact Administrator.

Auto-Cite®: Cases and annotations referred to herein can be further researched through the Auto-Cite® computer-assisted research service. Use Auto-Cite to check citations for form, parallel references, prior and later history, and annotation references.

---

§ 1. Short Title.

This act may be cited as the New England Compact on Radiological Health Protection.

History—
1967, 801, § 1.

Cross References—
Advisory council on radiation protection, see ALM GL c 111 § 4F.
Public health department controlling hazards of ionizing radiation, see ALM GL c 111 § 5B.

§ 2. Form of Compact.

A compact is hereby entered into with all jurisdictions legally joining therein in substantially the following form:—

NEW ENGLAND COMPACT ON RADIOLOGICAL HEALTH PROTECTION

ARTICLE I. PURPOSES.—

The purposes of this compact are to:

1. Promote the radiological health protection of the public and individuals within the party States.

2. Provide mutual aid and assistance in radiological health matters including, but not limited to, radiation incidents.

3. Encourage and facilitate the efficient use of personnel and equipment by furthering the orderly acquisition and sharing of resources useful for programs of radiation protection.

ARTICLE II. ENACTMENT.—

This compact shall become effective when enacted into law by any two or more of the States of Connecticut, Maine, Massachusetts, New Hampshire, Rhode Island and Vermont. Thereafter it shall become effective with respect to any other aforementioned State upon its enacting this compact into law. Any State not mentioned in this Article which is contiguous to any party State may become a party to this compact by enacting the same.

ARTICLE III. DUTIES OF STATES.—

(a) It shall be the duty of each party State to formulate and put into effect an intrastate radiation incident plan which is compatible with the interstate radiation incident plan formulated pursuant to this compact.

(b) Whenever the compact administrator of a party State requests aid from the compact administrator of any other party State pursuant to this compact, it shall be the duty of the requested State to render all possible aid to the requesting State which is consonant with the maintenance of protection of its own people. The compact administrator of a party State may delegate any or all of his authority to request aid or respond to requests for aid pursuant to this compact to one or more subordinates, in order that requests for aid and responses thereto shall not be impeded by reason of the absence or unavailability of the compact administrator. Any compact administrator making such a delegation shall inform all the other compact administrators thereof, and also shall inform them of the identity of the subordinate or subordinates to whom the delegation has been made.

(c) Each party State shall maintain adequate radiation protection personnel and equipment to meet normal demands for radiation protection within its borders.

ARTICLE IV. LIABILITY.—

(a) Whenever the officers or employees of any party State are rendering outside aid pursuant to the request of another party State under this compact, the officers or employees of such State shall, under the direction of the authorities of the State to which they are rendering aid, have the same powers, duties, rights, privileges and immunities as comparable officers and employees of the State to which they are rendering aid.

(b) No party State or its officers or employees rendering outside aid pursuant to this compact shall be liable on account of any act or omission on their part while so engaged, or on account of the maintenance or use of any equipment or supplies in connection therewith.

(c) All liability that may arise either under the laws of the requesting State or under the laws of the aiding State or under the laws of a third State, on account of or in connection with a request for aid, shall be assumed and borne by the requesting State.

(d) Any party State rendering outside aid to cope with a radiation incident shall be reimbursed by the party State receiving such aid for any loss or damage to or expense incurred in the operation of any equipment answering a request for aid, and for the cost of all materials, transportation and maintenance of officers, employees and equipment incurred in connection with such request; provided that nothing herein contained shall prevent any assisting party State from assuming such loss, damage, expense or other cost or from loaning such equipment or from donating such services to the receiving party State without charge or cost.

(e) Each party State shall provide for the payment of compensation and death benefits to injured officers and employees and the representatives of deceased officers and employees in case officers or employees sustain injuries or are killed while rendering outside aid pursuant to this compact, in the same manner and on the same terms as if the injury or death were sustained within the State for or in which the officer or employee was regularly employed.

ARTICLE V. FACILITIES, EQUIPMENT AND PERSONNEL.—

(a) Whenever a department, agency or officer of a party State responsible for and having control of facilities or equipment designed for or useful in radiation control, radiation research, or any other phase of a radiological health program or programs determines that such a facility or item of equipment is not being used to its full capacity by such party State, or that temporarily it is not needed for current use by such State, a department, agency or officer may, upon request of an appropriate department, agency or officer of another party State, make such facility or item of equipment available for use by such requesting department, agency or officer. Unless otherwise required by law, the availability and use resulting therefrom may be with or without charge, at the discretion of the lending department, agency or officer. Any personal property made available pursuant to this paragraph may be removed to the requesting State, but no such property shall be made available, except for a specified period and pursuant to written agreement. Except when necessary to meet an emergency, no supplies or materials intended to be consumed prior to return shall be made available pursuant to this paragraph.

(b) In recognition of the mutual benefits, in addition to those resulting from Article IV, accruing to the party States from the existence and flexible use of professional or technical personnel having special skills or training related to radiation protection, such personnel may be made available to a party State by appropriate departments, agencies and officers of other party States; provided that the borrower reimburses such party State regularly employing the personnel in question for any cost of making such personnel available, including a prorated share of the salary or other compensation of the personnel involved.

(c) Nothing in this Article shall be construed to limit or to modify in any way the provisions of Article IV of this compact.

ARTICLE VI. COMPACT ADMINISTRATORS.—

Each party State shall have a compact administrator who shall be the head of the State agency having principal responsibility for radiation protection, and who:

1. Shall coordinate activities pursuant to this compact in and on behalf of his State.

2. Serving jointly with the compact administrators of the other party States, shall develop and keep current an interstate radiation incident plan; consider such other matters as may be appropriate in connection with programs of cooperation in the field of radiation protection and allied areas of common interest; and formulate procedures for claims and reimbursement under the provisions of Article IV.

ARTICLE VII. OTHER RESPONSIBILITIES AND ACTIVITIES.—

Nothing in this compact shall be construed to:

1. Authorize or permit any party State to curtail or diminish its radiation protection program, equipment, services or facilities.

2. Limit or restrict the powers of any State ratifying the same to

provide for the radiological health protection of the public and individuals, or to prohibit the enactment or enforcement of State laws, rules or regulations intended to provide for such radiological health protection.

3. Affect any existing or future cooperative relationship or arrangement between Federal, State or local governments and a party State or States.

ARTICLE VIII. WITHDRAWAL.—

Any party State may withdraw from this compact by enacting a statute repealing the same, but no such withdrawal shall take effect until one year after the Governor of the withdrawing State has given notice in writing of the withdrawal to the Governors of all other party States. No withdrawal shall affect any liability already incurred by or chargeable to a party State prior to the time of such withdrawal.

ARTICLE IX. CONSTRUCTION AND SEVERABILITY.—

It is the legislative intent that the provisions of this compact be reasonably and liberally construed. The provisions of this compact shall be severable and if any phrase, clause, sentence or provision of this compact is declared to be unconstitutional or the applicability thereof to any State, agency, person or circumstance is held invalid, the constitutionality of the remainder of this compact and the applicability thereof to any other State, agency, person or circumstance shall not be affected thereby.

History—
1967, 801, § 2.

§ 3.   Public Health Commissioner to Formulate Radiation Incident Plan.

The commissioner of public health shall formulate and keep current a radiation incident plan for this commonwealth, in accordance with the duty assumed pursuant to Article III (a) of the New England Compact on Radiological Health Protection set forth in section two.

History—
1967, 801, § 3.

Cross References—
Duties of commissioner of public health, generally, see ALM GL c 111 § 2.

§ 4.   Public Health Commissioner or Designee as Compact Administrator.

The compact administrator for this commonwealth, as required by Article VI of said Compact, shall be the commissioner of public health or his designee.

History—
1967, 801.

Cross References—
Designation of persons to perform duties of members of boards or commissions appointed under interstate compacts, see ALM GL c 30 § 6A.

Duties of commissioner of public health, generally, see ALM GL c 111 § 2.

CHAPTER S111

New England State Police Compact

(Acts 1967, Ch. 498)

> **Auto-Cite®:** Cases and annotations referred to herein can be further researched through the Auto-Cite® computer-assisted research service. Use Auto-Cite to check citations for form, parallel references, prior and later history, and annotation references.

§ 1. Form of Compact.

A compact is hereby entered into with all jurisdictions legally joining therein in substantially the following form:—

NEW ENGLAND STATE POLICE COMPACT

ARTICLE I. PURPOSES

The purposes of this compact are to:

1. Provide close and effective cooperation and assistance in detecting and apprehending those engaged in organized criminal activities;

2. Establish and maintain a central criminal intelligence bureau to gather, evaluate and disseminate to the appropriate law enforcement officers of the party states information concerning organized crime, its leaders and their associates;

3. Provide mutual aid and assistance in the event of police emergencies, and to provide for the powers, duties, rights, privileges and immunities of police personnel when rendering such aid.

ARTICLE II. ENTRY INTO FORCE AND WITHDRAWAL

(a) This compact shall enter into force when enacted into law by any three of the states of Connecticut, Maine, Massachusetts, New

Hampshire, Rhode Island and Vermont. Thereafter, this compact shall become effective as to any other of the aforementioned states upon its enactment thereof.

(b) Any party state may withdraw from this compact by enacting a statute repealing the same, but no such withdrawal shall take effect until one year after the governor of the withdrawing state has given notice in writing of the withdrawal to the Governors of all other party states. No withdrawal shall affect any liability already incurred by or chargeable to a party state prior to the time of such withdrawal, and any records, files or information obtained by officers or employees of a withdrawing state shall continue to be kept, used and disposed of only in such manner as is consistent with this compact and any rules or regulations pursuant thereto.

ARTICLE III. THE CONFERENCE

(a) There is hereby established the "New England State Police Administrators' Conference", hereinafter called the "Conference", to be composed of the administrative head of the state police department of each party state.

(b) If authorized by the laws of his party state, the administrative head of the state police department of a party state may provide for the discharge of his duties and the performance of his functions on the Conference, for periods none of which shall exceed fifteen days, by an alternate. No such alternate shall be entitled to serve unless notification of his identity and appointment shall have been given to the Conference in such form as the Conference may require.

(c) An alternate serving pursuant to subdivision (b) of this article shall be selected only from among the officers and employees of the state police department, the head of which such alternate is to represent.

(d) The members of the Conference shall be entitled to one vote each. No action of the Conference shall be binding unless taken at a meeting at which a majority of the total number of votes of the Conference are cast in favor thereof. Action of the Conference shall be only at a meeting at which a majority of the members of the Conference, or their alternates, are present.

(e) The Conference shall have a seal.

(f) The Conference shall elect annually, from among its members, a chairman, (who shall not be eligible to succeed himself) a vice chairman and a treasurer. The Conference shall appoint an Executive Secretary and fix his duties and compensation. Such Executive Secretary shall serve at the pleasure of the Conference, and together with the Treasurer shall be bonded in such amount as the Conference shall determine. The Executive Secretary also shall serve as general secretary of the Conference.

(g) Irrespective of the civil service, personnel or other merit system laws of any of the party states, the Executive Secretary, subject to the direction of the Conference, shall appoint, remove or discharge such personnel as may be necessary for the performance of the Conference functions, and shall fix the duties and compensation of such personnel.

(h) The Conference may establish and maintain independently, or in conjunction with any one or more of the party states, a suitable retirement system for its full time employees. Employees of the Conference shall be eligible for social security coverage in respect of old age and survivor's insurance provided that the Conference takes such steps as may be necessary pursuant to the laws of the United States, to participate in such program of insurance as a governmental agency or unit. The Conference may establish and maintain or participate in such additional programs of employee benefits as may be appropriate. Employment by the Conference of a retired officer or employee of a party state shall not affect the pension or other retirement-connected benefits paid to such officer or employee by a party state.

(i) The Conference may borrow, accept or contract for the services of personnel from any party state, the United States, or any subdivision or agency of the aforementioned governments, or from any agency of two or more of the party states or their subdivisions.

(j) The Conference may accept for any of its purposes and functions under this compact any and all donations, grants of money, equipment, supplies, materials and services, conditional or otherwise, from any state, the United States, or any other governmental agency, or from any person, firm or corporation, and may receive, utilize and dispose of the same. The Conference shall publish in its annual report the terms, conditions, character and amount of any resources accepted by it pursuant hereto together with the identity of the donor.

(k) The Conference may establish and maintain such facilities as may be necessary for the transacting of its business. The Conference may acquire, hold and convey real and personal property and any interest therein.

(l) The Conference shall adopt by-laws for the conduct of its business and shall have the power to amend and rescind these by-laws. The Conference shall publish its by-laws in convenient form and shall file a copy thereof and a copy of any amendment thereto, with the appropriate agency or officer in each of the party states. The by-laws shall provide for appropriate notice of the Conference members of all Conference meetings.

(m) The Conference annually shall make to the Governor and legislature of each party state a report covering the activities of the Conference for the preceding year, and embodying such recommendations as may have been issued by the Conference. The Conference may make such additional reports as it may deem desirable.

ARTICLE IV. CONFERENCE POWERS

The Conference shall have power to:

(a) Establish and operate a New England Criminal Intelligence Bureau, hereinafter called "the Bureau", in which shall be received, assembled and kept case histories, records, data, personal dossiers and other information concerning persons engaged or otherwise associated with organized crime.

(b) Consider and recommend means of identifying leaders and emerging leaders of organized crime and their associates.

(c) Facilitate mutual assistance among the state police of the party states pursuant to Article VII of this compact.

(d) Formulate procedures for claims and reimbursements, pursuant to Article VII of this compact.

(e) Promote cooperation in law enforcement and make recommendations to the party states and other appropriate law enforcement authorities for the improvement of such cooperation.

(f) Do all things which may be necessary and incidental to the exercise of the foregoing powers.

ARTICLE V. DISPOSITION OF RECORDS AND INFORMATION

The Bureau established and operated pursuant to Article IV (a) of this compact is hereby designated and recognized as the instrument for the performance of a central criminal intelligence service to the state police departments of the party states. The files, records, data and other information of the Bureau and, when made pursuant to the by-laws of the Conference, any copies thereof shall be available only to duly designated officers and employees of the state police departments of the party states acting within the scope of their official duty. In the possession of the aforesaid officers and employees, such records, data, and other information shall be subject to use and disposition in the same manner and pursuant to the same laws, rules and regulations applicable to similar records, data and information of the officer's or employee's agency and the provision of this compact.

ARTICLE VI. ADDITIONAL MEETINGS AND SERVICES

The members of the Conference from any two or more party states, upon notice to the chairman as to the time and purpose of the meeting, may meet as a section for the discussion of problems common to their states. Any two or more party states may designate the Conference as a joint agency to maintain for them such additional common services as they may deem desirable for combating organized crime. Except in those cases where all party states join in such designation for common services, the representative of any group of such designating states in the Conference shall constitute a separate section of such Conference for the performance of the common service or services so designated provided that, if any additional expense is involved, the state so acting shall provide the necessary funds for this purpose. The creation of such a section or joint agency shall not affect the privileges, powers, responsibilities or duties of the states participating therein as embodied in the other articles of this compact.

ARTICLE VII. MUTUAL AID

(a) As used in this Article:

1. "Emergency" means an occurrence or condition, temporary in nature, in which the state police department of a party state is, or may reasonably be expected to be, unable to cope with substantial and imminent danger to the public safety, and in which the cooperation of or aid from local police forces within the state is, or may reasonably be expected to be insufficient. Also "emergency" shall mean a situation in which an investigation of an aspect of organized crime or events connected with organized crime require augmentation, for a limited time, of the investigative personnel of the state police department from without the state.

2. "Requesting state" means the state whose state police department requests assistance in coping with an emergency.

3. "Responding state" means the state furnishing aid, or requested to furnish aid, pursuant to this Article.

(b) In case of emergency, upon the request of the administrative head of the state police department of a party state, the administrative head of the state police department of each responding state shall order such part of his state police forces as he, in his discretion, may find necessary to aid the state police forces of the requesting state in order to carry out the purposes set forth in this compact. In such case, it shall be the duty of the administrative head of the state police department of each responding state to issue the necessary orders for such use of state police forces of his state without the borders of his state, and to direct such forces to place themselves under the operational control of the administrative head of the state police department of the requesting state.

(c) The administrative head of the state police department of any party state, in his discretion, may withhold or recall the police forces of his state, or any part or any member thereof, serving without its borders.

(d) Whenever any of the state police forces of any party state are engaged outside their own state in carrying out the purposes of this compact, the individual members so engaged shall have the same powers, duties, rights, privileges and immunities as members of the state police department of the state in which they are engaged, but, in any event, a requesting state shall save harmless any member of a responding state police department serving within its borders for any act or acts done by him in the performance of his duty while engaged in carrying out the purposes of this compact.

(e) All liability that may arise under the laws of the requesting state or under the laws of the responding state or under the laws of a third state on account of or in connection with a request for aid shall be assumed and borne by the requesting state.

(f) Any responding state rendering aid pursuant to this compact shall be reimbursed by the requesting state for any loss or damage to, or expense incurred in the operation of, any equipment answering a request for aid, and for the cost of the materials, transportation and maintenance of state police personnel and equipment incurred in connection with such request; provided, that nothing herein contained shall prevent any responding state from assuming such loss, damage, expense or other cost.

(g) Each party state shall provide, in the same amounts and manner as if they were on duty within their state, for the pay and allowances of the personnel of its state police department while engaged without the state pursuant to this compact and while going to and returning from such duty pursuant to this compact.

(h) Each party state providing for the payment of compensation and death benefits to injured members and the representatives of deceased members of its state police department in case such members sustain injuries or are killed within their own state shall provide for the payment of compensation and death benefits in the same manner and on the same terms in case such members sustain injury or are killed while rendering aid pursuant to this compact.

ARTICLE VIII. FINANCE.

(a) The Conference shall submit to the Governor or designated officer or officers of each party state a budget of its estimated expenditures for such period as may be required by the laws of that party state for presentation to the legislature thereof.

(b) Each of the Conference's budgets of estimated expenditures shall contain specific recommendations of the amount or amounts to be appropriated by each of the party states. The total amount of appropriation under any such budget shall be apportioned among the party states as follows: one third in equal shares; one third divided among the party states in the proportions that their populations bear to the total population of all the party states; and one third divided among the party states in the proportions that the major crimes committed in each party state bear to the total number of major crimes committed in all the party states. In determining population pursuant to this paragraph, the most recent decennial census compiled by the United States Government shall be used. Numbers of major crimes shall be as reported in the most recent annual "Uniform Crime Report" compiled by the Federal Bureau of Investigation of the United States Department of Justice, or by any agency which may assume responsibility for such compilation in the place of such Bureau. In the event that any source of information required to be used for the purpose of this paragraph shall be discontinued, the Conference shall make its calculations on the basis of the best alternative sources of information and shall identify the sources used.

(c) The Conference shall not pledge the credit of any party state. The Conference may meet any of its obligations in whole or in part with funds available to it under Article III (j) of this compact, provided that the Conference takes specific action setting aside such funds prior to incurring any obligation to be met in whole or in part in such manner. Except where the Conference makes use of funds available to it under Article III (j) hereof, the Conference shall not incur any obligation prior to the allotment of funds by the party states adequate to meet the same.

(d) The Conference shall keep accurate accounts of all receipts and disbursements. The receipts and disbursements of the Conference shall be subject to the audit and accounting procedures established under its rules. However, all receipts and disbursements of funds handled by the Conference shall be audited yearly by a qualified, public accountant and the report of the audit shall be included in and become part of the annual report of the Conference.

(e) The accounts of the Conference shall be open at any reasonable time for inspection by duly constituted officers of the party states and any persons authorized by the Conference.

(f) Nothing contained herein shall be construed to prevent Conference compliance with laws relating to audit or inspection of accounts by or on behalf of any government contributing to the support of the Conference.

ARTICLE IX. CONSTRUCTION AND SEVERABILITY

This compact shall be liberally construed so as to effectuate the purposes thereof. The provisions of this compact shall be severable and if any phrase, clause, sentence or provision of this compact is declared to be contrary to the Constitution of any state or of the United States or the applicability thereof to any government, agency, person or circumstance is held invalid, validity of the remainder of this compact and the applicability thereof to any government, agency, person or circumstance shall not be affected thereby. If this compact shall be held contrary to the constitution of any state participating herein, the compact shall remain in full force and effect as to the remaining party states and in full force and effect as to the state affected as to all severable matters.

History—
1967, 498, § 1.

Cross References—
State police, generally, see ALM GL c 22.

§ 2.   Administrative Head of the State Police Department, Defined.

The "administrative head of the state police department" for the Commonwealth of Massachusetts, for the purposes of the New England State Police Compact set forth in section one, shall be deemed to be the commissioner of public safety.

History—
1967, 498, § 2.

Cross References—

Public safety commissioner, generally, see ALM GL c 22 §§ 2, 3.

Designation of persons to perform duties of members of boards or commissions appointed under interstate compacts, see ALM GL c 30 § 6A.

§ 3. Public Safety Commissioner or Designee to Serve on New England State Police Administrators' Conference.

The commissioner of public safety is hereby authorized to designate an alternate to serve in his place and stead on the New England State Police Administrators' Conference as permitted by Article III (b) and (c) of the New England State Police Compact; however, it is the intention of the General Court that said commissioner shall attend and participate in the work of the Conference in person to the maximum extent practicable.

History—

1967, 498, § 3.

Cross References—

Designation of persons to perform duties of members of boards or commissions appointed under interstate compacts, see ALM GL c 30 § 6A.

CHAPTER S113

New England Interstate Corrections Compact
(Acts 1962, Ch. 753)

Sec.
1. Title.
2. Form of Compact.
3. Implementation of Compact by Corrections Commissioner.

Auto-Cite®: Cases and annotations referred to herein can be further researched through the Auto-Cite® computer-assisted research service. Use Auto-Cite to check citations for form, parallel references, prior and later history, and annotation references.

---

§ 1. Title.

This act may be cited as the New England interstate corrections compact.

History—
1962, 753, § 1.

Cross References—
Compact for interstate supervision of probationers and parolees, see ALM GL c 127 §§ 151A–151K.

As to procedure on interstate rendition, see ALM GL c 276, §§ 11–20R.

§ 2. Form of Compact.

The New England interstate corrections compact is hereby enacted into law and entered into by this state with any other of the hereinafter-mentioned states legally joining therein in the form substantially as follows:

NEW ENGLAND INTERSTATE CORRECTIONS COMPACT

ARTICLE I.

PURPOSE AND POLICY.

The party states, desiring by common action to fully utilize and

315

improve their institutional facilities and provide adequate programs for the confinement, treatment and rehabilitation of various types of offenders, declare that it is the policy of each of the party states to provide such facilities and programs on a basis of co-operation with one another, thereby serving the best interests of such offenders and of society and effecting economies in capital expenditures and operational costs. The purpose of this compact is to provide for the mutual development and execution of such programs of co-operation for the confinement, treatment and rehabilitation of offenders with the most economical use of human and material resources.

ARTICLE II.

DEFINITIONS.

As used in this compact, unless the context clearly requires otherwise:

(a) "State" means a state of the United States, located in New England, to wit, Maine, New Hampshire, Vermont, Massachusetts, Connecticut, Rhode Island.

(b) "Sending state" means a state party to this compact in which conviction or court commitment was had.

(c) "Receiving state" means a state party to this compact to which an inmate is sent for confinement other than a state in which conviction or court commitment was had.

(d) "Inmate" means a male or female offender who is committed, under sentence to or confined in a penal or correctional institution except county houses of correction and jails.

(e) "Institution" means any penal or correctional facility (including but not limited to a facility for the mentally ill or mentally defective) in which inmates as defined in (d) above may lawfully be confined.

ARTICLE III.

CONTRACTS.

(a) Each party state may make one or more contracts with any one or more of the other party states for the confinement of inmates on behalf of a sending state in institutions situated within receiving states. Any such contract shall provide for:

1. Its duration.

2. Payments to be made to the receiving state by the sending state for inmate maintenance, extraordinary medical and dental expenses, and any participation in or receipt by inmates of rehabilitative or correctional services, facilities, programs or treatment not reasonably included as part of normal maintenance.

3. Participation in programs of inmate employment, if any; the disposition or crediting of any payments received by inmates on account thereof; and the crediting of proceeds from or disposal of any products resulting therefrom.

4. Delivery and retaking of inmates.

5. Such other matters as may be necessary and appropriate to fix the obligations, responsibilities and rights of the sending and receiving states.

(b) The terms and provisions of this compact shall be a part of any contract entered into by the authority of or pursuant thereto, and nothing in any such contract shall be inconsistent therewith.

ARTICLE IV.

PROCEDURES AND RIGHTS.

(a) Whenever the duly constituted authorities in a state party to this compact, and which has entered into a contract pursuant to Article III, shall decide that confinement in, or transfer of an inmate to, an institution within the territory of another party state is necessary or desirable in order to provide adequate quarters and care of an appropriate program of rehabilitation or treatment, said officials may direct that the confinement be within an institution within the territory of said other party state, the receiving state to act in that regard solely as agent for the sending state.

(b) The appropriate officials of any state party to this compact shall have access, at all reasonable times, to any institution in which it has a contractual right to confine inmates for the purpose of inspecting the facilities thereof and visiting such of its inmates as may be confined in the institution.

(c) Inmates confined in an institution pursuant to the terms of this compact shall at all times be subject to the jurisdiction of the sending state and may at any time be removed therefrom for transfer to a prison or other institution in which the sending state may have a contractual or other right to confine inmates, for release on probation or parole, for discharge, or for any other purpose permitted by the laws of the sending state; provided, that the sending state shall continue to be obligated to such payments as may be required pursuant to the terms of any contract entered into under the terms of Article III.

(d) Each receiving state shall provide regular reports to each sending state on the inmates of that sending state in institutions pursuant to this compact including a conduct record of each inmate and certify said record to the official designated by the sending state, in order that each inmate may have official review of his or her record in determining and altering the disposition of said inmate in accordance with the law which may obtain in the sending state and in order that the same may be a source of information for the sending state.

(e) All inmates who may be confined in an institution pursuant to the provisions of this compact shall be treated in a reasonable and humane manner and shall be treated equally with such similar inmates of the receiving state as may be confined in the same institution. The fact of confinement in a receiving state shall not deprive any inmate so confined of any legal rights which said inmate would have had if confined in an appropriate institution of the sending state.

(f) Any hearing or hearings to which an inmate confined pursuant to this compact may be entitled by the laws of the sending state may be had before the appropriate authorities of the sending state, or of the receiving state if authorized by the sending state. The receiving state shall provide adequate facilities for such hearings as may be conducted by the appropriate officials of a sending state. In the event such hearing or hearings are had before officials of the receiving state, the governing law shall be that of the sending state and a record of the hearing or hearings as prescribed by the sending state shall be made. Said record together with any recommendations of the hearing officials shall be transmitted forthwith to the official or officials before whom the hearing would have been had if it had taken place in the sending state. In any and all proceedings had pursuant to the provisions of this subdivision, the officials of the receiving state shall act solely as agents of the sending state and no final determination shall be made in any matter except by the appropriate officials of the sending state.

(g) Any inmate confined pursuant to this compact shall be released within the territory of the sending state unless the inmate, and the sending and receiving states, shall agree upon release in some other place. The sending state shall bear the cost of such return to its territory.

(h) Any inmate confined pursuant to the terms of this compact shall have any and all rights to participate in and derive any benefits or incur or be relieved of any obligations or have such obligations modified or his status changed on account of any action or proceeding in which he could have participated if confined in any appropriate institution of the sending state located within such state.

(i) The parent, guardian, trustee or other person or persons entitled under the laws of the sending state to act for, advise or otherwise function with respect to any inmate shall not be deprived of or restricted in his exercise of any power in respect of any inmate confined pursuant to the terms of this compact.

ARTICLE V.

ACTS NOT REVIEWABLE IN RECEIVING STATE: EXTRADITION.

(a) Any decision of the sending state in respect of any matter over which it retains jurisdiction pursuant to this compact shall be conclusive upon and not reviewable within the receiving state, but if at the time the sending state seeks to remove an inmate from an institution in the receiving state there is pending against the inmate within such state any criminal charge or if the inmate is formally accused of having committed within such state a criminal offense, the inmate shall not be returned without the consent of the receiving state until discharged from prosecution or other form of proceeding, imprisonment or detention for such offense. The duly accredited officers of the sending state shall be permitted to transport inmates pursuant to this compact through any and all states party to this compact without interference.

(b) An inmate who escapes from an institution in which he is confined pursuant to this compact shall be deemed a fugitive from the sending state and from the state in which the institution is situated. In the case of an escape to a jurisdiction other than the sending or receiving state, the responsibility for institution of extradition or rendition proceedings shall be that of the sending state, but nothing contained herein shall be construed to prevent or affect the activities of officers and agencies of any jurisdiction directed toward the apprehension and return of an escapee.

ARTICLE VI.

FEDERAL AID.

Any state party to this compact may accept federal aid for use in connection with any institution or program, the use of which is or may be affected by this compact or any contract pursuant hereto and any inmate in a receiving state pursuant to this compact may participate in any such federally aided program or activity for which the sending and receiving states have made contractual provision; provided, that if such program or activity is not part of the customary correctional regimen the express consent of the appropriate official of the sending state shall be required therefor.

ARTICLE VII.

ENTRY INTO FORCE.

This compact shall enter into force and become effective and binding upon the states so acting when it has been enacted into law by any four states from among the states of New England. Thereafter, this compact shall enter into force and become effective and binding as to any other of said states upon similar action by such state.

ARTICLE VIII.

WITHDRAWAL AND TERMINATION.

This compact shall continue in force and remain binding upon a party state until it shall have enacted a statute repealing the same and providing for the sending of formal written notice of withdrawal from the compact to the appropriate officials of all other party states. An actual withdrawal shall not take effect until one year after the notices provided in said statute have been sent. Such withdrawal shall not relieve the withdrawing state from its obligations assumed hereunder prior to the effective date of withdrawal. Before the effective date of withdrawal, a withdrawing state shall remove to its territory, at its own expense, such inmates as it may have confined pursuant to the provisions of this compact.

ARTICLE IX.

OTHER ARRANGEMENTS UNAFFECTED.

Nothing contained in this compact shall be construed to abrogate or impair any agreement or other arrangement which a party state may have with a non-party state for the confinement, rehabilitation or treatment of inmates nor to repeal any other laws of a party state authorizing the making of co-operative institutional arrangements.

ARTICLE X.

CONSTRUCTION AND SEVERABILITY.

The provisions of this compact shall be liberally construed and shall be severable. If any phrase, clause, sentence or provision of this compact is declared to be contrary to the constitution of any participating state or of the United States or the applicability thereof to any government, agency, person or circumstance is held invalid, the validity of the remainder of this compact and the applicability thereof to any government, agency, person or circumstance shall not be affected thereby. If this compact shall be held contrary to the constitution of any state participating therein, the compact shall remain in full force and effect as to the remaining states and in full force and effect as to the state affected as to all severable matters.

History—
1962, 753, § 2.

§ 3.   Implementation of Compact by Corrections Commissioner.

The commissioner of correction, subject to the approval of the governor and council, is hereby authorized and directed to do all things necessary or incidental to the carrying out of the compact in every particular.

History—
1962, 753, § 3.

Cross References—
Commissioner of correction, generally, see ALM GL c 27 § 1.

Designation of persons to perform duties of members of boards or commissions appointed under interstate compacts, see ALM GL c 30 § 6A.

Commissioner of correction, generally, see ALM GL c 124 § 1.

CHAPTER S115

Interstate Compact as to Detainers Outstanding against Prisoners Based on Untried Indictments, Information or Complaint

(Acts 1965, Ch. 892)

> **Auto-Cite®:** Cases and annotations referred to herein can be further researched through the Auto-Cite® computer-assisted research service. Use Auto-Cite to check citations for form, parallel references, prior and later history, and annotation references.

§ 1. Form of Compact.

An agreement is hereby entered into by this commonwealth with all other jurisdictions legally joining therein in substantially the following form:

AGREEMENT ON DETAINERS

The contracting states solemnly agree that:

ARTICLE I

The party states find that charges outstanding against a prisoner, detainers based on untried indictments, informations or complaints, and difficulties in securing speedy trial of persons already incarcerated in other jurisdictions, produce uncertainties which obstruct programs of prisoner treatment and rehabilitation. Accordingly, it is the policy of the party states and the purpose of this agreement to encourage the expeditious and orderly disposition of such charges

323

and determination of the proper status of any and all detainers based on untried indictments, informations or complaints. The party states also find that proceedings with reference to such charges and detainers, when emanating from another jurisdiction, cannot properly be had in the absence of cooperative procedures. It is the purpose of this agreement to provide such cooperative procedures.

ARTICLE II

(a) "State" shall mean a state of the United States; the United States of America; a territory or possession of the United States; the District of Columbia; the Commonwealth of Puerto Rico.

(b) "Sending state" shall mean a state in which a prisoner is incarcerated at the time that he initiates a request for final disposition pursuant to Article III hereof or at the time that a request for custody or availability is initiated pursuant to Article IV hereof.

(c) "Receiving state" shall mean the state in which trial is to be had on an indictment, information or complaint pursuant to Article III or Article IV hereof.

ARTICLE III

(a) Whenever a person has entered upon a term of imprisonment in a penal or correctional institution of a party state, and whenever during the continuance of the term of imprisonment there is pending in any other party state any untried indictment, information or complaint on the basis of which a detainer has been lodged against the prisoner, he shall be brought to trial within one hundred eighty days after he shall have caused to be delivered to the prosecuting officer and the appropriate court of the prosecuting officer's jurisdiction written notice of the place of his imprisonment and his request for a final disposition to be made of the indictment, information or complaint; provided, that, for good cause shown in open court, the prisoner or his counsel being present, the court having jurisdiction of the matter may grant any necessary or reasonable continuance. The request of the prisoner shall be accompanied by a certificate of the appropriate official having custody of the prisoner, stating the term of commitment under which the prisoner is being held, the time already served, the time remaining to be served on the sentence, the amount of good time earned, the time of parole eligibility of the prisoner, and any decisions of the state parole agency relating to the prisoner.

(b) The written notice and request for final disposition referred to in paragraph (a) hereof shall be given or sent by the prisoner to the warden, commissioner of correction or other official having custody of the prisoner, who shall promptly forward it together with the certificate to the appropriate prosecuting official and court by registered or certified mail, return receipt requested.

(c) The warden, commissioner of correction or other official having custody of the prisoner shall promptly inform him of the source and contents of any detainer lodged against him and shall also inform him of his right to make a request for final disposition of the indictment, information or complaint on which the detainer is based.

(d) Any request for final disposition made by a prisoner pursuant to paragraph (a) hereof shall operate as a request for final disposition of all untried indictments, informations or complaints on the basis of which detainers have been lodged against the prisoner from the state to whose prosecuting official the request for final disposition is specifically directed. The warden, commissioner of correction or other official having custody of the prisoner shall forthwith notify all appropriate prosecuting officers and courts in the serveral jurisdictions within the state to which the prisoner's request for final disposition is being sent of the proceeding being initiated by the prisoner. Any notification sent pursuant to this paragraph shall be accompanied by copies of the prisoner's written notice, request, and the certificate. If trial is not had on any indictment, information or complaint contemplated hereby prior to the return of the prisoner to the original place of imprisonment, such indictment, information or complaint shall not be of any further force or effect, and the court shall enter an order dismissing the same with prejudice.

(e) Any request for final disposition made by a prisoner pursuant to paragraph (a) hereof shall also be deemed to be a waiver of extradiction with respect to any charge or proceeding contemplated thereby or included therein by reason of paragraph (d) hereof, and a waiver of extradition to the receiving state to serve any sentence there imposed upon him, after completion of his term of imprisonment in the sending state. The request for final disposition shall also constitute a consent by the prisoner to the production of his body in any court where his presence may be required in order to effectuate the purposes of this agreement and a further consent voluntarily to be returned to the original place of imprisonment in accordance with the provisions of this agreement. Nothing in this paragraph shall prevent the imposition of a concurrent sentence if otherwise permitted by law.

(f) Escape from custody by the prisoner subsequent to his execution of the request for final disposition referred to in paragraph (a) hereof shall void the request.

ARTICLE IV

(a) The appropriate officer of the jurisdiction in which an untried indictment, information or complaint is pending, shall be entitled to have a prisoner against whom he has lodged a detainer and who is serving a term of imprisonment in any party state made available in accordance with paragraph (a) of Article V upon presentation of a written request for temporary custody or availability to the appropriate authorities of the state in which the prisoner is incarcerated; provided, that, the court having jurisdiction of such indictment, information or complaint shall have duly approved, recorded and transmitted the request; and, provided further, that there shall be a period of thirty days after receipt by the appropriate authorities before the request is honored, within which period the governor of the sending state may disapprove the request for temporary custody or availability, either upon his own motion or upon the motion of the prisoner.

(b) Upon receipt of the officer's written request as provided in paragraph (a) hereof, the appropriate authorities having the prisoner in custody shall furnish the officer with a certificate stating the term of commitment under which the prisoner is being held, the time already served, the time remaining to be served on the sentence, the amount of good time earned, the time of parole eligibility of the prisoner, and any decisions of the state parole agency relating to the prisoner. Said authorities simultaneously shall furnish all other officers and appropriate courts in the receiving state who have lodged detainers against the prisoner with similar certificates and with notices informing them of the request for custody or availability and of the reasons therefor.

(c) In respect to any proceeding made possible by this Article, trial shall be commenced within one hundred twenty days of the arrival of the prisoner in the receiving state, but for good cause shown in open court, the prisoner or his counsel being present, the court having jurisdiction of the matter may grant any necessary or reasonable continuance.

(d) Nothing contained in his Article shall be construed to deprive any prisoner of any right which he may have to contest the legality of his delivery as provided in paragraph (a) hereof, but such delivery may not be opposed or denied on the ground that the executive authority of the sending state has not affirmatively consented to or ordered such delivery.

(e) If trial is not had on any indictment, information or complaint contemplated hereby prior to the prisoner's being returned to the original place of imprisonment pursuant to Article V (e) hereof, such indictment, information or complaint shall not be of any further force or effect, and the court shall enter an order dismissing the same with prejudice.

ARTICLE V

(a) In response to a request made under Article III or Article IV hereof, the appropriate authority in a sending state shall offer to deliver temporary custody of such prisoner to the appropriate authority in the state where such indictment, information or complaint is pending against such person in order that speedy and efficient prosecution may be had. If the request for final disposition is made by the prisoner, the offer of temporary custody shall accompany the written notice provided for in Article III of this agreement. In the case of a federal prisoner, the appropriate authority in the receiving state shall be entitled to temporary custody as provided by this agreement or to the prisoner's presence in federal custody at the place for trial, whichever custodial arrangement may be approved by the custodian.

(b) The officer or other representative of a state accepting an offer of temporary custody shall present the following upon demand:

(1) Proper identification and evidence of his authority to act for the state into whose temporary custody the prisoner is to be given.

(2) A duly certified copy of the indictment, information or complaint on the basis of which the detainer has been lodged and on the basis of which the request for temporary custody of the prisoner has been made.

(c) If the appropriate authority shall refuse or fail to accept temporary custody of said person, or in the event that an action on the indictment, information or complaint on the basis of which the detainer has been lodged is not brought to trial within the period provided in Article III or Article IV hereof, the appropriate court of the jurisdiction where the indictment, information or complaint has been pending shall enter an order dismissing the same with prejudice, and any detainer based thereon shall cease to be of any force or effect.

(d) The temporary custody referred to in this agreement shall be only for the purpose of permitting prosecution on the charge or charges contained in one or more untried indictments, informations or complaints which from the basis of the detainer or detainers or for prosecution on any other charge or charges arising out of the same transaction. Except for his attendance at court and while being transported to or from any place at which his presence may be required, the prisoner shall be held in a suitable jail or other facility regularly used for persons awaiting prosecution.

(e) At the earliest practicable time consonant with the purposes of this agreement, the prisoner shall be returned to the sending state.

(f) During the continuance of temporary custody or while the prisoner is otherwise being made available for trial as required by this agreement, time being served on the sentence shall continue to run but good time shall be earned by the prisoner only if, and to the extent that, the law and practice of the jurisdiction which imposed the sentence may allow.

(g) For all purposes other than that for which temporary custody as provided in this agreement is exercised, the prisoner shall be deemed to remain in the custody of and subject to the jurisdiction of the sending state and any escape from temporary custody may be dealt with in the same manner as an escape from the original place of imprisonment or in any other manner permitted by law.

(h) From the time that a party state receives custody of a prisoner pursuant to this agreement until such prisoner is returned to the territory and custody of the sending state, the state in which the one or more untried indictments, informations or complaints are pending or in which trial is being had shall be responsible for the prisoner and shall also pay all costs of transporting, caring for, keeping and returning the prisoner. The provisions of this paragraph shall govern unless the states concerned shall have entered into a supplementary agreement providing for a different allocation of costs and responsibilities as between or among themselves. Nothing herein contained shall be construed to alter or affect any internal relationship among the departments, agencies and officers of and in the government of a party state, or between a party state and its subdivisions, as to the payment of costs, or responsibilities therefor.

ARTICLE VI

(a) In determining the duration and expiration dates of the time periods provided in Articles III and IV of this agreement, the running of said time periods shall be tolled whenever and for as long as the prisoner is unable to stand trial, as determined by the court having jurisdiction of the matter.

(b) No provision of this agreement, and no remedy made available by this agreement, shall apply to any person who is adjudged to be mentally ill.

ARTICLE VII

Each state party to this agreement shall designate an officer who, acting jointly with like officers of other party states, shall promulgate rules and regulations to carry out more effectively the terms and provisions of this agreement, and who shall provide, within and without the state, information necessary to the effective operation of this agreement.

ARTICLE VIII

This agreement shall enter into full force and effect as to a party state when such state has enacted the same into law. A state party to this agreement may withdraw herefrom by enacting a statute repealing the same. However, the withdrawal of any state shall not affect the status of any proceedings already initiated by inmates or by state officers at the time such withdrawal takes effect, nor shall it affect their rights in respect thereof.

ARTICLE IX

This agreement shall be liberally construed so as to effectuate its purposes. The provisions of this agreement shall be severable and if any phrase, clause, sentence or provision of this agreement is declared to be contrary to the constitution of any party state or of the United States or the applicability thereof to any government, agency, person or circumstance is held invalid, the validity of the remainder of this agreement and the applicability thereof to any government, agency, person or circumstance shall not be affected thereby. If this agreement shall be held contrary to the constitution of any state party hereto, the agreement shall remain in full force and effect as to the remaining states and in full force and effect as to the state affected as to all severable matter.

History—
1965, 892, § 1.

§ 2.   Appropriate Court, Defined.

The phrase "Appropriate court", as used in the Agreement on Detainers, shall, with reference to the courts of this commonwealth mean the municipal court of the city of Boston, district courts, the superior court or the supreme judicial court.

History—
1965, 892, § 2.

§ 3.   Enforcement of Agreement; Co-operation With Other Party States.

All courts, departments, agencies, officers and employees of this commonwealth and its political subdivisions are hereby directed to enforce the Agreement on Detainers and to cooperate with one another and with other party states in enforcing said agreement and effectuating its purpose.

History—
  1965, 892, § 3.

§ 4.   Applicability of Habitual Offenders Law.

Nothing in the Agreement on Detainers shall be construed to require the application of the habitual offenders law to any person on account of any conviction had in a proceeding brought to final disposition by reason of the use of said agreement.

History—
  1965, 892, § 4.

Cross References—
  Habitual offenders, see ALM GL c 279 § 25.

§ 5.   Escape or Attempted Escape of Prisoner; Penalties.

A prisoner who escapes or attempts to escape from custody while in another state or while in this commonwealth pursuant to the Agreement on Detainers may be pursued and recaptured and shall be punished by imprisonment in the state prison in this commonwealth for not more than ten years or by imprisonment in a jail or house of correction in this commonwealth for not more than two and one half years.

History—
  1965, 892, § 5.

§ 6.   Mandatory Giving Over of Inmates as Required by Agreement.

It shall be lawful and mandatory upon the superintendent or other official in charge of a penal or correctional institution of this commonwealth to give over the person of any inmate thereof whenever so required by the operation of the Agreement on Detainers.

History—
  1965, 892, § 6.

§ 7. Compact Administrator.

The governor may designate an officer of the commonwealth to act as compact administrator of and information agent for the Agreement on Detainers.

History—
1965, 892, § 7.

§ 8. Copies of Agreement; Transmittal.

Copies of this agreement shall, upon its approval, be transmitted to the governor of each contracting state, the attorney general of the United States, the administrator of general services of the United States, and the council of state governments.

History—
1965, 892, § 8.

CHAPTER S117

Interstate Regional Planning Compact

(Acts 1963, Ch. 448)

SEC.
1. Form of Compact.
2. Short Title.

Auto-Cite®: Cases and annotations referred to herein can be further researched through the Auto-Cite® computer-assisted research service. Use Auto-Cite to check citations for form, parallel references, prior and later history, and annotation references.

---

§ 1. Form of Compact.

The division of planning of the department of commerce, as authorized under chapter twenty-three A of the General Laws, acting with and through the office of the attorney general is hereby directed to negotiate with the proper authorities of the states of Connecticut, New Hampshire, New York, Rhode Island and Vermont a compact for interstate regional planning substantially in the form as follows, which is hereby ratified:

INTERSTATE REGIONAL PLANNING COMPACT

Whereas, The social, economic, and esthetic growth and development of the several states has, in certain regions, extended beyond the boundaries of two or more states; and

Whereas, Such growth and development has resulted in physical problems, which require co-operative regional planning and mutual assistance toward their solution for the betterment of the health, welfare, and economic prosperity of the people living in such regions; and

Whereas, Congress has recognized the need for co-operative planning by giving its consent to two or more states entering into compacts for interstate regional planning; and

Whereas, Co-operative regional planning between states can be best accomplished through interstate regional planning agencies; now therefore, the signatory states do agree and are bound as follows:

ARTICLE I.

Any Massachusetts municipality is authorized by vote of its city council or town meeting to become a member of a regional planning agency established under the statutes of Connecticut, New Hampshire, New York, Rhode Island and Vermont providing that the division of planning of the department of commerce of Massachusetts, and the state agency with regional planning responsibilities in the signatory state, and the regional planning agency concerned determine that membership in such agency would be effective for planning purposes.

ARTICLE II.

Any city, town, or borough in the states of Connecticut, New Hampshire, New York, Rhode Island and Vermont is authorized by vote of its municipal legislative body to become a member of a regional planning district established under chapter 40B of the General Laws of Massachusetts providing that the district planning commission, and the division of planning of the department of commerce of Massachusetts, and the state agency with regional planning responsibilities in the signatory state determine that such membership would be effective for planning purposes.

ARTICLE III.

Any municipality becoming a member of an interstate regional planning agency located in another state shall adopt the statutes establishing such agency, and shall be subject to all provisions of such statute for representation, financial contributions, duties, reports, and otherwise hold full membership, except that requirements for initial establishment of the regional planning agency shall be based only on the municipalities in the state in which the agency is located.

ARTICLE IV.

A municipality which becomes a member of a regional planning agency in another state may regard any plans, studies, proposals, and recommendations by such agency as advisory and need not be bound by them.

ARTICLE V.

An annual report on the activities of any regional planning agency engaged in interstate regional planning under the provisions of this compact shall be filed with the state agency with regional planning responsibilities in each signatory state, in addition to any reports otherwise required from the regional planning agency.

History—
1963, 448, § 1.

Cross References—
Regional planning, generally, see ALM GL c 40B.

§ 2. Short Title.

This act may be cited as the Interstate Regional Planning Compact.

History—
1963, 448, § 2.

CHAPTER S119

Water Pollution Control Compact

(Acts 1947, Ch. 421)

SEC.
1. Form of Compact.
2. Filing of Compact; Effective Date; Notice of Ratification.
3. Appointment of Commission Members; Vacancies; Salaries; Designees; Terms.
4. Salaries and Expenses of Commissioners.
5. Annual Reports.

Auto-Cite®: Cases and annotations referred to herein can be further researched through the Auto-Cite® computer-assisted research service. Use Auto-Cite to check citations for form, parallel references, prior and later history, and annotation references.

---

§ 1. Form of Compact.

The state planning board, on behalf of the commonwealth, acting in accordance with the provisions of chapter two hundred and seventy-eight of the acts of nineteen hundred and thirty-six, and subject to the approval of the attorney general, is hereby authorized to enter into a compact, substantially in the following form, with any one or more of the states of Maine, New Hampshire, Vermont, Rhode Island and Connecticut, and the general court hereby approves and ratifies in advance such compact so entered into, such approval and ratification to be effective upon the filing of a properly executed copy of such compact in the office of the state secretary:—

NEW ENGLAND INTERSTATE WATER POLLUTION CONTROL COMPACT

Whereas, The growth of population and the development of the territory of the New England states has resulted in serious pollution of certain interstate streams, ponds and lakes, and of tidal waters ebbing and flowing past the boundaries of two or more states; and

Whereas, Such pollution constitutes a menace to the health, welfare and economic prosperity of the people living in such area; and

Whereas, The abatement of existing pollution and the control of future pollution in the interstate waters of New England area are of prime importance to the people and can best be accomplished through the co-operation of the New England states in the establishment of an interstate agency to work with the states in the field of pollution abatement;

Now, therefore, the states of Connecticut, Maine, Massachusetts, New Hampshire, Rhode Island and Vermont do agree and are bound as follows:

ARTICLE I.

It is agreed between the signatory states that the provisions of this compact shall apply to streams, ponds and lakes which are contiguous to two or more signatory states or which flow through two or more signatory states or which have a tributary contiguous to two or more signatory states or flowing through two or more signatory states, and also shall apply to tidal waters ebbing and flowing past the boundaries of two states.

ARTICLE II.

There is hereby created the New England Interstate Water Pollution Control Commission (hereinafter referred to as the commission) which shall be a body corporate and politic, having the powers, duties and jurisdiction herein enumerated and such other and additional powers as shall be conferred upon it by the act or acts of a signatory state concurred in by the others.

ARTICLE III.

The commission shall consist of five commissioners from each signatory state, each of whom shall be a resident voter of the state from which he is appointed. The commissioners shall be chosen in the manner and for the terms provided by law of the state from which they shall be appointed. For each state there shall be on the commission a member representing the state health department, a member representing the state water pollution control board (if such exists), and, except where a state in its enabling legislation decides that the best interests of the state will be otherwise served, a member representing municipal interests, a member representing industrial interests, and a member representing an agency acting for fisheries or conservation.

ARTICLE IV.

The commission shall annually elect from its members a chairman and vice chairman and shall appoint and at its pleasure remove or discharge such officers. It may appoint and employ a secretary who shall be a professional engineer versed in water pollution and may employ such stenographic or clerical employees as shall be necessary, and at its pleasure remove or discharge such employees. It shall adopt a seal and suitable by-laws and shall promulgate rules and regulations for its management and control. It may maintain an office for the transaction of its business and may meet at any time or place within the signatory states. Meetings shall be held at least twice each year. A majority of the members shall constitute a quorum for the transaction of business, but no action of the commission imposing any obligation on any signatory state or on any municipal agency or subdivision thereof or on any person, firm or corporation therein shall be binding unless a majority of the members from such signatory state shall have voted in favor thereof. Where meetings are planned to discuss matters relevant to problems of water pollution control affecting only certain of the signatory states, the commission may vote to authorize special meetings of the commissioners of the states especially concerned. The commission shall keep accurate accounts of all receipts and disbursements and shall make an annual report to the governor and the legislature of each signatory state setting forth in detail the operations and transactions conducted by it pursuant to this compact, and shall make recommendations for any legislative action deemed by it advisable, including amendments to the statutes of the signatory states which may be necessary to carry out the intent and purpose of this compact. The commission shall not incur any obligations for salaries, office, administrative, traveling or other expenses prior to the allotment of funds by the signatory states adequate to meet the same; nor shall the commission pledge the credit of any of the signatory states. Each signatory state reserves the right to provide hereafter by law for the examination and audit of the accounts of the commission. The commission shall appoint a treasurer who may be a member of the commission, and disbursements by the commission shall be valid only when authorized by the commission and when vouchers therefor have been signed by the secretary and countersigned by the treasurer. The secretary shall be custodian of the records of the commission with authority to attest to and certify such records or copies thereof.

ARTICLE V.

It is recognized, owing to such variable factors as location, size, character and flow and the many varied uses of the waters subject to the terms of this compact, that no single standard of sewage and waste treatment and no single standard of quality of receiving waters is practical and that the degree of treatment of sewage and industrial wastes should take into account the classification of the receiving waters according to present and proposed highest use, such as for drinking water supply, industrial and agricultural uses, bathing and other recreational purposes, maintenance and propagation of fish life, shellfish culture, navigation and disposal of wastes.

The commission shall establish reasonable physical, chemical and bacteriological standards of water quality satisfactory for various classifications of use. It is agreed that each of the signatory states through appropriate agencies will prepare a classification of its interstate waters in entirety or by portions according to present and proposed highest use and for this purpose technical experts employed by state departments of health and state water pollution control agencies are authorized to confer on questions relating to classification of interstate waters affecting two or more states. Each signatory state agrees to submit its classification of its interstate waters to the commission for approval. It is agreed that after such approval all signatory states through their appropriate state health departments and water pollution control agencies will work to establish programs of treatment of sewage and industrial wastes which will meet standards established by the commission for classified waters. The commission may from time to time make such changes in definitions of classifications and in standards as may be required by changed conditions or as may be necessary for uniformity.

ARTICLE VI.

Each of the signatory states pledges to provide for the abatement of existing pollution and for the control of future pollution of interstate inland and tidal waters as described in Article I, and to put and maintain the waters thereof in a satisfactory condition consistent with the highest classified use of each body of water.

ARTICLE VII.

Nothing in this compact shall be construed to repeal or prevent the enactment of any legislation or prevent the enforcement of any requirement by any signatory state imposing any additional condition or restriction to further lessen the pollution of waters within its jurisdiction. Nothing herein contained shall affect or abate any action now pending brought by any governmental board or body created by or existing under any of the signatory states.

ARTICLE VIII.

The signatory states agree to appropriate for the salaries, office, administrative, travel and other expenses such sum or sums as shall be recommended by the commission. The commonwealth of Massachusetts obligates itself only to the extent of sixty-five hundred dollars in any one year, the state of Connecticut only to the extent of three thousand dollars in any one year, the state of Rhode Island only to the extent of fifteen hundred dollars in any one year, and the states of New Hampshire, Maine, and Vermont each only to the extent of one thousand dollars in any one year.

ARTICLE IX.

Should any part of this compact be held to be contrary to the constitution of any signatory state or of the United States, all other parts thereof shall continue to be in full force and effect.

ARTICLE X.

The commission is authorized to discuss with appropriate state agencies in New York state questions of pollution of waters which flow into the New England area from New York state or vice versa and to further the establishment of agreements on pollution abatement to promote the interests of the New York and New England areas.

Whenever the commission by majority vote of the members of each signatory state shall have given its approval and the state of New York shall have taken the necessary action to do so, the state of New York shall be a party to this compact for the purpose of controlling and abating the pollution of waterways common to New York and the New England states signatory to this compact but excluding the waters under the jurisdiction of the interstate sanitation commission (New York, New Jersey and Connecticut)

ARTICLE XI.

This compact shall become effective immediately upon the adoption of the compact by any two contiguous states of New England but only in so far as applies to those states and upon approval by federal law. Thereafter upon ratification by other contiguous states, it shall also become effective as to those states.

History—
1947, 421, § 1.

§ 2. Filing of Compact; Effective Date; Notice of Ratification.

Whenever the state planning board shall have entered into the compact substantially in the form set forth in section one with the duly authorized agency of any of the states specified in said section, it shall file a certified copy of such compact in the office of the state secretary and shall notify the governor of its action. Such compact shall thereupon become effective and operative as between the commonwealth and such other state or states, subject to the consent of the Congress of the United States, which the governor shall take such steps as may be necessary to obtain. The governor is hereby authorized and requested, upon receiving notice of the filing of the required copy thereof in the office of the state secretary, to notify forthwith the governors of the specified states and the President of the United States, that the commonwealth on its part has ratified and executed said compact. The original notice of ratification received from the governor or other duly authorized official of any state joining in said compact shall be filed with the official copy of said compact in the office of the state secretary, and such notice, if any, as may be received from the President or the Congress of the United States, signifying the consent of the Congress to said compact, shall be filed in the same manner.

History—
1947, 421, § 2.

§ 3.   Appointment of Commission Members; Vacancies; Salaries; Designees; Terms.

After the aforesaid compact shall become effective and operative as provided in section two, the governor, with the advice and consent of the council, shall designate or appoint three commissioners who, with the commissioner of public health and chairman of the water resources commission, shall represent the commonwealth as members of the New England Interstate Water Pollution Control Commission, hereinafter called the commission. Any of the three commissioners so designated or appointed may be state officials, and all shall be named with due regard to interests concerned with interstate water pollution problems. Upon the expiration of the term of an appointee who is not a salaried state official his successor shall be appointed for a term of three years. Vacancies shall be filled for the remainder of unexpired terms, in the same manner as original appointments are made. The designations of state officials other than the commissioner of public health and chairman of the water resources commission, may be changed whenever in the opinion of the governor such change is desirable. Sections eight to twelve, inclusive, of chapter thirty of the General Laws shall apply at all times to commissioners who are not serving as salaried state officials during their terms hereunder. Any commissioner who is a state official may delegate from time to time a deputy or other subordinate in his department to attend and participate in any meeting of or hearing by or other proceeding of the commission, with authority to vote as the representative of or substitute for said commissioner. The terms of commissioners first appointed, who are not then holding salaried state offices, shall be considered to have begun on the date when the compact aforesaid shall become effective and operative in accordance with section two.

History—
1947, 421, § 3; 1959, 442.

Cross References—
Chairman of water resources commission, see ALM GL c 21 § 9.

Recommendations by water resources commission to interstate water pollution control commission, see ALM GL c 21 § 43.

Designation of persons to perform duties of members of boards or commissions appointed under interstate compacts, see ALM GL c 30 § 6A.

Duties of commissioner of public health, generally, see ALM GL c 111 § 2.

§ 4.   Salaries and Expenses of Commissioners.

Each commissioner designated or appointed by the governor, who, while such commissioner, holds no salaried state office, shall be paid by the commonwealth as compensation the sum of thirty-seven dollars and fifty cents for each day's service performed in connection with his duties as such commissioner, but not to exceed seven hundred and fifty dollars in any fiscal year. Such compensation shall be paid by the state treasurer not oftener than once in two weeks, upon bills approved by the chairman or vice chairman and the secretary of the commission. All commissioners shall be entitled to their actual expenses incurred in the performance of their duties as such.

History—
1947, 421, § 4; 1963, 801, § 81.

§ 5.   Annual Reports.

The commissioners on the part of the commonwealth shall obtain accurate accounts of all the commission's receipts and disbursements and shall report to the governor and the budget commissioner annually on or before the fifteenth day of September, setting forth in such detail as the budget commissioner may require the transactions of the commission for the fiscal year ending on the preceding June thirtieth. They shall include in such report recommendations for any legislative action that the commission deems advisable, including such amendments or additions to the laws of the commonwealth as may be necessary or desirable to carry out the intent and purposes of the New

England Interstate Water Pollution Control Compact among the states joining therein.

History—
1947, 421, § 5.

Northeastern Water and Related Resources Compact
with Other New England States

(Acts 1959, Ch. 621)

Sec.

1. Form of Compact.

2. Chairman of Water Resources Commission or Designee as
    Member of Northeastern Resources Commission.

Auto-Cite®: Cases and annotations referred to herein can be further researched through the Auto-Cite® computer-assisted research service. Use Auto-Cite to check citations for form, parallel references, prior and later history, and annotation references.

---

§ 1. Form of Compact.

The governor is hereby authorized, in the name and on behalf of the commonwealth, to enter into and to execute a compact with the other New England states in the following form:—

ARTICLE I

FINDINGS

The northeastern part of the United States is by virtue of geographic location and other characteristics a great natural resource area which, with more intense use of natural resources, increasingly requires co-ordinated planning as a basic ingredient of effective resource management and orderly growth of the region. The work of the New England—New York Interagency Committee demonstrated that a continuation and furtherance of activities such as those undertaken by it would be of great value. To this end, it is the intent of this compact to establish and provide for the operation of a joint agency for said northeastern region.

ARTICLE II

PURPOSE

It is the purpose of this compact to provide, in the northeastern region, improved facilities and procedures for the co-ordination of the policies, programs and activities of the United States, the sev-

345

eral states, and private persons or entities, in the field of water and related land resources, and to study, investigate and plan the development and use of the same and conservation of such water and related land resources; to provide means by which conflicts may be resolved; and to provide procedures for co-ordination of the interests of all public and private agencies, persons and entities in the field of water and related land resources; and to provide an organization for co-operation in such co-ordination on both the federal and state levels of government.

ARTICLE III

CREATION OF COMMISSION

There is hereby created the Northeastern Resources Commission, hereinafter called the commission.

ARTICLE IV

MEMBERSHIP

The commission shall consist of one member from each party state to be appointed and to serve, in accordance with and subject to the laws of the state which he represents, and seven members representing departments or agencies of the United States having principal responsibilities for water and related land resources development to be appointed and to serve in such manner as may be provided by the laws of the United States.

ARTICLE V

FUNCTIONS

It shall be the responsibility of the commission to recommend to the states and the United States, or any intergovernmental agency, changes in law or policy which would promote co-ordination, or resolution of problems, in the field of water and related land resources. The efforts of the commission in co-ordination of work and resolution of conflicts may be directed towards all state and federal activities involved in water and related land resources development responsibilities and shall include co-ordination of the following:—

(1) Collection and interpretation of basic data;

(2) Investigation and planning of water and related land resources projects;

(3) Programming (including scheduling) of water and related land resources construction and development;

(4) Encouraging of the referral of plans or proposals for resources projects to the commission.

The commission shall use qualified public and private agencies to make investigations and conduct research in the field of water and related land resources, but if it is unable to secure the undertaking of such investigations or original research by a qualified public or private agency, it shall have the power to make its own investigations and conduct its own research. The commission may make contracts with any public or private agencies or private persons or entities for the undertaking of such investigations, or original research within its purview.

ARTICLE VI

VOTING

No action of the commission respecting the internal management thereof shall be binding unless taken at a meeting at which a majority of the members are present and vote in favor thereof; provided, that any action not binding for such a reason may be ratified within thirty days by the concurrence in writing of a majority of the commission membership. No action of the commission respecting a matter other than its internal management shall be binding unless taken at a meeting at which a majority of the state members and a majority of the members representing the United States are present and a majority of said state members together with a majority of said members representing the United States vote in favor thereof; provided, that any action not binding for such a reason may be ratified within thirty days by the concurrence in writing of a majority of the state members and the concurrence in writing of a majority of the members representing the United States.

ARTICLE VII

FINANCES

A. The commission shall submit to the governor or designated officer of each party state a request for funds to cover estimated expenditures for such period as may be required by the laws of that jurisdiction for presentation to the legislature thereof. Any such request shall indicate the sum or sums which the commission has requested or intends to request be appropriated by the United States for the use or support of the commission during the period covered thereby.

B. With due regard for such monies and other assistance as may be made available to it, the commission shall be provided with such funds by each of the several states participating therein to provide the means of establishing and maintaining facilities, a staff of personnel, and such activities as may be necessary to fulfill the powers and duties imposed upon and entrusted to the commission.

With due allowance for monies otherwise available, each budget of the commission shall be the responsibility of the party states, to be apportioned among them on a weighted formula based fifty per cent on population and fifty per cent on gross land area, such population and gross land area to be determined in accordance with the last official U. S. Census of Population; provided, that the total contributions of all of the states shall not be required to exceed fifty thousand dollars annually; and provided, further, that regardless of the number of states party to the compact at any time the maximum annual contribution required of any state shall not exceed its share of the fifty thousand dollars as determined above. Any state may contribute such funds in excess of its share, as determined above, as it may desire.

C. The commission shall not pledge the credit of any jurisdiction. The commission may meet any of its obligations in whole or in part with funds available to it under Article VIII (E) of this compact; provided, that the commission takes specific action setting aside such funds prior to the incurring of any obligation to be met in whole or in part in such manner.

D. The members of the commission shall be paid by the commission their actual expenses incurred and incident to the performance of their duties, subject to the approval of the commission.

E. The commission shall keep accurate accounts of all receipts and disbursements. The receipts and disbursements of the commission shall be subject to the audit and accounting procedures established under its by-laws. However, all receipts and disbursements of funds handled by the commission shall be audited by a qualified public accountant and the report of the audit shall be included in and become a part of the annual report of the commission.

F. The accounts of the commission shall be open at any reasonable time for inspection by such agency, representative or representatives of the jurisdictions which appropriate funds to the commission.

ARTICLE VIII

ADMINISTRATION AND MANAGEMENT

A. The commission may sue and be sued, and shall have a seal.

B. The commission shall elect annually, from among its members, a chairman, vice-chairman and treasurer. The commission shall appoint an executive director who shall also act as secretary, and together with the treasurer, shall be bonded in such amounts as the commission may require.

C. The commission shall appoint and remove or discharge such personnel as may be necessary for the performance of its functions irrespective of any civil service laws which might otherwise apply. The commission shall establish and maintain, independently, by contract or agreement with the United States or any agency thereof, or in conjunction with any one or more of the party states, suitable retirement programs for its employees. Employees of the commission shall be eligible for social security coverage in respect to old age and survivors insurance; provided, that the commission takes such steps as may be necessary pursuant to federal law to participate in such program of insurance as a governmental agency or unit. The commission may establish and maintain or participate in such additional programs of employee benefits as may be appropriate to afford employees of the commission terms and conditions of employment similar to those enjoyed by employees of the party states generally.

D. The commission may borrow, accept or contract for the services of personnel from any state or the United States or any subdivision or agency thereof, from any intergovernmental agency, or from any institution, person, firm or corporation.

E. The commission may accept for any of its purposes and functions under this compact any and all appropriations, donations, and grants of money, equipment, supplies, materials and services, conditional or otherwise, from any state or the United States or any subdivision or agency thereof, or intergovernmental agency, or any institution, person, firm or corporation, and may receive, utilize and dispose of the same.

F. The commission may establish and maintain such facilities as may be necessary for the transacting of its business. The commission may accept, hold and convey real and personal property and any interest therein.

G. The commission may adopt, amend and rescind by-laws, rules and regulations for the conduct of its business.

H. The commission shall make and transmit annually, to the legislature and governor of each party state, and to the president and congress of the United States, a report covering the activities of the commission for the preceding year, and embodying such recommendations as may have been adopted by the commission. The commission may issue such additional reports as it may deem desirable.

ARTICLE IX

OTHER COMPACTS AND ACTIVITIES

Nothing in this compact shall be construed to impair, or otherwise affect, the jurisdiction of any interstate agency in which any party state participates nor to abridge, impair, or otherwise affect the provisions of any compact to which any one or more of the party states may be a party, nor to supersede, diminish, or otherwise affect any obligation assumed under any such compact. Nor shall anything in this compact be construed to discourage additional interstate compacts among some or all of the party states for the management of natural resources, or the co-ordination of activities with respect to a specific natural resource or any aspect of natural resource management, or for the establishment of intergovernmental planning agencies in sub-areas of the region. Nothing in this compact shall be construed to limit the jurisdiction or activities of any participating government, agency or officer thereof, or any private person or agency.

ARTICLE X

ENACTMENT

A. This compact shall become effective when entered into and enacted into law by any three of the states of Connecticut, Maine, Massachusetts, New Hampshire, Rhode Island and Vermont, and when the United States has provided by law for the designation of its representation on the commission. Thereafter it shall become effective with respect to any other aforementioned state upon its enacting this compact into law.

B. Upon consent of the congress of the United States of America, any other state in the northeastern area may become a party to this compact, by entering into and enacting this compact into law.

ARTICLE XI

WITHDRAWAL

This compact shall continue in force and remain binding upon each party state until renounced by it. Renunciation of this compact must be preceded by sending three years' notice in writing of intention to withdraw from the compact to the governor of each of the other states party hereto and to such officers or agencies of the United States as may be designated by federal law.

ARTICLE XII

CONSTRUCTION AND SEVERABILITY

The provisions of this compact shall be severable and if any phrase, clause, sentence or provision of this compact is declared to be unconstitutional or the applicability thereof to any state, agency, person or circumstance is held invalid, the constitutionality of the remainder of this compact and the applicability thereof to any other state, agency, person or circumstance shall not be affected thereby. It is the legislative intent that the provisions of this compact be reasonably and liberally construed.

History—
1959, 621, § 1.

§ 2.   Chairman of Water Resources Commission or Designee as Member of Northeastern Resources Commission.

The chairman of the water resources commission or a person designated by him shall be the member of the Northeastern Resources Commission representing the commonwealth.

History—
1959, 621, § 2; 1962, 279.

Cross References—
Chairman of water resources commission, see ALM GL c 21 § 9.

Designation of persons to perform duties of members of boards or commissions appointed under interstate compacts, see ALM GL c 30 § 6A.

CHAPTER S123

Compact with New Hampshire Relating to Merrimack River

(Acts 1956, Ch. 608)

> **Auto-Cite®:** Cases and annotations referred to herein can be further researched through the Auto-Cite® computer-assisted research service. Use Auto-Cite to check citations for form, parallel references, prior and later history, and annotation references.

§ 1. Form of Compact.

The members of the commission appointed under section three of this act are hereby authorized as agents on the part of the commonwealth, for and in its name and behalf, to enter into and execute with the State of New Hampshire an agreement or compact in the following form:—

Whereas, The federal government exercises jurisdiction over the nation's navigable rivers and their tributaries through passage of the flood control act of nineteen hundred and thirty-six and various other acts amendatory thereto; and

Whereas, These acts provide for construction by the United States of dams for flood control and, where feasible, in addition to flood control for storage of water to be used for irrigation, recreation, hydroelectric power, or for any of these purposes; and

Whereas, The Merrimack river is an interstate river and control of major floods on it can be obtained only by the construction of dams by the United States under authorization of the above mentioned acts; and

353

Whereas, The Commonwealth of Massachusetts and the State of New Hampshire recognize that it is in the interest of their general welfare that the United States construct in the Merrimack river valley a comprehensive system of local protection works and dams and reservoirs to control floods and prevent loss of life and property, the disruption of orderly processes and the impairment of commerce between the aforesaid states; and

Whereas, The United States has constructed dikes, flood walls and other local protection works at Nashua in the State of New Hampshire and at Haverhill, Lowell and Fitchburg in the Commonwealth of Massachusetts and dams and reservoirs for the storage of flood waters at Franklin Falls, Peterboro and Webster in the State of New Hampshire, and has prepared designs for dikes and flood walls and other local protection works at Lawrence and North Andover in the Commonwealth of Massachusetts; and

Whereas, The congress has at various times authorized construction by the United States of other dams and reservoirs for the storage of flood waters in the State of New Hampshire and has more recently instructed the Corps of Engineers to determine what additional local protection works and dams and reservoirs are required for a comprehensive system to control floods in the Merrimack river and its tributaries; and

Whereas, It is believed that such a comprehensive flood control system should include dams and reservoirs controlling flood run-off from approximately thirty per cent of the total drainage area of the Merrimack river basin and strategically located in reference to characteristics of tributaries and to damage centers; and

Whereas, Dams and reservoirs to control thirty per cent of flood run-off will be located in the State of New Hampshire and the major benefits from such dams and reservoirs will accrue to the Commonwealth of Massachusetts; and

Whereas, Construction by the United States of additional dams and reservoirs in the State of New Hampshire, to complete such a comprehensive flood control system, will remove from the tax rolls of local governments of the State of New Hampshire such property as is acquired by the United States and may work other hardships against the people of New Hampshire; and

Whereas, It is highly desirable that any flood control dam and reservoir constructed by the United States in the Merrimack river valley have the approval of the State of New Hampshire and the Commonwealth of Massachusetts and that the Commonwealth of Massachusetts benefiting from construction of such dam and reservoir make reimbursement for such loss of taxes and for such hardships; and

Whereas, A comprehensive system for the prevention of destructive floods and for water resources utilization in the Merrimack river valley can best be accomplished by co-operation between the Commonwealth of Massachusetts and the State of New Hampshire and by and through a common and joint agency of said two states; now, therefore

The said Commonwealth of Massachusetts and State of New Hampshire to hereby enter into the following compact, to wit:—

ARTICLE I.

The principal purposes of this compact are:—(a) to promote interstate comity among and between the signatory states; (b) to provide adequate storage capacity for impounding the waters of the Merrimack river and its tributaries for the protection of life and property from floods; (c) to provide a joint or common agency through which the signatory states, while promoting, protecting and preserving to each the local interest and sovereignty of the respective signatory states, may more effectively co-operate in accomplishing the object of flood control and water resources utilization in the basin of the Merrimack river and its tributaries.

ARTICLE II.

There is hereby created The Merrimack River Valley Flood Control Commission, hereinafter referred to as the commission, which shall consist of six members, three of whom shall be residents of the Commonwealth of Massachusetts, one of whom shall be a resident of the Merrimack Valley; and three of whom shall be residents of the State of New Hampshire.

The members of the commission shall be chosen by their respective states in such manner and for such term as may be fixed and determined from time to time by the law of each of said states, respectively, by which they are appointed. A member of the commission may be removed or suspended from office as provided by the law of the state from which he shall be appointed, and any vacancy occurring in the commission shall be filled in accordance with the laws of the state wherein such vacancy exists.

A majority of the members of each state shall constitute a quorum for the transaction of business, the exercise of any powers or the performance of any duties, but no action of the commission shall be binding unless at least two members from each state shall vote in favor thereof.

The compensation of members of the commission shall be fixed, determined and paid by the state which they respectively represent. All necessary expenses incurred in the performance of their duties shall be paid from the funds of the commission.

The commission shall elect from its members a chairman, vice-chairman, clerk and treasurer. Such treasurer shall furnish to the commission, at its expense, a bond with corporate surety, to be approved by the commission, in such amount as the commission may determine, conditioned for the faithful performance of his duties.

The commission shall adopt suitable by-laws and shall make such rules and regulations as it may deem advisable not inconsistent with laws of the United States, of the signatory states or with any rules or regulations lawfully promulgated thereunder.

The commission shall make an annual report to the governor and legislature of each of the signatory states, setting forth in detail the operations and transactions conducted by it pursuant to this compact.

The commission shall keep a record of all its meetings and proceedings, contracts and accounts, and shall maintain a suitable office, where its maps, plans, documents, records and accounts shall be kept, subject to public inspection at such times and under such regulations as the commission shall determine.

ARTICLE III.

The commission shall constitute a body, both corporate and politic, with full power and authority; (1) to sue and be sued; (2) to have a seal and alter the same at pleasure; (3) to appoint and employ such agents and employees as may be required in the proper performance of the duties hereby committed to it and to fix and determine their qualifications, duties and compensation; (4) to enter into such contracts and agreements and to do and perform any and all other acts, matters and things as may be necessary and essential to the full and complete performance of the powers and duties hereby committed to and imposed upon it and as may be incidental thereto; (5) to have such additional powers and duties as may hereafter be delegated to or imposed upon it from time to time by the action of the legislature of either of said states, concurred in by the legislature of the other state and by the Congress of the United States.

The commission shall make, or cause to be made, such studies as it may deem necessary, in co-operation with the corps of engineers and other federal agencies, for the development of a comprehensive plan for flood control and for utilization of the water resources of the Merrimack river valley.

The commission shall not pledge the credit of the signatory states or either of them.

ARTICLE IV.

The State of New Hampshire wherein is located the site of each of the following dams and reservoirs agrees to the construction by the United States of each such dam and reservoir in accordance with authorization by the congress:—(1) at West Hopkinton on the Contoocook river, controlling a drainage area of approximately four hundred and twenty-six square miles, and near East Weare, on the north branch of the Piscataquog river, controlling a drainage area of approximately sixty-four square miles; and providing flood control storage for approximately six inches of run-off over both said drainage areas; and (2) near Loudon on the Soucook river, controlling a drainage area of approximately seventy-seven square miles and providing flood control storage for approximately six inches of run-off over said drainage area.

ARTICLE V.

The Commonwealth of Massachusetts agrees to reimburse the State of New Hampshire seventy per cent of the amount of taxes lost to its political subdivisions by reason of acquisition and ownership by the United States of lands, rights or other property therein for the flood control dams and reservoirs at Franklin Falls, Blackwater and West Peterboro and for construction in the future of any flood control dam and reservoir specified in Article IV, and also for any other flood control dam and reservoir hereafter constructed by the United States in the Merrimack river valley.

Annually, not later than November first of each year the commission shall determine the loss of taxes resulting to political subdivisions of the State of New Hampshire by reason of acquisition and ownership therein by the United States of lands, rights or other property in connection with each flood control dam and reservoir for which provision for tax reimbursement has been made in the preceding paragraph. Such losses of taxes as determined by the commission shall be based on the tax rate then current in each such political subdivision and on the average assessed valuation for a period of five years prior to the acquisition by the United States of such property; provided, that whenever a political subdivision where in a flood control dam and reservoir or portion thereof is located shall have made a general revaluation of property subject to the annual municipal taxes of such subdivision, the commission may use such revaluation for the purpose of determining the amount of taxes for which reimbursement shall be made in the paragraph next above. Using the percentage of payment agreed to in said paragraph, the commission shall then compute the sum, if any, due from the Commonwealth of Massachusetts to the State of New Hampshire and shall send notice to the treasurer of the Commonwealth of Massachusetts setting forth in detail the sums, if any, to be paid to the State of New Hampshire in reimbursement of tax losses.

The Commonwealth of Massachusetts on receipt of formal notification from the commission of the sum which it is to pay in reimbursement for tax losses shall, not later than July first of the following year, make its payment for such tax losses to the State of New Hampshire, except that in case of the first annual payment for tax losses at any dam or reservoir such payment shall be made by the Commonwealth of Massachusetts not later than July first of the year in which the next regular session of its legislature is held.

Payment by the Commonwealth of Massachusetts of its share of reimbursement for taxes in accordance with formal notification received from the commission shall be a complete and final discharge of all liability of the Commonwealth of Massachusetts to the State of New Hampshire for each flood control dam and reservoir within the State of New Hampshire for the time specified in each formal notification. The State of New Hampshire shall have full responsibility for distributing or expending all such sums received and no agency or political subdivision shall have any claim against the Commonwealth of Massachusetts nor against the commission relative to tax losses covered by such payments.

Whenever the Commonwealth of Massachusetts and the State of New Hampshire shall agree, through the commission, on a lump sum payment in lieu of annual payments and such lump sum payment has been made and received, the requirement that the commission annually shall determine the tax losses, compute sums due from the Commonwealth of Massachusetts and sent notice thereof to the treasurer of the Commonwealth of Massachusetts, shall no longer apply to the aforesaid states with respect to any flood control dam and reservoir for which lump sum payment has been made and received.

The Commonwealth of Massachusetts agrees to pay the State of New Hampshire its respective share in reimbursement, as determined by the commission under the procedure following, for economic losses and damages occurring by reason of ownership of property by the United States for construction and operation of a flood control dam and reservoir at any site specified in Article IV, and for any other flood control dam and reservoir constructed hereafter by the United States in the Merrimack river valley; provided, however, that no reimbursement shall be made for speculative losses and damages or losses or damages for which the United States is liable.

On receipt of information from the chief of engineers that request is to be made for funds for the purpose of preparing detailed plans and specifications for any flood control dam and reservoir proposed to be constructed in the Merrimack river valley, including those specified in Article VI, the commission shall make an estimate of the amount of taxes which would be lost to and of economic losses and damages which would occur in political subdivisions of the State of New Hampshire wherein such dam and reservoir would be located, wholly or in part, by reason of acquisition and ownership by the United States of lands, rights or other property for the construction and operation of such flood control dam and reservoir and shall decide whether the flood control benefits to be derived in the signatory states from such flood control dam and reservoir, both by itself and as a unit of a comprehensive flood control plan, justifies, in the opinion of the commission, the assumption by a signatory state of the obligation to make reimbursement for loss of taxes and for economic losses and damages. Such estimate and decision shall thereafter be reviewed by the commission at five-year intervals until such time as the United States shall have acquired title to the site of such flood control dam, or plans for its construction are abandoned. The commission shall notify the governor, the members of the United States Senate and the members of the United States House of Representatives from each signatory state, and the chief of engineers as to the commission's decision and as to any change in such decision.

On receipt of information from the chief of engineers that any flood control dam and reservoir is to be constructed, reconstructed, altered or used for any purpose in addition to flood control, including those flood control dams and reservoirs heretofore constructed and those specified in Article IV, the commission shall make a separate estimate of the amount of taxes which would be lost to and of economic losses and damages which would occur in political subdivisions of the signatory state wherein such dam and reservoir would be located, wholly or in part, by reason of acquisition and ownership by the United States of lands, rights or other property for the construction and operation of such dam and reservoir in excess of the estimated amount of taxes which would be lost and of the economic losses and damages which would occur if the dam were constructed and operated for flood control only, and the commission shall decide the extent to which, in its opinion, the signatory states would be justified in making reimbursement for loss of taxes and for economic losses and damages in addition to reimbursement for such dam and reservoir if constructed and used for flood control only. Such estimate and decision shall thereafter be reviewed by the commission at five-year intervals until such time as such dam and reservoir shall be so constructed, reconstructed, altered or used, or plans for such construction, reconstruction, alteration or use are abandoned. The commission shall notify the governor, the members of the United States Senate and the members of the United States House of Representatives from each signatory state as to the commission's decision and as to any change in such decision.

Within thirty days after acquisition by the United States of the site of any flood control dam the commission shall proceed to make a final determination of economic losses and damages occasioned by such dam and reservoir. The commission shall not include in such determination either speculative losses and damages or losses and damages for which the United States is liable.

The commission shall compute the share the Commonwealth of Massachusetts shall pay to the State of New Hampshire by multiplying the sum of such losses and damages, as previously determined, by the percentage of flood control benefits which the Commonwealth of Massachusetts receives of the flood control benefits resulting from the dam and reservoir.

The commission shall send a notice to the treasurer of the Commonwealth of Massachusetts setting forth in detail the sum, if any, the Commonwealth of Massachusetts is to pay to the State of New Hampshire in reimbursement for economic losses and damages and shall also send such notice to the treasurer of the State of New Hampshire.

The Commonwealth of Massachusetts on receipt of such formal notification by the commission shall pay its share of such economic losses or damages to the State of New Hampshire. Full payment by the Commonwealth of Massachusetts of the sum specified in such formal notification from the commission as to the amount of economic losses and damages for which the Commonwealth of Massachusetts is to make reimbursement shall be a complete and final discharge of all liability by the Commonwealth of Massachusetts to the State of New Hampshire for economic losses and damages for each flood control dam and reservoir within the said state designated in such formal notification. The State of New Hampshire shall have full responsibility for distributing or expending all such sums received and no agency, political subdivision, private person, partnership, firm, association or corporation shall have any claim against the Commonwealth of Massachusetts nor against the commission relative to such economic losses and damages.

The State of New Hampshire may, in agreement with the commission and the chief of engineers, acquire title or option to acquire title to any or all lands, rights or other property required for any flood control dam and reservoir within its boundaries and transfer such titles or options to the United States. Whenever the fair cost to said state for such titles or options, as determined by the commission, is greater than the amount received therefor from the United States, the Commonwealth of Massachusetts shall pay its share of such excess cost to said State of New Hampshire, such share to be determined by the commission in accordance with procedure herein contained for determining reimbursement for economic losses and damages.

Whenever the commission shall not agree, within a reasonable time or within sixty days after a formal request from the governor of the State of New Hampshire or the Commonwealth of Massachusetts, concerning reimbursement for loss of taxes or for economic losses and damages at any flood control dam and reservoir heretofore or hereafter constructed by the United States in the Merrimack river valley, or concerning the extent, if any, to which reimbursement shall be made for additional loss of taxes and for additional economic losses and damages caused by construction, reconstruction, alteration or use of any such dam for purposes other than flood control, the governor of each signatory state shall designate a person from his state as a member of a board of arbitration, hereinafter called the board, and the members so designated shall choose one additional member who shall be chairman of such board. Whenever the members appointed by the governors to such board shall not agree within sixty days on such additional member of the board, the governors of such signatory states shall jointly designate the additional member. The board shall by majority vote decide the question referred to it and shall do so in accordance with the provisions of this compact concerning such reimbursement. The decision of the board on each question referred to it concerning reimbursement for loss of taxes and for economic losses and damages shall be binding on the commission and on each signatory state, notwithstanding any other provision of this compact.

ARTICLE VI.

Nothing contained in this compact shall be construed as a limitation upon the authority of the United States.

ARTICLE VII.

The signatory states agree to appropriate for compensation of agents and employees of the commission for office, administrative, travel and other expenses on recommendation of the commission subject to limitations as follows:—The Commonwealth of Massachusetts obligates itself to not more than seventeen thousand five hundred dollars for the first year and to not more than fourteen thousand dollars in any one year thereafter, the State of New Hampshire obligates itself to not more than seven thousand five hundred dollars for the first year and to not more than six thousand dollars in any one year thereafter.

ARTICLE VIII.

Should any part of this compact be held to be contrary to the constitution of either signatory state or of the United States, all other parts thereof shall continue to be in full force and effect.

ARTICLE IX.

This compact shall become operative and effective when ratified by the Commonwealth of Massachusetts and the State of New Hampshire, and approved by the Congress of the United States. Notice of ratification shall be given by the governor of each state to the governor of the other state and to the President of the United States, and the President of the United States is requested to give notice to the governors of the Commonwealth of Massachusetts and the State of New Hampshire of approval by the Congress of the United States.

History—
1956, 608, § 1.

Cross References—
Public works department powers and duties relative to Merrimack River, see ALM GL c 91 §§ 10, 12.

§ 2.   Ratification by State Legislatures; Congressional Approval; Filing of Compact.

The said agreement or compact, when ratified by the legislatures of each of said states and approved by the Congress of the United States, shall thereupon become operative and effective. The governor is authorized and directed forthwith to notify the governor of the State of New Hampshire and the President of the United States that the Commonwealth of Massachusetts on its part has approved and ratified said compact or agreement. Upon its execution in triplicate by the commissioners of each of said states as aforesaid, a duly executed original thereof shall be filed in the office of the secretary of the Commonwealth of Massachusetts, together with the original notice of ratification received from the governor of New Hampshire, and such notice, if any, as may be received from the President or the Congress of the United States, signifying the approval of congress thereto.

History—
    1956, 608, § 2.

§ 3.   Appointment by Governor of Member of Merrimack River Valley Flood Control Commission.

Within thirty days after the aforesaid agreement or compact shall have become effective as provided in section two of this act, the governor shall, with advice and consent of the council, appoint a member of the Merrimack River Valley Flood Control Commission, who with the commissioner of environmental quality engineering or his designated representative, and the chairman of the water resources commission or his designated representative, shall compose said commission. The member appointed by the governor shall serve until the first day of March, nineteen hundred and fifty-eight. In the month of February, nineteen hundred and fifty-eight, the governor, by and with the advice and consent of the council, shall appoint one such member to serve for a period of three years from the first day of March thereafter.

History—
    1956, 608, § 3; 1958, 350; 1975, 706, § 304.

Cross References—
    Chairman of water resources commission, see ALM GL c 21 § 9.
    Commissioner of environmental quality engineering, generally, see ALM GL c 21A § 7.
    Designation of persons to perform duties of members of boards or commissions appointed under interstate compacts, see ALM GL c 30 § 6A.

§ 4.   Vacancies in Commission; Reappointment.

In the event of a vacancy in the commission the governor shall, with the advice and consent of the council, appoint a member to serve only for the unexpired term. Any member of the commission shall be eligible for reappointment.

History—
    1956, 608, § 4.

§ 5.   Compensation of Governor's Appointee.

The member of said commission appointed by the governor of Massachusetts who does not hold a salaried state office shall receive as compensation for his services the sum of thirty-seven dollars and fifty cents a day for each day's service performed in connection with his duties as such member.

History—

1956, 608, § 5; 1963, 801, § 88.

§ 6.   Effective Date.

This act shall take effect one day after the governor of Massachusetts shall have been notified that the State of New Hampshire has passed legislation ratifying the foregoing proposed compact.

History—

1956, 608, § 6.

CHAPTER S125

Compact with Connecticut Relative to Flood Control and Water Resources in Basin of the Thames River

(Acts 1957, Ch. 616)

SEC.
1. Form of Compact.
2. Ratification by State Legislatures; Congressional Approval; Filing of Compact.
3. Appointment by Governor of Member of Thames River Valley Flood Control Commission.
4. Vacancies in Commission; Reappointment.
5. Compensation of Governor's Appointee.
6. Effective Date.

Auto-Cite®: Cases and annotations referred to herein can be further researched through the Auto-Cite® computer-assisted research service. Use Auto-Cite to check citations for form, parallel references, prior and later history, and annotation references.

---

§ 1. Form of Compact.

The members of the commission appointed under section three of this act are hereby authorized as agents on the part of the commonwealth, for and in its name and behalf, to enter into and execute with the State of Connecticut an agreement or compact in the following form:—

Whereas, The federal government exercises jurisdiction over the nation's navigable rivers and their tributaries through passage of the flood control act of nineteen hundred and thirty-six and various other acts amendatory thereto; and

Whereas, These acts provide for construction by the United States of dams for flood control and, where feasible, in addition to flood control for storage of water to be used for irrigation, recreation, or hydroelectric power or for any of these purposes; and

Whereas, The Thames River is an interstate river and control of major floods on it can be obtained only by the construction of dams by the United States under authorization of the above-mentioned acts; and

Whereas, The Commonwealth of Massachusetts and the State of Connecticut recognize that it is in the interest of their general welfare that the United States construct in the Thames River Valley a comprehensive system of local protection works and dams and reservoirs to control floods and prevent loss of life and property, the disruption of orderly processes and the impairment of commerce between the aforesaid states; and

Whereas, The United States has constructed dikes, flood walls and other local protection works at Norwich in the State of Connecticut and a dam and reservoir for the storage of flood waters at Mansfield Hollow in the State of Connecticut; and

Whereas, The Congress has at various times authorized construction by the United States of other dams and reservoirs for the storage of flood waters in the Commonwealth of Massachusetts and in the State of Connecticut and has more recently instructed the corps of engineers to determine what additional local protection works and dams and reservoirs are required for a comprehensive system to control floods in the Thames River and its tributaries; and

Whereas, It is believed that such a comprehensive flood control system should include dams and reservoirs controlling flood run-off from approximately twenty-five per cent of the total drainage area of the Thames River, and strategically located in reference to characteristics of tributaries and to damage centers; and

Whereas, Construction by the United States of dams and reservoirs in the Commonwealth of Massachusetts, to complete such a comprehensive flood control system, will remove from the tax rolls of local governments of that state such property as is acquired by the United States and may work a hardship against the people of Massachusetts; and

Whereas, It is highly desirable that any flood control dam and reservoir constructed by the United States in the Thames River Valley have the approval of the state wherein it is located and that the state benefiting from construction of such dam and reservoir make reimbursement for such loss of taxes; and

Whereas, A comprehensive system for the prevention of destructive floods and for water resources utilization in the Thames River Valley can best be accomplished by cooperation between the Commonwealth of Massachusetts and the State of Connecticut and in the valley and by and through a common and joint agency of said two states;

Now, therefore, the said Commonwealth of Massachusetts and the State of Connecticut do hereby enter into the following compact, to wit:

ARTICLE I.

The principal purposes of this compact are: (a) to promote inter-state comity among and between the signatory states; (b) to assure adequate storage capacity for impounding the waters of the Thames River and its tributaries for the protection of life and property from floods; (c) to provide a joint or common agency through which the signatory states, while promoting, protecting and preserving to each the local interest and sovereignty of the respective signatory states, may more effectively co-operate in accomplishing the object of flood control and water resources utilization in the basin of the Thames River and its tributaries.

ARTICLE II.

There is hereby created the Thames River Valley Flood Control Commission, hereinafter referred to as the commission, which shall consist of six members, three of whom shall be residents of the Commonwealth of Massachusetts and three of whom shall be residents of the State of Connecticut.

The members of the commission shall be chosen by their respective states in such manner and for such term as may be fixed and determined from time to time by the law of each of said states respectively by which they are appointed. A member of the commission may be removed or suspended from office as provided by the law of the state for which he shall be appointed, and any vacancy occurring in the commission shall be filled in accordance with the laws of the state wherein such vacancy exists.

A majority of the members from each state shall constitute a quorum for the transaction of business, the exercise of any of its powers or the performance of any of its duties, but no action of the commission shall be binding unless at least two of the members from each state shall vote in favor thereof.

The compensation of members of the commission shall be fixed, determined, and paid by the state which they respectively represent. All necessary expenses incurred in the performance of their duties shall be paid from the funds of the commission.

The commission shall elect from its members a chairman, vice-chairman, and a clerk-treasurer. Such clerk-treasurer shall furnish to the commission, at its expense, a bond with corporate surety, to be approved by the commission, in such amount as the commission may determine, conditioned on the faithful performance of his duties.

The commission shall adopt suitable by-laws and shall make such rules and regulations as it may deem advisable not inconsistent with laws of the United States, of the signatory states or with any rules or regulations lawfully promulgated thereunder.

The commission shall make an annual report to the governor and legislature of each of the signatory states, setting forth in detail the operations and the transactions conducted by it pursuant to this compact.

The commission shall keep a record of all its meetings and proceedings, contracts and accounts, and shall maintain a suitable office, where its maps, plans, documents, records and accounts shall be kept, subject to public inspection at such times and under such regulations as the commission shall determine.

ARTICLE III.

The commission shall constitute a body, both corporate and politic, with full power and authority: (1) to sue and be sued; (2) to have a seal and alter the same at pleasure; (3) to appoint and employ such agents and employees as may be required in the proper performance of the duties hereby committed to it and to fix and determine their qualifications, duties and compensation; (4) to enter into such contracts and agreements and to do and perform any and all other acts, matters and things as may be necessary and essential to the full and complete performance of the powers and duties hereby committed to and imposed upon it and as may be incidental thereto; (5) to have such additional powers and duties as may hereafter be delegated to or imposed upon it from time to time by the action of the legislature of either of said states, concurred in by the legislature of the other state and by the Congress of the United States.

The commission shall make, or cause to be made, such studies as it may deem necessary, in co-operation with the Corps of Engineers of the United States Army and other federal agencies, for the development of a comprehensive plan for flood control and for utilization of the water resources of the Thames River Valley.

The commission shall not pledge the credit of the signatory states or either of them.

ARTICLE IV.

The Commonwealth of Massachusetts wherein is located the site of each of the following dams and reservoirs agrees to the construction by the United States of each such dam and reservoir in accordance with authorization by the Congress:

(1) At East Brimfield on the Quinebaug River controlling a drainage area of approximately sixty-seven square miles and

providing flood storage of approximately eight inches of run-off from said drainage area;

(2) At Buffamville on the Little River controlling a net drainage area of approximately twenty-six square miles and providing flood control storage of approximately eight inches of run-off from said drainage area;

(3) At Hodges Village on the French River controlling a drainage area of approximately thirty square miles and providing flood control storage for approximately eight inches of run-off from said drainage area;

(4) At Westville on the Quinebaug River controlling a drainage area of approximately ninety square miles and providing flood control storage for approximately two and five tenths inches of run-off from said drainage area.

ARTICLE V.

The State of Connecticut agrees to reimburse the Commonwealth of Massachusetts forty per cent of the amount of taxes lost to its political subdivisions by reason of acquisition and ownership by the United States of lands, rights or other property therein for construction in the future of any flood control dam and reservoir specified in Article IV and also for any other flood control dam and reservoir hereafter constructed by the United States in the Thames River Valley in Massachusetts.

Annually, not later than November first of each year, the commission shall determine the loss of taxes resulting to political subdivisions of the Commonwealth of Massachusetts by reason of acquisition and ownership therein by the United States of lands, rights or other property in connection with each flood control dam and reservoir for which provision for tax reimbursement has been made in the paragraph next above. Such losses of taxes as determined by the commission shall be based on the tax rate then current in each such political subdivision and on the average assessed valuation for a period of five years prior to the acquisition by the United States of the site of the dam for such reservoir; provided, that whenever a political subdivision wherein a flood control dam and reservoir or portion thereof is located shall have made a general revaluation of property subject to the annual municipal taxes of such subdivision, the commission may use such revaluation for the purpose of determining the amount of taxes for which reimbursement shall be made. Using the percentage of payment agreed to in this Article, the commission shall then compute the sum, if any, due from the State of Connecticut to the Commonwealth of Massachusetts and shall sent a notice to the treasurer of each signatory state setting forth in detail the sums, if any, Connecticut is to pay to and Massachusetts is to receive in reimbursement of tax losses.

The State of Connecticut on receipt of formal notification from the commission of the sum which it is to pay in reimbursement for tax losses shall, not later than July first of the following year, make its payment for such tax losses to the Commonwealth of Massachusetts wherein such loss or losses occur, except that in case of the first annual payment for tax losses at any dam or reservoir such payment shall be made by the State of Connecticut not later than July first of the year in which the next regular session of its legislature is held.

Payment by the State of Connecticut of its share of reimbursement for taxes in accordance with formal notification received from the commission shall be a complete and final discharge of all liability by that state to the Commonwealth of Massachusetts for each flood control dam and reservoir within that state for the time specified in such formal notification. The Commonwealth of Massachusetts shall have full responsibility for distributing or expending all such sums received, and no agency or political subdivision of the Commonwealth shall have any claim against the State of Connecticut or against the commission relative to taxes losses covered by such payments.

The two states may agree, through the commission, on a lump sum payment in lieu of annual payments and when such lump sum payment has been made and received, the requirement that the commission annually shall determine the tax losses, compute sums due and send notice thereof to the treasurer of each state shall no longer apply with respect to any flood control dam and reservoir for which lump sum payment has been made and received.

On receipt of information from the chief of engineers that request is to be made for funds for the purpose of preparing detailed plans and specifications for any flood control dam and reservoir proposed to be constructed in the Thames River Valley in Massachusetts, including those specified in Article IV, the commission shall make an estimate of the amount of taxes which would be lost to the political subdivisions of that state by reason of acquisition and ownership by the United States of lands, rights or other property for the construction and operation of such flood control dam and reservoir and shall decide whether the flood control benefits to be derived from such flood control dam and reservoir, both by itself and as a unit of a comprehensive flood control plan, justifies, in the opinion of the commission, the assumption by the State of Connecticut of the obligation to make reimbursement for loss of taxes. Such estimate and decision shall thereafter be reviewed by the commission at five-year intervals until such time as the United States shall have acquired title to the site of such flood control dam or plans for its construction are abandoned. The commission shall notify the governor, the members of the United States Senate and the members of the United States House of Representatives from each signatory state and the chief of engineers as to the commission's decision and as to any change in such decision.

On receipt of information from the chief of engineers that any flood control dam and reservoir is to be constructed, reconstructed, altered or used for any purpose in addition to flood control, including those flood control dams and reservoirs heretofore constructed and those specified in Article IV, the commission shall make a separate estimate of the amount of taxes which would be lost to the political subdivisions of the Commonwealth of Massachusetts by reason of acquisition and ownership by the United States of lands, rights or other property for the construction and operation of such dam and reservoir in excess of the estimated amount of taxes which would be lost if the dam were constructed and operated for flood control only and the commission shall decide the extent to which, in its opinion, the State of Connecticut would be justified in making reimbursement for loss of taxes in addition to reimbursement for such dam and reservoir if constructed and used for flood control only. Such estimate and decision shall thereafter be reviewed by the commission at five-year intervals until such time as such dam and reservoir shall be so constructed, reconstructed, altered or used or plans for such construction, reconstruction, alteration or use are abandoned. The commission shall notify the governor, the members of the United States Senate and the members of the United States House of Representatives from each signatory state as to the commission's decision and as to any change in such decision.

A signatory state may, in agreement with the commission and the chief of engineers, acquire title or option to acquire title to any or all lands, rights or other property required for any flood control dam and reservoir within its boundaries and transfer such titles or options to the United States. Whenever the fair cost to said signatory state for such titles or options, as determined by the commission, is greater than the amount received therefor from the United States, the State of Connecticut shall pay its share of such excess cost to said signatory state, such share to be determined by the commission.

Whenever the commission shall not agree, within a reasonable time or within sixty days after a formal request from the governor of either signatory state, concerning reimbursement for loss of taxes at any flood control dam and reservoir heretofore or hereafter constructed by the United States in the Thames River Valley in Massachusetts, or concerning the extent, if any, to which reimbursement shall be made for additional loss of taxes caused by construction, reconstruction, alteration or use of any such dam for purposes other than flood control, the governor of each signatory state shall designate a person from his state as a member of a board of arbitration, hereinafter called the board, and the members so designated shall choose one additional member who shall be chairman of such board. Whenever the members appointed by the governors to such board shall not agree within sixty days on such additional member of the board, the governors of such signatory states shall jointly designate the additional member. The board shall by majority vote decide the question referred to it and shall do so in accordance with the provisions of this compact concerning such reimbursement. The decision of the board on each question referred to it concerning reimbursement for loss of taxes shall be binding on the commission and on each signatory state, notwithstanding any other provision of this compact.

ARTICLE VI.

Nothing contained in this compact shall be construed as a limitation upon the authority of the United States.

ARTICLE VII.

The signatory states agree to appropriate for compensation of agents and employees of the commission and for office, administrative, travel and other expenses on recommendation of the commission subject to limitations as follows: The Commonwealth of Massachusetts obligates itself to not more than seven thousand dollars in any one year and the State of Connecticut obligates itself to not more than five thousand dollars in any one year.

ARTICLE VIII.

Should any part of this compact be held to be contrary to the constitution of any signatory state or of the United States, all other parts thereof shall continue to be in full force and effect.

ARTICLE IX.

This compact shall become operative and effective when ratified by the Commonwealth of Massachusetts and the State of Connecticut, and approved by the Congress of the United States. Notice of ratification shall be given by the governor of each state to the governor of the other state and to the President of the United States, and the

President of the United States is requested to give notice to the governors of the Commonwealth of Massachusetts and the State of Connecticut of approval by the Congress of the United States.

History—
1957, 616, § 1.

§ 2. Ratification by State Legislatures; Congressional Approval; Filing of Compact.

The said agreement or compact, when ratified by the legislatures of each of said states and approved by the Congress of the United States, shall thereupon become operative and effective. The governor is authorized and directed forthwith to notify the governor of the State of Connecticut and the President of the United States that the Commonwealth of Massachusetts on its part has approved and ratified said compact or agreement. Upon its execution in triplicate by the commissioners of each of said states as aforesaid, a duly executed original of said agreement or compact shall be filed in the office of the secretary of the Commonwealth of Massachusetts, together with the original notice of ratification received from the governor of Connecticut and such notice, if any, as may be received from the President or the Congress of the United States, signifying the approval of Congress thereto.

History—
1957, 616, § 2.

§ 3. Appointment by Governor of Member of Thames River Valley Flood Control Commission.

Within thirty days after the aforesaid agreement or compact shall have become effective as provided in section two of this act, the governor shall, with the advice and consent of the council, appoint a member of the Thames River Valley Flood Control Commission, who with the commissioner of environmental quality engineering or his designated representative, and the chairman of the water resources commission, or a person designated by him, shall compose said commission. The member appointed by the governor shall serve until the first day of March, nineteen hundred and sixty. In the month of February, nineteen hundred and sixty, the governor, by and with the advice and consent of the council, shall appoint one such member to serve for a period of three years from the first day of March thereafter.

History—
1957, 616, § 3; 1975, 706, § 305.

Cross References—
Chairman of water resources commission, see ALM GL c 21 § 9.
Commissioner of environmental quality engineering, generally, see ALM GL
c 21A § 7.
Designation of persons to perform duties of members of boards or commissions appointed under interstate compacts, see ALM GL c 30 § 6A.

§ 4.   Vacancies in Commission; Reappointment.

In the event of a vacancy in the commission the governor shall, with the advice and consent of the council, appoint a member to serve only for the unexpired term. Any member of the commission shall be eligible for reappointment.

History—
1957, 616, § 4.

§ 5.   Compensation of Governor's Appointee.

The member of said commission appointed by the governor of Massachusetts who does not hold a salaried state office shall receive as compensation for his services the sum of thirty-seven dollars and fifty cents a day for each day's service performed in connection with his duties as such member.

History—
1957, 616, § 5; 1963, 801, § 89.

§ 6.   Effective Date.

This act shall take effect one day after the governor of Massachusetts shall have been notified that the State of Connecticut has passed legislation ratifying the foregoing proposed compact.

History—
1957, 616, § 6.

CHAPTER S127

Interstate Compact on Vehicles Equipment Safety

(Acts 1963, Ch. 721)

Auto-Cite®: Cases and annotations referred to herein can be further researched through the Auto-Cite® computer-assisted research service. Use Auto-Cite to check citations for form, parallel references, prior and later history, and annotation references.

---

§ 1. Form of Compact.

A compact is hereby entered into with all other jurisdictions legally joining therein in substantially the following form:—

VEHICLE EQUIPMENT SAFETY COMPACT

ARTICLE I. FINDINGS AND PURPOSES.

(a) The party states find that:

(1) Accidents and deaths on their streets and highways present a very serious human and economic problem with a major deleterious effect on the public welfare.

(2) There is a vital need for the development of greater interjurisdictional co-operation to achieve the necessary uniformity in the laws, rules, regulations and codes relating to vehicle equipment, and to accomplish this by such means as will minimize the time between the development of demonstrably and scientifically sound safety features and their incorporation into vehicles.

375

(b) The purposes of this compact are to:

(1) Promote uniformity in regulation of and standards for equipment.

(2) Secure uniformity of law and administrative practice in vehicular regulation and related safety standards to permit incorporation of desirable equipment changes in vehicles in the interest of greater traffic safety.

(3) To provide means for the encouragement and utilization of research which will facilitate the achievement of the foregoing purposes, with due regard for the findings set forth in subdivision (a) of this Article.

(c) It is the intent of this compact to emphasize performance requirements and not to determine the specific detail of engineering in the manufacture of vehicles or equipment except to the extent necessary for the meeting of such performance requirements.

ARTICLE II. DEFINITIONS.

As used in this compact:

(a) "Vehicle" means every device in, upon or by which any person or property is or may be transported or drawn upon a highway, excepting devices moved by human power or used exclusively upon stationary rails or tracks.

(b) "State" means a state, territory or possession of the United States, the District of Columbia, or the Commonwealth of Puerto Rico.

(c) "Equipment" means any part of a vehicle or any accessory for use thereon which affects the safety of operation of such vehicle or the safety of the occupants.

ARTICLE III. THE COMMISSION.

(a) There is hereby created an agency of the party states to be known as the "Vehicle Equipment Safety Commission" hereinafter called the Commission. The Commission shall be composed of one commissioner from each party state who shall be appointed, serve and be subject to removal in accordance with the laws of the state which he represents. If authorized by the laws of his party state, a commissioner may provide for the discharge of his duties and the performance of his functions on the Commission, either for the duration of his membership or for any lesser period of time, by an alternate. No such alternate shall be entitled to serve unless notification of his identity and appointment shall have been given to the Commission in such form as the Commission may require. Each

Commissioner, and each alternate, when serving in the place and stead of a commissioner, shall be entitled to be reimbursed by the Commission for expenses actually incurred in attending Commission meetings or while engaged in the business of the Commission.

(b) The commissioners shall be entitled to one vote each on the Commission. No action of the Commission shall be binding unless taken at a meeting at which a majority of the total number of votes on the Commission are cast in favor thereof. Action of the Commission shall be only at a meeting at which a majority of the commissioners, or their alternates, are present.

(c) The Commission shall have a seal.

(d) The Commission shall elect annually, from among its members, a chairman, a vice chairman and a treasurer. The Commission may appoint an Executive Director and fix his duties and compensation. Such Executive Director shall serve at the pleasure of the Commission, and together with the Treasurer shall be bonded in such amount as the Commission shall determine. The Executive Director also shall serve as secretary. If there be no Executive Director, the Commission shall elect a Secretary in addition to the other officers provided by this subdivision.

(e) Irrespective of the civil service, personnel or other merit system laws of any of the party states, the Executive Director with the approval of the Commission, or the Commission if there be no Executive Director, shall appoint, remove or discharge such personnel as may be necessary for the performance of the Commission's functions, and shall fix the duties and compensation of such personnel.

(f) The Commission may establish and maintain independently or in conjunction with any one or more of the party states, a suitable retirement system for its full time employees. Employees of the Commission shall be eligible for social security coverage in respect of old age and survivor's insurance provided that the Commission takes such steps as may be necessary pursuant to the laws of the United States, to participate in such program of insurance as a governmental agency or unit. The Commission may establish and maintain or participate in such additional programs of employee benefits as may be appropriate.

(g) The Commission may borrow, accept or contract for the services of personnel from any party state, the United States, or any subdivision or agency of the aforementioned governments, or from any agency of two or more of the party states or their subdivisions.

(h) The Commission may accept for any of its purposes and functions under this compact any and all donations, and grants of money, equipment, supplies, materials and services, conditional or otherwise, from any state, the United States, or any other governmental agency and may receive, utilize and dispose of the same.

(i) The Commission may establish and maintain such facilities as may be necessary for the transacting of its business. The Commission may acquire, hold, and convey real and personal property and any interest therein.

(j) The Commission shall adopt by-laws for the conduct of its business and shall have the power to amend and rescind these by-laws. The Commission shall publish its by-laws in convenient form and shall file a copy thereof and a copy of any amendment thereto, with the appropriate agency or officer in each of the party states. The by-laws shall provide for appropriate notice to the commissioners of all Commission meetings and hearings and the business to be transacted at such meetings or hearings. Such notice shall also be given to such agencies or officers of each party state as the laws of such party state may provide.

(k) The Commission annually shall make to the governor and legislature of each party state a report covering the activities of the Commission for the preceding year, and embodying such recommendations as may have been issued by the Commission. The Commission may make such additional reports as it may deem desirable.

ARTICLE IV. RESEARCH AND TESTING.

The Commission shall have power to:

(a) Collect, correlate, analyze and evaluate information resulting or derivable from research and testing activities in equipment and related fields.

(b) Recommend and encourage the undertaking of research and testing in any aspect of equipment or related matters when, in its judgment, appropriate or sufficient research or testing has not been undertaken.

(c) Contract for such equipment research and testing as one or more governmental agencies may agree to have contracted for by the Commission, provided that such governmental agency or agencies shall make available the funds necessary for such research and testing.

(d) Recommend to the party states changes in law or policy with emphasis on uniformity of laws and administrative rules, regulations or codes which would promote effective governmental action or co-ordination in the prevention of equipment-related highway accidents or the mitigation of equipment-related highway safety problems.

ARTICLE V. VEHICULAR EQUIPMENT.

(a) In the interest of vehicular and public safety, the Commission may study the need for or desirability of the establishment of or changes in performance requirements or restrictions for any item of equipment. As a result of such study, the Commission may publish a report relating to any item or items of equipment, and the issuance of such a report shall be a condition precedent to any proceedings or other action provided or authorized by this Article. No less than sixty days after the publication of a report containing the results of such study, the Commission upon due notice shall hold a hearing or hearings at such place or places as it may determine.

(b) Following the hearing or hearings provided for in subdivision (a) of this Article, and with due regard for standards recommended by appropriate professional and technical associations and agencies, the Commission may issue rules, regulations or codes embodying performance requirements or restrictions for any item or items of equipment covered in the report, which in the opinion of the Commission will be fair and equitable and effectuate the purposes of this compact.

(c) Each party state obligates itself to give due consideration to any and all rules, regulations and codes issued by the Commission and hereby declares its policy and intent to be the promotion of uniformity in the laws of the several party states relating to equipment.

(d) The Commission shall send prompt notice of its action in issuing any rule, regulation or code pursuant to this Article to the appropriate motor vehicle agency of each party state and such notice shall contain the complete text of the rule, regulation or code.

(e) If the constitution of a party state requires, or if its statutes provide, the approval of the legislature by appropriate resolution or act may be made a condition precedent to the taking effect in such party state of any rule, regulation or code. In such event, the commissioner of such party state shall submit any Commission rule, regulation or code to the legislature as promptly as may be in lieu of administrative acceptance or rejection thereof by the party state.

(f) Except as otherwise specifically provided in or pursuant to subdivisions (e) and (g) of this Article, the appropriate motor vehicle agency of a party state shall in accordance with its constitution or procedural laws adopt the rule, regulation or code within six months of the sending of the notice, and, upon such adoption, the rule, regulation or code shall have the force and effect of law therein.

379

(g) The appropriate motor vehicle agency of a party state may decline to adopt a rule, regulation or code issued by the Commission pursuant to this Article if such agency specifically finds, after public hearing on due notice, that a variation from the Commission's rule, regulation or code is necessary to the public safety, and incorporates in such finding the reasons upon which it is based. Any such finding shall be subject to review by such procedure for review of administrative determinations as may be applicable pursuant to the laws of the party state. Upon request, the Commission shall be furnished with a copy of the transcript of any hearings held pursuant to this subdivision.

ARTICLE VI. FINANCE.

(a) The Commission shall submit to the executive head or designated officer or officers of each party state a budget of its estimated expenditures for such period as may be required by the laws of that party state for presentation to the legislature thereof.

(b) Each of the Commission's budgets of estimated expenditures shall contain specific recommendations of the amount or amounts to be appropriated by each of the party states. The total amount of appropriations under any such budget shall be apportioned among the party states as follows: one-third in equal shares; and the remainder in proportion to the number of motor vehicles registered in each party state. In determining the number of such registrations, the Commission may employ such source or sources of information as, in its judgment present the most equitable and accurate comparisons among the party states. Each of the Commission's budgets of estimated expenditures and requests for appropriations shall indicate the source or sources used in obtaining information concerning vehicular registrations.

(c) The Commission shall not pledge the credit of any party state. The Commission may meet any of its obligations in whole or in part with funds available to it under Article III (h) of this compact, provided that the Commission takes specific action setting aside such funds prior to incurring any obligation to be met in whole or in part in such manner. Except where the Commission makes use of funds available to it under Article III (h) hereof, the Commission shall not incur any obligation prior to the allotment of funds by the party states adequate to meet the same.

(d) The Commission shall keep accurate accounts of all receipts and disbursements. The receipts and disbursements of the Commission shall be subject to the audit and accounting procedures established under its rules. However, all receipts and disbursements of funds handled by the Commission shall be audited yearly by a qualified public accountant and the report of the audit shall be included in and become part of the annual reports of the Commission.

(e) The accounts of the Commission shall be open at any reasonable time for inspection by duly constituted officers of the party states and by any persons authorized by the Commission.

(f) Nothing contained herein shall be construed to prevent Commission compliance with laws relating to audit or inspection of accounts by or on behalf of any government contributing to the support of the Commission.

ARTICLE VII. CONFLICT OF INTEREST.

(a) The Commission shall adopt rules and regulations with respect to conflict of interest for the commissioners of the party states, and their alternates, if any, and for the staff of the Commission and contractors with the Commission to the end that no member or employee or contractor shall have a pecuniary or other incompatible interest in the manufacture, sale or distribution of motor vehicles or vehicular equipment or in any facility or enterprise employed by the Commission or on its behalf for testing, conduct of investigations or research. In addition to any penalty for violation of such rules and regulations as may be applicable under the laws of the violator's jurisdiction of residence, employment or business, any violation of a Commission rule or regulation adopted pursuant to this Article shall require the immediate discharge of any violating employee and the immediate vacating of membership, or relinquishing of status as a member on the Commission by any commissioner or alternate. In the case of a contractor, any violation of any such rule or regulation shall make any contract of the violator with the Commission subject to cancellation by the Commission.

(b) Nothing contained in this Article shall be deemed to prevent a contractor for the Commission from using any facilities subject to his control in the performance of the contract even though such facilities are not devoted solely to work of or done on behalf of the Commission; nor to prevent such a contractor from receiving a remuneration or profit from the use of such facilities.

ARTICLE VIII. ADVISORY AND TECHNICAL COMMITTEES.

The Commission may establish such advisory and technical committees as it may deem necessary, membership on which may include private citizens and public officials, and may co-operate with and use the services of any such committees and the organizations which the members represent in furthering any of its activities.

ARTICLE IX. ENTRY INTO FORCE AND WITHDRAWAL.

(a) This compact shall enter into force when enacted into law by any six or more states. Thereafter, this compact shall become effective as to any other state upon its enactment thereof.

(b) Any party state may withdraw from this compact by enacting a statute repealing the same, but no such withdrawal shall take effect until one year after the executive head of the withdrawing state has given notice in writing of the withdrawal to the executive heads of all other party states. No withdrawal shall affect any liability already incurred by or chargeable to a party state prior to the time of such withdrawal.

ARTICLE X. CONSTRUCTION AND SEVERABILITY.

This compact shall be liberally construed so as to effectuate the purposes thereof. The provisions of this compact shall be severable and of any phrase, clause, sentence or provision of this compact is declared to be contrary to the Constitution of any state or of the United States or the applicability thereof to any government, agency, person or circumstance is held invalid, the validity of the remainder of this compact and the applicability thereof to any government, agency, person or circumstance shall not be affected thereby. If this compact shall be held contrary to the constitution of any state participating herein, the compact shall remain in full force and effect as to the remaining party states and in full force and effect as to the state affected as to all severable matters.

History—
1963, 721, § 1.

Cross References—
Safety standards for motor vehicles, see ALM GL c 90 §§ 7 et seq.
Governor's highway safety committee, see ALM GL c 90A.

§ 2. General Court to Approve Rules, Regulations or Codes of Vehicle Equipment Safety Commission; Authority of Registrar of Motor Vehicles.

Pursuant to Article V (e) of the Vehicle Equipment Safety Compact it is hereby provided that no rule, regulation or code issued by the Vehicle Equipment Safety Commission shall take effect until approved by the general court by the enactment of appropriate legislation; provided, however, that this provision shall not be deemed to affect the statutory authority of the registrar of motor vehicles to make rules and regulations relative to the equipment of motor vehicles in the interest of the safety of operation of such vehicles or the safety of the occupants.

History—
1963, 721, § 2.

Cross References—
Authority of registrar of motor vehicles to make rules and regulations relative to operation of motor vehicles, see ALM GL c 90 § 31.

§ 3. Registrar of Motor Vehicles or Designee as Commissioner for Commonwealth.

The registrar of motor vehicles shall be the commissioner for the commonwealth on said commission. He may, in accordance with Article III of said compact, designate an alternate for the discharge of his duties and the performance of his functions on said commission, either for the duration of his membership or for any lesser period of time. Any such alternate shall be designated from among the officers and employees of the registry of motor vehicles.

History—
1963, 721, § 3.

Cross References—
Registrar of motor vehicles, generally, see ALM GL c 16 § 9.
Designation of persons to perform duties of members of boards or commissions appointed under interstate compacts, see ALM GL c 30 § 6A.

§ 4. Retirement Coverage for Commission Employees.

Pursuant to Article III (f) of said compact the state board of retirement may make an agreement with said commission for the coverage of the employees of said commission. Any such agreement shall, as nearly as may be, provide for arrangements similar to those available to employees of the commonwealth and shall be subject to amendment or termination in accordance with its terms.

History—
1963, 721, § 4.

§ 5. Filing of By-laws and Amendments.

The secretary of the commonwealth shall be the appropriate officer with whom said commission shall file a copy of its by-laws and any amendments thereto, as provided in Article III (j) of said compact.

History—
1963, 721, § 5.

§ 6.   Auditing of Commission Accounts.

Pursuant to Article VI (e) of said compact, the auditor of the commonwealth is hereby authorized to audit the accounts of said commission.

History—
1963, 721, § 6.

§ 7.   Executive Head, Defined.

The words "executive head" as used in said compact shall, with reference to the commonwealth, mean the governor.

History—
1963, 721, § 7.

§ 8.   Commonwealth's Annual Expenses.

Notwithstanding the provisions of this act the annual expense of the commonwealth for the purposes thereof shall not exceed two thousand dollars.

History—
1963, 721, § 8.

CHAPTER S129

Compact on Taxation of Motor Fuels Consumed by Interstate Buses

(Acts 1963, Ch. 465)

SEC.
1. Form of Compact.
2. Administrator, Defined.
3. Inapplicable Laws.
4. Effective Date.

> **Auto-Cite®:** Cases and annotations referred to herein can be further researched through the Auto-Cite® computer-assisted research service. Use Auto-Cite to check citations for form, parallel references, prior and later history, and annotation references.

§ 1. Form of Compact.

A compact is hereby entered into with all jurisdictions legally joining therein in substantially the following form:—

COMPACT ON TAXATION OF MOTOR FUELS CONSUMED BY INTERSTATE BUSES

ARTICLE I. PURPOSES.

The purposes of this agreement are to:

(a) Avoid multiple taxation of motor fuels consumed by interstate buses and to assure each state of its fair share of motor fuel taxes.

(b) Establish and facilitate the administration of a criterion of motor fuel taxation for interstate buses which is reasonably related to the use of highway and related facilities and services in each of the party states.

(c) Encourage the availability of a maximum number of buses for intrastate service by removing motor fuel taxation as a deterrent in the routing of interstate buses.

ARTICLE II. DEFINITIONS.

(a) *State.* State shall include the States of the United States, the District of Columbia, the territories of the United States, the Provinces of Canada, and the States, Territories and Federal District of Mexico.

(b) *Contracting State.* Contracting State shall mean a State which is a party to this agreement.

(c) *Administrator.* Administrator shall mean the official or agency of a State administering the motor fuel taxes involved.

(d) *Person.* Person shall include any individual, firm, co-partnership, joint venture, association, corporation, estate, trust, business trust, receiver, syndicate or any other group or combination acting as a unit.

(e) *Bus.* Bus shall mean any motor vehicle of a bus type engaged in the interstate transportation of passengers and subject to the jurisdiction of the Interstate Commerce Commission, or any agency successor thereto, or one or more State regulatory agencies concerned with the regulation of passenger transport.

(f) *Gallon.* Gallon shall mean the liquid measure containing 231 cubic inches.

ARTICLE III. GOVERNING PRINCIPLE.

For purposes of this Compact, the primary principle for the imposition of motor fuel taxes shall be consumption of such fuel within the State. Motor fuel consumed by buses shall be taxed on the existing basis, as it may be from time to time, and under the procedures for collection of such taxes by each party state, except that to the extent that this Compact makes provision therefor, or for any matter connected therewith, such provision shall govern.

ARTICLE IV. HOW FUEL CONSUMED TO BE ASCERTAINED.

The amount of fuel used in the operation of any bus within this State shall be conclusively presumed to be the number of miles operated by such bus within the State divided by the average mileage per gallon obtained by the bus during the tax period in all operations, whether within or without the party State. Any owner or operator of two or more buses shall calculate average mileage within the meaning of this article by computing single average figures covering all buses owned or operated by him.

ARTICLE V. IMPOSITION OF TAX.

Every owner or operator of buses shall pay to the party state taxes equivalent to the amount of tax per gallon multiplied by the number of gallons used in its operations in the party state.

ARTICLE VI. REPORTS.

On or before the last business day of the month following the month being reported upon, each bus owner or operator subject to the payment of fuel taxes pursuant to this Compact shall make such reports of its operations as the state administrator of motor fuel taxes may require and shall furnish the state administrator of motor fuel taxes may require and shall furnish the state administrator in each other party state wherein his buses operate a copy of such report.

ARTICLE VII. CREDIT FOR PAYMENT OF FUEL TAXES.

Each bus owner or operator shall be entitled to a credit equivalent to the amount of tax per gallon on all motor fuel purchased by such operator within the party state for use in operations either within or without the party state, and upon which the motor fuel tax imposed by the laws of such party state has been paid.

ARTICLE VIII. ADDITIONAL TAX OR REFUND.

If the bus owner or operator's monthly report shows a debit balance after taking credit pursuant to Article VII, a remittance in such net amount due shall be made with the report. If the report shows a credit balance, after taking credit as herein provided, a refund in such net amount as has been overpaid shall be made by the party state to such owner or operator.

ARTICLE IX. ENTRY INTO FORCE AND WITHDRAWAL.

This Compact shall enter into force when enacted into law by any two states. Thereafter it shall enter into force and become binding upon any state subsequently joining when such state has enacted the Compact into law. Withdrawal from the Compact shall be by act of the legislature of a party state, but shall not take effect until one year after the governor of the withdrawing state has notified the governor of each other party state, in writing, of the withdrawal.

ARTICLE X. CONSTRUCTION AND SEVERABILITY.

This Compact shall be liberally construed so as to effectuate the purposes thereof. The provisions of this Compact shall be severable and if any phrase, clause, sentence or provision of this Compact is declared to be contrary to the Constitution of any state or of the United States or the applicability thereof to any government, agency, person or circumstance is held invalid, the validity of the remainder of this Compact and the applicability thereof to any government, agency, person or circumstance shall not be affected thereby. If this Compact shall be held contrary to the Constitution of any state participating herein, the Compact shall remain in full force and effect as to the remaining party states and in full force and effect as to the state affected as to all severable matters.

History—
1963, 465, § 1.

Cross References—
Common carriers of passengers by motor vehicle, see ALM GL c 159A.

§ 2.   Administrator, Defined.

The term "administrator", as used in the compact set forth in section one of this act shall, with reference to this commonwealth, mean the commissioner of revenue.

History—
1963, 465, § 2; 1978, 514, § 250.

Cross References—
Commissioner of revenue, generally, see ALM GL c 14 § 3.
Designation of persons to perform duties of members of boards or commissions appointed under interstate compacts, see ALM GL c 30 § 6A.

§ 3.   Inapplicable Laws.

The provisions of chapter sixty-four A and sixty-four E of the General Laws shall, to the extent that they are inconsistent with said compact, be inapplicable to the taxation of fuels used in the operation of a bus, as defined in said compact.

History—
1963, 465, § 3.

§ 4.   Effective Date.

This act shall take effect on January first, nineteen hundred and sixty-four.

History—
1963, 465, § 4.

CHAPTER S131

Agreement on Bus Registration Proration

(Acts 1965, Ch. 795)

Auto-Cite®: Cases and annotations referred to herein can be further researched through the Auto-Cite® computer-assisted research service. Use Auto-Cite to check citations for form, parallel references, prior and later history, and annotation references.

---

§ 1. Form of Agreement.

An agreement is hereby entered into with all jurisdictions legally joining therein in substantially the following form:—

AGREEMENT ON BUS REGISTRATION PRORATION

ARTICLE I. PURPOSES AND PRINCIPLES.

Section 1. Purposes of Agreement. It is the purpose of this agreement to set up a system whereby any contracting State may permit owners of fleets of buses operating in two or more States to prorate the registration of the buses in such fleets in each State in which the fleets operate on the basis of the proportion of miles operated within such State to total fleet miles, as defined herein.

Section 2. Principle of Proration of Registration. It is hereby declared that in making this agreement the contracting States adhere to the principle that each State should have the freedom to develop the kind of highway user tax structure that it determines to be most appropriate to itself, that the method of taxation of interstate buses should not be a determining factor in developing its user tax structure, and that annual taxes or other taxes of the fixed fee type upon buses which are not imposed on a basis that reflects the

389

amount of highway use should be apportioned among the States, within the limits of practicality, on the basis of vehicle miles traveled within each of the States.

ARTICLE II. DEFINITIONS.

(a) State. State shall include the States of the United States, the District of Columbia, the territories of the United States, the Provinces of Canada, and the States, Territories and Federal District of Mexico.

(b) Contracting State. Contracting State shall mean a State which is a party to this agreement.

(c) Administrator. Administrator shall mean the official or agency of a State administering the fee involved, or in the case of proration the official or agency of a State administering proration of registration in that State.

(d) Person. Person shall include any individual, firm, co-partnership, joint venture, association, corporation, estate, trust, business trust, receiver, syndicate, or any other group or combination acting as a unit.

(e) Base State. Base State shall mean the State from or in which the bus is most frequently dispatched, garaged, serviced, maintained, operated or otherwise controlled, or also in the case of a fleet bus the State to which it is allocated for registration under statutory requirements. In order that this agreement may not be used for the purpose of evasion of registration fees, the administrators of the contracting States may make the final decision as to the proper base State, in accordance with Article III (h) hereof, to prevent or avoid such evasion.

(f) Bus. Bus shall mean any motor vehicle of a bus type engaged in the interstate transportation of passengers and subject to the jurisdiction of the Interstate Commerce Commission, or any agency successor thereto, or one or more State regulatory agencies concerned with the regulation of passenger transport.

(g) Fleet. As to each contracting State, fleet shall include only those buses which actually travel a portion of their total miles in such State. A fleet must include three or more buses.

(h) Registration. Registration shall mean the registration of a bus and the payment of annual fees and taxes as set forth in or pursuant to the laws of the respective contracting States.

(i) Proration of Registration. Proration of registration shall mean registration of fleets of buses in accordance with Article IV of this agreement.

(j) Reciprocity. Reciprocity shall mean that each contracting State, to the extent provided in this agreement, exempts a bus from registration and registration fees.

Article III. General Provisions.

(a) Effect on Other Agreements, Arrangements and Understandings. On and after its effective date, this agreement shall supersede any reciprocal or other agreement, arrangement or understanding between any two or more of the contracting States covering, in whole or in part, any of the matters covered by this agreement; but this agreement shall not affect any reciprocal or other agreement, arrangement or understanding between a contracting State and a State or States not a party to this agreement.

(b) Applicability to Exempt Vehicles. This agreement shall not require registration in a contracting State of any vehicles which are, in whole or part, exempt from registration under the laws or regulations of such State without respect to this agreement.

(c) Inapplicability to Caravaned Vehicle. The benefits and privileges of this agreement shall not be extended to a vehicle operated on its own wheels, or in tow of a motor vehicle, transported for the purpose of selling or offering the same for sale to or by any agent, dealer, purchaser or prospective purchaser.

(d) Other Fees and Taxes. This agreement does not waive any fees or taxes charged or levied by any State in connection with the ownership or operation of vehicles other than registration fees as defined herein. All other fees and taxes shall be paid to each State in accordance with the laws thereof.

(e) Statutory Vehicle Regulations. This agreement shall not authorize the operation of a vehicle in any contracting State contrary to the laws or regulations thereof, except those pertaining to registration and payment of fees, and with respect to such laws or regulations, only to the extent provided in this agreement.

(f) Violations. Each contracting State reserves the right to withdraw, by order of the administrator thereof, all or any part of the benefits or privileges granted pursuant to this agreement from the owner of any vehicle or fleet of vehicles operated in violation of any provision of this agreement. The administrator shall immediately give notice of any such violation and withdrawal of any such benefits or privileges to the administrator of each other contracting State in which vehicles of such owner are operated.

(g) Co-operation. The administrator of each of the contracting States shall co-operate with the administrators of the others and each contracting State hereby agrees to furnish such aid and assistance to each other within its statutory authority as will aid in the proper enforcement of this agreement.

(h) Interpretation. In any dispute between or among contracting States arising under this agreement, the final decision regarding interpretation of questions at issue relating to this agreement shall be reached by joint action of the contracting States, acting through the administrator thereof, and shall upon determination be placed in writing.

(i) Effect of Headings. Article and section heading contained herein shall not be deemed to govern, limit, modify or in any manner affect the scope, meaning or intent of the provisions of any article or part hereof.

(j) Entry into Force. This agreement shall enter into force and become binding between and among the contracting States when enacted or otherwise entered into by any two States. Thereafter, it shall enter into force and become binding with respect to any State when enacted into law by such State. If the statutes of any State so authorize or provide, such State may become party to this agreement upon the execution thereof by an executive or administrative official thereof acting on behalf of and for such State.

Article IV. Proration of Registration.

(a) Applicability. Any owner of a fleet may register the buses of said fleet in any contracting State by paying to said State total registration fees in an amount equal to that obtained by applying the proportion of in-state fleet miles divided by the total fleet miles, to the total fees which would otherwise be required for regular registration of each and all of such vehicles in such contracting State.

All fleet pro-rata registration fees shall be based upon the mileage proportions of the fleet during the period of twelve months ending on August thirty-first next preceding the commencement of the registration year for which registration is sought, except that mileage proportions for a fleet not operated during such period in the State where application for registration is made will be determined by the administrator upon the sworn application of the applicant showing the operations during such period in other States and the estimated operations during the registration year for which registration is sought, in the State in which application is being made; or if no operations were conducted during such period a full statement of the proposed method of operation.

If any buses operate in two or more States which permit the proration of registration on the basis of a fleet of buses consisting of a lesser number of vehicles than provided in Article II (g), such fleet may be prorated as to registration in such States, in which event the buses in such fleet shall not be required to register in any other contracting States if each such vehicle is registered in some contracting State, except to the extent it is exempt from registration as provided in Article III (b).

If the administrator of any State determines, based on his method of the operation thereof, that the inclusion of a bus or buses as a part of a fleet would adversely affect the proper fleet fee which should be paid to his State, having due regard for fairness and equity, he may refuse to permit any or all of such buses to be included in his State as a part of such fleet.

(b) Total Fleet Miles. Total fleet miles, with respect to each contracting State, shall mean the total miles operated by the fleet (1) in such State, (2) in all other contracting States, (3) in other States having proportional registration provisions, (4) in States with which such contracting State has reciprocity, and (5) in such other States as the administrator determines should be included under the circumstances in order to protect or promote the interest of his State; except that in States having laws requiring proration on the basis of a different determination of total fleet miles, total fleet miles shall be determined on such basis.

(c) Leased Vehicles. If a bus is operated by a person other than the owner as a part of a fleet which is subject to the provisions of this article, then the operator of such fleet shall be deemed to be the owner of said bus for the purposes of this article.

(d) Extent of Privileges. Upon the registration of a fleet in a contracting State pursuant to this article, each bus in the fleet may be operated in both interstate and intrastate operations in such State, except as provided in Article III (e).

(e) Application for Proration. The application for proration of registation shall be made in each contracting State upon substantially the application forms and supplements authorized by joint action of the administrators of the contracting States.

(f) Issuance of Identification. Upon registration of a fleet, the State which is the base State of a particular bus of the fleet shall issue the required license plates and registration card for such bus, and each contracting State in which the fleet, of which such bus is a part, operates shall issue a special identification identifying such bus as a part of a fleet which has fully complied with the registration requirements of such State. The required license plates, registration cards and identification shall be appropriately displayed in the manner required by or pursuant to the laws of each respective State.

(g) Additions to Fleet. If any bus is added to a prorated fleet after the filing of the original application, the owner shall file a supplemental application. The owner shall register such bus in each contracting State in like manner as provided for buses listed in an original application and the registration fee payable shall be determined on the mileage proportion used to determine the registration fees payable for buses registered under the original application.

(h) Withdrawals from Fleet. If any bus is withdrawn from a prorated fleet during the period for which it is registered or identified, the owner shall notify the administrator of each State in which it is registered or identified of such withdrawal and shall return the plates, and registration card or identification as may be required by or pursuant to the laws of the respective States.

(i) Audits. The administrator of each contracting State shall, within the statutory authority of such administrator, make any information obtained upon an audit of records of any applicant for proration of registration available to the administrators of the other contracting States.

(j) Errors in Registration. If it is determined by the administrator of a contracting State, as a result of such audits or otherwise, that an improper fee has been paid his State, or errors in registration found, the administrator may require the fleet owner to make the necessary corrections in the registration of his fleet and payment of fees.

ARTICLE V. RECIPROCITY.

(a) Grant of Reciprocity. Each of the contracting States grants reciprocity as provided in this article.

(b) Applicability. The provisions of this agreement with respect to reciprocity shall apply only to a bus properly registered in the base State of the bus, which State must be a contracting State.

(c) Non-applicability to Fleet Buses. The reciprocity granted pursuant to this article shall not apply to a bus which is entitled to be registered or identified as part of a prorated fleet.

(d) Extent of Reciprocity. The reciprocity granted pursuant to this article shall permit the interstate operation of a bus and intrastate operation which is incidental to a trip of such bus involving interstate operation.

(e) Other Agreements. Nothing in this agreement shall be construed to prohibit any of the contracting States from entering into separate agreements with each other for the granting of temporary permits for the intrastate operation of vehicles registered in the other State; nor to prevent any of the contracting States from entering into agreements to grant reciprocity for intrastate operation within any zone or zones agreed upon by States.

Article VI. Withdrawal or Revocation.

Any contracting State may withdraw from this agreement upon thirty-days written notice to each other contracting State, which notice shall be given only after the repeal of this agreement by the legislature of such State, if adoption was by legislative act, or after renunciation by the appropriate administrative official of such contracting State if the laws thereof empower him so to renounce.

Article VII. Construction and Severability.

This agreement shall be liberally construed so as to effectuate the purposes thereof. The provisions of this agreement shall be severable and if any phrase, clause, sentence or provision of this agreement is declared to be contrary to the Constitution of any State or of the United States or the applicability thereof to any government, agency, person or circumstance is held invalid, the validity of the remainder of this agreement and the applicability thereof to any government, agency, person or circumstance shall not be affected thereby. If this agreement shall be held contrary to the Constitution of any State participating herein, the agreement shall remain in full force and effect as to the remaining party States and in full force and effect as to the State affected as to all severable matters.

History—
1965, 795, § 1.

Cross References—
Registration of motor vehicles, see ALM GL c 90 § 2.
Fees for registration of motor vehicles, see ALM GL c 90 § 33.
Common carriers of passengers by motor vehicle, see ALM GL c 159A.

§ 2.   Administrator, Defined.

As used in the Agreement on Bus Registration Proration, hereinafter called the Agreement, with reference to this commonwealth, the term "administrator" shall mean the registrar of motor vehicles.

History—
1965, 795, § 2.

Cross References—
Registrar of motor vehicles, generally, see ALM GL c 16 § 9.

Designation of persons to perform duties of members of boards or commissions appointed under interstate compacts, see ALM GL c 30 § 6A.

§ 3.   Exemptions from Coverage of Agreement; Changes in Methods for Reporting Information.

The registrar of motor vehicles shall have the power to make such exemptions from the coverage of the Agreement as may be appropriate and to make such changes in methods for the reporting of any information required to be furnished to this commonwealth pursuant to the Agreement as, in his judgment, shall be suitable; provided, that any such exemptions or changes shall not be contrary to the purposes set forth in Article I of the Agreement and shall be made in order to permit the continuance of uniformity of practice among the contracting States with respect to buses. Any such exemption or change shall be made by rule or regulation and shall not be effective unless made by the same procedure required for other rules and regulations of his division.

History—
1965, 795, § 3.

§ 4.   Governor as Officer to Give Notice of Withdrawal.

Unless otherwise provided in any statute withdrawing this commonwealth from participation in the Agreement, the governor shall be the officer to give notice of withdrawal therefrom in accordance with Article VI thereof.

History—
1965, 795, § 4.

§ 5.   Excise on Fleet Buses According to GL c. 60A.

Notwithstanding any provision of the Agreement, set forth in section one, or any action taken pursuant thereto, an excise shall be assessed, levied and collected, as provided in chapter sixty A of the General Laws, on any fleet bus which is registered in this commonwealth under the provisions of chapter ninety of the General Laws.

History—
1965, 795, § 5.

CHAPTER S133

Connecticut River Atlantic Salmon Compact

(Acts 1981, Ch. 716)

Sec.

1. Connecticut River Atlantic Salmon Commission.

> **Auto-Cite®:** Cases and annotations referred to herein can be further researched through the Auto-Cite® computer-assisted research service. Use Auto-Cite to check citations for form, parallel references, prior and later history, and annotation references.

§ 1. Connecticut River Atlantic Salmon Commission.

The governor is hereby authorized and directed to enter into an execute, on behalf of the commonwealth, a compact in the form substantially as set forth herein with the states of Connecticut, New Hampshire and Vermont and with the United States Fish and Wildlife Service and the National Marine Fisheries Service legally joining therein.

THE CONNECTICUT RIVER ATLANTIC SALMON COMPACT

ARTICLE 1

The purpose of this compact is to create an interstate compact for the management of Atlantic salmon in the main stem of the Connecticut River in the states of Massachusetts, Connecticut, New Hampshire and Vermont, to promote the restoration of anadromous Atlantic salmon, herein after referred to as Atlantic salmon, in the Connecticut River basin by the development of a joint interstate program for stocking, protection, management research and regulation and to restore Atlantic salmon to the Connecticut River in numbers as near as possible to their historical abundance.

ARTICLE II

This agreement shall become operative immediately whenever all of the states of Massachusetts, Connecticut, New Hampshire and Vermont have executed it in a form that is in accordance with the laws of the executing state and the congress has given its consent.

ARTICLE III

Each state joining herein shall appoint two representatives to a commission hereby constituted and designated as the Connecticut River Atlantic Salmon Commission. One shall be the executive officer of the administrative agency of such state charged with the management of the fisheries resources to which this compact pertains or his designee. The second shall be a citizen who shall have a knowledge and interest in Atlantic salmon to be appointed by the governor for a term of three years. The director of the northeast region of the Fish and Wildlife Service, United States Department of the Interior or his designee and the director of the northeast region of the National Marine Fisheries Service, United States Department of Commerce, or his designee, shall be members of said Commission. The Commission shall be a body corporate with the powers and duties set forth herein.

ARTICLE IV

The duty of said Commission shall be to make inquiry and ascertain from time to time such methods, practices, circumstances and conditions as may be disclosed for bringing about the restoration of Atlantic salmon in the Connecticut River and its tributaries.

To promote the restoration, preservation and protection of Atlantic salmon in the Connecticut River Basin the Commission may draft and recommend to the governors of the various signatory states legislation to accomplish this end. The Commission shall, more than sixty days prior to any regular meeting of the legislature of any signatory state, present to the governor of the states its recommendations relating to proposed enactments to be made by the legislature of the state in furthering the intents and purposes of this compact.

The Commission shall have the power to recommend to the states party hereto stocking programs, management procedures and research projects and when two or more states party hereto shall jointly stock waters or undertake cooperative management or research the Commission shall act as the coordinating agency. The Commission using all available means, shall encourage acquisition by the signatory states of river bank, river bed and access thereto.

The Commission shall consult with and advise the pertinent administrative agencies in the signatory states with regard to other anadromous species and their potential impact or the potential impact of sport fisheries and commercial fisheries for other anadromous species on the restoration of Atlantic salmon to the Connecticut River Basin.

In the interest of developing a sound program of Atlantic salmon management the Commission shall promulgate regulations governing Atlantic salmon fishing in the main stem of the Connecticut River in all four signatory states as hereinafter provided. Such regulations may: (1) establish the open and closed seasons for Atlantic salmon which may vary by river section, (2) establish hours, days or period during the open season when fishing for Atlantic salmon shall not be permitted in designated areas, (3) prescribe the legal methods of taking Atlantic salmon including the type of gear such as gaffs, landing nets or tailers which may be used to assist in landing such fish, (4) establish the minimum legal length for Atlantic salmon, (5) establish the daily creel limit, the season creel limit and the possession limit for Atlantic salmon.

The commission shall recommend, review and issue comments on such regulations as may be promulgated by the signatory states governing Atlantic salmon fishing in tributary streams. The states of Massachusetts and Connecticut agree to make available for brood stock, from fish taken in the fish passage facilities at the Rainbow Reservoir dam and the Holyoke Power Company dam, such numbers of adult Atlantic salmon as the Commission deems necessary to carry out the Atlantic salmon restoration program.

The Commission shall have the power to issue a Connecticut River Basin Atlantic Salmon License and the sale of such licenses shall be handled by the individual signatory states or their authorized agents. The individual states shall be accountable to the Commission for all such licenses and the moneys received therefrom. The initial fee for such licenses shall be determined by majority vote of the Commission but shall not exceed the maximum resident angling license fee of the signatory states except that the Commission may upon a determination of need and with the unanimous approval of its membership increase such license and issuing fee. The individual signatory states or their issuing agents may retain a recording fee of up to fifty cents for each license issued. Forms for such license shall be provided to the signatory states by the Commission. Such license shall be a legal prerequisite for any person including minors fishing for or possessing Atlantic salmon in the waters or on the shores of the Connecticut River and all of its tributaries. In addition to said Connecticut River Basin Atlantic Salmon License, all persons, except those specifically exempted because of age, disability or other limitation as determined by statute or regulations of the individual signatory states shall be required to possess a valid resident or non-resident sport fishing license issued by the state in which such person is fishing. The Commission shall recognize that in certain waters or sections of waters a daily rod permit may also be required, such daily rod permit to be issued by the state in which such waters or sections of waters are located; however, the signatory states shall not, by fee, distinguish between residents and non-residents. The authority to limit the numbers of persons fishing for Atlantic salmon in certain tributaries or sections of certain tributaries shall remain the prerogative of the individual signatory states.

The respective police agencies of the signatory states shall have the authority to enforce all of the regulations and license requirements of the Commission any place in the Connecticut River Basin.

The Commission shall have the authority to accept gifts, state grants and federal funds. The Commission shall have the authority to expend money from fees collected for Connecticut River Basin Atlantic Salmon Licenses or from such other funds available to the Commission to finance the cost of stocking, management or research carried on by signatory states to further the purposes of this compact.

ARTICLE V

The Commission shall elect from its number a chairman and a vice chairman and at its pleasure may remove such officers. Said Commission shall adopt rules and regulations for the conduct of its business. At such time as funds are available to the Commission the Commission may establish and maintain an office for the transaction of its business. The Commission may meet at any time or place but must meet at least semiannually.

The Commission shall have the authority to expend money from available commission funds to reimburse its membership for necessary travel expenses.

ARTICLE VI

At such time as funds are available the Commission may employ and discharge at its pleasure such personnel as may be required to carry out the provisions of this compact and shall fix and determine their duties, qualifications and compensation.

ARTICLE VII

There shall be established a technical committee to consist of one fishery biologist from each of the signatory states, the United States Fish and Wildlife Service and the National Marine Fisheries Service to act in an advisory capacity to the Commission. The technical committee shall have the authority to request employees of the signatory states, the United States Fish and Wildlife Service and the National Marine Fisheries Service or others who have special fields of expertise to act as special advisors to the committee. At such time as funds are available the Commission may reimburse technical committee members and special advisors for necessary travel expenses.

ARTICLE VIII

No action shall be taken by the Commission in regard to its general affairs except by affirmative vote of a majority of members present at any meeting, provided there is a quorum. A quorum shall consist of a simple majority of all members of the Commission, provided, however, that no action shall be taken by the Commission unless each signatory state is represented at any such meeting. No recommendation or allotment of grant funds shall be made by the commission except by the affirmative vote of a majority of its members.

ARTICLE IX

Continued absence of representation or of any representative on the Commission from any party hereto shall be brought to the attention of the governor thereof.

ARTICLE X

The states signatory hereto agree to make an annual appropriation to the initial support of the Commission in the amount of one thousand dollars for each of the first three years this compact is in effect.

ARTICLE XI

The Commission shall keep accurate accounts of all receipts and disbursements and shall report to the governor and the legislature of each state party to this compact on or before the tenth day of January of each year, setting forth in detail the transactions conducted by it during the twelve months preceding January first of that year. The comptroller of the state of Massachusetts is hereby authorized and empowered from time to time to examine the accounts and books of the Commission, including its receipts, disbursements, grants and such other items referring to its financial standing as such comptroller may deem proper and to report the results of such examination to the governor of the commonwealth.

History—
1981, 716, § 1; 1983, 610.

Editorial Note—
The **1983 amendment** rewrote the introductory paragraph, deleting language referring to the renouncement of the compact by the Commonwealth. While the amendment stated that it was striking out § 1, it dealt only with the

introductory paragraph, and thus, in the opinion of the editor, it did not intend to delete the compact itself.

Federal Aspects—

United States Fish and Wildlife Service, 16 USCS §§ 742a et seq.

Salmon and Steelhead Conservation Enhancement Act of 1980, 16 USCS § 3301 note.

Code of Massachusetts Regulations—

Taking of anadromous fish in the territorial waters of Massachusetts, 322 CMR 3.05.

Taking of coho salmon from the coastal waters of Massachsuetts, 322 CMR § 3.06.

CHAPTER S135

Compact Agreement on Issuance of Certain Interstate Truck Permits

(Acts 1988, Ch. 251)

Auto-Cite®: Cases and annotations referred to herein can be further researched through the Auto-Cite® computer-assisted research service. Use Auto-Cite to check citations for form, parallel references, prior and later history, and annotation references.

---

§ 1. [1989, 251, § 1, amended ALM GL c 90, § 34]

§ 2. Form of Compact.

An agreement is hereby entered into with all jurisdictions legally joining therein in substantially the following form:

ARTICLE I. PURPOSES.

The purposes of this agreement are to:

403

(a) Ease the burden of the trucking industry in obtaining approvals required to move over-size and overweight trucks across state borders.

(b) Establish uniform and equitable procedures whereby one contracting state on its own behalf and on behalf of another contracting state or other contracting states may issue a single common permit authorizing non-divisible over-size and overweight trucks to travel through the issuing state and in interstate travel into or through another one or more of the contracting states.

(c) Establish procedures under which the fees required by each contracting state into which or through which the said over-size or overweight truck will travel are collected by the issuing state and distributed to the said contracting states, and the accounting procedures in connection therewith.

ARTICLE II. DEFINITIONS.

The following definitions shall apply in this agreement and in this act.

(a) "State", the states of the United States, the District of Columbia, the territories of the United States, the Provinces of Canada, and the states, territories and federal district of Mexico.

(b) "Contracting state", a state which is a party to this agreement.

(c) "Envelope vehicle", any non-divisible over-size or overweight vehicle which shall not exceed specified size and weight to be determined by the contracting states.

(d) "Issuing state", the state which, in accordance with rules established by the policy committee, will issue the common permit for the envelope vehicle and collect fees for all contracting states through which the specific envelope vehicle will travel.

(e) "Regional highway network", the routes designated on maps by the contracting states over which the envelope vehicles may be permitted to travel only to the extent and under the conditions specified in the common permit issued by the issuing state. In accordance with procedures developed by the contracting states, each contracting state may impose temporary restrictions on the regional highway network or the access highway network, as defined below, and may remove such restrictions by written notification to the other contracting states of such imposition or removal, and the issuing state shall conform to such restrictions when issuing a common permit for travel in the contracting states.

(f) "Access highway network", the access highway network designated on maps by the contracting states over which envelope vehicles may travel to or from the regional highway network when their points of destination or their points of origin require such travel.

(g) "Designated routes", the route designated by the issuing state on the common permit from which the envelope vehicle shall not deviate unless an approved alternative route is required or agreed upon by a particular contracting state.

(h) "Common permit form", the form of the permit issued by the issuing state and on which a route is designated to be used in accordance with permit conditions by an envelope vehicle traveling through the contracting states. The common permit form is to be a standard form developed by the contracting states which may from time to time be amended or revised by the contracting states.

(i) "Department", the department of public works of the commonwealth of Massachusetts.

(j) "Fee collection", the collection of the total permit fees by the issuing state for its own state and for all contracting states through which the vehicle is thereby permitted to travel, all in accordance with Article V.

(k) "Fee distribution", the periodic distribution to each and every contracting state of the total permit fees collected and held by each issuing state on behalf of the other contracting states, all in accordance with Article V.

(l) "Total permit fees", the total of the permit fees which the issuing state shall collect for issuance of the common permit which shall include the fee required by the issuing state and all fees required for such permit by other contracting states through which the permitted envelope vehicle will travel under the permit.

(m) "Administrator", the official or agency of a contracting state who administers the granting of over-size or overweight permits in his state.

(n) "Common permit", the single permit issued by the issuing state in the common permit form. The truck operator of any overweight or over-size vehicle not eligible for a common permit under this agreement between the contracting states must obtain individual state permits.

(o) "The commonwealth", the commonwealth of Massachusetts.

(p) "Policy committee", the committee composed of one administrator from each contracting state.

ARTICLE III. GENERAL PROVISIONS.

(a) On and after its effective date, this agreement shall supersede any reciprocal or other agreement, arrangement or understanding between any two or more of the contracting states covering, in whole or in part, any of the matters covered by this agreement; but this agreement shall not affect any reciprocal or other agreement, arrangement or understanding between a contracting state and a state or states not parties to this agreement.

(b) This agreement shall not require a permit fee in a contracting state of any over-size or overweight vehicles which are, in whole or part, exempt from such permit fee under the laws or regulations of such state without respect to this agreement.

(c) This agreement does not waive any fees or taxes charged or levied by any contracting state in connection with the ownership or operation of vehicles which fees and taxes are to be enforced in addition to the permit fees as defined herein under the laws or regulations of such state without respect to this agreement.

(d) This agreement shall not authorize the operation of a vehicle in any contracting state contrary to the laws or regulations thereof, except those pertaining to over-size and overweight permits and the payment of fees therefor, and then only to the extent provided in this agreement.

(e) Each contracting state reserves the right to withdraw, by order of the administrator thereof, in a manner consistent with respective state law, all or any part of the benefits or privileges granted pursuant to this agreement from the owner of any vehicle or fleet of vehicles operated in violation of any provision of this agreement. Such benefits and privileges shall not be unreasonably denied. The administrator shall immediately give notice of any such violation or withdrawal of any such benefits or privileges to the administrator of each other contracting state in which vehicles of such owner are operated.

(f) The administrator of each of the contracting states shall cooperate with the administrators of the others and each contracting state hereby agrees to furnish such aid and assistance to each other within its statutory authority as will aid in proper enforcement of this agreement.

(g) In any dispute between or among contracting states arising under this agreement, the final decision regarding interpretation of questions at issue relating to this agreement shall be reached by joint action of the contracting states, acting through the administrators thereof, and shall upon determination be placed in writing.

(h) This agreement shall become effective and binding between and among the states of Maine, Massachusetts, New Hampshire, Rhode

Island and Vermont, as contracting states, when enacted or otherwise entered into by any of the said states. This agreement shall become effective and binding with respect to any other state upon the happening of the following: (1) submission by said state to the policy committee of an application of membership to the agreement; (2) unanimous approval of said application by the policy committee; (3) enactment of the agreement into law by said state or when said state otherwise enters into the agreement, including, when provided by the statutes of said state, the execution of the agreement by an executive or administrative official of said state acting on behalf of and for said state.

ARTICLE IV. ISSUANCE OF PERMIT.

(a) The issuing state may issue a common permit for a specific envelope vehicle to travel a designated route in the issuing state and in any other contracting state or other contracting states, without seeking any prior approval from any other contracting state other than that required by this agreement.

(b) The common permit issued by the issuing state shall specify a designated route upon which the envelope vehicle may travel, and no other route may be used by such envelope vehicle, except as follows: the common permit may include, as part of its designated route, a route or routes other than those included in the regional and access route networks only when the contracting state or states or the issuing state itself requires or has agreed specifically to allow such exceptional route.

(c) The common permit shall be issued subject to such conditions as the contracting states agree are necessary for public safety and convenience. Said conditions shall be in printed form and be made available upon request in reasonable quantities to the public.

(d) The operator of any vehicle which does not conform to the specifications for an envelope vehicle must obtain a separate permit from each state in which the non-conforming vehicle will travel and must comply with each such state's permit procedures.

ARTICLE V. COLLECTION AND DISTRIBUTION OF TOTAL PERMIT FEES.

(a) The issuing state shall collect the total permit fee when issuing the common permit to the operator of an envelope vehicle.

(b) Each contracting state shall provide all other contracting states with its current fee schedule and the total permit fee collected by an issuing state shall be in accordance with such fee schedules. A printed fee schedule for permits issued under this agreement shall be available to the public upon request.

(c) Each contracting state shall continue to exercise sole and independent authority to establish its own fees and fee systems and nothing in this agreement shall affect that sole and independent authority of any state.

(d) Periodically, as established in administrative procedures, each contracting state which has collected fees and held such fees on behalf of another contracting state shall distribute those fees to such other contracting states.

(e) The administrator of each contracting state or his agent or agents may inspect and audit the records of each other contracting state in so far as such records relate to the collection and distribution of the total permit fees, subject to reasonable conditions which may be set by the administrator of the contracting state whose records are being inspected or audited.

(f) Any errors in collection or distribution of the total permit fees shall be settled by the administrators of the affected contracting states; provided, however, that if the settlement requires further action or approval by the legislative or executive officer of any affected contracting state, the finality of such settlement shall be subject to such further action or approval.

(g) If the issuing state fails to charge or charges less than is actually due to a contracting state as its part of the total permit fee, such failure to charge or such undercharge shall not excuse the permittee on the common permit from the obligation of paying to such contracting state the fee amount which would have been due to it. The substance of this subsection shall be made a condition on the common permit.

ARTICLE VI. SAFETY REGULATIONS.

(a) The contracting states shall establish, and may amend from time to time, a common set of safety regulations which shall be incorporated into the common permit and, thus, be applicable to envelope vehicles when such vehicles are traveling in any of the contracting states under a common permit issued by any of the contracting states.

(b) A common set of safety regulations shall be established based on and consistent with the recommended American Association of State Highway Traffic Officials (AASHTO) standards for safety requirements and may include, without limitation, requirements relative to flags, signs for oversized loads, lights, escort vehicles, convoys, speed, days and hours on which travel will be permitted, inclement weather and use of travel lanes. The common safety regulations shall be made available in printed form in reasonable quantities to the public upon request.

(c) Each contracting state may establish fines and penalties, in a manner consistent with the laws of each respective state, for the violation of the terms of the common permits by operators of the envelope vehicles when such vehicles are traveling under common permit in said state.

ARTICLE VII. RECIPROCITY.

(a) Each of the contracting states grants reciprocity as provided in this article.

(b) The reciprocity granted pursuant to this article shall permit the interstate operation of an envelope vehicle and intrastate operation which is incidental to a trip of such envelope vehicle involving interstate operation.

(c) Nothing in this agreement shall be construed to prohibit any of the contracting states from entering into separate agreements with each other for the granting of temporary permits for the intrastate operation of vehicles registered in the other state; nor to prevent any of the contracting states from entering into agreements to grant reciprocity for intrastate operation within any zone or zones agreed upon by states.

ARTICLE VIII. ADMINISTRATION OF AGREEMENT.

(a) The policy committee shall elect a chairman.

(b) The chairman shall appoint an administrative procedures committee from persons nominated by the policy committee. The number of persons on the said committee shall be determined by the policy committee.

(c) The administrative procedures committee shall develop and maintain a written administrative procedures manual. The administrative procedures manual or any amendment to it shall be effective upon approval and adoption by at least a three-fourths vote of the policy committee. The written procedures manual shall become part of this agreement, and shall be distributed to the administrators of all contracting states.

ARTICLE IX. WITHDRAWAL OR REVOCATION.

(a) Any contracting state may withdraw from this agreement upon one hundred and eighty days written notice to each other contracting state, which notice shall be given only after the repeal of this agreement by the legislature of such state, if adoption was by legislative act, or, after renunciation by the appropriate administrative official of such contracting state, if the laws thereof empower him so to renounce.

(b) Withdrawal or revocation by one contracting state, or more, shall not affect this agreement between other states.

(c) Any state which withdraws from or revokes this agreement shall give each of its licensees a ninety-days notice of such withdrawal.

ARTICLE X. CONSTRUCTION AND SEVERABILITY.

This agreement shall be liberally construed so as to effectuate the purposes thereof. The provisions of this agreement shall be severable and if any phrase, clause, sentence or provision of this agreement is declared to be contrary to the constitution of any state or of the United States, or the applicability thereof to any government, agency, person or circumstance is held invalid, the validity of the remainder of this agreement and the applicability thereof to any government, agency, person or circumstance shall not be affected thereby. If this agreement shall be held contrary to the constitution of any state participating herein, the agreement shall remain in full force and effect as to the remaining party states and full force and effect as to the state affected as to all severable matters.

History—
1988, 251, § 2.

§ 3.   Part of Total Permit Fee to be in Form Payable to Interstate Permit Fund.

Upon this agreement becoming effective with respect to the commonwealth, that part of the total permit fee which is due to contracting states, other than the commonwealth, when collected by the department, shall be in a form payable to the Interstate Permit Fund. The Interstate Permit Fund shall be a revolving fund.

History—
1988, 251, § 3.

§ 4.   Deposit and Distribution of Funds; Cost of Administration.

Upon this agreement taking effect with respect to the commonwealth, the state treasurer, hereinafter referred to as the "treasurer", is hereby authorized and directed to deposit all funds payable to the Interstate Permit Fund into such fund for the benefit of the contracting states entitled thereto. The funds of the Interstate Permit Fund shall be deposited in a bank licensed to do business in the commonwealth for the benefit of the contracting states entitled thereto. From time to time distributions to the contracting states, including interest accrued on funds due to each respective contracting state, shall be made in such amounts as the commissioner of the department of public works certifies to the treasurer as due to the respective contracting states. The treasurer shall and is hereby authorized to disburse, without appropriation from the legislature, funds from the Interstate Permit Fund to the respective contracting states in such amounts as the commissioner of the department of public works has certified to the treasurer. The cost of administering the Interstate Permit Fund shall be paid by the commonwealth. That part of the total permit fees which is due to the commonwealth as an issuing state shall be deposited into the treasury of the commonwealth and be credited to the Highway Fund in accordance with section thirty-four of chapter ninety of the General Laws.

History—
1988, 251, § 4.

§ 5.   Deposit and Distribution Procedures Subject to Approval by Commissioner of Administration.

The procedures, other than those provided for in this act, for deposit into the Interstate Permit Fund and the distribution therefrom to other contracting states of their respective shares of the total permit fees shall be subject to approval by the commissioner of administration. The procedure for the deposit of the commonwealth's share of the total permit fees into the treasury of the commonwealth to be credited to the Highway Fund shall be subject to approval of the commissioner of administration.

History—
1988, 251, § 5.

§ 6.   Fees Due Commonwealth Payable to Department of Public Works; Accounting Procedures Subject to Approval by Commissioner of Administration.

Upon this agreement taking effect with respect to the commonwealth, those amounts of the total permit fees which have been collected by other contracting states and which are due to the commonwealth shall be paid by said contracting states to the Massachusetts department of public works, acting on behalf of the commonwealth, and such amounts, when received by the said department, shall be deposited into the treasury of the commonwealth to be credited to the Highway Fund in accordance with the provisions of section thirty-four of chapter ninety of the General Laws. The procedures for accounting

411

for such receipts and deposits shall be subject to the approval by the commissioner of administration.

History—
1988, 251, § 6.

§ 7.   Settlement of Errors Subject to Approval of Commissioner of Administration.

Any settlement of errors under this agreement shall be subject to the approval of the commissioner of administration and, if action or approval by the general court is required, the commissioner of administration shall submit the said agreement for the required action or approval by the general court.

History—
1988, 251, § 7.

§ 8.   Department May Promulgate Common Safety Regulations.

The department may promulgate the common safety regulations authorized in section one of Article VI. Such regulations may not abrogate regulations of the department in effect at the date of enactment of this act for permits issued pursuant to section thirty of chapter eighty-five of the General Laws.

History—
1988, 251, § 8.

§ 9.   Operation of Envelope Vehicle in Violation of Provisions Subject to Fine; Prima Facie Evidence.

Any person who is convicted of operating or permitting the operation of an envelope vehicle on any public ways of the commonwealth in violation of the provisions of the common permit under which it is operating shall be punished by a fine in the amount provided by the General Laws for each offense. A certified copy of the common permit issued by any issuing state shall be prima facie evidence in the courts of the commonwealth.

History—
1988, 251, § 9.

§ 10.   Governor May Withdraw Commonwealth From Agreement.

Unless otherwise provided by law, the governor shall be the appropriate administrative official to withdraw the commonwealth from this agreement and to give notice thereof in accordance with subsection (a) of Article IX.

History—
1988, 251, § 10.

CHAPTER S137

Compact With Rhode Island Relating to Bays Systems

(Acts 1990, Ch. 444)

SEC.

1. Form of Compact.

Auto-Cite®: Cases and annotations referred to herein can be further researched through the Auto-Cite® computer-assisted research service. Use Auto-Cite to check citations for form, parallel references, prior and later history, and annotation references.

---

§ 1. Form of Compact.

The governor, on behalf of this commonwealth, is hereby authorized to enter into a compact, substantially in the following form, with the state of Rhode Island, and the general court hereby signifies in advance its approval and ratification of such a compact so entered into, such approval and ratification to be effective upon the filing of a copy of such compact in the office of the state secretary:—

ARTICLE I

PURPOSE AND POLICY

A. It is the purpose of this compact to:

1. Establish and maintain close cooperation and understanding among executive, legislative, professional, educational, and lay leadership basis at the state and local levels.

2. Enhance the economic and environmental qualities of the bays system.

3. Provide a forum for the discussion, development, crystallization and recommendation of public policy alternatives in the field of environmental and economic aspects of Narragansett Bay and Mount Hope Bay.

4. Provide a clearing house of information on matters relating to the problems of the bays systems and how they are being met in different places, so that the legislative branch of state government may have ready access to the experience and record of the compact members and so that both lay and professional groups in this field

415

may have additional avenues for the sharing of experience and interchange of ideas in the formation of this public policy.

5. Facilitate the improvement of state and local systems so that all of them will be able to meet adequate and desirable goals which require continuous advancement in related marine opportunities, methods and facilities.

B. It is the policy of this compact to encourage and promote local and state initiative in the development, maintenance, improvement and administration of bays systems in a manner which will accord with the needs and advantages of diversity among localities and the state of Rhode Island and the Commonwealth of Massachusetts.

C. The party states recognize that each of them has an interest in the water quality in the other states, as well as in its own marine system.

ARTICLE II

STATE DEFINED

As used in the compact, "state" means state of Rhode Island or the Commonwealth of Massachusetts.

ARTICLE III

THE COMMISSION

A. The commission of the states, hereinafter called "the commission", is hereby established. The commission shall be comprised of seventeen (17) members, eight (8) members from Rhode Island, eight (8) members from Massachusetts and one (1) member being the north east regional director of the Environmental Protection Agency or his/her designee. The Rhode Island members shall be the governor or his designee, three (3) senators chosen by the senate majority leader, three (3) members of the house of representatives chosen by the speaker of the house and one (1) member chosen jointly by the senate majority leader and the speaker of the house. The Massachusetts members shall be the governor or his designee, two (2) senators appointed by the president of the senate, four (4) members of the house of representatives appointed by the speaker of the house and one member appointed jointly by the president of the senate and the speaker of the house of representatives. The member of the commission shall be uncompensated and serve for a term of two (2) years.

B. The members of the commission shall be entitled to one (1) vote on each commission. No action of the commission shall be binding unless taken at a meeting at which a majority of the total number of votes on the commission are cast in favor thereof. Action of the commission shall be only at a meeting at which a majority of the commissioners are present. The commission shall meet at least once a year. In its bylaws, and subject to such directions and limitations as may be contained therein, the commission may delegate the exercise of any of its powers to the executive committee or the executive director, except for the power to approve budgets or requests for appropriations, the power to make policy recommendations pursuant to article III(J).

C. The commission shall have a seal.

D. The commission shall elect annually, from its members, a chairman, a vice chairman, and a treasurer. The commission may provide for the appointment of an executive director. Such executive director shall serve at the pleasure of the commission, and together with the treasurer and such other personnel as the commission may deem appropriate shall be bonded in such amount as the commission shall determine. The executive secretary shall be secretary.

E. Notwithstanding the civil service, personnel or other merit system laws of any of the party states, the executive director subject to the approval of the executive committee appoint, remove or discharge such personnel as may be necessary for the performance of the functions of the commission, and fix the duties and compensation of such personnel. The commission in its by-laws shall provide for the personnel policies and programs of the commission.

F. The commission may borrow, accept or contract for the services of personnel from any party jurisdiction, the United States, or any subdivision or agency of the aforementioned governments, or from any agency of two (2) or more of the party jurisdictions or their subdivisions.

G. The commission may accept for any of its purposes and functions under this compact any and all donations, and grants of money, equipment, supplies, materials and services, conditional or otherwise, from any state, the United States, or any other governmental agency, or from any person, firm, association, foundation, or corporation, and may receive, utilize and dispose of the same. Any donation or grant accepted by the commission pursuant to this paragraph or services borrowed pursuant to paragraph (F) of this article shall be reported in the annual report of the commission. Such report shall include the nature, amount and conditions, if any, of the donation, grant, or services borrowed, and the identity of the donor or lender.

H. The commission may establish and maintain such facilities as may be necessary for the transacting of its business. The commission may acquire, hold, and convey real and personnel property and any interest therein.

I. The commission shall adopt by-laws for the conduct of its business and shall have the power to amend and rescind its by-laws. The commission shall publish its by-laws in convenient form and shall file a copy thereof and a copy of any amendments thereto, with the appropriate agency or officer in each of the party states.

J. The commission annually shall make to the governor and legislature of each party state a report covering the activities of the commission for the preceding year. The commission may make such additional reports as it may deem desirable.

ARTICLE IV

POWERS

In addition to authority conferred on the commission by other provisions of the compact, the commission shall have authority to:

1. Collect, correlate, analyze and interpret information and data concerning needs and resources.

2. Encourage and foster research in all aspects of Narragansett Bay and Mount Hope Bay, but with special reference to the desirable scope of environmental and economic aspects.

3. Develop proposals for adequate financing of the compact as a whole and at each of its many levels.

4. Conduct or participate in research of the types referred to in this article in any instance where the commission finds that such research is necessary for advancement of the purposes and policies of this compact, utilizing fully the resources of national associations, regional compact organizations, and other agencies and institutions, both public and private.

5. Formulate suggested policies and plans for the improvement of Mount Hope Bay as a whole, or for any segment thereof, and make recommendations with respect thereto available to the appropriate governmental units, agencies and public officials.

6. Do such other things as may be necessary or incidental to the administration of any of its authority or functions pursuant to this compact.

ARTICLE V

COOPERATION WITH FEDERAL GOVERNMENT

A. If the laws of the United States specifically so provide, or if administrative provision is made therefor within the federal government, the United States shall be represented on the commission by the north east regional executive director of the environmental protection agency or his/her designee. Such representative or representatives of the United States shall be appointed and serve in such manner as may be provided by or pursuant to federal law.

B. The commission may provide information and make recommendations to any executive or legislative agency or officer of the federal government concerning the common policies of the member states, and may advise with any such agencies or officers concerning any matter of mutual interest.

ARTICLE VI
COMMITTEES

A. To assist in the expeditious conduct of its business when the full commission is not meeting, the commission shall elect an executive committee of five (5) members which, subject to the provisions of this compact and consistent with the policies of the commission, shall be constituted and function as provided in the by-laws of the commission. A federal representative on the commission may serve with the executive committee, but without vote. The voting members of the executive committee shall serve for terms of two (2) years, except that members elected to the first executive committee of the commission shall be elected as follows: one (1) for one (1) year and one (1) for two (2) years. The chairman, vice chairman, and treasurer of the commission shall be members of the executive committee and, anything in this paragraph to the contrary notwithstanding, shall serve during their continuance in these offices. Vacancies in the executive committee shall not affect its authority to act, but the commission at its next regularly ensuing meeting following the occurrence of any vacancy shall fill it for the unexpired term. No person shall serve more than two (2) terms as a member of the executive committee; provided that service for a partial term of one (1) year or less shall not be counted toward the two (2) term limitation.

B. In addition there shall be an advisory board. This board, selected by the commission, shall be comprised of a minimum of eight (8) members whose term of service shall be for one (1) year. The guiding principle for the composition of the membership on the advisory board of each party state shall be that the members representing such state shall, by virtue of their training, experience, knowledge or affiliations be in a position collectively to reflect broadly the interests of the state government, marine trades, water quality and environmental standards.

B. * The commission may establish advisory and technical commit

---

* So in original.

419

tees composed of state, local, and federal officials, and private persons to advise it with respect to any one (1) or more of its functions. Any advisory or technical committee may, on request of the states concerned, be established to consider any matter of special concern to the state of Rhode Island and Commonwealth of Massachusetts.

C. The commission may establish such additional committees as its by-laws may provide.

ARTICLE VII

FINANCE

A. The commission shall not pledge the credit of any party states. The commission may meet any of its obligations in whole or in part with funds available to it pursuant to article III (G) of this compact, provided that the commission takes specific action setting aside such funds prior to incurring an obligation to be met in whole or in part in such manner. Except where the commission makes use of funds available to it pursuant to article III (G) thereof, the commission shall not incur any obligation prior to the allotment of funds by the party states adequate to meet the same.

B. The commission shall keep accurate accounts of all receipts and disbursements. The receipts and disbursements of the commission shall be subject to the audit and accounting procedure established by its by-laws. However, all receipts and disbursements of funds handled by the commission shall be audited yearly by a qualified public accountant, and the report of the audit shall be included in and become part of the annual reports of the commission.

C. The accounts of the commission shall be open at any reasonable time for inspection by duly constituted officers of the party states and by any persons authorized by the commission.

D. Nothing contained herein shall be construed to prevent commission compliance with laws relating to audit or inspection of accounts by or on behalf of any government contributing to the support of the commission.

ARTICLE VIII

ELIGIBLE PARTIES: ENTRY INTO AND WITHDRAWAL

A. This compact shall have as eligible parties the state of Rhode Island and the Commonwealth of Massachusetts.

B. Adoption of the compact may be either by enactment thereof, or by adherence thereto by the governor; provided that in the absence of enactment, adherence by the governor shall be sufficient to make his state a party only until December 31, 1991.

C. Except for withdrawal effective on December 31, 1991, in accordance with paragraph B of this article, any party state may withdraw from this compact by enacting a statute repealing the same, but no such withdrawal shall take effect until one (1) year after the governor of the withdrawing state has given notice in writing of the withdrawal to the governor of the other party state. No withdrawal shall affect any liability already incurred by or chargeable to a party state prior to the time of such withdrawal.

ARTICLE IX

CONSTRUCTION AND SEVERABILITY

This compact shall be liberally construed so as to effectuate the purposes thereof. The provisions of this compact shall be severable and if any phrase, clause, sentence or provision of this compact is declared to be contrary to the constitution of either state or of the United States, or the applicability thereof to any government, agency, person or circumstance is held invalid, the validity of the remainder of this compact and the applicability thereof to any government, agency, person or circumstance shall not be affected thereby. If this compact shall be held contrary to the constitution of any state participating therein, the compact shall remain in full force and effect as to the state affected as to all severable matters.

History—

1990, 444, § 1, approved December 29, 1990, by § 2, effective upon passage.

Index

AIRPORT OUTLAY LOAN ACT
Transportation bond authorization act, issuance and sale of bonds, Spec L 79:28

AIRPORTS
Port Authority (this index)
Transportation Bond Authorization Act (this index)

AIR RIGHTS
Turnpike Authority, utilization of air rights, Spec L 75:15A

ALTERATION
Change or Modification (this index)

AMENDMENTS
Education commission of states, filing of bylaw amendments, Spec L 99:3

Vehicle equipment safety, filing amendments to bylaws, Spec L 127:5

ANNUAL EXPENSES
Vehicle equipment safety, Spec L 127:8

ANNUAL REPORTS
Parking Authority, Spec L 71:14
Port Authority, Spec L 73:21
Turnpike Authority, Spec L 75:15
Water pollution control, Spec L 119:5

APPLICABILITY OF HABITUAL OFFENDERS LAW
Detainers outstanding against prisoners, Spec L 115:4

APPOINTMENTS
Library compact, appointment of compact administrator, Spec L 103:5

Merrimack River compact, appointment by governor of member of merrimack river valley flood control commission, Spec L 123:3, 123:5,123:3, 123:5

New England Board of Higher Education (this index)

Water pollution control members, Spec L 119:3

Water Resources Authority, Spec L 67:5, 676:7

APPORTIONMENT
Transportation bond authorization act, Spec L 79:20 to 79:22

APPROPRIATE AUTHORITY IN RECEIVING STATE
Placement of children compact, definitions, Spec L 95:4

APPROPRIATE COURT
Detainers outstanding against prisoners, definitions, Spec L 115:2

APPROPRIATIONS
Port Authority, Spec L 73:26
Transportation bond authorization act, appropriation from highway fund debt service, Spec L 79:24
Water Resources Authority, Spec L 67:5

APPROVAL
Consent or Approval (this index)

ASSESSMENTS
Water Resources Authority, Spec L 67:10

ASSISTANCE
Port Authority, assistance in projects by other agencies and departments, Spec L 73:23
Transportation bond authorization act, commonwealth to aid mbta to pay portion of net cost of service, Spec L 79:16

ATTEMPTED ESCAPE OF PRISONER
Detainers outstanding against prisoners, Spec L 115:5

ATTORNEY GENERAL
Appearance in lawsuits involving pollution, Spec L 67:24

ATTORNEYS' FEES
Supervision, care and assistance to juveniles, Spec L 97:5

AUCTIONS
Parking Authority, unclaimed property, Spec L 71:14A

AUDITS
Parking Authority, Spec L 71:14

424

426

427

DECLARATION OF NECESSITY
Parking Authority, Spec L 71:1

DEFECTIVE GUARDRAIL
Complaints for injuries, Spec L 75:3 Form 1

DEFERRED COMPENSATION PLANS
Bays system commission, Spec L 137:1

Port Authority, Spec L 73:22A

Water Resources Authority, Spec L 67:7

DEFINITIONS
Appropriate authority in receiving state, Spec L 95:4

Bus registration proration, Spec L 131:2

Detainers outstanding against prisoners, Spec L 115:2

Executive head, placement of children, compact on, Spec L 95:8

Library compact, Spec L 103:3

Parking Authority, Spec L 71:2

Port Authority, Spec L 73:1

Taxation of motor fuels, Spec L 129:2

Turnpike Authority, Spec L 75:4

Vehicle equipment safety, Spec L 127:7

Water Resources Authority, Spec L 67:2

DELINQUENT CHILDREN
Placement of children, compact on, jurisdiction of courts, Spec L 95:7

DEPARTMENT OF PUBLIC WORKS
Truck permits, interstate agreement, Spec L 135:5

DEPARTMENT OF STATE POLICE
State police compact, administrative head, defined, Spec L 111:2

DEPOSIT OF FUNDS
Truck permits, interstate agreement, Spec L 135:3 to 135:5

DESIGN OF PROJECTS
Parking Authority, assistance to, Spec L 71:14

DETAINERS OUTSTANDING AGAINST PRISONERS
Generally, Spec L 115:1 to 115:8,115:1 to 115:8

Administrator of compact, Spec L 115:7

Applicability of habitual offenders law, Spec L 115:4

Appropriate court, defined, Spec L 115:2

Attempted escape of prisoner, Spec L 115:5

Compact administrator, Spec L 115:7

Cooperation with other party states, Spec L 115:3

Copies of agreement, Spec L 115:8

Court, appropriate, defined, Spec L 115:2

Definitions, generally, Spec L 115:2

Enforcement of agreement, Spec L 115:3

Escape of prisoner, Spec L 115:5

Form of compact, Spec L 115:1

Habitual offenders law, Spec L 115:4

Inmates, mandatory giving over as required by agreement, Spec L 115:6

Mandatory giving over of inmates as required by agreement, Spec L 115:6

Party states, cooperation with, Spec L 115:3

Penalties, Spec L 115:5

Repeat offenders, Spec L 115:4

Transmittal, Spec L 115:8

DETENTION OF PERSONS
Corrections Compact (this index)

Detainers Outstanding Against Prisoners (this index)

DISBURSEMENTS
New England Board of Higher Education, Spec L 101:5

DISPOSAL OF PROPERTY
Water Resources Authority, Spec L 67:9

DISPOSAL SERVICES

Water Resources Authority, exclusivity of services, Spec L 67:20

DISTRIBUTION OF FUNDS

Truck permits, interstate agreement, Spec L 135:3 to 135:5

DISTRICTS

Library compact, districts partially within Commonwealth, Spec L 103:4

Metropolitan District Commission, definition, Spec L 67:2

DIVERSION OF WATER

Water Resources Authority, compensation for diversion from watershed system, Spec L 67:26

DIVISION

Water Resources Authority (this index)

EDUCATION

Certification of Educational Personnel (this index)

Education Compacts and Agreements (this index)

New England Board of Higher Education (this index)

EDUCATION COMPACT COUNCIL OF MASSACHUSETTS

Generally, Spec L 99:2

EDUCATION COMPACTS AND AGREEMENTS

Generally, Spec L 99:1 to 3

Amendments of education commission of states, filing of, Spec L 99:3

Bylaws of education commission of states, filing of, Spec L 99:3

Certification of Education Personnel (this index)

Commission on education of states, filing of bylaws and amendments of, Spec L 99:3

Education Compact Council of Massachusetts, Spec L 99:2

Filing of bylaws and amendments of education commission of states, Spec L 99:3

EDUCATION COMPACTS AND AGREEMENTS—Cont'd

Form of compact, Spec L 99:1

New England Board of Higher Education (this index)

EFFECTIVE DATE

Merrimack River compact, Spec L 123:6

New England Board of Higher Education compact, Spec L 101:2

Parking Authority, Spec L 71:25

Steamship Authority, Spec L 77:20

Taxation of motor fuels, Spec L 129:4

Thames River Compact Act, Spec L 125:6

Transportation bond authorization act, Spec L 79:30

Water Pollution Control Act, Spec L 119:2

EFFECTIVENESS OF COMPACT

Supervision, care and assistance to juveniles, cessation of effectiveness, Spec L 97:7

ELDERLY

Nantucket regional transit authority, van services, Spec L 81:2

ELECTED OFFICIALS

Governor (this index)

ELIGIBILITY FOR INVESTMENT

Parking Authority bonds, Spec L 71:13

Port Authority bonds, Spec L 73:18

Steamship Authority bonds, Spec L 77:11

Turnpike Authority bonds, Spec L 75:14

EMPLOYMENT

Labor and Employment (this index)

ENFORCEMENT

Detainers outstanding against prisoners, Spec L 115:3

Rights of bondholder. **Enforcement of Bondholder's Rights** (this index)

ENFORCEMENT—Cont'd

Supervision, care and assistance to juveniles, Spec L 97:6

ENFORCEMENT OF BONDHOLDER'S RIGHTS

Parking Authority, Spec L 71:12

Port Authority, Spec L 73:16

Steamship Authority, Spec L 77:12

Turnpike Authority, Spec L 75:12

ENTRY ON PROPERTY

Water Resources Authority, investigation of water pollution, Spec L 67:1 et seq.

ENVELOPE VEHICLES

Truck Permits, Interstate Agreement (this index)

ENVIRONMENTAL AFFAIRS OFFICE

Generally, Spec L 67:3

ENVIRONMENTAL PROTECTION DEPARTMENT

Generally, Spec L 67:8

ENVIRONMENTAL REMEDIES

Reimbursement of communities, Water Resources Authority, Spec L 67:8

EQUAL OPPORTUNITY EMPLOYMENT

Water Resources Authority, Spec L 67:7

EQUIPMENT

Vehicle Equipment Safety (this index)

EQUITY SUIT TO ENFORCE BONDHOLDERS' RIGHTS

Enforcement of Bondholder's Rights (this index)

ESCAPE OF PRISONER

Detainers outstanding against prisoners, Spec L 115:5

EVIDENCE

Truck permits, violation of interstate agreement, Spec L 135:8

EXCESS LAND

Turnpike Authority, utilization of excess land of Authority, Spec L 75:15B

EXCISE TAX

Bus registration proration, fleet buses, Spec L 131:5

EXCLUSIVE SERVICE AREAS

Water Resources Authority, Spec L 67:20

EXECUTIVE DIRECTOR

Water Resources Authority, appointment, Spec L 67:5, 676:7

EXECUTIVE HEAD

Placement of children, compact on, Spec L 95:8

Vehicle equipment safety, Spec L 127:7

EXEMPTION FROM COVERAGE

Bus registration proration, Spec L 131:3

EXEMPTION FROM TAXATION

Parking Authority, Spec L 71:16

Port Authority, Spec L 73:17

Steamship Authority, Spec L 77:6

Turnpike Authority, Spec L 75:13

Water Resources Authority, Spec L 67:19

EXPENDITURES

Transportation Bond Authorization Act (this index)

EXPENSES

Costs or Expenses (this index)

FEDERAL SUPPORT

Transportation bond authorization act, basis for expenditures, Spec L 79:29

FEES

Guardian ad litem, fees relating to appointment, Spec L 97:5

Parking Authority, penalty for failure to pay, Spec L 71:14

Supervision, care and assistance to juveniles, Spec L 97:5

GARAGE REVENUE BONDS
Parking Authority, Spec L 71:8, 71:17

GENERAL COURT
Vehicle Equipment Safety Commission, approval of rules, regulations, or codes of, Spec L 127:2

GENERATORS
Transportation Bond Authorization Act, changing generator power source, Spec L 79:26

GOVERNING LAW
Parking Authority, Spec L 71:23

Placement of children, compact on, Spec L 95:5

Port Authority, Spec L 73:29

Steamship Authority Act as, Spec L 77:19

Taxation of motor fuels, Spec L 129:3

Turnpike Authority Act as, Spec L 75:21

Water Resources Authority, Spec L 67:28

GOVERNOR
Bus registration proration, give notice of withdrawal, Spec L 131:4

Merrimack River compact
– appointment of member of Merrimack River Valley Flood Control Commission, Spec L 123:3
– compensation of appointee, Spec L 123:5

New England Board of Higher Education
– appointees to board, Spec L 101:3
– responsibility of, Spec L 101:2

Thames River compact
– appointment of member of Thames River Valley Flood Control Commission, Spec L 125:3
– compensation of appointee to Control Commission, Spec L 125:5

Truck permits, withdrawal from interstate agreement, Spec L 135:9

GRANT OF POWERS
Steamship Authority, Spec L 77:4

GRANT OF POWERS—Cont'd
Turnpike Authority, Spec L 75:5, 75:7

GROUP INSURANCE
Water Resources Authority employees, Spec L 67:7

GUARDIAN AD LITEM
Appointment, fees relating to, Spec L 97:5

GUARDRAIL
Forms, complaints for injuries from defective guardrail, Spec L 75:3 Form 1

HABITUAL OFFENDERS LAW
Detainers outstanding against prisoners, Spec L 115:4

HEALTH
Mental Health Compact (this index)
Radioactivity and Radiological Health (this index)

HEARINGS
Port Authority, airport flight patterns, Spec L 73:3A

Steamship Authority, hearings on each island, Spec L 77:15B

HIGHWAY FUND
Transportation Bond Authorization Act, appropriations from highway fund debt service, Spec L 79:24

Truck permits, interstate agreement, Spec L 135:3 to 135:5

HIGHWAY IMPROVEMENT LOAN ACT
Issuance and sale of bonds, Spec L 79:23

HIGHWAYS AND STREETS
Fund. Highway Fund (this index)
Guardrail defects, complaints for injuries from, Spec L 75:3 Form 1
Transportation Bond Authorization Act (this index)
Turnpike Authority, incorporation of highways of state, Spec L 75:6

HITCHHIKING
Prohibition on turnpike authority, Spec L 75:15

433

LEASE OF PROPERTY
Rental (this index)

LEGISLATION
New England Board of Higher Education, recommendations, Spec L 101:5

LIABILITY IN TORT
Tort Liability (this index)

LIBERAL CONSTRUCTION
Construction and Interpretation (this index)

LIBRARY COMPACT
Generally, Spec L 103:1 to 6

Administrator of compact, appointment, Spec L 103:5

Appointment of compact administrator, Spec L 103:5

Capital outlays, compliance with laws governing, Spec L 103:2

Cities, pledging of credit, compliance with laws governing, Spec L 103:2

Counties, pledging of credit, compliance with laws governing, Spec L 103:2

Credit of political subdivisions, pledging, compliance with laws governing, Spec L 103:2

Definitions, generally, Spec L 103:3

Districts lying partially within Commonwealth, Spec L 103:4

Form of compact, Spec L 103:1

Pledging of credit of political subdivisions, compliance with laws governing, Spec L 103:2

State library agency, defined, Spec L 103:3

Withdrawal of Commonwealth from compact, Spec L 103:6

LIENS
Parking Authority, payment of fee, Spec L 71:14

LIFE INSURANCE CONTRACTS
Port Authority, Spec L 73:22A

LISTS
Transportation Bond Authorization Act, list of municipalities aided, Spec L 79:20, 79:21

MAINTENANCE AND REPAIR
Parking Authority, repair of garages by, Spec L 71:14

Port Authority, repair of projects by, Spec L 73:23

Turnpike Authority, maintenance responsibility, Spec L 75:15

MANDAMUS TO ENFORCE BONDHOLDERS' RIGHTS
Enforcement of Bondholders' Rights (this index)

MANDATORY
Detainers outstanding against prisoners, giving over of inmates as required, Spec L 115:6

Parking Authority, obligatory construction of tunnels, Spec L 71:19

MAPS
Port Authority, transfer to, Spec L 73:23

MARTHA'S VINEYARD STEAMSHIP LINE OR AUTHORITY
Steamship Authority (this index)

MASSACHUSETTS PARKING AUTHORITY
Parking Authority (this index)

MBTA
Transportation Bond Authorization Act (this index)

MDC SEWER SYSTEM
Definition, Spec L 67:2

MENTAL HEALTH COMPACT
Generally, Spec L 107:1 to 107:4

Administrator of compact authorized to promulgate rules and regulations, Spec L 107:2

Cooperation with Commonwealth departments and agencies, Spec L 107:2, 107:2

Copies of act, Spec L 107:4

Finances, Spec L 107:3

Form of compact, Spec L 107:1

Rules and regulations, compact administrator authorized to promulgate, Spec L 107:2

436

437

NECESSITY—Cont'd
Water Resources Authority bonds, consent of governing body, Spec L 67:15

NEGLIGENCE
Port Authority, liability for negligence, Spec L 73:23

NEGOTIATIONS
Certification of educational personnel, authorization of educational official, Spec L 105:2

NEIGHBORHOOD REVITALIZATION
Housing finance agency, Spec L 7:1 to 7:5

NEW BEDFORD, WOODS HOLE, MARTHA'S VINEYARD AND NANTUCKET STEAMSHIP AUTHORITY
Abolition and transfer of assets of, Spec L 77:16

NEW ENGLAND BOARD OF HIGHER EDUCATION
Generally, Spec L 101:1 to 5
Appointees
– gubernatorial appointees to board, Spec L 101:3
– salaries of appointees, Spec L 101:4
Disbursements of board, reports of, Spec L 101:5
Financial reports, Spec L 101:5
Form of compact, Spec L 101:1
Governor
– appointees to board, Spec L 101:3
– responsibility of, Spec L 101:2
Governor (this index)
Legislation, recommendations for, Spec L 101:5
Office, term of, Spec L 101:3
Payback by service defined, Spec L 101:6
Recommendations for legislation, Spec L 101:5
Reports of receipts and disbursements of board, Spec L 101:5
Salaries of appointees, Spec L 101:4
Term of office, Spec L 101:3

NEW ENGLAND BOARD OF HIGHER EDUCATION—Cont'd
Time when compact becomes operative and effective, Spec L 101:2
Vacancies, Spec L 101:3

NEW ENGLAND STATES EMERGENCY MILITARY AID COMPACT
Generally, Spec L 91:1

NEW YORK EMERGENCY MILITARY AID COMPACT
Generally, Spec L 93:1

NORTHEASTERN RESOURCES COMMISSION
Generally, Spec L 121:1, 121:2

NOTICE AND KNOWLEDGE
Bus registration proration, withdrawal, Spec L 131:4
Steamship Authority, schedule changes, Spec L 77:15A
Water pollution control, ratification, Spec L 119:2
Water Resources Authority, entry upon lands, trespass, Spec L 67:1 et seq.

OATH OF OFFICE
Water Resources Authority members, Spec L 67:3

OBLIGATORY
Mandatory (this index)

OFFENSES OF TURNPIKE AUTHORITY
Generally, Spec L 75:15

OFFICE, TERM OF
Term of Office (this index)

OLD PERSONS
Nantucket regional transit authority, van services, Spec L 81:2

OTHER STATES
Interstate Compacts and Agreements (this index)

PARKING AUTHORITY
Generally, Spec L 71:1 to 71:25
Abandoned property auction, Spec L 71:14A
Agreements, trust, Spec L 71:9

PATTERNS OF FLIGHT
Port Authority regulation, Spec L 73:3A

PAYBACK BY SERVICE
Definition, Spec L 101:6

PAYMENTS
Port Authority, application by, Spec L 73:7

PENALTIES
Detainers outstanding against prisoners, Spec L 115:5

Parking Authority, failure to pay prescribed fee, Spec L 71:14

Port Authority (this index)

Turnpike Authority (this index)

PENSION
Retirement Systems (this index)

PERSONAL INJURIES
Forms, complaint for injuries from defective guardrail, Spec L 75:3 Form 1

PIER 5
Lease by Port Authority, Spec L 73:3 note

PLACEMENT OF CHILDREN, COMPACT ON
Generally, Spec L 95:1 to 95:8

Agencies of other states, agreements relating to placement, Spec L 95:5

Agreements with officers or agencies of other states relating to placement, Spec L 95:5

Appropriate authority in receiving state, defined, Spec L 95:4

Courts, jurisdiction to place delinquent children, Spec L 95:7

Definitions

– appropriate authority in receiving state, Spec L 95:4

– executive head, Spec L 95:8

Delinquent children, jurisdiction of courts to place, Spec L 95:7

Executive head, defined, Spec L 95:8

Financial responsibility for child, Spec L 95:3

Form of compact, Spec L 95:1

PLACEMENT OF CHILDREN, COMPACT ON—Cont'd
Governing law, Spec L 95:5

Homes, inspection of, Spec L 95:6

Inspection requirements, generally, Spec L 95:6

Institutions, inspection of, Spec L 95:6

Jurisdiction of courts to place delinquent children, Spec L 95:7

Officers or agencies of other states, agreements relating to placement, Spec L 95:5

Receiving state, appropriate authority in, defined, Spec L 95:4

Supervision, requirements for, generally, Spec L 95:6

Visitation, requirements for, generally, Spec L 95:6

PLANNING COMPACT
Regional Planning Compact (this index)

PLANS
Port Authority, transfer of plans to, Spec L 73:23

POLICE
Parking Authority garage project, protection of, Spec L 71:14

Port Authority projects, protection of, Spec L 73:23

State Police Compact (this index)

Turnpike Authority, special police, Spec L 75:15

POLITICAL SUBDIVISIONS
Cities and Towns (this index)

Credit of Commonwealth or Subdivision, Pledge of (this index)

POLLUTION
Water Pollution Control (this index)

PORT AUTHORITY
Generally, Spec L 73:1 to 73:34

Acquisition of property, Spec L 73:4

Action to enforce bondholders' rights, Spec L 73:16

Agreement of trust, bonds, Spec L 73:12

440

PORT AUTHORITY—Cont'd

Life insurance contracts, funding, Spec L 73:22A

Mandamus to enforce bondholders' rights, Spec L 73:16

Maps, transfer to Port Authority, Spec L 73:23

Municipalities, credit not pledged, Spec L 73:11

Mutual funds, deferred compensation plan funding, Spec L 73:22A

Mystic River Bridge, vesting of title in Authority, Spec L 73:34

National Guard facilities, Spec L 73:23

Negligence, liability for, Spec L 73:23

Operation of bridges, generally, Spec L 73:13

Patterns of flight, regulation of, Spec L 73:3A

Payments, application of, generally, Spec L 73:7

Penalties

– conflict of interest, Spec L 73:23

– failure to pay toll, Spec L 73:23

Pier 5, lease of, Spec L 73:3 note

Plans, transfer to Port Authority, Spec L 73:23

Pledge of credit by Commonwealth, Spec L 73:11

Police, protection of Port Authority projects, Spec L 73:23

Political subdivisions, credit not pledged, Spec L 73:11

Powers of Authority, generally, Spec L 73:3, 73:6

Properties

– acquisition of, Spec L 73:4

– port properties, Spec L 73:6, 73:33

Publication of actions, Spec L 73:23

Refunding bonds, Spec L 73:19

Remedies of bondholders, Spec L 73:16

Repair of projects by Port Authority, Spec L 73:23

Reports and records

– annual report, Spec L 73:21

– transfer to Port Authority, Spec L 73:23

PORT AUTHORITY—Cont'd

Retirement systems, public safety employees assigned to Port Authority, Spec L 73:34A

Revenues, Spec L 73:14

Smokers as ineligible to work in certain positions at Logan International Airport, Spec L 73:3B

Suit to enforce bondholders' rights, Spec L 73:16

Taxation, exemption from, Spec L 73:17

Title

– airport properties, certain laws inoperative upon vesting, Spec L 73:32

– Mystic River Bridge in Authority, certain laws inoperative upon, Spec L 73:34

– port properties, vesting in authority, certain laws inoperative upon, Spec L 73:33

– transfer to Commonwealth, Spec L 73:25

Tolls, failure to pay, Spec L 73:23

Tort liability of Port Authority, Spec L 73:23

Towns, credit not pledged, Spec L 73:11

Trade and transportation center, generally, Spec L 73:4A

Transfer of employees, Spec L 73:22

Transfer of projects to Commonwealth, Spec L 73:25

Transportation center, Spec L 73:4A

Trusts and trust funds

– bonds, trust agreements as to, Spec L 73:12

– deferred compensation plans funding bank investment trusts, Spec L 73:22A

– revenues of Authority held in trust, Spec L 73:15

Vesting of title

– airport properties, Spec L 73:32

– Mystic River Bridge, Spec L 73:34

– port properties, Spec L 73:33

Words and phrases, generally, Spec L 73:1

POWER SOURCE FOR GENERATORS

Transportation bond authorization act, alteration or changing, Spec L 79:26

PRELIMINARY EXPENSES

Parking Authority, Spec L 71:18

Turnpike Authority, Spec L 75:18

PRISONERS

Detention of Persons (this index)

PROPERTY

Real Property (this index)

PROPERTY DAMAGE

Turnpike Authority, compensation for private property damage, Spec L 75:15

PUBLICATION

Port Authority actions, Spec L 73:23

Steamship Authority, announcement for bids on contracts, Spec L 77:15

PUBLIC HEALTH COMMISSIONER

Radioactivity and Radiological Health (this index)

PUBLIC LANDS

Acquisition by Turnpike Authority, Spec L 75:15

PUBLIC OFFICERS AND EMPLOYEES

As to particular persons or positions, see specific topics

Bus registration proration, notice of withdrawal, Spec L 131:4

Certification of educational personnel, authorization to negotiate and enter into agreements, Spec L 105:2

Governor (this index)

Parking Authority, Spec L 71:22

Placement of children, agreements relating to, officers or agencies of other states, Spec L 95:5

Port Authority (this index)

Retirement Systems (this index)

Term of Office (this index)

PUBLIC OFFICERS AND EMPLOYEES—Cont'd

Transportation Bond Authorization Act, transfer of officers of MBTA, Spec L 79:19

Vacancies (this index)

Water Resources Authority (this index)

PUBLIC SAFETY COMMISSIONER

State Police Compact, New England State Police Administrators Conference, Spec L 111:3

QUORUM

Water Resources Authority meetings, Spec L 67:3

RADIATION INCIDENT PLAN

Generally, Spec L 109:3

RADIOACTIVITY AND RADIOLOGICAL HEALTH

Generally, Spec L 109:1 to 109:4

Administrator of compact, public health commissioner as, Spec L 109:4

Form of compact, Spec L 109:2

Formulation of radiation incident plan by public health commissioner, Spec L 109:3

Incident plan for radiation, formulation by public health commissioner, Spec L 109:3

Public Health Commissioner

– compact administrator, Spec L 109:4

– radiation incident plan, Spec L 109:3

Radiation incident plan, Spec L 109:3

Title of Act, Spec L 109:1

RATES FOR SERVICES

Water Resources Authority, Spec L 67:10

RATIFICATION

Merrimack River Compact, Spec L 123:2

Thames River compact, Spec L 125:2

Water pollution control, notice of ratification, Spec L 119:2

REAL PROPERTY
Parking Authority, Spec L 71:14
Port Authority (this index)
Turnpike Authority (this index)
Water Resources Authority (this index)

REAPPOINTMENT
Merrimack River compact, Spec L 123:4
Thames River Compact, commission members, Spec L 125:4

RECEIPTS
New England Board of Higher Education, receipts and disbursements of board, Spec L 101:5
Truck permits, interstate agreement, fees, Spec L 135:3 to 135:5

RECEIVING STATE
Placement of children, compact on, definition of appropriate authority in receiving state, Spec L 95:4

RECOMMENDATIONS
Legislation, recommendations by New England Board of Higher Education, Spec L 101:5

RECORDS
Port Authority (this index)
Water Resources Authority, transfer of records to, Spec L 67:4

REFUNDING BONDS
Parking Authority, Spec L 71:17
Port Authority, Spec L 73:19
Turnpike Authority, Spec L 75:16
Water Resources Authority, Spec L 67:12, 67:13, 67:16

REGIONAL PLANNING COMPACT
Generally, Spec L 117:1, 117:2
Form of compact, Spec L 117:1
Short title, Spec L 117:2

REGISTRAR OF MOTOR VEHICLES
Authority of, Spec L 127:2
Commissioner for Commonwealth, Spec L 127:3

REGISTRATION
Bus Registration Proration (this index)

REGISTRATION—Cont'd
Registrar of Motor Vehicles (this index)

REIMBURSEMENT
Steamship Authority, contracts with Commonwealth, Spec L 77:9A
Total coliform level violations, reimbursing communities involved in remedying, Spec L 67:8
Transportation Bond Authorization Act, airport systems planning, Spec L 79:27
Water Resources Authority, communities involved in remedying total coliform level violations, Spec L 67:8

REMEDIES
Bondholders. **Enforcement of Bondholders' Rights** (this index)
Steamship Authority, Spec L 77:12
Water Resources Authority, reimbursing communities involved in environmental remedies, Spec L 67:8

REMOVAL
Water Resources Authority members, Spec L 67:3

RENTAL
Parking Authority, rental of real property to Authority by municipality, Spec L 71:14
Port Authority, lease of Pier 5, Spec L 73:3 note

REPAIR
Maintenance and Repair (this index)

REPEAL OF OTHER STATUTES
Parking Authority, Spec L 71:23

REPEAT OFFENDERS
Detainers outstanding against prisoners, Spec L 115:4

REPORTS
Annual Reports (this index)
Bus registration proration, changes in methods for reporting information, Spec L 131:3

446

(References are to Special Law Chapters and Sections)

TREASURY OF STATE

Truck permit fees, interstate agreement, Spec L 135:3, 135:5

TRESPASS

Water Resources Authority, Spec L 67:1 et seq.

TRUCK PERMITS, INTERSTATE AGREEMENT

Generally, Spec L 135:1 to 135:9

Accounting, approval by Commissioner of Administration, Spec L 135:5

Approval by Commissioner of Administration, Spec L 135:5

Commissioner of Administration, Spec L 135:4 to 135:6

Common safety regulations, Spec L 135:7

Cost of administration, Spec L 135:3

Department of Public Works, Spec L 135:5

Deposit and distribution of funds, Spec L 135:3 to 135:5

Fees, Spec L 135:5

Fines, violation of provisions, Spec L 135:8

Form of compact, Spec L 135:1

Funds, deposit and distribution of, Spec L 135:3 to 135:5

Governor, withdrawal from agreement, Spec L 135:9

Highway Fund, Spec L 135:3 to 135:5

Interstate Permit Fund, Spec L 135:2 to 135:4

Prima facie evidence, Spec L 135:8

Receipts and deposits, Spec L 135:3 to 135:5

Settlement of errors, Spec L 135:6

Violation of provisions, Spec L 135:8

Withdrawal from agreement, Spec L 135:9

TRUSTS AND TRUST FUNDS

Parking Authority, Spec L 71:9, 71:11

Port Authority (this index)

Steamship Authority (this index)

Turnpike Authority (this index)

TRUSTS AND TRUST FUNDS —Cont'd

Water Resources Authority, Spec L 67:18

TUNNELS

Parking Authority, obligatory construction, Spec L 71:19

TURNPIKE AUTHORITY

Generally, Spec L 75:1 to 75:21

Abandoned property, disposition of, Spec L 75:15

Action to enforce bondholders' right, Spec L 75:12

Air rights, utilization of, Spec L 75:15A

Annual report, Spec L 75:15

Bonds and notes

– investment, eligibility for, Spec L 75:14

– revenue bonds, Spec L 75:8, 75:16

Bridges, incorporation in turnpike, Spec L 75:6

Charity, donation of abandoned property to, Spec L 75:15

Commonwealth

– credit not pledged, Spec L 75:2

– transfer to, Spec L 75:17

Compensation for private property damage, Spec L 75:15

Constitutional construction, Spec L 75:20

Construction of Act, Spec L 75:19 to 75:21

Credit of Commonwealth not pledged, Spec L 75:2

Definitions, generally, Spec L 75:4

Eligibility of bonds for investment, Spec L 75:14

Equity suit to enforce bondholders' rights, Spec L 75:12

Excess land of Authority, utilization of, Spec L 75:15B

Exemption from taxation, Spec L 75:13

Expenses, preliminary, Spec L 75:18

Governing law, Act as, Spec L 75:21

Grant of powers, generally, Spec L 75:5, 75:7

WATER RESOURCES AUTHORITY—Cont'd

Transfer of property to Authority, Spec L 67:4

Treasurer of Authority, appointment, Spec L 67:7

Treatment of sewage, exclusivity of services, Spec L 67:20

Trespass, Spec L 67:1 et seq

Trust funds, revenues from bonds as, Spec L 67:18

Vice-chairman of Authority, generally, Spec L 67:3

Waterworks systems
generally, Spec L 67:4
- compensation for water diverted, Spec L 67:26
- definition, Spec L 67:2
- exclusive services, Spec L 67:20
- operation, etc., Spec L 67:8
- service areas division designation, Spec L 67:8

WATERSHED SYSTEM

Water Resources Authority (this index)

WATERWORKS SYSTEMS

Water Resources Authority (this index)

WITHDRAWAL

Bus registration proration, notice from governor, Spec L 131:4

Certification of educational personnel, provisions in agreements, Spec L 105:3

Library Compact, withdrawal of Commonwealth, Spec L 103:6

Truck permits, interstate agreement, Spec L 135:9

WOODS HOLE, MARTHA'S VINEYARD AND STEAMSHIP AUTHORITY

Steamship Authority (this index)

WOODS HOLE STEAMSHIP LINE

Steamship Authority (this index)

WRONGFUL DEATH

Parking Authority, Spec L 71:14